Get the eBooks FREE!

(PDF, ePub, Kindle, and liveBook all included)

We believe that once you buy a book from us, you should be able to read it in any format we have available. To get electronic versions of this book at no additional cost to you, purchase and then register this book at the Manning website.

Go to https://www.manning.com/freebook and follow the instructions to complete your pBook registration.

That's it!
Thanks from Manning!

Get Programming with

F#

A guide for .NET developers

Isaac Abraham

MANNING

Shelter Island

Manning Publications Co.
20 Baldwin Road
PO Box 761
Shelter Island, NY 11964

Acquisitions editor:	Michael Stephens
Development editor:	Elesha Hyde
Review editor:	Aleksandar Dragosavljević
Technical development editor:	Mark Elston
Technical proofreader:	Dane Balia
Production editor:	David Novak
Copyeditor:	Sharon Wilkey
Proofreader:	Melody Dolab
Typesetter:	Dottie Marsico
Cover designer:	Monica Kamsvaag

ISBN 9781617293993
Printed in the United States of America
1 2 3 4 5 6 7 8 9 10 – EBM – 23 22 21 20 19 18

Contents

Unit 1

F# AND VISUAL STUDIO

Unit 2

HELLO F#

Unit 3

TYPES AND FUNCTIONS

Unit 4

COLLECTIONS IN F#

Unit 5

THE PIT OF SUCCESS WITH THE F# TYPE SYSTEM

Unit 6

LIVING ON THE .NET PLATFORM

Foreword

When I first met Isaac Abraham in 2015, I knew immediately that he shared my passion for educating .NET developers in the art of F#. His book, which you hold in your hands, is the text I had wanted when I first kindled my F# romance. Inside, Isaac will lead you on a journey of F# that's both pragmatic and relevant. If you're a C# or Visual Basic .NET developer, you'll learn through a series of lessons how to apply F# to everyday .NET development. You won't have to wade through the deep theoretical explanations that are often the staple of functional programming books. Instead, Isaac will guide you with practical advice and best practices derived from his own experience as an F# developer.

I first fell in love with F# when it was still a research language being developed out of Microsoft Research in Cambridge, England. The language was a bit rough around the edges, but every monthly release brought a fresh set of exciting new features to explore. The community was small but already vibrant, eager to evangelize any who would listen about how F# was so expressive, powerful, and fun. I found myself caught up in it all.

Since F# was still very new, there weren't many books available to help me learn the language. Being a self-taught C# programmer, I wanted something that was light on theory and heavy on practice, but such books hadn't been written yet. I even made my own meager attempt to fill that void, by writing a blog series (viewable today only via the Internet Archive) titled, "Why I Love F#."

In each blog article, I attempted to present F# to everyday C# developers like myself, highlighting features that marry well with .NET development such as the F# Interactive environment, type-safe format strings, tuples, and pattern matching. I wanted to encourage others to explore this beautiful language that I'd become quite smitten with, and to teach them how to use it effectively to create .NET programs. Eventually, my blog fell by the wayside. After joining the .NET languages team at Microsoft, I could no longer find the time to keep it current and gave it up.

Fast-forward to today. Today, F# is more popular than ever and growing at a rapid pace. F# code is running quite literally everywhere: on desktops, mobile devices, the web, IoT devices, and in the cloud. F# has reached its fourth major version, boasts an active and fiercely passionate community, and enjoys first-class tooling support in many IDEs and editors, such as Visual Studio, Visual Studio for Mac, and JetBrains Rider. And of course, F# books are available on a wide variety of topics, from the more general purpose to fully scientific.

F# exemplifies an aspect of programming that all too often is forgotten: programming should be fun. With Isaac as your teacher, I'm confident you'll have an absolute blast.

—DUSTIN CAMPBELL
PRINCIPAL SOFTWARE ENGINEER,
.NET LANGUAGES TEAM, MICROSOFT

In the Introduction to F#, Isaac mentions that F# leads you to a *pit of success*, which is something that I wholeheartedly agree with. I believe that the way this happens has a lot to do with how a pragmatic way of thinking, functional ideas, and a powerful runtime come together in F#. The functional ideas serve as a fantastic tool for understanding and modeling the problem domain in a simple way. At the same time, F# gives you a versatile toolbox for solving concrete problems within the domain. This includes a language that supports multiple paradigms including functional, object-oriented, and imperative, but also powerful .NET and F# libraries. Again, this book introduces F# from exactly the right perspective. It rightly puts a strong emphasis on thinking about the domain in a functional way, but at the same time, it introduces all of the important tools from the F# toolbox.

When I started learning the F# language 10 years ago, the typical advice was that F# is just a functional programming language for .NET, so you should "forget everything you know about programming," read a couple of academic functional programming textbooks, and then figure out how to use the functional concepts to write .NET applications on your own.

I'm happy that this isn't the advice we give to people who are curious about F# these days. There are two main reasons for this. First, it turns out that "forgetting everything" is just a poor strategy for learning F# if you have existing programming knowledge. Second, it also turns out that the "functional programming" label is only partly appropriate for the kind of code you write when using F# to solve real-world problems. This book reflects both points, which is what makes it a fantastic material for learning F#.

The difference between F# and other .NET languages is equally easy to overstate and to understate. On one hand, many functional language constructs now exist in C# and VB

.NET, so you might think that the difference isn't that big. On the other hand, F# is rooted in functional programming and leads you to different way of thinking about problems, so you might think that you need to start from a clean slate. As is often the case, the truth is somewhere in the middle. When using F#, you'll find yourself designing software differently and, as a result, falling into the pit of success described in unit 5. At the same time, learning F# shouldn't be as daunting as it was 10 years ago. You'll find many similarities to what you know already, and this book does a great job of using them to explain F# clearly and effectively.

If you're a C# or VB .NET developer who cares about solving problems in a pragmatic way, this is the book for you. There's no need to wait for the "right problem" that will be "well suited to functional programming" and give you an excuse to learn F#. As this book clearly explains, the point of F# isn't just in functional programming, but in the pit of success, where the F# way of solving problems leads you.

—TOMAS PETRICEK
PARTNER, FSHARPWORKS

Preface

Several years ago, when I was a full-time C# developer working for a .NET consultancy in the United Kingdom, I embarked on a goal to improve the quality of software I developed. I was fed up with writing software and having the customer find bugs that I felt I should have caught, and disappointed that I didn't know how to use OO programming to model real-world problems. So I learned about SOLID, became a TDD fanatic, and read up on things like dependency injection and design patterns. And my software did improve! My clients were happier, and my managers were pleased with the lower bug rates.

But soon afterward, I once again became frustrated with a lack of progress. Did we *really* need this amount of rigor, of process, and of unit tests in order to become proficient software developers? I knew that I'd taken a step forward in terms of quality by adopting SOLID and TDD, but I wanted to achieve it in a more productive fashion. I wanted more support from my programming language to do the right thing by default; something that guided me to the "pit of success" without my needing to use a myriad of design patterns in a specific way, and allowed me to get to the heart of a problem that I was trying to solve.

Fast-forwarding a little, I ended up working for a financial services company working on a rules engine to monitor dodgy-looking trades—things like insider trading. We spent a great deal of time looking at how to create a component-based rules engine with pluggable "rules" that we could use to build "larger" rules. What I discovered by the end was that we had spent the last 18 months trying to implement a functional pipeline using object-oriented constructs and design patterns.

So, having heard about F#, I thought I'd give it a look. I was initially interested in it as a means to an end; I'd heard that it could help me write software on .NET more quickly and with fewer bugs. I attended an intensive two-day course, and tried to use F# as much in my own time as I could. Interestingly, while learning F#, I found that it reinvigorated me as a developer—not only was I learning something entirely new, but I could see the benefits of using the language in a tangible sense. I was able to rapidly deliver software and yet also had the confidence that what I had delivered to my customers worked, but without the rigor I'd experienced beforehand. At the same time, I found an entirely new community of .NET developers that I didn't even know existed, with different ideas and ways of working that made me question many of the fundamentals that I took for granted. I realized that I was excited about and enjoying software development again!

Over time, I learned more about F# and functional programming; coming from a C# background, I had many preconceptions about what F# was (and wasn't), and made lots of mistakes on the way to learning how to use F# more effectively. This book is the culmination of what I wish I had had when I was taking my first steps with F# while at the same time trying to find out where it fits in my day-to-day work.

I couldn't put *everything* that I wanted to in this book—and many of the lessons deliberately leave out the hard-core details that could be useful as reference material—but as long as you understand what this book is and isn't, I think that you'll find it a great start to the world of F# and FP on .NET. It'll help get you up and running, building on your existing knowledge of .NET, and although it won't necessarily take you all the way to the finish line, it'll offer you signposts and guidance on how to get there yourself.

Acknowledgments

Thank you to all the people who have helped guide the book throughout the many forms it took over its development. The reviewers and MEAP participants provided invaluable guidance during this time to help me focus on getting to the real crux in many of the lessons. The list of reviewers includes Andy Kirsch, Anne Epstein, Bruno Sonnino, Dane Balia, Dmytro Lypai, Dylan Scott, Ernesto Cardenas Cangahuala, Jason Hales, Jiri Pik, Joel Clermont, Miranda Whurr, Panagiotis Kanavos, Sambaran Hazra, Stephen Byrne, Tim Djossou, and Wes Stahler. Thanks to you all. I'd like to reserve a special thank you for Tomas Petricek for his invaluable and extremely detailed feedback throughout the book, as well as Dustin Campbell for taking the time to put together a wonderful foreword. Also, thanks to the Manning team, including all my editors, for their guidance.

Thanks also to Don Syme and Microsoft for creating and then integrating F# into Visual Studio—my life as a software developer is much more pleasant for it! The F# community gets a huge thank you for providing feedback during the development of this book, but also for making F# such a fun and welcoming environment; I've learned so much also about working within the community as well as on open source projects in general.

Finally, thank you to my wife, Carmen, for enduring the countless evenings and weekends spent working on this book, and helping me stay positive through the twists and turns that I've now learned are part of creating a book.

About this book

Who should read this book

This book takes a practical look at how to start using functional programming techniques with F# in production applications, using frameworks, libraries, and tools that you're already familiar with, as well as exploring F#-specific libraries that open up all sorts of interesting options that aren't possible today in C# and VB .NET.

It's important to note from the outset that this book won't teach you everything about the F# language. Instead, we'll focus on a core subset of the language that gives you the most effective return for your investment; where there's further learning available that could be worthwhile for you, I'll point it out. You won't learn everything about functional programming, either; again, we'll concentrate on the most important fundamentals from which the more advanced techniques and practices will naturally reveal themselves to you over time. So, if you're expecting to learn the ins and outs of functors, monads, and applicatives, this book isn't for you. If, on the other hand, you want to learn the parts that will enable you to achieve the same qualities in software that you strive for already, without spending time learning the inner workings of exactly why things work from a theoretical point of view, then keep reading!

If you're an enterprise developer on .NET, it's likely that you're looking to see how F# can provide tangible benefits to you in the minimum amount of time. This book focuses on showing you things that you can start using today with F#, be they frameworks that you might already know, or F#-specific libraries designed to take full advantage of F#'s powerful type system that will provide real-world benefits over existing libraries. As such, this book focuses on using Visual Studio on Windows as the primary development platform, although you can use almost (but not all) of the libraries mentioned here through other IDEs and OSs.

How this book is organized

This book is roughly split into two main sections, plus appendices. The first part of the book introduces the F# language and development experience from within Visual Studio—a tool that you already feel at home with. We'll start from ground zero, and work our way up to features such as program flow, data structures, and domain modeling. The second section of the book deals with practical applications and use cases for F#, from working with hybrid language solutions to unit testing to data-driven websites. We'll look at popular existing .NET libraries wherever possible so that you can easily compare how we approach solving challenges with frameworks that you might already be familiar with in C# or VB .NET. We'll also dig into some cool F#-only libraries that will push the boundaries of what you're familiar with. Finally, a set of appendices contain helpful tips and resources for continuing to learn more about F#, as well as how to start using it in a practical sense within your organization.

A word on the following list: each item represents a *unit*, which is formed of several *lessons*. A lesson is normally 8–12 pages and focuses on a single learning element; when taken together, all of the lessons in the unit provide a coherent piece of learning. Most units also end with a larger exercise for you to do that "brings everything together."

- *F# and Visual Studio*—This unit gets you up and running with F# on Visual Studio, in preparation for the rest of the book. You'll also do some coding to familiarize yourself with the environment.
- *Hello, F#*—This unit focuses on the core language features in F#, and provides you with a solid foundation in using F# for basic application flow.
- *Types and functions*—This unit presents the data types and structures that F# offers, and shows how to use them to model data. We'll then look at F# functions in more depth and see how powerful and flexible they are.
- *Collections in F#*—Collections are a powerful weapon in the arsenal of the F# developer. This unit looks at the collections available in F# and when best to use each one.
- *The pit of success with the F# type system*—This unit focuses on the more powerful features of the F# language, including how to handle conditionals and flow, as well as how to model rules into code.
- *Living on the .NET platform*—This unit looks at how F# interoperates with the rest of .NET, including C# and VB .NET interoperability as well as working with NuGet packages.

- *Working with data*—F# shines when it comes to working with data. This unit looks at some of the unique features in F# that make working with a wide variety of data sources easy and fun.
- *Web programming*—This unit looks at both consuming and creating web applications in F#, using both standard .NET and custom F# libraries.
- *Unit testing*—This unit covers a variety of types of testing that can be easily performed in F#, from typical TDD-style testing or more powerful property-based testing.
- *Where next*—The final unit contains appendices that discuss miscellaneous technical topics that are either too small for or don't easily fit into any single unit, as well as nontechnical elements such as the F# community. It also offers guidance on moving forward from this book, making the leap from working through predefined exercises to using F# "in the wild."

I strongly advise that you go through all the units in the first half of the book, as it covers the core part of the F# language that's used everywhere. You may find some of the second-half units, which cover practical applications of F#, more or less useful, depending on how you use .NET. But I still recommend you go through all of them, as they give you more experience with using F# in different situations, particularly the end-of-unit capstone exercises.

About the code

All the code samples in this book are available at the following URL (including suggested solutions for all capstones): https://github.com/isaacabraham/get-programming-fsharp.

This book contains many examples of source code both in numbered listings and inline with the text. In both cases, source code is formatted in a `fixed-width font like this` to separate it from ordinary text. Sometimes code is also in bold to highlight code that has changed from previous steps in the chapter, such as when a new feature adds to an existing line of code.

In many cases, the original source code has been reformatted; we've added line breaks and reworked indentation to accommodate the available page space in the book. In rare cases, even this was not enough, and listings include line-continuation markers (➡). Additionally, comments in the source code have often been removed from the listings when the code is described in the text. Code annotations accompany many of the listings, highlighting important concepts.

Book forum

Purchase of *Get Programming with F#* includes free access to a private web forum run by Manning Publications where you can make comments about the book, ask technical questions, and receive help from the author and from other users. To access the forum, go to www.manning.com/books/get-programming-with-f-sharp. You can also learn more about Manning's forums and the rules of conduct at https://forums.manning.com/forums/about.

Manning's commitment to our readers is to provide a venue where a meaningful dialogue between individual readers and between readers and the author can take place. It is not a commitment to any specific amount of participation on the part of the author, whose contribution to the forum remains voluntary (and unpaid). We suggest you try asking the author some challenging questions lest his interest stray! The forum and the archives of previous discussions will be accessible from the publisher's website as long as the book is in print.

About the author

ISAAC ABRAHAM is an F# MVP and has been a .NET developer since .NET 1.0, with an interest in cloud computing and distributed data problems. He nowadays lives in both the UK and Germany, and is the director of Compositional IT. He specializes in consultancy, training and development, and helping customers adopt high-quality, functional-first solutions on the .NET platform.

Isaac focuses on practical software development techniques and practices that can deliver good return quickly. He believes that although an understanding of, for example, functional programming underpinnings is important, these lessons need to be delivered in a way that quickly illustrates value and benefit to students.

WELCOME TO GET PROGRAMMING WITH F#!

Welcome to F#! I hope that you're reading this book because you've heard something interesting about F# and want to learn more about how to start using it within your daily work cycle. Perhaps you've heard something about its data processing capabilities, or that it can lead to systems with fewer bugs, or that it can lead to more rapid development cycles than C# or VB .NET. These are all true, but there's a whole lot more to F# than just that. F# presents a whole host of possibilities to you as a .NET developer that will open your eyes to a better way to develop software—one that leads to you enjoying what you do more, while making you more productive in your job.

This introduction summarizes at a high level what F# is (and isn't!), and then discusses some of the benefits that you'll receive from using it. We won't spend much time looking at the language in this introduction, so you'll have to take some of what I say at face value; but you'll end up with a good idea of where F# can potentially fit in with your day-to-day role. We'll also cover the relationship of F# within the wider context of the .NET ecosystem, as well as taking a look at the F# community and how F# fits into the open source world. At the end of this introductory lesson, you'll have a good understanding of the *what* and *why* of F#; the rest of the book will then explain the *how*!

Although I do think it's important to read this, if you're keen to just dig in, feel free to go straight to lesson 1 and start bashing out some code!

What is F#, and why does it matter?

Let's first start at the beginning and discuss at a relatively high level some of the key points of what F# is (and isn't!). Then we'll discuss the key question that you probably have on the tip of your tongue: why should you spend time learning a new language with a new way of doing things, when you could be productively bashing out code right now in C# or VB?

What is F#?

What's this whole buzz about F#? F# is a language that's rapidly growing in popularity and attracting developers to be used in a variety of domains, not just from within the .NET ecosystem but also from without.

Let's start by quoting directly from the fsharp.org website:

> *F# is a mature, open source, cross-platform, functional-first programming language. It empowers users and organizations to tackle complex computing problems with simple, maintainable, and robust code.*

Let's discuss a few points mentioned in that quote:

- *Mature*—F# is a mature language with an established community. Based on the ML family of programming languages, and now at version 4, it's been a first-class citizen of Visual Studio since Visual Studio 2010 (though you may not even have been aware of it) and runs on the .NET Framework, which itself is over 15 years old now. In terms of the risk of using F#, you don't have to be concerned about things such as sourcing package dependencies or that you won't be able to find resources or help online.
- *Open source*—F# as a project is entirely open source and has been for several years (way before Microsoft's recent public shift toward open source). The compiler is open source, anyone can submit changes to the compiler and language (subject to approval of course!), and it runs not only on Windows but also on Mono, with support for Microsoft's new .NET Core well on the way at the time of writing.
- *Functional-first*—F# is prescriptive in the sense that the language encourages us *but doesn't force us* as developers to write code in a functional programming (FP) style. We'll describe those features in more detail shortly, and how they affect the way we code, but for now just know that it's an alternative way to model and solve problems compared to the object-oriented (OO) paradigm that you're used to. But as F# runs on the .NET Framework (an inherently OO framework), F# needs to support OO features. So, you can also consume and create classes and interfaces just as you can with C#; it's simply that it's not the idiomatic way to

write F#. In this book, we'll be effectively ignoring the OO side of F#—which would mostly just be about learning a new syntax—and focusing on the FP side, which is much more interesting.

Another point that the preceding quote alludes to is that F# helps us focus on delivering business logic and ultimately business value, instead of having to focus on complex design patterns, class hierarchies, and so on in order to achieve quality. This is partly because F# contains a powerful compiler that does a lot of the heavy lifting for us, which can lead to more succinct solutions than you might normally achieve in C#. But in addition, the FP paradigm (in conjunction with F#) emphasizes composing small pieces of functionality together to naturally build more powerful abstractions rather than through designing large class hierarchies up front and building downward.

What is functional programming?

To explain this a little more, let's quickly define *FP* within the context of this book. Just as with OO design, defining exactly what FP is can be subjective; many languages that support FP to some extent will have some features that others do not. At the end of the day, you can think of FP as a sliding scale of language features that encourage a particular style of programming; I suggest that any FP language should have good support for a few core fundamentals:

- *Immutability*—The ability to create values that can never be changed in their lifetime, which leads to a clear separation of data and functionality (unlike the OO world, which merges both state and behavior into classes).
- *Expressions*—The notion that every operation in your program has a tangible output that can be reasoned about.
- *Functions as values*—The ability to easily create, use, and share functions as a unit of abstraction and composition within a system.

There's certainly more to FP than just that, and many languages have features such as sum types, pattern matching, type classes, and the often-dreaded monad; we'll deal with some of these features throughout this book, but the preceding three are the key ones that we'll really emphasize. Remember that FP is just another way to model solutions to programming problems; there's no real magic involved, nor do you need to be a mathematical genius.

F# alongside other programming languages

Figure 1 illustrates where I believe F# fits in within the spectrum of other mainstream programming languages.

F# and C#—two sides of the same coin

Let's start by looking at F# which, as already stated, is a functional-*first* language. It's clearly on the FP side of the axis, yet it's not on the far right. Why? Well, F# makes it easy

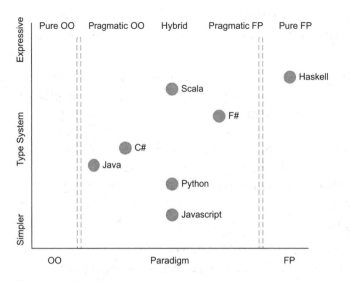

Figure 1   F# within the context of other programming languages

to write code in the FP style, but is a *hybrid* language, supporting both OO and FP features; it's not a pure functional language. It allows us to write code that might not be allowed in a stricter FP language such as Haskell.

Conversely, let's relate this diagram to two languages that we know well—C# and VB .NET. I suggest that both are going through a change of identity. What should we consider idiomatic C# code to be? On the one hand, it started life as an OO language with extremely limited support for FP. More recent iterations of the language have introduced some (limited) FP features—and the next version of C# has introduced yet more FP features—so perhaps it'll move further across this axis. Yet it has its roots in the OO paradigm, and the design of the language makes typical OO features (for example, mutability, statements, and classes) deliberately easy to use.

> **C# and VB .NET**
>
> I'll take this opportunity to acknowledge that figure 1 mentions C# only; as far as I'm concerned, aside from a few corner cases and syntactical features, C# and VB .NET are the same language both in terms of features and their ideology toward problem solving and modeling (although interestingly, Microsoft in early 2017 stated that in the future VB won't follow C# just to ensure parity). If later in this book, I mention only C# or VB .NET for the sake of brevity, do a find-and-replace operation in your head to show both languages.

In some ways, we can think about F# as being the alternative side of the same coin from a C# perspective—often, things that are difficult to achieve in C# are easy to implement in F#—and vice versa. Let's take a quick look at one example of that: creating mutable variables and immutable values in C# and F#.

Listing 1 Declaring values and variables in C# and F#

```
var name = "Isaac";          ◄─────── Declaring a mutable variable in C#
const string name = "Isaac"; ◄─────── Declaring an immutable value in C#

let mutable name = "Isaac"   ◄─────── Declaring a mutable variable in F#
let name = "Isaac"           ◄─────── Declaring an immutable value in F#
```

In C#, we normally use mutable variables by default to store data; to make them *immutable*, we need to use extra keywords (such as readonly or const). Conversely, in F#, to make *mutable* variables, we need to specify an extra mutable keyword; otherwise, the language assumes you're working with immutable data. This mentality applies across all of F#; it's prescriptive about making it easy to work with certain language features that fit in with the functional programming style, while allowing us to revert to modeling problems with objects and imperative code if we're willing to "pay the cost" of a few extra keywords. Table 1 lists distinctions between the default ways of working across the three .NET languages; all of the features on the right-hand side can be considered conducive to writing code in the FP style.

Table 1 Comparing and contrasting OO- and FP- based languages on .NET

Feature	C# / VB .NET	F#
Execution model	Statements	Expressions
Data structures	Mutable data	Immutable data
Program flow	Imperative	Declarative
Modeling behavior	Stateful classes	Functions with separate immutable state
Reuse	Inheritance	Composition

You might now say, "You can implement stateless functions or expressions in C#," and that's true. But this isn't the default way of working in C#. It requires extra keywords, or extra hoops that need jumping through in order to achieve the required behavior. In F#, the opposite is true for all of these features. Expressions are easy to achieve; statements aren't. Composition is easy to achieve; inheritance feels somewhat unnatural.

> **Is FP "better" than OO?**
>
> Or is F# better than C#, for that matter? I deliberately avoid saying either of these things when I give talks on F#. Not only can it be perceived as a controversial statement, but it also depends on your perspective. If you prefer solving problems by using statements, mutable data, and classes with inheritance, then you'll probably find C# a more elegant language, because that's how it was designed to be used! But if you're trying to use features from the right-hand side of the table in your day-to-day C# or VB .NET, F# will quickly feel like a natural fit. I can solve problems much more easily using FP features, and as such, F# is a much better fit for me.

Expressiveness

In figure 1, we can also see a second dimension: the *expressiveness* of a language. F# allows you to define your intent extremely succinctly, without a large amount of verbosity in terms of syntax. Instead, you concentrate on encoding your business rules in F# within the confines of a few simple rules; the compiler will get on with doing the heavy lifting for you. Note that this doesn't mean that writing F# leads to unreadable code! Coming from a C# or VB .NET background, where we're used to features such as curly braces, explicit typing, and statements everywhere, F# can initially appear unusual— even a little daunting. But it's more accurate to think of it as succinct and expressive with a powerful vocabulary that requires a little effort to learn. Once you're familiar with the syntax, the F# code is extremely easy to understand, and you can rapidly express complex business logic in a succinct manner.

Why F#?

We've described at a fairly high level what F# is: a functional-first, general-purpose programming language that runs on the .NET platform. The question now remains, why should you, as an experienced .NET developer who is productive in C# or VB .NET and confident at modeling problems using OO design paradigms, need to look at an alternative way of building solutions?

New possibilities

You might be looking at F# because you're interested in using it as a way to start exploring new concepts and domains such as type providers and functional programming. This is true. You'll find that F# opens the door to solving entirely new classes of problems such as data analysis, machine learning, and DSLs as varied as web testing and build management—some of which you might never have thought achievable within .NET. Although this book won't deal in depth with all of these areas, we'll definitely cover a few of them and point you in the direction of resources that you can further explore in your own time.

High-quality solutions

The F# language syntax and type system is designed for writing software that exhibits some of the key attributes of high-quality software. You can think of some of these attributes as follows:

- *Readability*—How easy it is to read and reason *about* some code
- *Maintainability*—How easy it is to modify an existing piece of code
- *Correctness*—How simple it is to write code that works as intended

In all of these areas, the design of F# leads you down a path that will naturally guide you toward code that exhibits these characteristics. First, it has a syntax that, although initially appearing a little unusual when coming from C-style languages, enables you to more easily read and understand its intent without performing a compilation in your head as you read the code. Let's discuss one of the points that I made earlier, that of imperative versus declarative code. Imperative code can be thought of as the low-level *how*—how you want to implement something. Conversely, declarative code concentrates more on expressing the *what*—what you want to achieve—and leaving the low-level details to another party. Here's an example of an imperative way of filtering out odd numbers from a list by using both imperative C# and declarative F#.

Listing 2 Imperative and declarative code samples in C# and F#

```
IEnumerable<int> GetEvenNumbers(IEnumerable<int> numbers) {
    var output = new List<int>();  ◄─────── Temporary collection to store output
    foreach (var number in numbers) { ◄─── Manual iteration through collection
        if (number % 2 == 0)        ◄───── Actual filter logic
            output.Add(number); }   ◄──── Manual addition to output collection
    return output; }
                                                      Focus on
let getEvenNumbers = Seq.filter(fun number -> number % 2 = 0) ◄─ business
                                                      logic
```

In the declarative version, we're more interested in our intent than the implementation details. We don't need to know the details of how the `Seq.filter` function is implemented because we understand the general logic of how it behaves. Armed with this, we can focus on our core goal, which is to identify numbers that are even. The code is much smaller—there's less to read, less to think about, and less that can go wrong. Of course, you can achieve similar code in C# via LINQ; in fact, if you typically use LINQ for these sorts of operations today, that's great! In F#, this is the default way of working, so you'll find that this style of code will be much more common throughout your applications.

Again, I don't want you to worry too much at this stage about the nitty-gritty of the F# syntax (or to wonder why there are apparently no arguments in the function!). I'll explain all of that in more detail later. But I do want you to think about the lack of type annotations and the lightweight syntax with the minimum of boilerplate; this sort of minimalistic approach is a common theme when working with F#.

> **Where are the types?**
> Just like C# and VB .NET, F# is a statically typed language. But it has an extremely powerful type inference engine, which means that it has the succinctness close to dynamic languages such as Python, but with the backing of a strong type system and compiler. You get the best of both worlds. Again, more on this later.

F# also emphasizes composition rather than inheritance to achieve reuse, with support for this baked into the language. Functions are the main component of reuse, rather than classes, so expect to write small functions that "plug together" to create powerful abstractions. Individual functions are nearly always easier to understand and reason about than entire sets of methods coupled together through state in a class, just like writing stateless functions are much easier to reason about than those that are stateful. As such, making changes to existing code is much easier to do with a greater degree of confidence. Here's a simple example of how we might build behaviors into more powerful ones in C# and F#. Again, in C# I've deliberately kept things at the method level, but also think about the effort required when trying to compose more complex sorts of behaviors across classes and objects.

Listing 3 Composing behaviors in C# and F#

```
IEnumerable<int> SquareNumbers(IEnumerable<int> numbers) {        Manually
    // implementation of square elided...                        composing the
                                                                  logic of two
}                                                                 functions together

IEnumerable<int> GetEvenNumbersThenSquare(IEnumerable<int> numbers {
    return SquareNumbers(GetEvenNumbers(numbers))
                                                                  Composition
}                                                                 as a first-class
let squareNumbers = Seq.map(fun x -> x * x)                       language feature
let getEvenNumbersThenSquare = getEvenNumbers >> squareNumbers
```

Without any understanding of how the >> symbol works, it should be clear to you that this operator fuses two functions together into one.

Finally, the F# type system is extremely powerful compared to C# and VB .NET. It allows us to write code in such a way that we can encode many more rules directly into our application so the compiler verifies that our code is valid without the need to resort to, for example, unit tests. But F# does this in an extremely succinct way, so that we aren't discouraged from being explicit about these rules. To be honest, the majority of the features in F# can be achieved in C# and VB .NET, but the cost would be so high in terms of the amount of code you would need to write, we simply don't do it. In F#, the lightweight syntax is a game changer because it means we can encode more rules into our code without a massive cost increase in terms of code.

Productivity

The difference with F# and other .NET languages is that the sorts of benefits I've mentioned so far are apparent from the syntax of the language right through to the F# core libraries and packages that you'll use. In effect, you have to write a whole lot less code in order to design a solution that's quicker to write, easier to understand, and cheaper to change than in C# or VB .NET. It's not uncommon to hear F# developers joke that if their code compiles, there's a good chance it works! Although this isn't always strictly true, and unit tests still have a place in F#, F# also definitely provides an ability to encode more business rules directly into your program, so you don't have to spend time writing and maintaining unit tests. You'll find you spend more time in F# itself defining your application logic than in C#, but a lot less time in the debugger.

Improving your C# and VB .NET

Not only will you start to learn how to write applications that are more maintainable, easier to understand, and reason about, but—particularly if the primary language in your software career has been C# or VB .NET on Visual Studio—F# will open your eyes and make you a better all-around software developer. You'll gain a better appreciation in C# for features such as lambda expressions, expression-bodied members (a recent addition in C# 6), and LINQ, and will realize that the application of these sorts of features can be used for more than just data access layers. You'll also probably start to approach modeling problems differently in C#, with less reliance on inheritance and other OO constructs as the only way to solve problems.

Working with a smarter compiler

Imagine you have a system with a simple domain model. You decide to add a new field onto one of your core domain classes, and hit Build in Visual Studio. In the C# and VB .NET world, this sort of change will compile without a problem, even though you haven't used or initialized the new field yet. You could even start to reference the field elsewhere in your application, without the compiler preventing you from accessing it despite having never initialized it. Later, perhaps you'll run the application and receive a null reference exception somewhere further down the chain. Perhaps you'll be unlucky and not test it out because it's a particularly obscure branch of code. Instead, a few months later, your users will eventually hit that part of code—and crash the application.

You might say that you could write unit tests to force this issue to the surface sooner. That's true. But another truth is that people often don't write unit tests, particularly for seemingly small changes. It'd be nice if the language could support us here. In the F# world, adding a new field will instantly break your code. Wherever you create instances of that type, you'll need to explicitly set the value of the new field at initialization time. Only after you've fixed all the assignments and usages would you be in a position to deal with how that new field is being used. Nulls aren't allowed for F# types either—so you wouldn't be able to set it as such. Instead, F# has the notion of optional values to cater to both possibilities.

The net result? You spend more time fixing compiler issues and evaluating possible branches of code, but the benefits are that you don't need to write any unit tests to guarantee consistency of the type, nor is there a risk of getting a null reference exception at runtime, and you won't need to debug it to prove that you won't get one.

You may feel an instinctive negative reaction to what I've just told you. After all, why would you want a compiler to get in the way of you writing code and slow you down from running your application? Don't worry; this is a normal reaction, and is part of the learning curve in "trusting" the compiler to help us write correct code in a much richer way than we're used to, which saves us a lot more time further down the road.

What's the catch?

Although I've been talking about the benefits of F# and said that it makes your life easier, we all know that there's no such thing as a free lunch. Surely there's a catch somewhere? The truth is somewhere in between.

On the one hand, F# isn't as hard as is claimed; you might have heard that F# should be used only for finance applications or mathematical modeling. Don't believe this.

Although it's certainly true that F# is a good fit for those use cases because of the nature of the language and its feature set, the language is also just as suitable for writing line-of-business applications, domain modeling, web development, or back-end services that fetch and shape data from a data store such as SQL Server or Mongo DB. It's almost as though OO languages with curly braces are apparently the only form of general-purpose programming languages in existence! And because F# runs on .NET, you won't have to waste time learning lots of new libraries to be productive (although F#-specific libraries do exist), and because we'll be using Visual Studio 2015, you'll be instantly familiar with the development environment (although, again, there are some differences that we'll cover later).

The biggest challenges you'll face are first learning the syntax of F#, and then, more important, *unlearning* the dogma of OO methodology. Things such as for loops, classes, and mutable state are so deeply ingrained into our thought processes for modeling domains and problem solving that it can be difficult to forget them. F# does allow you to work with mutable data, imperative styles, and classes; but doing these sorts of things in F# certainly isn't idiomatic, and the syntax will feel unnatural compared to C# or VB .NET. In essence, you'll get the worst of both worlds. Instead, you'll be better off starting from a clean slate when you approach solving problems, and you should rely on following a few simple rules and behaviors that we'll cover throughout the book. If you can do that, your solutions will naturally end up in a functional style.

When shouldn't I use F#?

To cut a long story short: for the majority of use cases for .NET development today, in my experience F# will let you get things done quicker than in C# or VB .NET with at least the same level of quality. In fact, I'll say right now that I recommend F# over C# or VB .NET as a general-purpose programming language for nearly every use case today, be it business logic, data access, or rules engines. That's a pretty bold statement, but having used C# since it first came out and F# for several years now, and having run a company that makes F# one of its main selling points, I think I'm allowed to do so!

The only situations that I don't recommend F# for are ones requiring custom tooling/support that's available only in C# or VB .NET (for example, Razor views in ASP .NET), or where the problem domain requires features that are inherently OO-based, or requires imperative and/or mutable code. As you'll see in this book, these cases are few and far between.

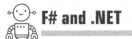 **F# and .NET**

We use .NET every day and, by and large, we all like it. It has a wide set of ready-made classes in the BCL across all sorts of areas such as collections, data access classes, UI frameworks, and web access, and the CLR has many great features such as a smart garbage collector. We also now have a rich ecosystem of rapidly evolving libraries through NuGet that can be released outside full .NET Framework releases. Why should you have to give all this up to use F#? The answer is that you don't. F# runs on .NET.

This is something that may seem obvious but is often overlooked or misunderstood, so it's worth stressing. *F# runs on .NET*. Virtually all of the types that you use in the BCL with C# are also accessible directly from within the F# language. You can also use NuGet packages and reference any .NET DLL, just as you would from C# or VB .NET. At runtime, F# is compiled into Intermediary Language (IL) and is hosted on the CLR so you get all the normal features of the CLR such as garbage collection. You can reference C# or VB .NET assemblies from F# and vice versa, and F# has interoperability features to allow seamless interaction across languages, while also taking advantage of F#-specific features to make dealing with .NET libraries nicer. You can consume (and create) classes with inheritance, interfaces, properties, and methods. Indeed, one of the strengths of F# is that it permits the developer to mix both FP and OO styles where appropriate. You're not going to have to give up the libraries that you already know, or the knowledge you've learned over the past years regarding the CLR, garbage collection, reflection, and so forth.

Although C# will, I suspect, always remain the focal point of Microsoft's investment in programming languages on .NET, this has always been the case. VB .NET, for example, has never been marketed by Microsoft as the main go-to language of .NET. Similarly, although F# doesn't receive quite the same level of investment as C#, it's still an important part of the .NET story and will continue to be in the .NET Core world.

In terms of VS integration, since Visual Studio 2010, F# has been supported out of the box as a first-class citizen of Visual Studio. This has continued up until the latest version at the time of writing, VS2015 (and will continue with VS2017). You can create all the things you would expect to do with VS and F#, including projects in solutions that might also contain C# or VB .NET projects. You can build assemblies in VS by using the same process that you're used to. You can create console applications, class libraries, Windows applications, and web applications all within Visual Studio. What you won't find in F# in Visual Studio 2015 out of the box are things like support for code generation, refactorings, or the "smarter" features in VS that are designed specifically for C# or

VB .NET, such as code analysis or code metrics. But as you learn more about F#, you'll see that there are ways, both through third-party tooling and the language itself, to negate the need for the tooling that we've come to rely on in C# or VB .NET.

Visual F#? F#? What's the difference?

It's worth taking a moment to explain the differences between F# and Visual F#. Visual F# is the Microsoft-managed version of F#, which is included with Visual Studio. It's been open sourced on GitHub, accepting contributions from the public, but is maintained by Microsoft, which ultimately has the final say on what features and changes are accepted. You can consider this repository to currently be the core repository for the F# compiler and language. A second repository (also on GitHub) is based on Visual F# and generally has a virtually identical code base known as F# Open Edition. This itself feeds into the cross-platform tooling support for Mono and Xamarin as well as other open source tools and code editors. You can find out more about this relationship at http://fsharp.github.io/.

For the purposes of this book, we're dealing exclusively with Visual F#, so whenever you see F#, you can consider it to mean Visual F#.

F#'s place within .NET

Let's now take a look at where F# fits within the .NET Framework and CLR runtime; see figure 2.

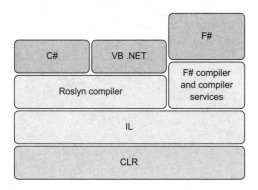

Figure 2   F# alongside other popular .NET languages

The F# language sits on top of the Common Language Runtime (CLR), just as C# and VB .NET do. The F# compiler, `fsc.exe`, emits .NET assemblies, just as the C# compiler `csc.exe` (and its replacement Roslyn) does. In addition, the F# Compiler Service (FCS) acts in a similar manner to Roslyn, allowing us to reason about F# code for the purposes of refactorings.

You'll notice that the F# compiler is drawn as a larger box than the Roslyn box. That's not to suggest that Roslyn / C# / VB .NET are smaller projects (in fact, quite the contrary)! But if you compare like-for-like idiomatic C# and F#, you'll see that the F# compiler does a lot more work for us. It's not unheard of for a single line of F# to emit the same IL as maybe a dozen lines or more of C#. Although this might sound like a gimmick, it's important. After you've been using F#, you'll start to realize that having a smarter compiler allows us to truly focus on the essentials of our problem domain, and to trust the compiler to help us write systems that have a greater *pit of success*—a larger chance of writing the correct code the first time.

Summary

That's the end of the introduction! You should now have an understanding of what F# is and what its benefits are. You learned that F# sits on top of .NET and is included with Visual Studio, so it's going to be easy for you to get up and running. Until now, you've just been taking my word for all of this, so the remainder of this book will prove it to you through practical examples.

There's one last piece of advice I'd like to give you before going any further. To fully benefit from learning F# in the most effective manner, to quote a wise man: you must *unlearn* what you have *learned*. If you can resist the temptation to see F# as an alternative syntax for designing code in the way you do today, and trust that there's an alternative way to solve the same kinds of problems, you're halfway there.

F# and Visual Studio

In this first unit of *Learn F#*, you're going to gently ease into getting up and running with F#. You'll mostly look at how F# works within the development environment that you're already most familiar with, Visual Studio. This book uses VS2015.

You'll also write a simple application in F# as quickly as possible, so that you understand which existing skills and knowledge from your C#/VB .NET expertise can be reapplied within the world of F#, and which can't be. Finally, you'll explore a different way of developing software in Visual Studio called the REPL.

By the end of this unit, you'll have a good understanding of how F# fits into Visual Studio and what you should (and shouldn't!) expect from the typical F# developer workflow. Here we go!

THE VISUAL STUDIO EXPERIENCE

I'm assuming that as a C# or VB .NET developer, you're already familiar with Visual Studio (VS). In this book, you'll be using Visual Studio 2015 (VS2015) and F# 4 (which is included with VS2015). This lesson covers how to ensure that your installation of VS contains everything needed for the remainder of the book so that you're on a level playing field with me, and we can dive straight into F#! We'll look at the following:

- Installing Visual Studio with F#
- Downloading F# extensions for Visual Studio 2015
- Configuring Visual Studio 2015 for use with F#

If you've already used F#, you might feel the need to skip this lesson. I advise you to at least quickly skim through it to ensure that you're working from the same baseline as I am to avoid any confusion later.

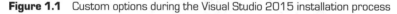 **1.1   Installing VS2015 with F#**

First, if you don't have VS2015, don't worry. Since VS2015, Microsoft has released a free-to-use version known as VS2015 Community Edition. This version is completely usable for the purposes of this book, and if you don't have it, I encourage you to download it now from www.visualstudio.com.

When you install VS2015, it's important to not select the default options during the installation process. As of VS2015, Visual Studio has become a much more componentized system, such that from now on, the default options install a much more bare-bones version. By default, F# isn't installed out of the box with VS2015; instead, select Custom, as shown in figure 1.1, and then pick Visual F# from the options.

Figure 1.1   Custom options during the Visual Studio 2015 installation process

---

I've already installed VS2015 without F#

What happens if you've already installed VS2015 and didn't install F# at the time? Don't worry! The first time you use VS2015 to create a new or open an existing F# project (for example, a console application or class library), the installer process will kick in and download the F# features for you automatically. Be careful, though—the same doesn't apply when creating or opening a standalone F# file.

1.2   Configuring Visual Studio for F#

Now that you've installed VS2015, let's quickly look at setting it up for working with F#
in an optimal manner.

1.2.1   Visual F# tools configuration

The first thing you should do is configure the core Visual F# tools, as shown in figure 1.2.

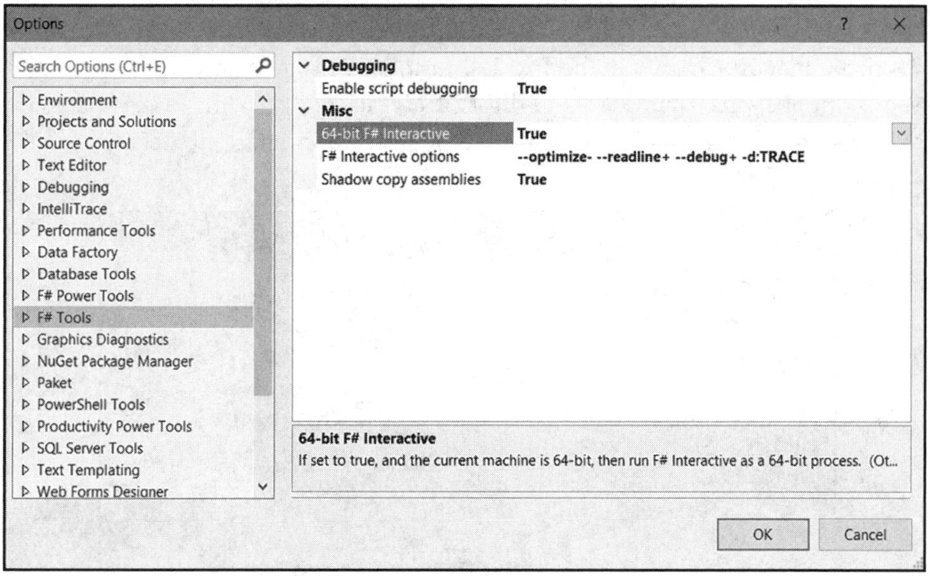

Figure 1.2   Configuring Visual F# tools

It's not too important at this point to know what these tools do, and you probably won't
ever need to touch these settings again. They'll make life easier for you as an F# developer by enabling you to do the following:

- Reference assemblies within scripts without holding locks on the file, or debug
  F# scripts
- Debug F# scripts in Visual Studio
- Output trace messages within F# scripts

> **Other IDEs for .NET**
>
> It's worth pointing out that in the last couple of years, other IDEs have cropped up that allow .NET development on Windows without Visual Studio. These include Atom and Microsoft's very own lightweight editor, Code. Both allow you to work with F# through a fantastic external plugin called Ionide. I often use Code rather than VS, as it's extremely lightweight and has great integration with many tools, but I still recommend Visual Studio as the best .NET IDE out there on Windows.

1.2.2   Configuring the F# editor

Next, ensure that you specify in the Text Editor to insert spaces and not keep tabs. On the same Options screen, choose Text Editor > F# > Tabs and click the Insert Spaces radio button, as shown in figure 1.3. This is important, as F# uses spaces to denote scope.

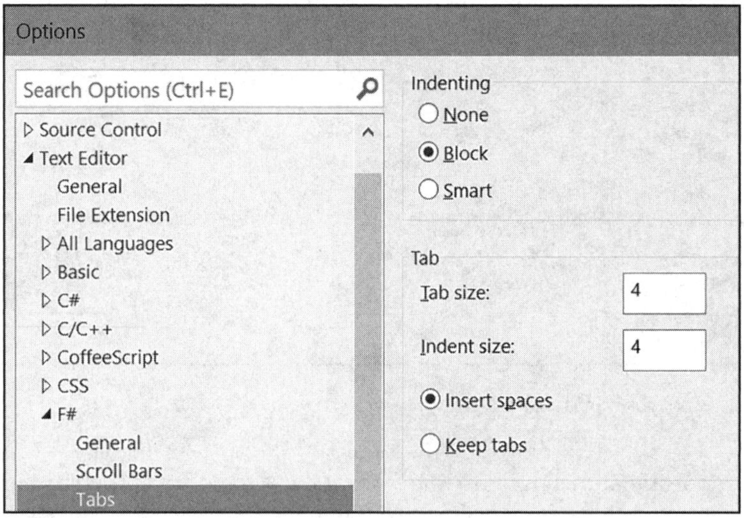

Figure 1.3   Configuring Text Editor options for F#

1.3   Getting the best out of VS 2015 and F#

Almost done! Next I'd like to show you extras that are worth configuring now, before we progress further through an extension.

1.3.1   Installing Visual F# Power Tools

Without a doubt, Visual F# Power Tools (VFPT) is the most important extension to add to VS2015 for F# development. It adds the following extra features:

- Refactorings
- Code collapsing
- Code generation
- Code formatting
- Syntax coloring
- Code rules

The Power Tools project is completely open source, so you can visit the repository and make changes to the tool if you have new features you'd like to see added. It also uses the code from other projects that are available as standalone tools, such as Fantomas (code formatting) and F# Lint (rules). Installing the VFPT will bring all of these and more in as one extension, so it's the quickest way to get up and running.

To install, go to Tools > Extensions and Updates and search for *fsharp*, as shown in figure 1.4. Alternatively, you can download the extension from the Visual Studio extensions website (https://visualstudiogallery.msdn.microsoft.com).

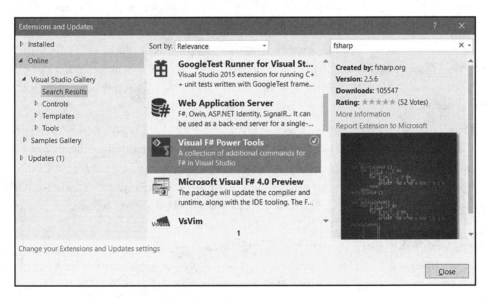

Figure 1.4 Installing F# Power Tools

What about Visual Studio 2017?

VS2017 has now been released! If you're using VS2017, there are some important things to note. First, the F# Power Tools are no longer available; VFPT isn't compatible with VS2017. As part of VS2017, the entire F#/VS integration was rewritten from the ground up to use Visual Studio's Roslyn IDE system (just as TypeScript does). This has several benefits: adding new refactorings will be much easier, and the entire IDE experience will align much more closely with C# and VB .NET.

There's a flip side to this, though. The rewritten integration with VS2017 was somewhat late to the party and suffered from delays, as well as reliability issues—not to mention that (again, at the time of this writing) it doesn't offer feature parity with VS2015 + VFPT. (I should point out that both the Visual F# team and, even more important, several people in the F# community have put forth a huge effort to improve this in a short space of time.)

I strongly recommend waiting until the experience is equivalent to VS2015, and the reliability issues have been fixed, before moving across; this might even be an update that's released shortly after RTM. If you're already using VS2017, most (if not all) of the VFPT features mentioned in this book will eventually be ported, and I predict that within 12 months, F# will have the same strong editor support in VS that C# or VB does today.

After you've installed and restarted VS2015, go to Tools > Options > F# Power Tools > General. You'll see a dialog box similar to figure 1.5.

You should activate all of these options, as they're all generally useful, with the possible exception of graying out unused opens and declarations, as they can be quite CPU-intensive. I recommend that you leave these options turned on to start with and see how your machine copes.

You'll also notice the Lint tab, which contains a whole host of "rules" that analyze your code in the background and provide helpful suggestions regarding writing more-effective F#. These suggestions are highlighted with orange squiggly underlines in code; they never indicate full compiler errors, but are there as best-practice tips (although like all code analyzers, it occasionally recommends something that isn't feasible).

1.3.2   Configuring F# syntax highlighting

Because of the nature of the F# syntax and its use of type inference, it's important for you to understand how the compiler "sees" your code to aid you when fixing compile-time errors. Now that you have VFPT installed, spend a couple of minutes configuring syntax highlighting. To do that, choose Tools > Options > Environment > Fonts and Colors and scroll down until you see the F# options, shown in figure 1.6.

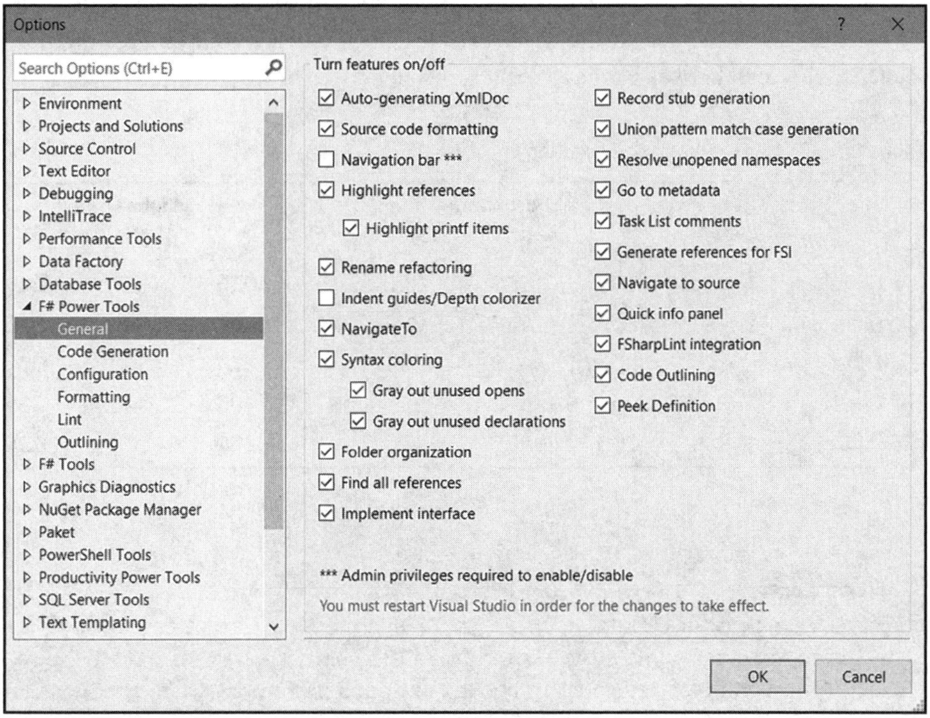

Figure 1.5 The Visual F# Power Tools options page

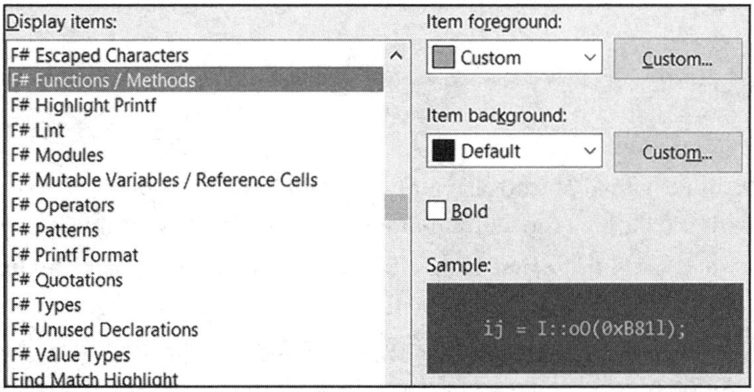

Figure 1.6 F# syntax highlighting options

You don't have to configure all of these options, but you should change those listed in table 1.1 ahead of the defaults. The following values will set your environment up to easily distinguish between many of the types of symbols.

Table 1.1   Custom F# syntax highlighting

| | Dark theme | | | Light theme | | |
	R	G	B	R	G	B
F# Functions / Methods	094	203	255	086	156	214
F# Modules	255	128	000	000	128	128
F# Mutable Variables	255	128	128	204	000	000
F# Operators	255	128	255	185	000	092
F# Patterns	255	255	128	200	100	000

What about .NET Core and non-Windows?

This book focuses on Windows, Visual Studio, and the full .NET on Windows, but the F# language works the same on Mono and .NET Core—although the tool-chain is slightly different (and I don't cover that in this book), the language features are the same. When it comes to .NET Framework features, things are a little different, though, as some technologies such as Windows Presentation Foundation (WPF) are Windows-specific and don't exist on .NET Core.

 **Summary**

In this lesson

- You installed Visual Studio 2015 and ensured that it was properly configured not only with the built-in tools but also with an extension, Visual F# Power Tools.
- You learned that F# is a first-class citizen of Visual Studio, as it's included "in the box" of the installer, or can optionally be applied at a later date if you choose.
- You saw that there's good integration for F# in the sense that the standard VS tooling and editor options are already F#-aware. You're now ready to start writing F# applications!

CREATING YOUR FIRST F# PROGRAM

Now that you've installed Visual Studio and have the F# tools installed in it, what can you do with it? By the end of this lesson, you'll see how and where F# integrates with Visual Studio. This lesson covers the following:

- Creating an F# console application in Visual Studio
- Working with F# syntax
- Understanding F#'s "less is more" approach

 ## 2.1 F# project types

You can create projects in a solution, just as you'd do in C#, in exactly the same way. F# has support out of the box for several project templates, the most important of which are the following:

- *Library*—A Visual Studio project that compiles into a .NET assembly ending with .dll and can be referenced by other .NET projects and assemblies. You can think of this as equivalent to the Class Library project that you'll be familiar with from C#.
- *Console Application*—A Visual Studio project that compiles into a .NET assembly ending with .exe and is capable of being run. This can also be referenced by other .NET projects and assemblies.

Sounds familiar, right?

Now you try

Let's see how to create your first F# project. You'll already know these project types from C# or VB. NET, and they work in the same way. Creating one is as simple as following these steps:

1 Choose File > New Project and then pick the appropriate project type.
2 If this is the first time you've used F#, you have to navigate down to the Other Languages node to locate the Visual F# templates.
3 Select Console Application and set the name to MyFirstSharpApp, as shown in figure 2.1, before clicking OK.

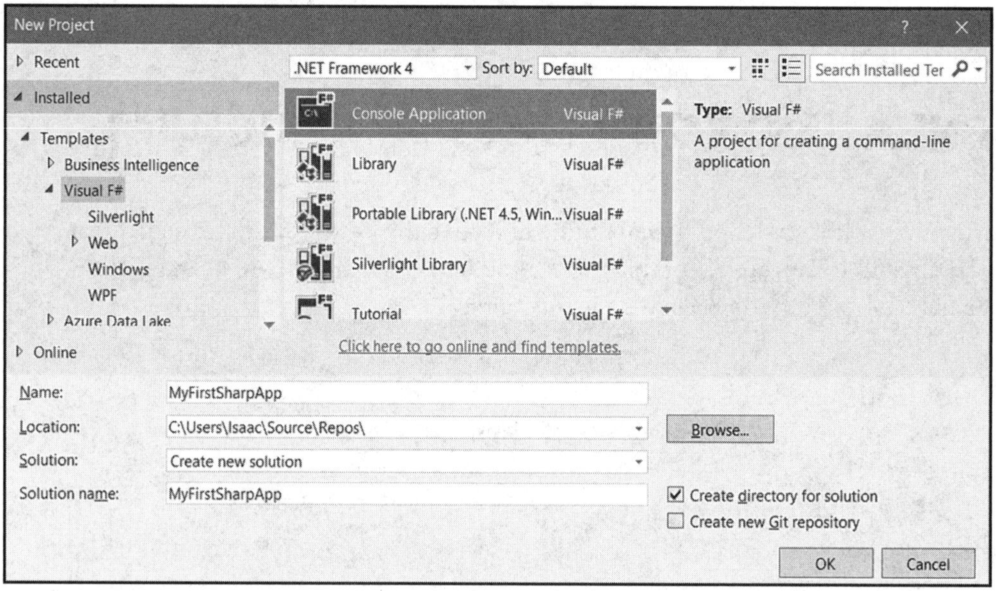

Figure 2.1   Creating an F# console application in VS2015

Where are the projects?

You might notice that figure 2.1 shows a Web node that you don't have. You might also be wondering where the Windows Forms or WPF project templates are. The answer is that out of the box, VS2015 doesn't come with any of them. But you can overcome this in various ways (as you'll see in more detail later in this book), such as third-party templates or packages.

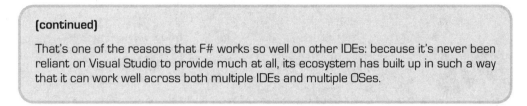

(continued)

That's one of the reasons that F# works so well on other IDEs: because it's never been reliant on Visual Studio to provide much at all, its ecosystem has built up in such a way that it can work well across both multiple IDEs and multiple OSes.

The result will be a solution comprising a single project with numerous files in it, as shown in figure 2.2.

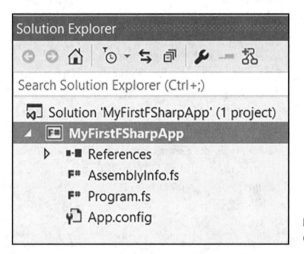

Figure 2.2 A stock F# console application

Let's go through the files one by one:

- *AssemblyInfo.fs*—This file sets properties of the assembly and fulfills the same function as AssemblyInfo files in C# or VB projects. It's not particularly interesting, so let's leave it for now.
- *Program.fs*—This is the launch point of your application, and is worth looking into in more depth.

Listing 2.1 Console application entry point

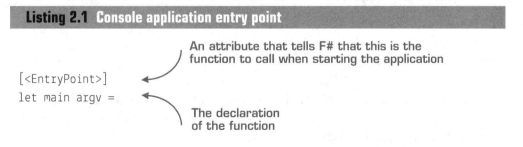

```
printfn "%A" argv
0 // return an integer exit code
```

Body of the function—prints the
arguments that were passed in

Body of the function—
returns 0 as the result
of the application

You probably have questions about this code snippet, and I'll answer the most likely ones by using a comparison with a C# console application:

- *No class declaration?* That's right. F# does normally require you to create a *module* as a container for functions inside .fs files, but for console applications, you can skip this entirely. Instead, the compiler uses the name of the file as the module implicitly. You can see this by hovering over the main function name, where you'll see the fully qualified name as Program.main.
- *Why do I need to use* EntryPoint*?* In C#, you don't need the entry point because you must instead specify it through the project properties. In F#, this is achieved by marking the function with an attribute (note that in F#, attributes are specified as [<Attribute>] rather than [Attribute], as the [ ] syntax is used elsewhere).
- *Where's the return keyword / curly braces / semicolons / type declarations (and so forth)?* These are not normally required or valid in F#! You'll find out more in the coming lessons. F# instead is *whitespace-significant*, which means that *indentation* of code is used to represent blocks.

F# file types
Unlike C# and VB.NET, which have only a single file type, F# has two files types:

- .fs—Equivalent to .cs or .vb, these files are compiled as part of a project by MSBuild and the filenames end in .dll or .exe.
- .fsx—An F# script file that's a standalone piece of code that can be executed without first needing to be compiled into a .dll. You'll learn more about script files in the coming lessons, but for now, remember that these are a lightweight and easy way to explore code without the need for a full-blown console application. In the next version of Visual Studio, C# will have a similar file type to this known as .csx.

Now you try

Running an application in F# is the same as usual. Pressing F5 runs the application with debugging attached, and Ctrl-F5 runs without debugging attached. Running the application without debugging attached shows you something like figure 2.3.

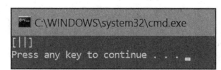

Figure 2.3 Running the stock
F# console application

That's pretty, but what is it? Well, looking back in the application, you can see that you
print out the arguments supplied to the app with the call to `printfn`. But you're not sup-
plying any arguments yet, so what's [|||]? The answer is that F# has *native language* sup-
port for some data structures and collections, including standard .NET arrays (you'll
learn more about arrays in unit 4). The arguments passed into main (`argv`) are an array of
strings (or `string` []),as in C#/VB. In F#, the syntax for arrays is as follows:

```
let items = [| "item"; "item"; "item"; "item" |]
```

The closest equivalent in C# is probably this:

```
var items = new [] { "item", "item", "item", "item" };
```

Because you're passing in an empty array to your application, that's all that's printed
out: [| |]. Let's see how to change that by supplying arguments to the application:

1 Go to the properties pane of the project by selecting the project node in Solution
  Explorer and pressing Alt-Enter.
2 Navigate to the Debug tab.
3 In the Command Line arguments box, enter the text `HELLO WORLD`.
4 Rerun the application.

You'll now see the results shown in figure 2.4.

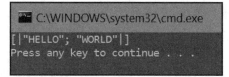
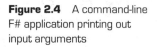

Figure 2.4 A command-line
F# application printing out
input arguments

The arguments supplied are automatically converted into the array. That's nice, but let's
look at the F# syntax a little more, before seeing how to write some F# yourself and
incorporating it into your existing application.

Now you try

We'll deal with more of the F# syntax in the next couple of lessons, but even exploring this small code snippet raises interesting issues:

1 Mouse over each of the values defined in Program.fs to get IntelliSense over them. You'll see that the values all have explicit types according to the tooltips — yet none are specified in the code. Where do they come from? This is F#'s type inference engine at work; you'll find out more about this in lesson 5.

2 If you installed the Power Tools extension as indicated in lesson 1, you'll see that `main` and `printfn` are highlighted in a different color than `argv`. This is because both `main` and `printfn` are functions. You'll find the coloring of different symbols extremely useful in understanding the context of your code and learning how the F# compiler parses your code.

Quick check 2.1

1 What are the two basic project types for F# shipped with Visual Studio?
2 What is the [`<EntryPoint>`] attribute for?
3 What are the two types of F# files in a project?

2.2   Debugging applications in F#

Debugging applications is less important in F# than in other languages. Because of the language design and features such as the REPL, you'll usually have tested most outcomes before you ever run your application. But there's still a good debugging experience in Visual Studio for F#, with the usual features such as breakpoints and watches. Still, at times the debugging experience falls a *little* short of what you're probably used to in C#, because some of the more advanced features of F# that don't exist in C# aren't supported by the debugger.

QC 2.1 answer

1 Console and Class Library
2 Marking the entry function to a console application
3 .fs (compiled file) and .fsx (script file)

Now you try

Let's explore with the Visual Studio debugger:

1 Go to line 6 in Program.fs and press F9 (or if you have the breakpoints column turned on in the editor, click there).

2 Debug the application with F5.

3 Mouse over the `argv` value when the breakpoint is hit. Observe that you can drill into the array to see the values passed in, as shown in figure 2.5.

4 The normal commands such as F10 for *step over* and F11 for *step into* all work as usual.

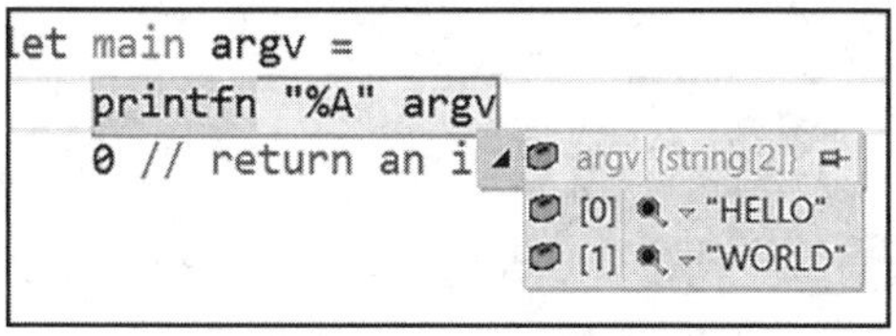

```
let main argv =
    printfn "%A" argv
    0 // return an i    ◢ ◉ argv {string[2]}  ₊
                         ◉ [0] ◉ ▾ "HELLO"
                         ◉ [1] ◉ ▾ "WORLD"
```

Figure 2.5 The VS debugger within an F# console application

> **Quick check 2.2**   What keyboard shortcut is used for adding debug breakpoints?

2.3   Writing your first F# program

Let's end this lesson with you writing a little bit of F#. You'll change the output of `printfn` to show the length of the array passed in as well as the items themselves. Change the code as follows.

Listing 2.2 An enhanced console application

```
[<EntryPoint>]
let main argv =
    let items = argv.Length
    printfn "Passed in %d items: %A" items argv
    0 // return an integer exit code
```

QC 2.2 answer   F9

You'll see that when you *dot into* argv, you'll get IntelliSense for the array. Make sure you supply the arguments to printfn in the correct order!

---

printfn in F#

printfn is a useful function (along with its sibling sprintf) that allows you to inject values into strings by using placeholders. These placeholders are also used to indicate the type of data being supplied:

- %d—int
- %f—float
- %b—Boolean
- %s—string
- %O—The .ToString() representation of the argument
- %A—An F# pretty-print representation of the argument that falls back to %O if none exists

Supply the args, space-separated, after the raw string. Don't use brackets or commas to separate the arguments to printfn—only spaces (the reason for this will be explained).

After you've amended the application, running it should display the output in figure 2.6.

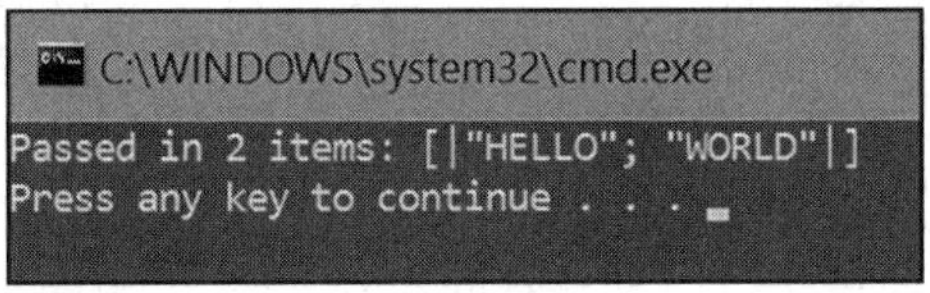

```
C:\WINDOWS\system32\cmd.exe
Passed in 2 items: [|"HELLO"; "WORLD"|]
Press any key to continue . . .
```

Figure 2.6   An enhanced Hello World console application in F#

Quick check 2.3   What placeholder is used for printing strings in printfn?

QC 2.3 answer   %s

 **Summary**

In this lesson

- You created a simple console application in F# and learned how to define an entry point to it.
- You explored how to run console applications, and saw that running and debugging F# applications isn't very different from the C# or VB .NET experience.
- You had a first look at the F# language in a standalone application.

Try this

Enhance the application to print out the length of the array as well as the items that were supplied by using a combination of `printfn` and the `Length` property on the array (use dot notation, as you're used to).

THE REPL—CHANGING HOW WE DEVELOP

In this lesson, you'll look at an alternative way to develop applications than what you're probably used to in terms of both tools and process. You'll first learn the pros and cons of techniques such as debugging and unit tests, and then see how to shorten your development cycle through alternatives that F# provides.

3.1   Code-focused developer processes

Think for a moment about your typical development process in terms of the way you write and then validate your code. After you've written some C# or VB .NET, how do you confirm that it works as you intended? What tools or process do you follow? I'm willing to bet it follows one of the following three patterns: application-based development, console test rigs, or automated unit tests.

3.1.1   Application-based development

You develop code for a while, thinking about the problem at hand. When you think it's ready, you run the application and run the section of the application to stress the code you just wrote. If it behaves as expected, you move on to solving the next problem.

The problem with this approach, depicted in figure 3.1, is that it's not particularly efficient. The section of code you've just written may take time to navigate through the application, or may not be feasible—for example, code that gets called only under circumstances out of your control, such as only when the network connection drops.

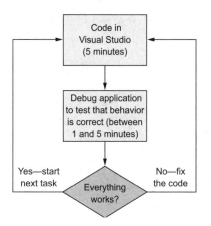

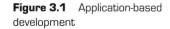

Figure 3.1   Application-based development

3.1.2   Console test rigs

You develop code for a while. When you're ready to test it, you write a console application that calls directly into the application code that you've written—perhaps several times with specific arguments. Figure 3.2 shows the process.

It's hard to maintain these console test harnesses. The cost of keeping these up-to-date often grows quickly, particularly as you want your test rig to grow to cater to more scenarios and areas of your code.

3.1.3   Automated unit tests

Unit tests are a great way to test parts of code without running a full application. They also give us regression tests so that as we make changes, we know whether we've broken existing behavior. As you can see in figure 3.3, the process is more complex than with test rigs.

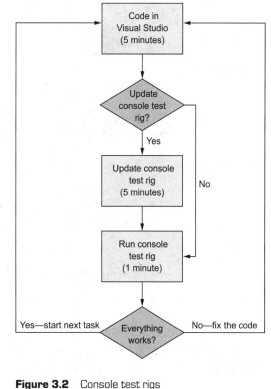

Figure 3.2   Console test rigs

Unfortunately, the truth is that test-driven development (TDD) is a difficult skill to master, and if done wrong can be extremely costly—with fragile unit tests that are difficult to reason about and hard to change. It's also expensive as a means to explore a domain; you wouldn't use unit tests as a means to test out a new NuGet package, for example.

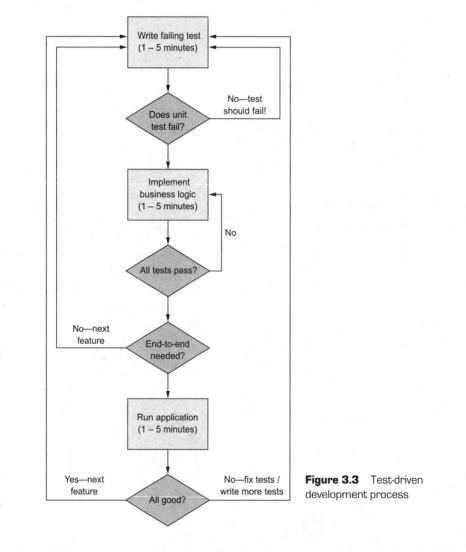

Figure 3.3 Test-driven development process

I should point out that I'm a big fan of TDD in C#. I used it religiously for many years and found that it can raise the quality of software. But it's *hard* to get right! And it doesn't lend itself well to trying new things quickly. What we need is a lightweight way to experiment with code, test out ideas, and when we're happy with the results, push them into a real code base—perhaps along with some unit tests to prove the behavior.

3.2   Enter the REPL

In this section, we'll look at an entirely different way to approach exploring and developing code: the REPL.

3.2.1   What is the REPL?

Figure 3.4   The Read Evaluate Print Loop is an effective way to rapidly explore and develop solutions.

REPL stands for *Read Evaluate Print Loop*—a mechanism for you to enter arbitrary, ad hoc code into a standalone environment and get immediate feedback. The easiest way to think of a REPL is to think of the Immediate window in Visual Studio, but rather than being used when *running* an application, a REPL is used when *developing* an application. You send code to the REPL, and it evaluates the code and then prints the result. This feedback loop, depicted in figure 3.4, is a tremendously productive way to develop.

A REPL can be an effective replacement for all three of the use cases outlined previously. Here are some example uses for a REPL:

- Writing new business logic that you want to add to your application
- Testing existing production code with a predefined set of data
- Exploring a new NuGet package that you've heard about in a lightweight exploratory mode
- Performing rapid data analysis and exploration—think of tools such as SQL Server Management Studio or LINQPad.

As you can see in figure 3.5, the emphasis is on quick exploration cycles: trying out ideas in a low-cost manner and getting rapid feedback, before pushing that into the application code base. What's nice about F# is that because the language allows you to encode more business rules into the code than in C#, you can often have a great deal of confidence that your code will work. You won't need to run end-to-ends particularly often. Instead, you'll find yourself working in Visual Studio and the REPL more and more, focusing on writing code that delivers business value.

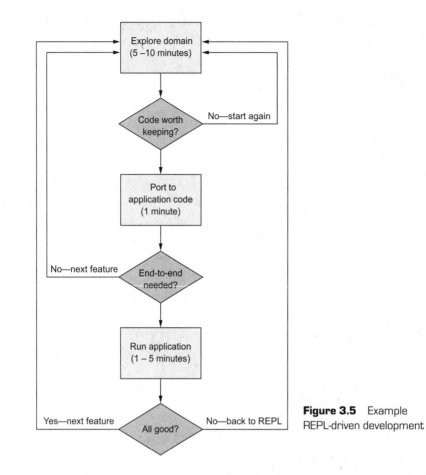

Figure 3.5 Example REPL-driven development

REPLs, REPLs everywhere!

Many languages and development environments already have a REPL. Some full-blown standalone applications are extremely powerful REPLs with built in-charting and reporting facilities, such as Python's IPython Notebook (and more recently, Jupyter). Since newer versions of VS2015, C# now finally does have a basic REPL called C# Interactive.

3.2.2   F# Interactive

Let's try out the REPL that comes with VS2015 for F#, called F# Interactive, or FSI for short. Figure 3.6 shows the user interface.

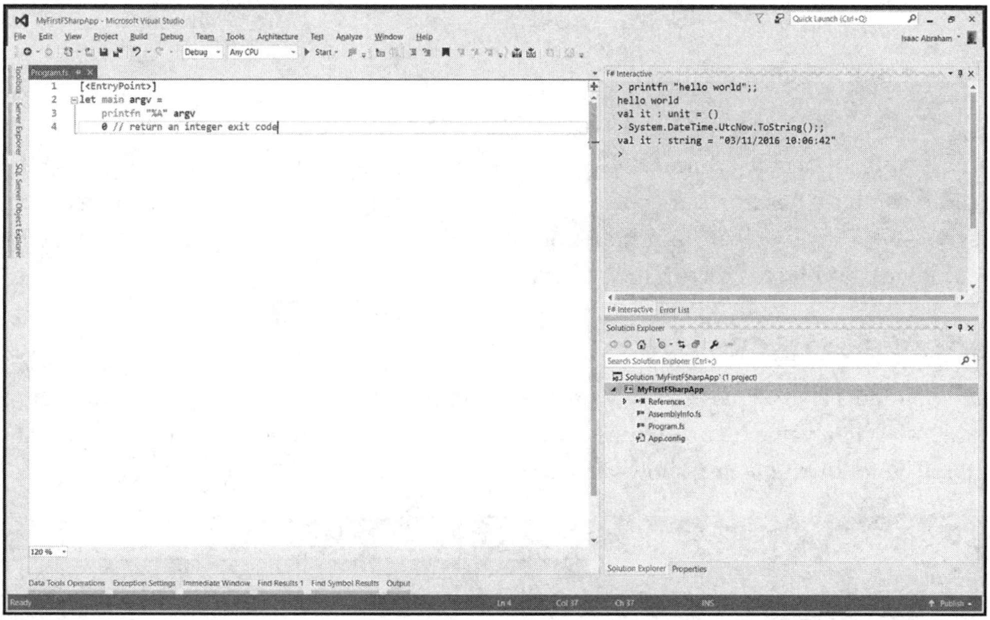

Figure 3.6   The F# development REPL experience in VS2015. The main code window is shown on the left, with the top-right pane representing F# Interactive (FSI).

Now you try

1   Open F# Interactive from the View > F# Interactive menu option.
2   You're presented with a new tool window. This is most likely docked to the bottom of the window. My preference is to dock it to right-hand side of the window, occupying about 25%–30% of the width of the IDE (although I use a widescreen monitor).
3   Clicking on the FSI pane enables you to execute any valid F# code. Enter this command:

```
printfn "Hello World";;
```

You'll see the following output:

```
Hello world!
val it : unit = ()
```

4 Enter this command:

```
System.DateTime.UtcNow.ToString();;
```

You'll see this output:

```
val it : string = "06/04/2016 10:30:42"
```

You're able to execute arbitrary F# code without needing to run an application; Visual Studio itself is a host to your code. FSI outputs anything that you print out (such as the text Hello World) as well as information itself (such as the content of values when they're evaluated). You'll see more in the coming lessons.

3.2.3   State in FSI

FSI maintains state across each command, and you can bind the value of a particular expression to a value by using the let keyword that you can then access in subsequent calls. The following listing shows an example.

Listing 3.1 A simple `let` binding

```
let currentTime = System.DateTime.UtcNow;;
currentTime.TimeOfDay.ToString();;
```

Note the two semicolons (;;) at the end of each command. This tells FSI to execute the text currently in the buffer. Without this, FSI will add that command to the buffer until it encounters ;; and will execute all the commands that are in the buffer.

If you want to reset all state in FSI, you can either right-click and choose Reset Interactive Session, or press Ctrl-Alt-R. Similarly, you can clear the output of FSI (but retain its state) by using Clear All or Ctrl-Alt-C.

What's it?

You probably noticed the val it = text in FSI for commands that you executed. What's this? it is the default value that any expressions are bound to if you don't explicitly supply one by using the let keyword. Executing this command

```
System.DateTime.UtcNow;;
```

is the same as executing this:

```
let it = System.DateTime.UtcNow;;
```

Quick check 3.1

Quick check 3.1

1. What does REPL stand for?
2. Name at least two conventional processes used for developing applications.
3. What is the F# REPL called?

3.3   F# scripts in Visual Studio

If you've tried the preceding exercises, your first thought is probably something like, "Well, this is quite useful, but the IDE support is awful!" And you're not far wrong. You get no syntax highlighting, no IntelliSense support—no nothing, really. A couple of experimental extensions are available to improve this (plus some extremely promising work being done in MonDevelop, Xamarin Studio, and with Roslyn), but at the moment working directly in FSI isn't a great experience.

3.3.1   Creating scripts in F#

Luckily, there's a much better way to work with FSI that *does* give you IntelliSense and syntax highlighting: F# scripts, or .fsx files. Let's see how to create your first script and experiment with it a little.

Now you try

1. Right-click your F# project in Visual Studio and choose Add > New Item.
2. From the dialog box that pops up, choose Installed > Code > Script File and set the filename to `scratchpad.fsx`. The file automatically opens in VS.

You'll be looking at a blank file in the main panel. Entering any text here will give you full IntelliSense and code completion, just like inside a full .fs file. Start by entering something simple into the script:

```
let text = "Hello, world"
```

QC 3.1 answer

1. REPL stands for Read Evaluate Print Loop.
2. Application-based testing, console test rigs, and unit testing.
3. F# Interactive, or FSI for short.

Hovering over text will show you that F# has identified the value as a string. If you move to the next line and type `text.`, you'll see immediately that you get full IntelliSense for it, as shown in figure 3.7.

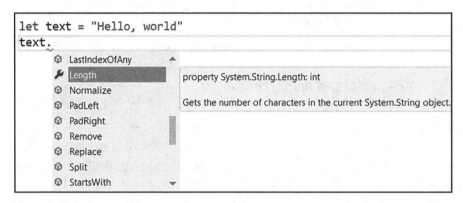

Figure 3.7   Working with F# in an .fsx script file

In this way, you can work with all .NET types and values within a script file for experimentation. Even better, scripts can work together with FSI to give you a fantastic experience, as you'll see next. And the best bit is that a script doesn't need a solution *or project* in which to function. You can open Visual Studio, choose File > New, pick an F# script, and start working!

3.3.2   Understanding the relationship between scripts and FSI

When working with scripts, you'll obviously want a way to evaluate the results of code you've entered. This is extremely easy within an F# script: pressing Alt-Enter sends the current line to FSI for evaluation (see Figure 3.8). In this way, you can think of the rapid feedback cycle here as similar to writing unit tests (particularly in a TDD style), albeit in a much more lightweight form. You can also highlight multiple lines and use the same keypress to send all the highlighted code to FSI.

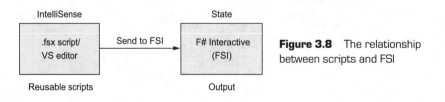

Figure 3.8   The relationship between scripts and FSI

> **Resharper and F#**
>
> You might find that Alt-Enter doesn't work for you. This might be because you have ReSharper installed, which "steals" this shortcut for its own use. You'll have to reconfigure ReSharper to not do this, or choose a different keyboard shortcut for FSI Send to Interactive from within the keyboard shortcut options of VS.

Now you try

Now, explore the relationship between .fsx scripts and FSI:

1 Move to the first line in your script and press Alt-Enter.
2 Observe that FSI outputs the result `val text : string = "Hello, world"`.
3 On the next line in the script, send the command `text.Length` to FSI and observe the result in FSI: `val it : int = 12`.
4 Reset FSI.
5 Highlight both lines and send them to FSI simultaneously.
6 Reset FSI again.
7 Highlight *only the second line* and send it to FSI. Notice that FSI returns an error that `text` isn't defined. You haven't sent the first line that defines it to FSI.

Instead of you having to manually enter code in FSI, you can first enter it into a *repeatable* script and send entire sections of the script to FSI as needed. You can use scripts as a way to completely remove the need for console test rigs; instead, you'll have a set of scripts to test your code in a predefined way.

3.3.3 Working with functions in scripts

You can also define functions in scripts, send them to FSI, and then call them from the script on demand. The next listing creates a function that takes in someone's name and returns a string that's the greeting of the person.

Listing 3.2 A simple function definition

```
let greetPerson name age =
    sprintf "Hello, %s. You are %d years old" name age
```

Highlighting the entire function and sending it to FSI compiles the function.

On the next line, enter this code before sending it to FSI to execute the function call:

```
let greeting = greetPerson "Fred" 25
```

Functions and type inference

Notice that mousing over `greetPerson` shows you the signature of the function; `name` is inferred to be a `string`, and `age` an `integer`, and the function returns a `string`. You'll explore this more in lesson 5. For now, it's enough to know that the `sprintf` function tells you that `name` is a `string`, and `age` an `int` from the `%s` and `%d` specifiers.

You can repeatedly highlight this line and send it to FSI. You'll learn more about `let` in lesson 4, but in case you're wondering, repeatedly executing this line doesn't mutate the value of `greeting` multiple times. Instead, it's creating a *new* value every time and discarding the previous one.

Quick check 3.2

1 Do scripts need a project in order to run?
2 Give two reasons that you might use a script rather than coding directly into FSI.

 **Summary**

In this lesson

- You explored the REPL, a powerful tool in a developers' arsenal.
- You learned about the relationship between F# Interactive (FSI) and F# scripts (.fsx files), and how and when to use each of them.
- You explored writing more F# code, defining your first function.

Try this

Spend a little more time in the F# script; write a function, countWords, that can return the number of words in a string by using standard .NET string split and array functionality. You'll need to provide a type hint for the input argument, such as

```
let countWords (text:string) =...
```

Then, save the string and number of words to disk as a plain-text file.

QC 3.2 answer

1 No—you can run scripts as standalone files.
2 F# scripts have an improved development experience and are repeatable.

Hello F#

In the previous unit, you gained a feeling for the development experience in VS. It's not that different from C# and VB .NET insofar as you have the same basic project types, as well as access to the Base Class Library (BCL) that you already know. But we covered only the bare essentials of the F# language.

This unit focuses on the core foundational elements of F# as a language: how it differs from C# and VB .NET in its aims, how it changes your approach to problem solving in the "small," and how you learn to work with a compiler and language that make you think in a slightly different way. As you'll see, you'll already be familiar with some of the concepts in C# and VB .NET; but F# takes those features and turns the dial up to 11 on them—putting them front and center of the language.

By the end of this unit, you'll have a good understanding of the basic syntax structure and philosophy of F#. You'll gain experience working with its rich type inference as well as with expressions and statements. In addition, you'll understand the benefits of immutable data.

> **NOTE** Pay attention in this unit! At the end of it, you'll work through a capstone exercise—a larger lesson that's designed to get you using all the elements you'll have learned thus far in a single, coherent application. Think of it as the end-of-level boss, and these lessons as the power-ups you need to gain in order to beat it.

SAYING A LITTLE, DOING A LOT

In this lesson, you'll gain an overview of the basics of the F# language:

- You'll take a closer look at the F# language syntax, including the `let` keyword.
- You'll learn how to write some more-complex functions and values.
- You'll learn what scoping is, why it's important for creating readable code, and how it works in F#.

Think about the programming languages that you use today. They come in all sorts of flavors and are known for being used in different fields or situations. For example, Java is well-known as an *enterprise* programming language—which has somewhat negative connotations of a slow-moving and verbose language. Others might have a reputation for being used at startups, academia, or in data science. Why are languages shoehorned into specific fields, when many of them say that they're *general-purpose* programming languages? A combination of many factors sometimes helps push a language to a specific community or use case.

One of these factors might be the type system. For example, some languages are generally considered to be statically typed (Java, C#), whereas others are dynamic (Python, JavaScript, Ruby). The latter have gained a reputation for being used in startups because of the alleged speed at which development can occur for relatively simple systems (although several notable examples exist of organizations having to rewrite entire systems in a static language after the application grew too large—Twitter being one).

Another important feature is the *syntax* of the language. This, just as much as the type system, can turn entire sets of potential developers away from a language. Too verbose, and developers may lose patience with it and move on to another one. Too lightweight and terse, and it might be too difficult for developers to pick up, particularly if they're used to a language that has a verbose syntax.

These two traits often seem to be naturally grouped, as shown in table 4.1.

Table 4.1   Language traits compared

Language	Type system	Syntax
C#	Static, simple	Curly brace, verbose
Java	Static, simple	Curly brace, extremely verbose
Scala	Static, powerful	Curly brace, verbose
Python	Dynamic, simple	Whitespace, very lightweight
Ruby	Dynamic, simple	Whitespace, very lightweight
JavaScript	Dynamic, simple	Curly brace, lightweight

The takeaway is often that static programming languages are slower to develop than dynamic languages, because the syntax is too heavyweight and verbose, and the benefits of a static type system don't outweigh those costs. But some static languages, such as F# and Haskell, aim to give the developer the best of both worlds: a powerful, static type system that has an extremely lightweight syntax designed to allow developers to express their intent without having to worry about lots of keywords and symbols for everyday use. In this way, and in conjunction with the REPL, you can rapidly develop applications that are underpinned by a powerful compiler and type system.

Before you dive in, let me reiterate one point: in F#, the overall emphasis is to enable you to solve *complex* problems with *simple* code. You want to focus on solving the problem at hand without necessarily having to *first* think about design patterns within which you can put your code, or complex syntax. All the features you're going to see now are geared toward helping to achieve that. F# does have some common "design-patternish" features, but in my experience, they're few and far between, with less emphasis on them.

4.1 Binding values in F#

The `let` keyword is the single most important keyword in the F# language. You use it to bind values to symbols. In the context of F#, a value can range from a simple value type such as an integer or a Plain Old C# Object (POCO), to a complex value such as an object with fields and methods or even a function. In C#, we're not generally used to treating functions as values, but in F#, they're the same—so any value can be bound to a symbol with `let`.

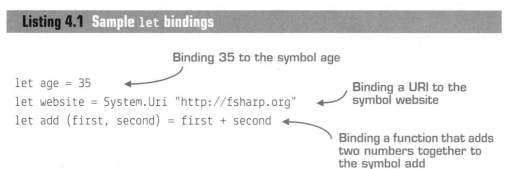

Binding 35 to the symbol age

```
let age = 35
let website = System.Uri "http://fsharp.org"
let add (first, second) = first + second
```

Binding a URI to the symbol website

Binding a function that adds two numbers together to the symbol add

Here are some takeaways from that small sample:

- *No types*—You'll notice that we haven't bothered with specifying any types. The F# compiler will figure these out for you, so if you mouse over `age` or `website`, you'll see `int` and `System.Uri` (although you can—and occasionally *must*—specify them). This type inference is scattered throughout the language, and is so fundamental to how we work in F# that lesson 5 is entirely dedicated to it (and will explain how the compiler understands that the `add` function takes in two numbers—it's not magic!).
- *No new keyword*—In F#, the `new` keyword is optional, and generally not used except when constructing objects that implement `IDisposable`. Instead, F# views a constructor as a function, like any other "normal" function that you might define.
- *No semicolons*—In F#, they're optional; the newline is enough for the compiler to figure out you've finished an expression. You *can* use semicolons, but they're completely unnecessary (unless you want to include multiple expressions on a single line). Generally, you can forget they ever existed.
- *No brackets for function arguments*—You might have already seen this and asked why this is. F# has two ways to define function arguments, known as *tupled form* and *curried form*. We'll deal with this distinction in a later lesson, but for now it's

fine to say that both when calling and defining them, functions that take a *single* argument don't *need* round brackets (a.k.a. parentheses), although you can put them in if you like; functions that take in zero or multiple arguments (as per the add function) need them, as well as commas to separate the arguments, just like C#.

Now you try

You'll now experiment with binding values to symbols:

1   Create a new F# script file.
2   Bind some values to symbols yourself:
    a   A simple type (for example, string or int).
    b   An object from within the BCL (for example, System.Random).
    c   Create a simple one-line function that takes in no arguments and calls a function on the object that you created earlier (for example, random.Next()).
3   Remember to execute each line in the REPL by using Alt-Enter.

4.1.1   let isn't var!

Don't confuse let with var. Unlike var, which declares *variables* that can be modified later, let binds an *immutable value* to a symbol. The closest thing in C# would be to declare every variable with the readonly keyword (although this isn't *entirely* equivalent). It's better to think of let bindings as copy-and-paste directives; wherever you see the symbol, replace it with the value that was originally assigned during the declaration.

You may have noticed that you can execute the same let binding multiple times in FSI. This is because F# allows you to repurpose a symbol multiple times within the same scope. This is known as *shadowing*, and is shown in the following listing.

Listing 4.2 Reusing let bindings

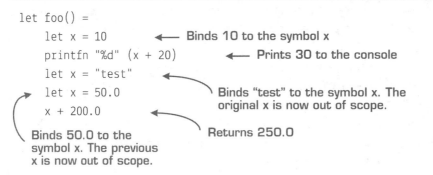

```
let foo() =
    let x = 10            ←—— Binds 10 to the symbol x
    printfn "%d" (x + 20)        ←—— Prints 30 to the console
    let x = "test"    ←
    let x = 50.0                  Binds "test" to the symbol x. The
    x + 200.0     ←               original x is now out of scope.

  Binds 50.0 to the          Returns 250.0
  symbol x. The previous
  x is now out of scope.
```

Shadowing is a more advanced (and somewhat controversial) feature, so don't worry too much about it. But this is why you can declare the same symbol multiple times within FSI.

Quick check 4.1

1 Give at least two examples of values that can be bound to symbols with `let`.
2 What's the difference between `let` and `var`?
3 Is F# a static or dynamic language?

4.2 Scoping values

I'm sure you've heard that global variables are a bad thing! *Scoping* of values is important in any language; scoping allows us not only to show intent by explaining where and when a value is of use within a program, but also to protect us from bugs by reducing the possibilities for a value to be used within an application. In C#, we use { } to explicitly mark scope, as shown in the next listing.

Listing 4.3 Scoping in C#

```csharp
using System
public static int DoStuffWithTwoNumbers(int first, int second)
{
    var added = first + second;
    Console.WriteLine("{0} + {1} = {2}", first, second, added);
    var doubled = added * 2;
    return doubled;
}
```

In this context, the variable `added` is only *in scope* within the context of the curly braces. Outside of that, it's *out of scope* and not accessible by the rest of the program. On the other hand, F# is a *whitespace-significant* language: rather than using curly braces, you have to *indent code* to tell the compiler that you're in a nested scope.

QC 4.1 answer

1 Primitive values, values of custom types, functions.
2 `let` is an immutable binding of a symbol. `var` represents a pointer to a specific mutable object.
3 F# is a statically typed language.

Listing 4.4 Scoping in F#

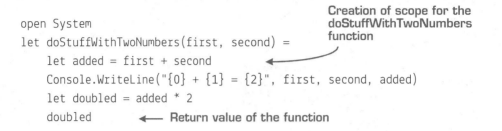

```
open System
let doStuffWithTwoNumbers(first, second) =
    let added = first + second
    Console.WriteLine("{0} + {1} = {2}", first, second, added)
    let doubled = added * 2
    doubled
```

Creation of scope for the doStuffWithTwoNumbers function

Return value of the function

There's no specific restriction on the number of spaces to indent. You can indent 1 space or 10 spaces—as long as you're consistent within the scope! Most people use four spaces. It's not worth wasting time on picking the indent size, so I advise you to go with that to start with.

You'll see in listing 4.4 that you've opened up the System namespace so that you can call Console.WriteLine directly. You can also get VFPT to open the namespaces for you, just like standard Visual Studio, through the lightbulb tip, as shown in figure 4.1.

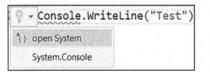

Figure 4.1   Visual F# Power Tools integration in Visual Studio 2015 offering to open up a namespace

You'll also notice a few more things from this multiline function:

- *No* return *keyword*—The return keyword is unnecessary and not valid F# syntax (except in one case, which you'll see that in the second half of this book). Instead, F# assumes that the *final expression* of a scope is the result of that scope. In this case it's the value of doubled.
- *No accessibility modifier*—In F#, public is the default for top-level values. There are several reasons for this, but it makes perfect sense in F#, because with nested scopes (described in detail in the following section), you can hide values effectively without resorting to accessibility modifiers.
- *No static modifier*—Again, static is the default way of working in F#. This is different from what you're used to, but it fits with how you'll design most solutions in F#.

> **Accessibility modifiers in F#**
>
> It's worth pointing out that although F# supports most modifiers, there's no `protected` access modifier. This isn't usually a problem; I've certainly never needed `protected` since I started using F#. This is probably because `protected` is a modifier used when working with object-oriented hierarchies—something you rarely use in F#.

4.2.1 Nested scopes

We're used to using classes and methods as a means of scoping and data hiding. You might have a class that contains private fields and methods, as well as one or many public methods. You can also use methods for data hiding—again, the data is visible only within the context of that function call. In F#, you can define arbitrary scopes at any point you want. Let's assume you want to estimate someone's age by using the current year, as shown in the following listing.

Listing 4.5 Unmanaged scope

```
let year = DateTime.Now.Year
let age = year - 1979
let estimatedAge = sprintf "You are about %d years old!" age
// rest of application…
```

Looking at this code, the only thing you're interested in is the string value `estimatedAge`. The other lines are used *as part of the calculation* of that; they're not used anywhere else in your application. But currently, they're at the top level of the code, so anything afterward that uses `estimatedAge` can also see those two values.

Why is this a problem? First, because it's something more for you as a developer to reason about—where is the `year` value being used? Is any other code somehow depending on it? Second (and again, this is slightly less of an issue in F#, where values are immutable by default), values that have large scopes tend to negatively impact a code base in terms of bugs and/or code smells. In F#, you can eliminate this by nesting those values *inside* the scope of `estimatedAge` as far as possible, as the next listing shows.

Listing 4.6 Tightly bound scope

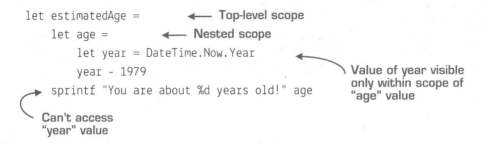

```
let estimatedAge =              ←── Top-level scope
    let age =        ←── Nested scope
        let year = DateTime.Now.Year
        year - 1979                                    Value of year visible
                                                       only within scope of
    sprintf "You are about %d years old!" age          "age" value

    Can't access
    "year" value
```

Now it's clear that age is used only by the estimatedAge value. Similarly, DateTime.Now.Year is used only when calculating age. You can't access any value outside the scope that it was defined in, so you can think of each of these nested scopes as being *mini classes* if you like—scopes for storing data that's used to generate a value.

4.2.2   Nested functions

If you've been paying attention, you'll remember that F# treats *functions* as *values*. This means that you can also create functions *within other functions*! Here's an example of how to do this in F#.

Listing 4.7 Nested (inner) functions

```
let estimateAges(familyName, year1, year2, year3) =  ←── Top-level function
    let calculateAge yearOfBirth =            ←── Nested function
        let year = System.DateTime.Now.Year
        year - yearOfBirth

    let estimatedAge1 = calculateAge year1   ←── Calling the nested function
    let estimatedAge2 = calculateAge year2
    let estimatedAge3 = calculateAge year3

    let averageAge = (estimatedAge1 + estimatedAge2 + estimatedAge3) / 3
    sprintf "Average age for family %s is %d" familyName averageAge
```

You declare a function called estimateAges, which itself defines a nested helper function called calculateAge inside it. The estimateAges function then calls calculateAge three times in order to generate an average age estimate for the three ages that were supplied. The ability to create nested functions means that you can start to think of functions and classes that have a single public method as *interchangeable* (see table 4.2).

Table 4.2 Comparing functional equivalents to core object-oriented class features

Class	Function
Constructor / single public method	Arguments passed to the function
Private fields	Local values
Private methods	Local functions

Capturing values in F#

Within the body of a nested function (or any nested value), code can access any values defined in its containing (parent) scope without you having to explicitly supply them as arguments to the nested function. You can think of this as similar to a lambda function in C# "capturing" a value declared in its parents' scope. When you return such a code block, this is known as a closure; it's common to do this in F#—without even realizing it.

Cyclical dependencies in F#

This is one of the best "prescriptive" features of F# that many developers coming from C# and VB are shocked by: F# doesn't (easily) permit cyclical dependencies. *In F#, the order in which types are defined matters.* Type A can't reference Type B if Type A is declared *before* Type B, and the same applies to values.

Even more surprising is that this applies to all the files in a project—so file order in a project matters! Files at the *bottom* of the project can access types and values defined *above* them, but not the other way around. You can manually move files up and down in VS by selecting the file and pressing Alt-up arrow or Alt-down arrow (or right-clicking a file and choosing the appropriate option).

As it turns out, though, this "restriction" turns into a feature. By forcing you to avoid cyclic dependencies, the design of your solutions will naturally become easier to reason about, because all dependencies will always face "upward."

Now you try

Within a script file, you'll create a Windows Forms form that contains a `WebBrowser` control for hosting the content of a web resource that you'll download. Here's a snippet to get you started.

Listing 4.8 Creating a form to display a web page

```
open System
open System.Net
open System.Windows.Forms          ◀── Opening up namespaces in F#
let webClient = new WebClient()
let fsharpOrg = webClient.DownloadString(Uri "http://fsharp.org")
let browser =
    new WebBrowser(ScriptErrorsSuppressed = true,
                   Dock = DockStyle.Fill,
                   DocumentText = fsharpOrg)    ◀──  Object initializer-style
let form = new Form(Text = "Hello from F#!")        syntax in F#
form.Controls.Add browser
form.Show()
```

Rewrite the preceding code so that the scopes are more tightly defined. For example, webClient is used only during creation of the fsharpOrg value, so it can live within the definition of that value.

Next, try to make the code a function so that it can be supplied with a URL instead of being hardcoded to fsharp.org. Creating functions from simple sets of values is incredibly easy in F#:

1 Indent all the code you wish to make a function.
2 On the line above the code block, define the function along with the argument(s) you wish to take in.
3 Replace the hardcoded values in the code block with the arguments you defined.
4 Ensure that the last line in the function block isn't a let statement, but an expression.

Here's a two-part example of refactoring a set of arbitrary assignments and expressions into a reusable function to get you started.

Listing 4.9 Refactoring to functions—before

```
let r = System.Random()
let nextValue = r.Next(1, 6)
let answer = nextValue + 10
```

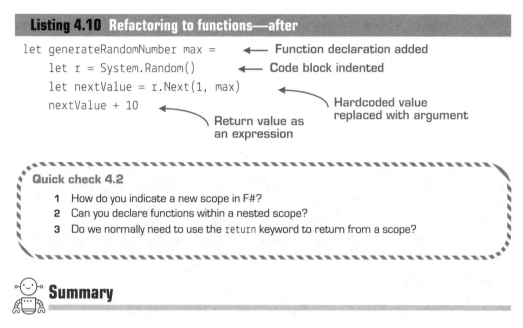

Listing 4.10 Refactoring to functions—after

```
let generateRandomNumber max =        ← Function declaration added
    let r = System.Random()           ← Code block indented
    let nextValue = r.Next(1, max)    ←
    nextValue + 10   ←                        Hardcoded value
                                              replaced with argument
                          Return value as
                          an expression
```

Quick check 4.2

1. How do you indicate a new scope in F#?
2. Can you declare functions within a nested scope?
3. Do we normally need to use the `return` keyword to return from a scope?

Summary

In this lesson

- You learned a great deal about the most fundamental parts of the syntax of F#.
- You learned about the `let` keyword.
- You saw how scoping works in F#.

Hopefully, you've seen that F# contains a relatively simple and minimalistic syntax, with a minimum of extra symbols and keywords. A large majority of what you've seen so far is "stripping away" what turned out to be "unnecessary" syntax features of C#—but some elements of the language may be new to you, such as nested scopes and the lack of support for cyclic dependencies.

Try this

Explore scoping in more depth: try creating a set of functions that are deeply nested within one another. What happens if you call a function—for example, `Random.Next()` —within another function as opposed to simply using the result of it? What implication does this have for, for example, caching?

QC 4.2 answer

1. Indent code to declare a new scope.
2. Yes, functions can be declared within a nested scope.
3. No, the `return` keyword isn't used in F# to specify the result of an expression.

5

LESSON

TRUSTING THE COMPILER

The compiler is one of the most important features in any language. In a language such as F#, where the compiler does a lot of heavy lifting for you, it's particularly important that you understand the role it plays in your day-to-day development cycle. In this lesson

- You'll look at the F# compiler from a developer's point of view (don't get scared!).
- You'll focus specifically on one area of it: type inference.
- You'll recap what type inference is from a C# / VB .NET perspective.
- You'll look at how F# takes type inference to the next level.

5.1 Type inference as we know it

Unless you've used only earlier versions of C#, you'll almost certainly be familiar with the var keyword. Let's refamiliarize ourselves with the var keyword based on the official MSDN documentation:

> *Variables that are declared at method scope can have an implicit type var. An implicitly typed local variable is strongly typed just as if you had declared the type yourself, but the compiler determines the type.*

5.1.1 Type inference in C# in detail

Here's a simple example of that description in action.

Listing 5.1 Using var in C#

```
var i = 10;         ◄─── Implicitly typed
int i = 10;         ◄─── Explicitly typed
```

The right-hand side of the = can be just about any expression, so you can write more-complicated code that may defer to another method, perhaps in another class. Naturally, you need to give a little bit of thought regarding the naming of variables when using var!

Listing 5.2 Variable naming with type inference

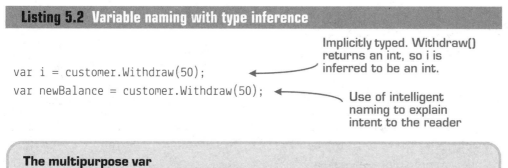

```
var i = customer.Withdraw(50);
var newBalance = customer.Withdraw(50);
```

Implicitly typed. Withdraw() returns an int, so i is inferred to be an int.

Use of intelligent naming to explain intent to the reader

> **The multipurpose var**
>
> There's another reason for the use of var in C#: to store references to types that have no formal declaration, a.k.a. anonymous types. Anonymous types don't exist in F#, although as you'll see later, you rarely miss them, as good alternatives exist that are in many ways more powerful.

It's important to stress that var mustn't be confused with the dynamic keyword in C#, which is (as the name suggests) all about dynamic typing. var allows you to use static typing without the need to explicitly specify the type by *allowing the compiler to determine the type for you at compile time* (see figure 5.1).

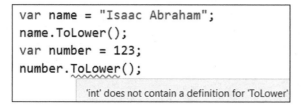

```
var name = "Isaac Abraham";
name.ToLower();
var number = 123;
number.ToLower();
```
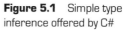
'int' does not contain a definition for 'ToLower'

Figure 5.1 Simple type inference offered by C#

5.1.2   Practical benefits of type inference

Even in its restricted form in C#, type inference can be a nice feature. The most obvious benefit is that of readability: you can focus on getting results from method calls and use the human-readable name of the value to gain its meaning, rather than the type. This is especially useful with generics, and F# uses generics a lot. But you gain another subtler benefit: the ease of refactoring.

Imagine you have a method Save() that stores data in the database and returns an integer value. Let's assume that this is the number of rows saved. You then call it in your main code.

Listing 5.3 Depending on method results with explicit typing

```
int result = Save();          ←——  Explicit binding to int

if (result == 0)              ←
    Console.WriteLine("Failure!");        Where the value is
else                                      explicitly used as a int
    Console.WriteLine("Worked!");
```

Note that you're explicitly marking result as an integer, although the declaration of the variable could just as well have been var. Then at some point in the future, you decide that you want to return a Boolean that represents success/failure instead. You have to change two things:

1 You need to manually change the method signature to specify that the method returns bool rather than int. There's no way around this in C#.

2 You need to go through every call site to Save() and manually fix it to bind the result to bool rather than int. If you had used var, this wouldn't have been a problem at all, because you'd have left the compiler to "figure out" the type of result.

Even when using var, at some point you'd normally have to make *some* kind of change to your code to handle a bool instead of an int—in this case, it's the conditional expression for the if statement. Although var won't fix *everything* for you—it's not magic—the difference is that the compiler would have taken care of fixing the "boilerplate" error for you automatically, leaving you to change the "real" logic (changing the expression from comparing with 0 to comparing with true).

> **Critics of type inference**
>
> Some developers shy away from type inference. A common complaint I hear is that it's "magic," or alternatively that one can't determine the type of a variable at a glance. The first point can be easily dispelled by reading the rules for type inference: the compiler doesn't guess the types; a set of precedence rules guides the compiler. The second point can also be dispelled by the number of excellent IDEs (including VS2015) that give you mouse-over guidance for types, as well as following good practices such as sane variable naming (which is generally a good thing to do). Overall, particularly in F#, the benefits massively outweigh any costs.

5.1.3   Imagining a more powerful type-inference system

Unfortunately, type inference in C# and VB .NET is restricted to the single use case I've illustrated. Let's look at a slightly larger code snippet.

Listing 5.4 Hypothetical type inference in C#

```
public static var CloseAccount(var balance, var customer)
{
    if (balance < 0)            ←— Balance compared with 0
        return false;           ←— Returning a Boolean
    else
    {
        customer.Withdraw(customer.AccountBalance);    ←— Calling methods and accessing properties on a type
        customer.Close();
        return true;            ←— Returning a Boolean
    }
}
```

This is invalid C#, because I've omitted all types. But couldn't the compiler possibly "work out" the return type or input arguments based the following?

- We're comparing `balance` with 0. Perhaps this is a good indicator that `balance` is also an integer (although it could also be a float or other numeric type).
- We're returning Boolean values from all possible branches of the method. Perhaps we want the method to return `Boolean`?

- We're accessing methods and properties on the customer object. How many types in the application have `Withdraw` and `Close` methods and an `AccountBalance` property (which is also compatible with the input argument of `Withdraw`)?

Quick check 5.1

1 Can you think of any limitations of the C# type-inference engine?
2 What is the difference between dynamic typing and type inference?

5.2 F# type-inference basics

We've discussed some of the benefits of type inference in C#, as well as some of the issues and concerns about it. All of these are magnified with F#, because type inference in F# is *pervasive*. You can write entire applications without making a single type annotation (although this isn't always possible, nor always desirable). In F#, the compiler can infer the following:

- Local bindings (as per C#)
- Input arguments for both built-in and custom F# types
- Return types

F# uses a sophisticated algorithm that relies on the Hindley–Milner (HM) type system. It's not *especially* important to know what that is, although feel free to read up on it in your own time! What *is* important to know is that HM type systems *do* impose some restrictions in order to operate that might surprise you, as we'll see shortly.

Without further ado, let's finally get onto some F#! Thus far, all the examples you've seen in F# haven't used type annotations, but now I'll show you a simple example that we can break down piece by piece so you can understand how it works.

Listing 5.5 Explicit type annotations in F#

```
let add (a:int, b:int) : int =
    let answer:int = a + b
    answer
```

QC 5.1 answer

1 Types can't be inferred from method scope, and are valid only on assignment.
2 The latter is statically typed, but types are resolved by the compiling. Dynamic typing truly doesn't specify types at compile time.

We'll cover functions in more depth later, but to get us going here, a type signature in F# has three main parts:

- The function name
- All input argument type(s)
- The return type

You can see from the code sample that both input arguments a and b are of type int, and the function also returns an int.

Type annotations in C# and F#

Many C# developers recoil when they see types declared after the name of the value. In fact, most languages outside of C, C++, Java, and C# use this pattern. It's particularly common in languages such as F#, where type inference is especially powerful, or optional type systems such as TypeScript.

Start by removing just the return type from the type signature of the function; when you compile this function in FSI, you'll see that the type signature is exactly the same as before.

Listing 5.6 Omitting the return type from a function in F#

```
let add (a:int, b:int) =
...
// val add : a:int * b:int -> int
```

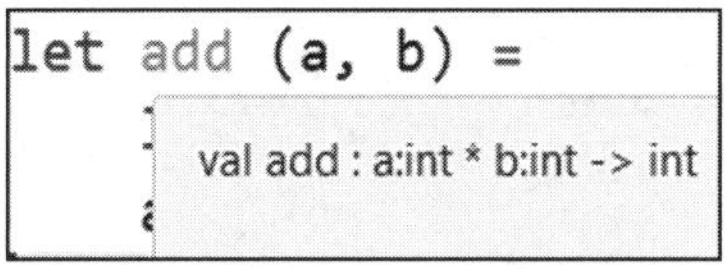

```
let add (a, b) =
    val add : a:int * b:int -> int
```

Figure 5.2 F# type inference operating on a function

F# infers the return type of the function, based on the result of the final expression in the function. In this case, that's answer. Now go one step further and remove the type annotation from b. Again, when you compile, the type signature will be the same. In this case, it raises an interesting question: how does the compiler know that b isn't a float or decimal? The answer is that in F#, *implicit conversions aren't allowed*. This is another feature of the type system that helps enforce safety and correctness, although it's not something that you'll necessarily be used to. In my experience, it's not a problem at all. And given this restriction, the compiler can safely make the assumption that b is an int. Finally, remove the remaining two type annotations, as shown in figure 5.2.

Amazingly, the compiler still says that the types are all integers! How has it figured this out? In this case, it's because the + operator binds by default to integers, so all the values are inferred to be ints.

Now you try

Experiment with this code a little more to see how the compiler responds to code changes:

1. Mix some type annotations on the function—for example, mark a as `int` and b as `string`. Does it compile?
2. Remove all the type annotations again, and rewrite the body to add an explicit value, such as the following:

   ```
   a + b + "hello"
   ```

3. Does this compile? What are the types? Why?
4. What happens if you call the function with an incompatible value?

Earlier, we demonstrated that type inference can not only improve readability by removing unnecessary keywords that can obscure the meaning of your code, but also speed up refactoring—for example, by allowing you to change the return type of a function without necessarily breaking the caller. This benefit is increased by a significant factor when working with F#, because you can automatically change the return type by simply changing the implementation of a function, without needing to manually update the function signature. Indeed, when coupled with its lightweight syntax and ability to create scopes by indenting code, F# enables you to create new functions and change type signatures of existing code incredibly easily—particularly because type inference in F# can escape local scope, unlike in C#.

5.2.1   Limitations of type inference

F# has a few more restrictions and limitations related to type inference. Let's go through them one by one here.

Working with the BCL

First, type inference works best with types *native* to F#. By this, I mean basic types such as ints, or F# types that you define yourself. We haven't looked at F# types yet, so this won't mean much to you, but if you try to work with a type from a C# library (and this includes the .NET BCL), type inference won't work quite as well—although often a single annotation will suffice within a code base.

Listing 5.7 Type inference when working with BCL types in F#

Doesn't compile—type
annotation is required

Compiles

```
let getLength name = sprintf "Name is %d letters." name.Length
let getLength (name:string) = sprintf "Name is %d letters." name.Length
let foo(name) = "Hello! " + getLength(name)
```

Compiles— "name" argument
is inferred to be string, based
on the call to getLength()

The first function won't compile, as the F# compiler doesn't know that name is a string (and therefore has a Length property). The second version works, because of the annotation. Any code that calls that function *won't* need an annotation; the initial one will "bleed out" naturally.

Classes and overloaded methods

Second, in F#, overloaded functions aren't allowed. You can create (or reference from C# libraries) *classes* that contain *methods* that are overloaded, but *functions* declared using the let syntax can't be overloaded. For this reason, type inference doesn't completely function on classes and methods.

5.2.2 Type-inferred generics

F# can apply type inference not just on simple values but also for *type arguments*. You can either use an underscore (_) to specify a placeholder for the generic type argument, or omit the argument completely.

Listing 5.8 Inferred type arguments in F#

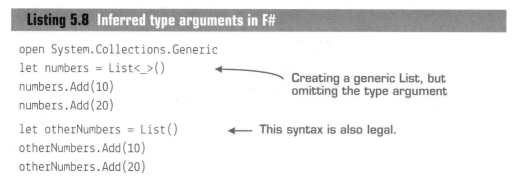

```
open System.Collections.Generic
let numbers = List<_>()
numbers.Add(10)
numbers.Add(20)

let otherNumbers = List()
otherNumbers.Add(10)
otherNumbers.Add(20)
```

Creating a generic List, but
omitting the type argument

This syntax is also legal.

You should understand that F# infers the type based on the first available usage of the type argument. The call to numbers.Add(10) is used to tell the compiler that List is of type int. If you were to call `numbers.Add` with 10 and then "Hello", you'd get a compiler error on the second call, as by this stage the compiler has selected int as the type argument.

F# also automatically makes functions generic when needed. Let's look at a simple function that adds items to a list. In this example, no type is specified for the `output` value anywhere in the code, so the compiler can't infer the type of List. In this case, it will make the entire `createList()` function generic!

Listing 5.9 Automatic generalization of a function

```
let createList(first, second) =
    let output = List()
    output.Add(first)
    output.Add(second)
    output
// val createList : first:'a * second:'a -> List<'a>
```

In this case, you can think of `'a` as the same as `T` in C# (a generic type argument). You can specify the generic argument placeholder (and use it as a type annotation) if you want to (for example, `let createList<'a>(first:'a, second)`, but you should generally just let the compiler infer the arguments; it's powerful and will save you a lot of time.

Quick check 5.2

1 How does F# infer the return type of a function?
2 Can F# infer types from the BCL?
3 Does F# allow implicit conversions between numeric types?

5.3   Following the breadcrumbs

Because type inference escapes function scope in F#, unlike in C#, the compiler will go through your entire code base and notify you where the types *eventually* clash. This is normally a good thing, but it does mean that occasionally you'll need to remember how

QC 5.2 answer

1 Based on the type of the last expression in the function.
2 No, although it can infer BCL types across functions declared in F#.
3 No.

the type inference system works in order to diagnose compiler errors. Let's look at a relatively simple example that shows how making changes to types can lead to errors occurring in unusual places.

Listing 5.10 Complex type-inference example

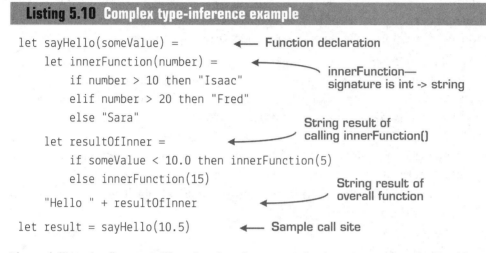

```
let sayHello(someValue) =                    ← Function declaration
    let innerFunction(number) =              ←
        if number > 10 then "Isaac"              innerFunction—
        elif number > 20 then "Fred"             signature is int -> string
        else "Sara"
                                                 String result of
    let resultOfInner =                      ←   calling innerFunction()
        if someValue < 10.0 then innerFunction(5)
        else innerFunction(15)
                                                 String result of
    "Hello " + resultOfInner                 ←   overall function
let result = sayHello(10.5)                  ← Sample call site
```

If you follow the flow, you'll notice that the current logic suggests that the Fred branch will never be called. Don't worry about that; we're more interested in the type system and F#'s inference engine here.

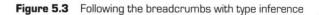

Now you try

Copy the code from listing 5.10 into an F# script in VS; everything will compile by default. Now let's see how to break this code! Start by first changing the *first* if/then case in innerFunction to compare against a string ("hello") rather than an integer (10), as shown in figure 5.3.

```
let innerFunction(number) =
    if number > "hello" then "Isaac"
    elif number > 20 then "Fred"
    else "Sara"

let resultOfInner =
    if someValue < 10.0 then innerFunction(5)
    else innerFunction(15)
```

Figure 5.3 Following the breadcrumbs with type inference

Rather than this line showing an error, you'll see errors in three other places! Why? This is what I refer to as *following the breadcrumbs*: you need to track through at least one of the errors and see the inferred types to understand why this has happened.

Let's look into the first error and try to work out why it's occurring: *this expression was expected to have type* string, *but here it has type* int. Remember to mouse over the values and functions to get IntelliSense of the type signatures being inferred!

1   Looking at the compiler error message, you can see that the call site to inner-Function now expects a string, although you know that it should be an int.

2   Now look at the function signature of innerFunction. It used to be int -> string, but now is string -> string (given a string, it returns a string).

3   Look at the function body. You can see that the first branch of the if/then code compares number against a string rather than an int. The compiler has used this to infer that the function should take in a string.

4   You can prove this by hovering over the number value, which sure enough is now inferred to be a string.

5   To help you, and to guide the compiler, let's temporarily explicitly type-annotate the function as shown in figure 5.4.

6   You'll see that the "false" compiler errors disappear, and the compiler now correctly identifies the error as being "hello", which should be an int.

7   After you correct the error, you can remove the type annotation again.

```
let innerFunction(number:int) =
    if number > "hello" then "Isaac"
    elif number > 20 then "Fred"
    else "Sara"
```

Figure 5.4 Explicit type annotations can help to drill down on the source of an error.

From this example, you can see that adding in type annotations can sometimes be useful, particularly when trying to narrow down an error caused by clashing types. I recommend, however, that you in general try to avoid working with explicit types everywhere. Your code will look much cleaner as a result.

Now you try

Try some more examples of changing values to experiment with how F# type inference works:

1   Replace Isaac with 123. Look at the errors that show up. Why do they appear?

2   Replace Fred with 123. Why is the error different from when you changed Isaac?

3   Replace 10.0 with 10. What happens? Why?

Quick check 5.3 Why are type annotations sometimes useful when looking at compiler errors?

 **Summary**

That was an intensive lesson! We covered the following:

- Basics of type inference
- Simple type inference in C# / VB .NET
- Type inference in F#
- Limitations of F# type inference
- Diagnosing type inference problems in F#

It's well worth spending the time to understand type inference in F#, because it's a crucial part of the flavor of the language. Type inference fits with the "more with less" philosophy, as well as another side of F# discussed at the start of this lesson, which is trusting the compiler.

You need a different mindset to create functions and arguments without type annotations and let the compiler fill in the gaps, and as you saw, at times it's important that you understand what the compiler is doing under the hood. But as you'll see over the coming lessons, type inference is incredibly useful in writing succinct, easily refactorable code without needing to resort to a third-party tool to "rewrite" your code for you.

Try this

Try creating other generic objects that you already know within the BCL. How does F# work with them? Then, experiment with the code that you created in the previous lessons. Can you remove any of the type annotations? How does it affect the look and feel of the code?

QC 5.3 answer Temporarily placing explicit type annotations allows you to guide the compiler with your intention; this can help track down when types are incompatible in code.

WORKING WITH IMMUTABLE DATA

Working with immutable data is one of the more difficult aspects of functional programming to deal with, but as it turns out, after you get over the initial hurdle, you'll be surprised just how easy it is to write entire applications working with purely immutable data structures. It also goes hand in hand with many other F# features you'll see, such as expression-based development. In this lesson, you'll learn

- The basic syntax for working with immutable and mutable data in F#
- Some reasons you should consider immutability by default in software development today
- Simple examples of working with immutable values to manage changing state

6.1 Working with mutable data—a recap

Let's start by thinking about some of the issues we come up against but often take for granted as simply "the way things are." Here are a few examples that I've either seen firsthand or fallen foul of myself.

6.1.1 The unrepeatable bug

Say you're developing an application, and one of the test team members comes up to you with a bug report. You walk over to that person's desk and see the problem happening. Luckily, your tester is running in Visual Studio, so you can see the stack trace and so on. You look through the locals and application state, and figure out why the bug is showing up. Unfortunately, you have no idea how the application got into this state in the first place; it's the result of calling a number of methods repeatedly over time with some shared mutable state stored in the middle.

You go back to your machine and try to get the same error, but this time you can't reproduce it. You file a bug in your work-item tracking system and wait to see if you can get lucky and figure out how the application got into this state.

6.1.2 Multithreading pitfalls

How about this one? You're developing an application and have decided to use multithreading because it's cool. You recently heard about the Task Parallel Library in .NET, which makes writing multithreaded code a lot easier, and also saw that there's a `Parallel .ForEach()` method in the BCL. Great! You've also read about locking, so you carefully put locks around the bits of the shared state of your application that are affected by the multithreaded code.

You test it locally and even write some unit tests. Everything is green! You release, and two weeks later find a bug that you eventually trace to your multithreaded code. You don't know why it happened, though; it's caused by a race condition that occurs only under a specific load and a certain ordering of messages. Eventually, you revert your code to a single-threaded model.

6.1.3 Accidentally sharing state

Here's another one. You've working on a team and have designed a business object class. Your colleague has written code to operate on that object. You call that code, supplying an object, and then carry on. Sometime later, you notice a bug in your application: the state of the business object no longer looks as it did previously!

It turns out that the code your colleague wrote modified a property on the object without you realizing it. You made that property public only so that *you* could change it; you didn't intend or expect *other* bits of code to change the state of it! You fix the problem by making an interface for the type that exposes the bits that are "really" public on the type, and give that to consumers instead.

6.1.4   Testing hidden state

Or maybe you're writing unit tests. You want to test a specific method on your class, but unfortunately, to run a specific branch of that method, you first need to get the object into a specific state. This involves mocking a bunch of dependencies that are needed to run the *other* methods; only then can you run your method. Then, you try to assert whether the method worked, but the only way to prove that the method worked properly is to access a shared state that's private to the class. Your deadlines are fast approaching, so you change the accessibility of the private field to be Internal, and make internals visible to your test project.

6.1.5   Summary of mutability issues

All of these problems are real issues that occur on a regular basis, and they're nearly always due to mutability. The problem is often that we simply assume that mutability is a way of life, something we can't escape, and so look for other ways around these sorts of issues—things like encapsulation, hacks such as InternalsVisibleTo, or one of the many design patterns out there. It turns out that working with *immutable* data solves many of these problems in one fell swoop.

6.2   Being explicit about mutation

So far, you've only looked at simple values in F#, but even these show that by default, values are immutable. As you'll see in later lessons, this also applies to your own custom F# types (for example, Records).

6.2.1   Mutability basics in F#

You'll now see immutability in action. Start by opening a script file and entering the following code.

Listing 6.1   Creating immutable values in F#

```
let name = "isaac"        ◄─── Creating an immutable value
name = "kate"             ◄─── Trying to assign "kate" to name
```

You'll notice when you execute this code, you receive the following output in FSI:

```
val name : string = "isaac"
val it : bool = false
```

The false doesn't mean that the assignment has somehow failed. It occurs because in F#, the = operator represents equality, as == does in C#. All you've done is compare isaac with kate, which is obviously false.

How do you update or mutate a value? You use the assignment operator, <-. Unfortunately, trying to insert that into your code leads to an error, as shown next.

Listing 6.2 Trying to mutate an immutable value

```
name <- "kate"
error FS0027: This value is not mutable
```

Oops! This still doesn't work. It turns out that you need to take one final step to make a value mutable, which is to use the mutable keyword.

Listing 6.3 Creating a mutable variable

```
let mutable name = "isaac"      ◄─── Defining a mutable variable
name <- "kate"        ◄─── Assigning a new value to the variable
```

If you installed and configured Visual F# Power Tools, you'll notice that the name value is now automatically highlighted in red as a warning that this is a mutable value. You can think of this as the inverse of C# and VB .NET, whereby you use *variables* by default, and explicitly mark individual items as immutable *values* by using the readonly keyword.

The reason that F# makes this decision is to help guide you down what I refer to as the *pit of success*; you can use mutation when needed, but you should be explicit about it and should do so in a carefully controlled manner. By default you should go down the route of adopting *immutable* values and data structures.

As it turns out, you can easily develop entire applications (and I have, with web front ends, SQL databases, and so forth) by using only immutable data structures. You'll be surprised when you realize how little you need mutable data, particularly in request/response-style applications such as web applications, which are inherently stateless.

6.2.2 Working with mutable objects

Before we move on to working with immutable data, here's a quick primer on the syntax for working with mutable *objects*. I don't recommend you create your own mutable types, but working with the BCL is a fact of life as a .NET developer, and the BCL is inherently OO-based and filled with mutable structures, so it's good to know how to interact with them.

Now you try

Start by creating a good old Windows Form, displaying it, and then setting a few properties of the window.

Listing 6.4 Working with mutable objects

```
open System.Windows.Forms
let form = new Form()          ←——— Creating the form object
form.Show()
form.Width <- 400      ←———
form.Height <- 400                   Mutating the form by
form.Text <- "Hello from F#!"        using the <- operator
```

> **Mutable bindings and objects**
>
> Most objects in the BCL, such as a Form, are inherently mutable. Notice that the form symbol is immutable, so the binding symbol itself can't be changed. But the object *it refers to* is itself mutable, so properties on that object can be changed!

Notice that you can see the mutation of the form happen through the REPL. If you execute the first three lines, you start with an empty form, but after executing the final line, the title bar will immediately change, as shown in figure 6.1.

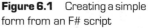

Figure 6.1 Creating a simple form from an F# script

F# also has a shortcut for creating mutable data structures in a way that assigns all properties in a single action. This shortcut is somewhat similar to object initializers in C#, except that in F# it works by making properties appear as optional constructor arguments.

Listing 6.5 Shorthand for creating mutable objects

```
open System.Windows.Forms
let form = new Form(Text = "Hello from F#!", Width = 300, Height = 300)
form.Show()
```
Creating and mutating properties of a form in one expression

If actual constructor arguments are required as well, you can put them in there at the same time (VS2015 sadly doesn't give IntelliSense for setting mutable properties in the constructor).

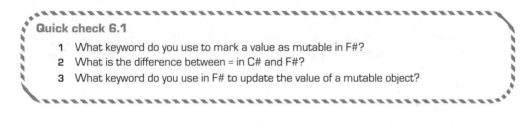

Quick check 6.1

1 What keyword do you use to mark a value as mutable in F#?
2 What is the difference between = in C# and F#?
3 What keyword do you use in F# to update the value of a mutable object?

6.3 Modeling state

Let's now look at the work needed to model data with state without resorting to mutation.

6.3.1 Working with mutable data

Working with mutable data structures in the OO world follows a simple model: you create an object, and then modify its state through operations on that object, as depicted in figure 6.2.

QC 6.1 answer

1 The mutable keyword.
2 In F#, = performs an equality between two values. It can also be used for binding a value to a symbol. In C#, = always means assignment.
3 F# uses the <- operator to update a mutable value.

Figure 6.2 Mutating an object repeatedly

What's tricky about this model of working is that it can be hard to reason about your code. Calling a method such as UpdateState() in the preceding example will generally have no return value; the result of calling the method is a *side effect* that takes place on the object.

Now you try

Let's put this into practice with a simple example: driving a car. You want to be able to write code that allows you to drive() a car, tracking the amount of petrol (gas) used. Depending on the distance you drive, you should use up a different amount of petrol.

Listing 6.6 Managing state with mutable variables

```
let mutable petrol = 100.0          ◀── Initial state

let drive(distance) =               ◀── Modify state through mutation
    if distance = "far" then petrol <- petrol / 2.0
    elif distance = "medium" then petrol <- petrol - 10.0
    else petrol <- petrol - 1.0
drive("far")        ◀── Repeatedly modify state
drive("medium")
drive("short")

petrol        ◀── Check current state
```

Working like this, it's worth noting a few things:

- Calling drive() has no outputs. You call it, and it silently modifies the mutable petrol variable; you can't know this from the type system.
- Methods aren't deterministic. You can't know the behavior of a method without knowing the (often hidden) state. If you call drive("far") three times, the value of petrol will change every time, depending on the previous calls.
- You have no control over the ordering of method calls. If you switch the order of calls to drive(), you'll get a different answer.

6.3.2 Working with immutable data

Let's compare working with mutable data structures with working with immutable ones, as per figure 6.3.

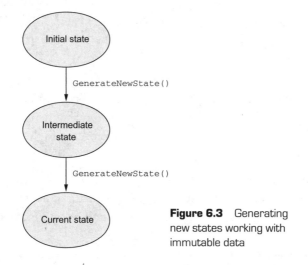

Figure 6.3 Generating new states working with immutable data

In this mode of operation, you can't mutate data. Instead, you create *copies* of the state with updates applied, and return that for the caller to work with; that state may be passed in to other calls that themselves generate new state.

> **Performance of immutable data**
>
> I often hear this question asked: isn't it much slower to make copies all the time rather than modify a single object? The answer is yes and no. Yes, it's slower to copy an object graph than to make an in-place update. But unless you're in a tight loop performing millions of mutations, the cost of doing so is negligible compared to, for example, opening a database connection. Plus, many languages (including F#) have specific data structures designed to work with immutable data in a highly efficient manner.

Now rewrite your code to use immutable data.

Listing 6.7 Managing state with immutable values

```
let drive(petrol, distance) =
    if distance = "far" then petrol / 2.0
    elif distance = "medium" then petrol - 10.0
```

Function explicitly dependent on state—takes in petrol and distance, and returns new petrol

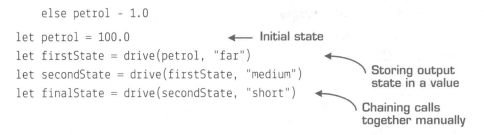

```
      else petrol - 1.0
let petrol = 100.0                    ←—— Initial state
let firstState = drive(petrol, "far")
let secondState = drive(firstState, "medium")          Storing output
                                                       state in a value
let finalState = drive(secondState, "short")
                                                       Chaining calls
                                                       together manually
```

There are now a few key changes to the code. The most important is that you aren't using a mutable variable for your state any longer, but a set of immutable values. You "thread" the state through each function call, storing the intermediate states in values that are then manually passed to the next function call. Working in this manner, you gain a few benefits immediately:

- You can reason about behavior much more easily. Rather than hidden side effects on private fields, each method or function call can return a new version of the state that you can easily understand. This makes unit testing much easier, for example.
- Function calls are repeatable. You can call drive(50, "far") as many times as you want, and it will always give you the same result. This is because the only values that can affect the result are supplied as input arguments; there's no "global state" that's implicitly used. This is known as a *pure function*. Pure functions have nice properties, such as being able to be cached or pregenerated, as well as being easier to test.
- The compiler is able to protect you in this case from accidentally misordering function calls, because each function call is explicitly dependent on the output of the previous call.
- You can also see the value of each intermediate step as you "work up" toward the final state.

Passing immutable state in F#

In this example, you'll see that you're manually storing intermediate state and explicitly passing that to the next function call. That's not strictly necessary, and you'll see in future lessons how F# has language syntax to avoid having to do this explicitly.

Now you try

Let's see how to make some changes to your drive code:

1 Instead of using a string to represent how far you've driven, use an integer.
2 Instead of far, check whether the distance is more than 50.
3 Instead of medium, check whether the distance is more than 25.
4 If the distance is > 0, reduce petrol by 1.
5 If the distance is 0, make *no change* to the petrol consumption. In other words, return the same state that was provided.

6.3.3   Other benefits of immutable data

Immutable data has a few other benefits that aren't necessarily obvious from the preceding example:

- When working with immutable data, encapsulation isn't necessarily as important as it is when working with mutable data. At times encapsulation is still valuable (for example, as part of a public API), but on other occasions, making your data read-only eliminates the need to "hide" your data.
- You'll see more of this later, but one of the other benefits of working with immutable data is that you don't need to worry about locks within a multi-threaded environment. Because there's never any shared *mutable* state, you never have to be concerned with race conditions. Every thread can access the same piece of data as often as it likes, as it can never change.

> **Quick check 6.2**
>
> 1 How do you handle changes in state when working with immutable data?
> 2 What is a pure function?
> 3 What impact does working with immutable data have with multithreading code?

QC 6.2 answer

1 By creating copies of existing data with applied changes.
2 A function that varies based only on the arguments explicitly passed to it.
3 Immutable data doesn't need to be locked when working across multiple threads.

Summary

In this lesson

- You learned about areas where mutable data structures can cause problems.
- You saw how immutable data can act as a form of state through copy-and-update that works particularly well with pure functions, while avoiding side effects to allow you to more easily reason about your code.
- You saw a simple example of how to create and work with immutable data in F#.

This is only the beginning, and you'll see examples throughout this book of how immutable data is a core part of F#. Also important is that F# encourages you to work with immutable data *by default*, but because F# is a pragmatic language, it always allows you to opt out of this by using the `mutable` keyword and `<-` operators. This is particularly useful when working with types from the BCL and/or other libraries written in C# or VB .NET that are inherently mutable. But just as working with *immutable* data in C# is a bit of extra work and not necessarily idiomatic, so the inverse is true in F#.

Try this

1 Try modeling another state machine with immutable data—for example, a kettle that can be filled with water, which is then poured into a teapot or directly into a cup.
2 Look at working with BCL classes that are inherently mutable, such as `System.Net.WebClient`. Explore various ways to create and modify them.

EXPRESSIONS AND STATEMENTS

Expressions and statements are two aspects of programming that we use often, and generally take for granted, but in F# the distinction between the two is much starker than you might be used to. In this lesson, you'll do the following:

- Explore the differences between statements and expressions
- Lean the pros and cons of both
- See how expressions in combination with the F# type system and compiler can help you write code that's more succinct as well as easier to reason about

7.1   Comparing statements and expressions

Before we dive in, let's quickly recap the definitions of *statements* and *expressions*. Here are two definitions taken directly from the C# documentation on MSDN—first statements, and then expressions:

> *The actions that a program takes are expressed in statements. Common actions include declaring variables, assigning values, calling methods, looping through collections, and branching to one or another block of code, depending on a given condition.*
>
> —https://msdn.microsoft.com/en-us/library/ms173143.aspx

An expression *is a sequence of one or more operands and zero or more operators that can be evaluated to a single value, object, method, or namespace.*

—https://msdn.microsoft.com/en-us/library/ms173144.aspx

One of these is written in relatively plain (but somewhat verbose) English. The other is plain confusing (to me, at least!). Let's redefine the two terms more succinctly and appropriately for this purposes of this lesson; see table 7.1.

Table 7.1   Statements and expressions compared

	Returns something?	Has side-effects?
Statements	Never	Always
Expressions	Always	Rarely

In a nutshell, that's it. In C#, we're used to methods *sometimes* returning values, and a few operators such as +, -, and / or null coalesce (??). But we're not used to handling *program flow* as expressions. Instead, language constructs in C# are generally all statement-based, and rely on side effects to make changes in the system—something you've already seen can be difficult to reason about. But how can you write applications when program flow *constructs* are expressions?

7.1.1   Difficulties with statements

When working in languages such as C# and VB .NET, we often don't think about the differences between statements and expressions, as these languages mix and match both features. I consider both of these languages to be primarily *statement-based languages*, in that statements are easy to achieve, but expressions aren't.

Here's a simple example to help you compare and contrast statements and expressions. We start with a method that takes in someone's age and tries to print out a string that describes the person.

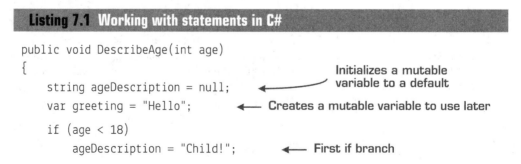

Listing 7.1 Working with statements in C#

```
public void DescribeAge(int age)
{
    string ageDescription = null;          ← Initializes a mutable variable to a default
    var greeting = "Hello";                ← Creates a mutable variable to use later
    if (age < 18)
        ageDescription = "Child!";         ← First if branch
```

```
else if (age < 65)
    greeting = "Adult!";          ←—— Second if branch
Console.WriteLine($"{greeting}! You are a '{ageDescription}'.");
}
```

This code has several issues, all caused by the fact that if/then in C# is a way of controlling program flow with a set of arbitrary, *unrelated* statements (see figure 7.1):

- There's no handler for the case when age >= 65. You're not accessing any properties on the string, so you won't get any null reference exceptions; instead you'll just print out null. If you deliberately avoid setting ageDescription to any value, the compiler will give you a warning regarding using an uninitialized variable—but initializing it to null satisfies the compiler!
- The code accidentally assigned the string to greeting, rather than ageDescription, in the second case.
- ageDescription needed to be declared with a default value before assigning it. This opens the possibility of all sorts of bugs for more-complex logic.

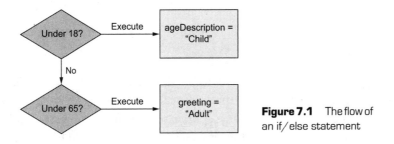

Figure 7.1 The flow of an if/else statement

Your initial instinct might be to say that no one makes mistakes like that, and that this is a strawman example. But you'd be amazed how many bugs creep in from situations just like this—particularly as a code base grows in size and as these sorts of code smells begin to manifest themselves in strange ways.

7.1.2 Making life better through expressions

In the previous example, you saw a number of issues that are all valid C# code, yet are mistakes that you were (hopefully!) able to identify quickly and easily. Why can't the compiler fix these things for you? Why can't it help you get these things right the first time?

The answer is that statements are *weak*. Compilers have no understanding that there's any *relationship* between all the branches of the if/else block. Instead, they're different paths to go down and execute; the fact that they're all supposed to assign a value to the *same* variable is purely coincidental.

You need a construct that's a little bit more powerful in order for the compiler to understand what you're trying to achieve. As it turns out, you can fix all of these problems in one fell swoop in C# by rewriting your code as follows.

Listing 7.2 Working with expressions in C#

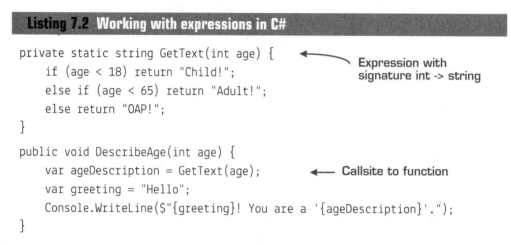

```
private static string GetText(int age) {          ←——      Expression with
    if (age < 18) return "Child!";                          signature int -> string
    else if (age < 65) return "Adult!";
    else return "OAP!";
}

public void DescribeAge(int age) {
    var ageDescription = GetText(age);            ←—— Callsite to function
    var greeting = "Hello";
    Console.WriteLine($"{greeting}! You are a '{ageDescription}'.");
}
```

You've now split your code into two methods: one that has the *single responsibility* of generating the description, and the other that calls it and uses the result later. There's the obvious benefit that moving the code into a separate method might improve readability, but the real benefits are now shown by the way you're naturally forced to structure your code (see figure 7.2):

- You can no longer omit the *else* case when generating the description; if you do, the C# compiler will stop you with the error not all code paths return a value.
- You can't accidentally assign the description to the wrong variable in half of the cases, because the assignment to ageDescription is performed in only one location.
- You don't need to have a null-initialized variable floating around now either.

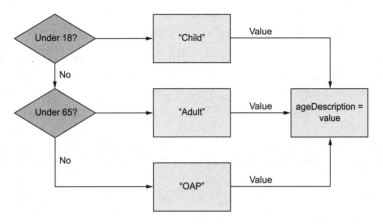

Figure 7.2 The flow of an if/else expression

Quick check 7.1

1   How often do expressions return a value?
2   How often do statements use side effects?
3   What is the smallest unit of expression in C#?

7.2   Using expressions in F#

Let's look at how F# treats expressions as a first-class element.

7.2.1   Working with expressions

F# firmly encourages expressions as the default way of working. In fact, virtually everything in F# is an expression! For example,

- F# has no notion of a void function. Every function *must* return something (although, once again, there's a nice escape hatch if you need to write code that has no result).

- All program-flow branching mechanisms are expressions.
- All values are expressions.

This illustrates why F# doesn't need a return keyword at the end of a function. Because everything is an expression, the last expression within a function *must* be the return value. Compare the original C# sample to F# and see the differences.

Listing 7.3 Working with expressions in F#

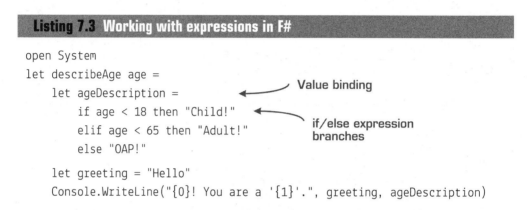

```
open System
let describeAge age =
    let ageDescription =
        if age < 18 then "Child!"
        elif age < 65 then "Adult!"
        else "OAP!"

    let greeting = "Hello"
    Console.WriteLine("{0}! You are a '{1}'.", greeting, ageDescription)
```

The key thing to observe in this code sample is that the if/then block of code has a *result* that's assigned to ageDescription. This is different from within the C# block. In this case, the if/then block acts more like a function, in that it has an (implicit) input (age) and an explicit result (either "Child", "Adult", or "OAP"), which is then assigned to ageDescription. By moving to this way of working with expressions, you get the same benefits that you did in C# except here they're a first-class part of the language. You don't have to move your code to extra methods to benefit from the extra safety that expressions provide. As a further benefit, also notice that you're no longer relying on mutable data. Both string values are immutable by default, which fits nicely with this expression-based mode of development.

7.2.2 Encouraging composability

A further benefit of expressions is that they encourage *composability*. Imagine that you want to modify the original C# method in order to write the result to disk rather than print to the console. Because you're writing to the console as part of the whole method (and therefore returning void), there's nothing to act on. But if you separate the method into two parts—one that generates a string, and another that outputs to the console—you can reuse the first part much more easily (as well as make unit testing simpler).

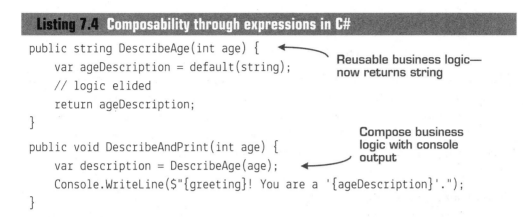

Listing 7.4 Composability through expressions in C#

```
public string DescribeAge(int age) {
    var ageDescription = default(string);
    // logic elided
    return ageDescription;
}
public void DescribeAndPrint(int age) {
    var description = DescribeAge(age);
    Console.WriteLine($"{greeting}! You are a '{ageDescription}'.");
}
```

Reusable business logic—
now returns string

Compose business
logic with console
output

7.2.3 Introducing unit

I mentioned that F# doesn't allow methods to return void. How on earth does this work in F#, then—particularly when the BCL probably has thousands of methods that return void? The answer is that F# has a type called unit. You've probably seen this term floating around in IntelliSense occasionally. The unit type is found in place of any method that would in C# normally return void, but unlike void, appears in F# to be a regular object that can get returned from any piece of code. In this way, you can say that every function returns a value—*even if that value is* unit. Similarly, every function can be thought of as always taking in at least one input value, *even if that value is* unit.

Let's look at functions and methods from both the preceding code and the BCL. You can even bind the value of unit to a symbol, like any other normal value!

Listing 7.5 Replacing void methods with functions that return unit

```
describeAge : age:int -> unit
System.Console.WriteLine : unit -> unit
"Test".GetHashCode : unit -> int
let x = describeAge 20 // val x : unit = ()
```

Now you try

Let's quickly look at unit with a few practical examples:

1 Create an instance of unit by using standard let binding syntax; the right-hand side of the equals sign needs to be ().

2 Call the describeAge function and assign the result of the function call to a separate value.

3 Check whether the two values are equal to one another. What is the result?

Why is all this unit business important? What's wrong with void? One reason is that void is a special case within the C# type system. Normal rules don't apply to it, which is why in many situations you have two versions of the same type in the BCL. A good example is the Task type in .NET, which has both Task and Task<T>. In F#, all you need is Task<T>, because even a function that returns nothing would be Task<unit>.

---

unit isn't quite an object

Unfortunately, despite unifying the type system, at runtime unit doesn't behave quite like a proper .NET object. For example, don't try to call GetHashCode() or GetType() on it, because you'll get a null reference exception. Hopefully, a future version of F# will fix this, but you can still think of unit as a singleton object if it helps you to visualize it.

7.2.4   Discarding results

F# also tells you that you might be doing something wrong if you call a function and don't use the return value.

Listing 7.6 Discarding the result of an expression

```
let writeTextToDisk text =                        ← Writes text to disk
    let path = System.IO.Path.GetTempFileName()
    System.IO.File.WriteAllText(path, text)
    path
                                                  Writes several
let createManyFiles() =                           ← files to disk
    writeTextToDisk "The quick brown fox jumped over the lazy dog"
    writeTextToDisk "The quick brown fox jumped over the lazy dog"
    writeTextToDisk "The quick brown fox jumped over the lazy dog"

createManyFiles()                  ←
                                     Calls the function
```

You'll notice a warning in the Visual Studio code editor under the first two calls in the createManyFiles() function:

```
This expression should have type 'unit', but has type 'string'.
Use 'ignore' to discard the result of the expression, or 'let'
to bind the result to a name.
```

The compiler is warning you that the writeToDisk() function is returning something (in this case, the generated filename) and you're simply discarding it! In this case, you might decide to now change the code to make a note of all the filenames that were generated and collate them into a list to return to the caller.

In a pure functional language, such as Haskell, it wouldn't make sense to discard the value of a function call, because everything is an expression and there are no side effects. In the impure .NET world, this isn't the case; there are many functions that perform side effects such as file I/O and database access.

In this case, perhaps you aren't interested in the resulting filename. Or replace this call with one to ADO .NET that performs a SQL command; the result is the number of rows updated. Again, perhaps you're not interested in this. So, you can remove the preceding warning by explicitly wrapping the result in the ignore function. ignore takes in a value and discards it, before returning unit, and because F# allows you to silently ignore expressions that return unit, the warning goes away.

Listing 7.7 Explicitly ignoring the result of an expression

```
let createManyFiles() =
    ignore(writeTextToDisk "The quick brown fox jumped over the lazy dog")
    ignore(writeTextToDisk "The quick brown fox jumped over the lazy dog")
    writeTextToDisk "The quick brown fox jumped over the lazy dog"
```

Quick check 7.2

1 What is the difference between a function returning unit and a void method?
2 What is the purpose of the ignore function in F#?

QC 7.2 answer

1 unit is a type that represents the absence of a specific value. Functions can return unit and take it in as an argument. void is a custom feature in the C# language for methods that have no return type.
2 ignore allows you to explicitly discard the result of a function call.

7.3   Forcing statement-based evaluation

Moving to expressions means that you can't get away any longer with things like unfinished if/else branches, or even early return statements from functions. However, at times you might need to work with statement-like evaluation (although it should definitely be the exception to the rule). You can do this in F# by ensuring that code in a given branch returns unit.

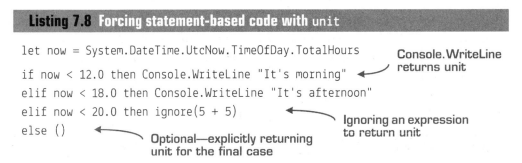

Listing 7.8 Forcing statement-based code with unit

```
let now = System.DateTime.UtcNow.TimeOfDay.TotalHours          Console.WriteLine
                                                               returns unit
if now < 12.0 then Console.WriteLine "It's morning"
elif now < 18.0 then Console.WriteLine "It's afternoon"
elif now < 20.0 then ignore(5 + 5)                          Ignoring an expression
else ()                                                     to return unit
                           Optional—explicitly returning
                           unit for the final case
```

By the way, the else branch here is optional. Because the first three branches all return unit, F# allows you to implicitly ignore the else branch as well and it fills it in for you. In this way, you've turned the if/else expression into a statement. There's no result of the conditional, just a set of side effects that return unit.

Of course, going with a statement-based approach means that you're right back where we started, with no type checks around dealing with all cases, and leading you down the path of relying on mutable data.

Cryptic compiler errors

One aspect of F# 4 that I'm not especially fond of is the error messages that it spits out, which are a throwback to F#'s OCaml roots. For example, if you create an if/else expression that returns a string value for the if branch, but forget to handle an else branch, you'll see an error similar to this:

```
This expression was expected to have type string but here has type unit
```

What the compiler is saying is that you're missing the else case, so please add one that returns a string. Thankfully, a concerted effort is being put forward by the community to contribute changes to the error messages in the compiler to improve this situation. This situation should be much improved in time for the next release of F#.

Quick check 7.3 Is it possible to work with statements rather than expressions in F#?

 **Summary**

In this lesson

- You learned about the differences between statements and expressions.
- You saw how by moving from statements to expressions you benefit from being able to better reason about your code, with the added bonus that the compiler can catch more bugs at an earlier stage.
- You saw that expressions in F# are a fundamental feature of the language, whereas statements are shied away from—leading you down the road of writing code in a manner that's less likely to result in bugs.

As you move through the next set of lessons, you'll see expressions more and more in the language.

Try this

Try to port some statement-oriented code you've written in C# to F#, making it expression-based in the process. What's its impact? Then, create a program that can read the user's full name from the console and print the user's first name only. Thinking about expressions, can you write the application so that the main logic is expression-based? What impact does this have on coupling to the console?

QC 7.3 answer Yes, using tricks such as ignore to ensure that branches return unit.

CAPSTONE 1

This lesson is slightly different from what we've covered so far. Instead of learning a new language feature, you'll try to solve a larger exercise that's designed to bring together all the lessons covered to this point in the book. In this lesson you'll be expected to

- Make changes to an existing F# application in Visual Studio
- Use the REPL as a development playground to help you develop solutions
- Port code from scripts into an F# application that's compiled into an assembly
- Write code by using expressions and immutable data structures

8.1 Defining the problem

For this exercise, you're going to work on a code base that builds on the petrol car example from earlier in this unit. The objective is to write a simple application that can drive the car to various destinations without running out of petrol. A basic application structure has already been written for you for the console runner, but the implementation of the core code needs to be done:

1 Your car starts with 100 units of petrol.
2 The user can drive to one of four destinations. Each destination will consume a different amount of petrol:
   a Home—25 units
   b Office—50 units
   c Stadium—25 units
   d Gas station—10 units
5 If the user tries to drive anywhere else, the system will reject the request.
6 If the user tries to drive somewhere and doesn't have enough petrol, the system will reject the request.
7 When the user travels to the gas station, the amount of petrol in the car should increase by 50 units.

 ## 8.2 Some advice before you start

Here are a few tips before starting this exercise:

1 Use the REPL and a script file to explore various ideas. See if you can build up everything in script form, before looking to build a standalone application. If you get anything wrong, don't worry! The whole point of a script is to allow you to cheaply try out ideas; if an idea doesn't work, try again. You want to explore the domain in a carefree manner. When you find something that feels right, move on to the next stage.
2 Avoid mutation by default.
3 Favor expressions and pure functions over statements.
4 Don't worry if your code feels more procedural than functional at this stage. Given the limited number of lessons you've gone through so far, that's not a problem.

 ## 8.3 Starting small

The easiest way to get something up and running quickly is, as usual, to start in the REPL. One of the core differences in how I tend to approach problems in the FP world compared to the OO world is to start by implementing small functions that I know are more or less correct, without worrying too much about *how* they'll be used later. As long as the functions don't rely on any shared external state, they can be used just about anywhere without a problem. With that in mind, let's start!

8.3.1   Solution overview

You'll see that in the src/code-listings/lesson-08 folder is a prebuilt Capstone1.sln solution for you to open. This contains a few files:

- *Program.fs*—The console runner of the application. This has already been written for you, and we'll briefly review it shortly.
- *Car.fs*—Contains the logic that you'll create to implement the preceding rules.
- *Scratchpad.fsx*—Will be used to explore the domain and to experiment with some code.

There's also a Car - Solution.fs file, which contains a suggested solution. Don't look at this unless you really need to!

Let's now review the Program.fs file. As you've already seen, this contains a main function, which takes in some arguments (argv). You won't use them here, though.

Listing 8.1 The main routine in your program

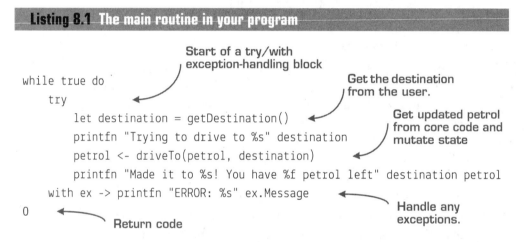

There are some interesting bits to mention here. First, notice the try/with block, F#'s equivalent of try/catch. It works in pretty much the same way, with support for the equivalent of exception filters and so on. In general, functional programmers tend to shy away from exceptions, especially as a way of managing control flow, so I don't want you to think about this sample as instructive—rather it's because you haven't learned all the functional tools yet to give you a valid alternative!

Second, you'll notice you're using a while loop here. This isn't exactly idiomatic F#, and using a while loop forces you to use a mutable variable. But note that your mutable data is *isolated*: it's in a single place, and Visual Studio highlights it in a different color to warn you. This is a key point of working in F#; in many applications, there will be a few places where mutation (or a side effect) is difficult to get rid of—and there's nothing inherently wrong with that. What is important is that you try to restrict mutation to just those places, and favor immutability everywhere else (see figure 8.1). You'll learn tricks throughout the rest of this book for avoiding common mutation pitfalls, including the preceding "while loop over state" challenge.

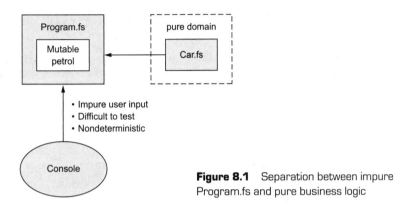

Figure 8.1   Separation between impure Program.fs and pure business logic

By doing this, you can design your core domain to be entirely pure and easy to reason about and test, and you can isolate the bits of impurity and untestability to the console runner.

 ## 8.4   Implementing core logic

To implement the solution, start by working from a script file. Test individual functions, building up to larger functions, before eventually migrating over to a full-blown application. To that end, open scratchpad.fsx in the solution in VS.

8.4.1   Your first function—calculating distances

Start by implementing a function that can figure out how many units of petrol will be used by driving to a specific location—simple. This function should have one input—the destination to drive to—and should return the amount of petrol required to get there. (Don't worry; in this example, the distance needed is always the same, regardless of where you are.) Here's a stub function to get you going.

Listing 8.2 Creating a function to calculate distances

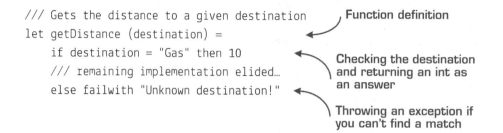

```
/// Gets the distance to a given destination          Function definition
let getDistance (destination) =
    if destination = "Gas" then 10                     Checking the destination
    /// remaining implementation elided…               and returning an int as
    else failwith "Unknown destination!"               an answer

                                                        Throwing an exception if
                                                        you can't find a match
```

You can use the `elif` keyword for the other custom branches of code. The `failwith` keyword is a quick way to throw an exception with a message—although there are other ways (such as the `raise` keyword for custom exception types).

Now that you've written the function, you should test it. You don't need to worry about unit tests and the like at this point; you'll use the script itself to check it! A couple of example test calls are already included in the script for you:

1   First, compile the `getDistance` function by highlighting it and pressing Alt-Enter.

2   Execute both test cases, one at a time. They should both return `true`.

On its own, this function is pretty useless, so the next step will take you through writing more functions that will then put you in a position to tie it all together.

8.4.2   Calculating petrol consumption

Next up, you need a function that can calculate the amount of petrol remaining after driving a specific distance (assume that one unit of distance needs one unit of petrol). This should be another simple function; here's an example definition:

```
let calculateRemainingPetrol(currentPetrol:int, distance:int) : int = …
```

The function should behave as follows:

1   As long as the petrol is greater than or equal to the distance needed, it should return the new petrol amount.

2   Otherwise, it should throw an exception with the message "Oops! You've run out of petrol!"

3   Again, after you've developed this function, you should test it in isolation.

8.4.3   Composing functions together

Now that you've created a couple of useful (albeit limited) functions, let's see how to build a larger function to pull them together. First, test in the script that you can call the functions together.

Listing 8.3   Testing orchestration of several functions

Calling the getDistance function

```
let distanceToGas = getDistance("Gas")
calculateRemainingPetrol(25, distanceToGas) // should return 15
calculateRemainingPetrol(5, distanceToGas) // should throw
```

If that all worked, you can now build a proper function to orchestrate the two functions together, driveTo. This function should take in some current petrol and a target destination. Next, work out the distance by using getDistance and use that to call calculateRemainingPetrol, the result of which you should return. Your function definition should look like this:

```
let driveTo (petrol:int, destination:string) : int = …
```

8.4.4   Stopping at the gas station

The last part you need to do is to add extra logic to check whether the user went to the gas station, and if so, to increase total petrol by 50. You can write this logic directly into the driveTo function after you've called calculateRemainingPetrol; if the destination is Gas, add 50 onto the output; otherwise, return what was output by calculateRemainingPetrol. Be sure to only add the 50 units of petrol *after* the user has safely driven to the gas station and not before (the user has to drive there first!).

8.5   Testing in scripts

Before you move over to a full-blown application, you can test this all in isolation in your script. Here's a simple test case you can try.

Listing 8.4   A test case in script

```
let a = driveTo(100, "Office")
let b = driveTo(a, "Stadium")
let c = driveTo(b, "Gas")
let answer = driveTo(c, "Home")
```

A number of chained calls to your top-level function

Answer should be 40

Observe that everything written so far is entirely *pure*. There's no shared state, no mutation. You can call these functions easily in isolation and build them into larger functions.

8.6　Moving to a full application

Now that you've tested this, you should be ready to move the code into a full application:

1　In the solution, open Car.fs.
2　Copy across the two helpers you wrote, `getDistance` and `calculateRemainingPetrol`.
3　Make sure that you paste them *above* the stub function for `driveTo`.
4　Copy across the implementation for `driveTo` from your script into the file, replacing the existing stub implementation.

You should now be in a position to compile the application and run it. Figure 8.2 shows the output.

```
C:\WINDOWS\system32\cmd.exe
Enter destination: Office
Trying to drive to Office
Made it to Office! You have 50 petrol left
Enter destination: Stadium
Trying to drive to Stadium
Made it to Stadium! You have 25 petrol left
Enter destination: Gas
Trying to drive to Gas
Made it to Gas! You have 65 petrol left
Enter destination: Home
Trying to drive to Home
Made it to Home! You have 40 petrol left
Enter destination: Shops
Trying to drive to Shops
ERROR: Unknown destination!
Enter destination:
```

Figure 8.2　Sample output from the console runner

Summary

You made it! Hopefully, that wasn't too taxing. This capstone exercise has shown you various elements from previous lessons, including the following:

- Working with scripts as a way of exploring a domain and developing code
- Writing expression-based, pure functional code
- Migrating from scripts to console applications

Types and functions

So far, in terms of F# the language, you've looked at type inference, structuring code with expressions, and working with immutable data. But you've only dealt with simple data values—int, string, and so on. What about classes? Do we still have them in F#? If not, what else do we use? And what about functions? F# is supposed to be a functional programming language, and yet we've barely covered them!

Don't worry: this unit covers all these topics. You'll see how F#'s approach to separating data and behavior works, and why it generally means that classes are undesirable within a functional-first system. In fact, this unit doesn't focus on classes at all. Instead, it presents alternative ways of modeling problems without needing to resort to classes. (And believe me when I say I've written entire full-stack applications in F# without needing to write a single class!)

You'll see how the rules you learned about immutable data still apply, even when working with larger data structures. You'll also learn more about F# functions: how they're much more powerful than the simple methods that you're used to, and how you can often use simple functions instead of classes. And, as if that's not enough, you'll also learn how to construct larger applications through namespacing and modules.

There'll be more and more F# code in the coming lessons, so make sure you have an open copy of Visual Studio at the ready with a blank .fsx file so that you can code as you go!

SHAPING DATA WITH TUPLES

You'll start this unit by looking at the simplest data structure in F#, the tuple. Tuples are a great way to quickly pass small bits of data around your code when classes or similar elements feel like overkill. In this lesson

- You'll see how tuples are used within F#.
- You'll understand when to use and not use them.
- You'll see how tuples work together with type inference to enable succinct code.
- You'll see how tuples relate to the rest of .NET.

 9.1   The need for tuples

Let's start by considering an example that seems trivial and yet gets us in all sorts of contortions nearly every day. The following method takes in a string that contains an individual's name (for example, `"Isaac Abraham"`) and splits it into its constituent parts, returning *both* the forename and surname.

Listing 9.1 Trying to return arbitrary data pairs in C#

```
public ??? ParseName(string name) {
    var parts = name.Split(' ');
    var forename = parts[0];
    var surname = parts[1];
    return ???; }
```

What should this method return? There are a few options, none of which is particularly satisfying (I should point out that these are all real answers that have been suggested to me when I've posed this question!):

1 Create a dedicated DTO called Name, with properties Forename and Surname. This works, but it's a heavyweight approach for something as small as this one-off function. And what if you have a second method that returns the forename, surname, and age? You'll quickly end up with many DTOs, all of which are similar, and probably have to map between them because C# doesn't allow you to compare objects that have the same structure rather than type.

2 Return an anonymous type? Unfortunately, C# doesn't allow anonymous types to escape method scope; instead, you can return it as a weakly typed object, and then use reflection or a similar process to get at the data. Doing something like this effectively moves you from the world of the C# type system to the world of runtime checking. Also, anonymous types are internal, so this solution doesn't work across assemblies.

3 The same as point 2, but this time use C#'s dynamic typing support to avoid reflection.

4 Return an array of strings. Again, this isn't ideal and means that the type system isn't working for you. If you want to return a mixture of types, you're again stuck.

5 Out parameters. Everyone hates these! You need to first explicitly declare a variable before calling a method, and the syntax is somewhat ugly (the C# team is working to improve this in the future for C#).

The one option that I rarely hear is to return a tuple. Tuples are exactly what you need in this case, but C# currently has no specific language support for them, so you have to rely on the raw BCL type, System.Tuple. Here's what it looks like (I've used explicit typing here for documentation purposes, but it's not necessary; I would normally use var).

Listing 9.2 Returning arbitrary data pairs in C#

```
public Tuple<string, string> ParseName(string name) {
    string[] parts = name.Split(' ');
    string forename = parts[0];
    string surname = parts[1];
    return Tuple.Create(forename, surname); }

Tuple<string, string> name = ParseName("Isaac Abraham");
string forename = name.Item1;
string surname = name.Item2;
```

Calling a method that returns a tuple of string, string

Manually deconstructing the tuple into meaningful variables

Tuples are nice in that they allow you to pass arbitrary bits of data around, temporarily grouped together. Tuples also support equality comparison by default, so you can compare arbitrary tuples against one another (provided their generic types are the same, and each type itself supports equality comparison). The problem is that the properties show up as Item1, Item2, ItemN, and so forth, so you lose all semantic meaning. You usually either comment them to explain meaning, or immediately deconstruct the tuple into its constituent parts with meaningful variable names.

 ## 9.2 Tuple basics

F#, on the other hand, has *language* support for tuples. You can rewrite listing 9.2 as follows.

Listing 9.3 Returning arbitrary data pairs in F#

```
let parseName(name:string) =
    let parts = name.Split(' ')
    let forename = parts.[0]
    let surname = parts.[1]
    forename, surname
let name = parseName("Isaac Abraham")
let forename, surname = name
let fname, sname = parseName("Isaac Abraham")
```

Creating a tuple of forename and surname

Calling a function that returns a tuple

Deconstructing a tuple into meaningful values

Deconstructing a tuple directly from a function call

> **Indexers in F#**
>
> Unlike in C#, to index into an array or list, you need to use a dot between the value and the index e.g. `myList.[4]`

Let's look at this in more detail. Most of this should translate easily from the C# example that you saw, but the key parts of how you interact with tuples will be new.

First, instead of having to explicitly call the `Tuple.Create` function, you can create tuples by separating values with a comma. Second, you can also *deconstruct* a tuple back into separate parts by assigning them to different values, again with a comma. Tuples can also be of arbitrary length and contain a mixture of types—so to create a tuple of three values, you use syntax such as `let a = "isaac", "abraham", 35`.

> **Tuples and decimal numbers**
>
> Some countries (mostly those in mainland Europe) use commas to express decimals (for example, 10,5 rather of 10.5). If you're living in one of those countries, don't get confused! In F#, you don't need the space separator, so `let y = 10,5` is a tuple of two numbers. It's not a decimal separator.

Now you try

Let's do a bit of hands-on work with tuples:

1 Open a blank .fsx file for experimenting.
2 Create a new function, `parse`, which takes in a string `person` that has the format `playername game score` (for example, `Mary Asteroids 2500`).
3 Split the string into separate values.
4 Convert the third element to an integer. You can use either `System.Convert.ToInt32()`, `System.Int32.Parse()`, or the F# alias function for it, `int()`.
5 Return a three-part tuple of name, game, and score and assign it to a value.
6 Deconstruct all three parts into separate values by using `let a,b,c =` syntax.
7 Notice that you can choose arbitrary names for each element.

The history of tuples in .NET

Tuples were introduced in the BCL in .NET 4, but they were part of the FSharp.Core library since much earlier. Indeed, if you run any F# 2 code, you see that FSharp.Core has a version of the Tuple type. Since F# 3, this type no longer exists; F# uses the BCL `System.Tuple` instead.

C# 7 also has a similar kind of language-level tuple support (indeed, it even allows you to assign names to Tuple elements). For performance reasons, a new `ValueTuple` type was created that's a struct (unlike `System.Tuple`). F# 4.1 also has a new `struct` keyword to allow you to use the ValueType version; this is very useful for interop purposes.

9.2.1 When should I use tuples?

Tuples are lightweight data structures. They're easy to create, with native language support. As such, they're great for internal helper functions and for storing intermediary state. You can imagine using them within a function as a way to package a few values in order to easily pass them to another section of code, or as a way of specifying intent (that two values are somehow bound to one another, by first name and surname, or sort code and account number, and so forth).

Tuple helpers

F# also has two built-in functions for working with two-part tuples: `fst` and `snd`. As the names suggest, these functions take in a two-part tuple and return either just the first or second element in the tuple.

Quick check 9.1

1 How would you separate values in a tuple in F#?
2 What is the main distinction between tuples in F# and C# 6?

QC 9.1 answer

1 You use the comma to separate values.
2 F# has language support for tuples; C#6 doesn't.

9.3   More-complex tuples

Let's briefly expand this discussion with a slightly more detailed look into tuples and how they fit into the F# type system.

9.3.1   Tuple type signatures

It's worth understanding tuple notation in F#, which is type * type * type. A three-part tuple of two strings and an int would be notated as string * string * int. Figure 9.1 shows a simple example.

```
let nameAndAge = "Joe", "Bloggs", 28
        val nameAndAge : string * string * int
```

Figure 9.1   Creating a three-part tuple in F# and Visual Studio 2015

9.3.2   Nested tuples

You can also nest, or group, tuples together. The preceding example treats all three elements as siblings; there's no grouping of the name elements. You can fix that by creating a *nested* tuple within a larger tuple, by grouping together the inner part with brackets. You can visualize this in figure 9.2.

Listing 9.4   Returning more-complex arbitrary data pairs in F#

```
let nameAndAge = ("Joe", "Bloggs"), 28          ⟵ Creating a nested tuple
let name, age = nameAndAge                    ⟵ Deconstructing a tuple
let (forename, surname), theAge = nameAndAge ⟵
```
Deconstructing the same tuple, including the nested component

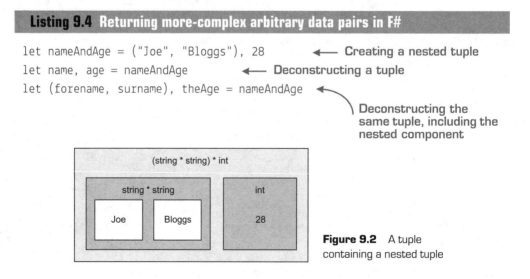

Figure 9.2   A tuple containing a nested tuple

Just to confirm: the type signature for nameAndAge here is (string * string) * int. It's a two-part tuple, the first part of which is *itself* a tuple of two strings, while the second part is an integer. If you were to use the raw System.Tuple type here (and you can prove it by calling GetType() on nameAndAge), it would look something like Tuple<Tuple<String, String>, Int32>. I know which syntax I prefer!

9.3.3 Wildcards

If there are elements of a tuple that you're not interested in, you can discard them while deconstructing a tuple by assigning those parts to the underscore symbol.

Listing 9.5 Using wildcards with tuples

```
let nameAndAge = "Jane", "Smith", 25
let forename, surname, _ = nameAndAge          ← Discarding the third
                                                 element of the tuple
```

This is particularly useful when you want to pull out only a certain section of a tuple, and it's better than assigning it to arbitrary values such as x or y. The underscore is a symbol in F# that tells the type system (and the developer) that you explicitly don't want to use this value. You'll also see in the coming lessons that wildcards are useful when *pattern matching*, a form of conditional logic checking that replaces switch/case.

9.3.4 Type inference with tuples

F# can infer tuples, just as it does with a simple value, even for function arguments.

Listing 9.6 Type inference with tuples in F#

```
let explicit : int * int = 10, 5       ← Explicit type signature
let implicit = 10,5                     ← Type inferred to be int * int

let addNumbers arguments =              ← "arguments" inferred to be int * int
    let a, b = arguments
    a + b
```

Notice also that F# will also automatically genericize tuples within functions if a tuple element is unused within a function.

Listing 9.7 Genericized functions with tuples

```
let addNumbers arguments =
    let a, b, c, _ = arguments      ← Deconstructing a
    a + b                             four-part tuple
```

What is the signature of arguments in this case? The compiler can infer the types of a and b as integers, but the tuple has two other elements: c and the wildcard value. The compiler will automatically make them generic type arguments to the addNumbers function: int * int * 'a * 'b. This is a four-part tuple, of which the first two elements are integers, the third is of type 'a, and the fourth of type 'b.

> **Quick check 9.2**
>
> 1 What is the type signature of nameAndAge in listing 9.4? Why?
> 2 How many elements are in nameAndAge?
> 3 What is the purpose of the wildcard symbol?
> 4 How many wildcards can you use when deconstructing a tuple?

9.4   Tuple best practices

You've seen what tuples can do, but F# has other data structures, such as records (lesson 10) and discriminated unions. This section briefly outlines some best practices for using tuples.

9.4.1   Tuples and the BCL

One of the nicest parts of F# is that it handles interoperability with both C# and VB. There's plenty to see on this later in the book, but as an example, you'll see now how F# uses tuple language support to elegantly remove the need for out parameters. Here's an example of trying to parse a number stored in a string by using C# and the Int32.TryParse function.

> **QC 9.2 answer**
>
> 1 (string * string) * int—a tuple first containing a nested tuple of two strings, and then an int.
> 2 Two elements: (string * string) and (int).
> 3 To explicitly discard unneeded elements of a tuple.
> 4 There's no limit. You can discard as many elements of a tuple as you wish.

Listing 9.8 Implicit mapping of out parameters to tuples

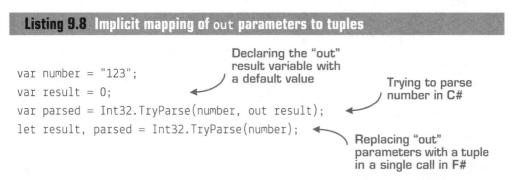

```
var number = "123";
var result = 0;
var parsed = Int32.TryParse(number, out result);
let result, parsed = Int32.TryParse(number);
```

Declaring the "out" result variable with a default value

Trying to parse number in C#

Replacing "out" parameters with a tuple in a single call in F#

Here, the same BCL call that you'd normally have to call as a two-stage process with an out parameter is replaced with a single call, and both the parsed value *and* parsing result are returned as a tuple—much nicer!

9.4.2   When not to use tuples

F# has other types of data structures in addition to tuples, so clearly tuples aren't the only way of passing data around. When wouldn't you use them?

Despite their ease of use, tuples aren't generally a great fit for public APIs *except* when the tuple size is small: typically two, or at most three, elements wide; anything larger quickly becomes difficult to reason about. Why? Remember that tuple fields have no specific names. The client of the tuple can choose arbitrary names for tuple fields when deconstructing them, so it's not easy to encode the semantic meaning behind a tuple. Imagine you have a function that returns a tuple of string * string. What does this represent? Forename and Surname? City and Country? It could be anything.

So, although tuples are useful (as you'll see, they can simplify complicated type signatures), you still need to think about, for example, intelligently naming functions that return tuples so that it's obvious what the parts of the tuple represent. In the following example, all three functions return the same data: a string * string tuple. But what do a and b represent?

Listing 9.9 Intelligently naming functions

```
let a, b = getData()                        Poor naming
let a, b = getBankDetails()                 Improved naming
let a, b = getSortCodeAndAccountNumber()    Better naming
```

In situations like this, where you have a clear contract for a DTO that's fairly stable, you'll probably prefer to use a record.

Quick check 9.3

1   What's generally considered the maximum size you should use for a tuple?
2   When should you be cautious of using tuples?

Summary

In this lesson

- You saw the most basic data structure in F#, the tuple.
- You understand that tuple support in F# is language support over the `System.Tuple` type that exists in the BCL.
- You've seen how type inference works with tuples.
- You understand when and where tuples are best suited to being used.

Try this

Look at methods in common BCL namespaces, and try to find some that you think should be "tupled." (Hint: Ones with `out` parameters are a good start!) Then, write a function to load a filename and last-modified date from the filesystem, using a tuple as the return type.

QC 9.3 answer

1   Two or three elements.
2   In public contracts, particularly when different elements of the tuple are of the same type and open to misinterpretation.

10

SHAPING DATA WITH RECORDS

In the previous lesson, you looked at a lightweight, simple way of packaging data pieces together with the tuple. You also saw that tuples are great in some situations, but in others not so much. Now you'll look at F#'s secondary data structure: the record, a more fully featured data structure more akin to a class. In this lesson

- You'll see what records are within F#.
- You'll understand how records compare with C# and VB classes.
- You'll learn how to affect changes to records while still retaining immutability.
- You'll see tips for working with records.

Let's start by continuing where we left off in the previous lesson and by describing a situation where tuples aren't suitable for exposing data. For example, a tuple wouldn't be suitable for a public contract of some sort where you want explicit named fields, or somewhere that you need to expose more than two or three properties. Here's a simple example of a Customer type in C#.

Listing 10.1 A basic DTO in C#

```
public class Customer {                ←—— Type definition
    public string Forename { get; set; }    ←——
    public string Surname { get; set; }          Public, mutable
                                                  properties
```

111

```
    public int Age { get; set; }
    public Address Address { get; set; }
    public string EmailAddress { get; set; }
}
```

This is often referred to as a Plain Old C# Object (POCO) or data transfer object (DTO) — a class that's used for the purposes of storing and transferring data, but not necessarily any behavior. I've omitted the Address class for brevity, but it's just another DTO.

That POCO is pretty nice, but there are issues with this sort of approach, all around data integrity. First, there's no way to guarantee that you'll always create a valid object; for example, you might forget to set the Address property. Second, you can also modify this after the object is created; in fact, anyone could! You'll probably want to enforce the construction and lifetime of Customer in a safer way, as shown in the next listing.

Listing 10.2 Near-immutable DTOs in C#

```
public class Customer {
    public string Forename { get; private set; }     ◄─── Public read-only,
    public string Surname { get; private set; }            private mutable
    public int Age { get; private set; }                   properties
    public Address Address { get; private set; }
    public string EmailAddress { get; private set; }

    public Customer(string forename, string surname, int age, Address
    ⮡address, string emailAddress) {        ◄─── Nondefault constructor
        Forename = forename;                      guarantees safe
        Surname = surname;                        initialization of object
        Age = age;
        Address = address;
        EmailAddress = emailAddress;
    }
}
```

This is a definite improvement, but there's a lot of boilerplate here! Even worse, you're still not guaranteeing that this type is immutable. The class itself could change its own state later in, for example, a method. If you want to *truly* make this DTO immutable, you have to manually create a read-only backing field, and then make a public getter for it. In the interest of time and space (and our sanity), I'm not going to show that version here.

There's another issue with this that we tend to once again take for granted as "the way things are." Let's say you want to check whether two customers have the same address. How would you check that? Here's what you'd like to be able to do.

Listing 10.3 Comparing objects of the same type in C#

```
public class Address {
    public string Street { get; set; }          Example
    public string Town { get; set; }            Address type
    public string City { get; set; }
}                                               Comparing two
var sameAddress = (customerA.Address == customer.Address);   address objects
```

Unfortunately, this will almost certainly return `false`, even if both addresses contain the same address values. That's because .NET classes perform reference equality checks by default. Only if both addresses are *the same object*, existing in *the same space in memory*, will this check return `true`. That's not what you want! What you're looking for is a form of *structural equality* checking. You can do this in C# or VB .NET, but as it turns out, it's a lot of work. You need to do the following:

- Override `GetHashCode()`.
- Override `Equals()`.
- Write a custom `==` operator (otherwise, `Equals` and `==` will give different behavior!).

- Ideally, implement `System.IEquatable`.
- Ideally, implement `System.Collections.Generic.IEqualityComparer`.

Try implementing all of this by hand for all fields in the class (and the associated unit tests) and you'll discover that suddenly your POCO is no longer a plain C# object but a COCO—a Complex Old C# Object!

You'd be surprised how often you'll want some form of structural equality rather than referential equality. There's a reason we use tools such as ReSharper to generate this for us: it's not fun and is prone to errors. Even with a tool like ReSharper, the code that's generated needs to be maintained. Imagine that you add a property to an object and forget to regenerate the equality-checking code. This can lead to the worst kinds of bugs that occur only at runtime in specific circumstances, depending on the objects being compared.

10.1 POCOs done right: records in F#

F# records are best described as simple-to-use objects designed to store, transfer, and access immutable data that have named fields—essentially the same thing you just tried to achieve with a C# POCO.

10.1.1 Record basics

Let's see how to implement the same `Address` type in F# so that it supports immutability as well as implementing structural equality checking.

> ### Listing 10.4   Immutable and structural equality record in F#

```
type Address =
    { Street : string
      Town : string
      City : string }
```

Believe it or not, that's everything you need. For this, you'll get the following:

- A constructor that requires all fields to be provided
- Public access for all fields (which are themselves read-only)
- Full structural equality, throughout the *entire object graph*

> **Declaring records on a single line**
>
> You can also define the record on a single line (useful for simple records) by using a semi-colon as a separator (for example, `type Address = { Line1 : string; Line2 : string }`). Note that for multiline declarations, like the rest of the language, you need to ensure that all fields start on the same column.
>
> I suggest you allow Visual F# Power Tools to take care of formatting for you, though—at least while you're taking your first steps with the language. You can highlight any declaration and choose Edit > Advanced > FormatSelection (or FormatDocument) to have it format your code in a consistent manner.

10.1.2 Creating records

Creating records in F# is super easy. Record constructors, again, have specific language support. Here's how to create an instance of an `Address`, and then create a `Customer` with that address (reuse the code sample from earlier for the declaration of the `Address` type).

Listing 10.5 Constructing a nested record in F#

```
type Customer =                        ◄─── Declaring the
    { Forename : string                     Customer
      Surname : string                      record type
      Age : int
      Address : Address
      EmailAddress : string }
let customer =                         ◄─── Creating a
    { Forename = "Joe"                      Customer with
      Surname = "Bloggs"                    Address inline
      Age = 30
      Address =
        { Street = "The Street"
          Town = "The Town"
          City = "The City" }
      EmailAddress = "joe@bloggs.com" }
```

Easy! Notice that you define the address inline while creating the customer. You could've defined the address separately if you wanted to, as a separate `let` binding.

Now that you've created a record, you can see in figure 10.1 that you can access fields on the record just like "normal" C# objects.

```
customer.Address.|
    Address.City: string  ◕ City
                          ◔ Equals
                          ◔ GetHashCode
                          ◔ GetType
                          ◕ Street
                          ◔ ToString
                          ◕ Town
```

Figure 10.1 Accessing fields on an F# record

Now see in figure 10.2 that, as with a constructor that requires all properties, you can't miss any of the fields when declaring an instance of a record.

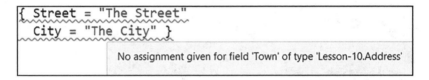

```
{ Street = "The Street"
   City = "The City" }
```
No assignment given for field 'Town' of type 'Lesson-10.Address'

Figure 10.2 Compiler error when omitting the Town field from an Address record

---

All your fields are belong to us

One nice thing about having to eagerly set all fields of a record is that when you decide to add a new field to a record, the compiler will instantly warn you of every location where you create an instance of that record. That way, you can ensure that you never accidentally create a record with half of it uninitialized. You might wonder how you'd deal with cases that have only some values of a record up front. Or perhaps you want to use only some of the fields in the record some of the time, and other times use all of them. In C#, it's normal to reuse a POCO for multiple purposes by omitting setting some fields.

This is again part of F# trying to guide you down the road of being explicit about this and ultimately encoding these sorts of business rules or situations within the type system. We'll cover the most common answer (discriminated unions) in a later lesson, but the main point is that the compiler forces you to populate all fields when creating a record value.

Now you try

Let's have a look at creating your own record type now:

1   Define a record type in F# to store data on a Car, such as manufacturer, engine size, number of doors, and so forth.
2   Create an instance of that record.
3   Experiment with formatting the record; use power tools to automatically format the record for you.

Quick check 10.1

1   What is the default accessibility modifier for fields on records?
2   What is the difference between referential and structural equality?

 ## 10.2 Doing more with records

Let's move on to looking at some more-advanced features that we get with records.

10.2.1 Type inference with records

You'll notice that the code used to create an instance of a record (such as address and customer) looks somewhat similar to the way you declare objects in JavaScript—a dynamic language. Don't be fooled! The compiler knows that these are static types, rather than dynamic objects. Once again, the compiler has inferred the types based on the *properties assigned to the object*. You can be explicit about this in a couple of ways: either by specifying the type of the left-side binding, or by prefixing fields with the type name.

QC 10.1 answer

1   Public.
2   Referential equality compares two records to see whether they're the same object in memory; structural equality compares the content of two records.

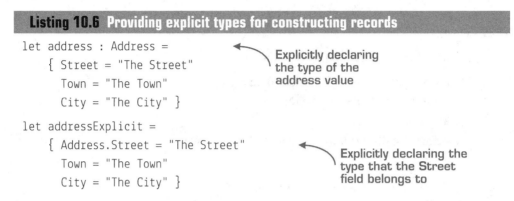

Listing 10.6 **Providing explicit types for constructing records**

```
let address : Address =
    { Street = "The Street"
      Town = "The Town"
      City = "The City" }

let addressExplicit =
    { Address.Street = "The Street"
      Town = "The Town"
      City = "The City" }
```

Explicitly declaring the type of the address value

Explicitly declaring the type that the Street field belongs to

I encourage you to avoid using explicit types unless you really need to, but one benefit of choosing to prefix a field with the type is that the compiler will immediately give you IntelliSense, as shown in figure 10.3.

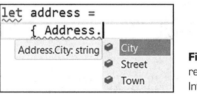

Figure 10.3 Creating a record in F# with field-level IntelliSense

F# will also infer a record type based on *usage* of an instance. Figure 10.4 shows an example of a function that takes in a customer as an argument. After you've dotted into the object once and accessed the first field, the compiler will kick in and realize what you're doing.

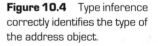

Figure 10.4 Type inference correctly identifies the type of the address object.

Note that until you access at least one property, the compiler (obviously) won't be able to deduce the type, so it'll normally show as an object (or perhaps a generic type).

> **Members on records**
>
> You'll notice that records have the standard members (for example, ToString() and Get-HashCode()). That's because records compile down to classes. And, as with classes, you can create member methods on them. But this isn't something that you'll normally need to do in F# (remember that records should act as DTOs) and isn't covered in this lesson.

10.2.2 Working with immutable records

Like regular value bindings, fields on F# records are immutable by default. But you know that in the real world, you sometimes have to model the context of a value changing its state over time. How can you do this without mutating fields on a record? F#'s answer to this is to provide *copy-and-update* syntax. Let's see how to change a customer's email address and age.

Listing 10.7 Copy-and-update record syntax

```
let updatedCustomer =
    { customer with
        Age = 31
        EmailAddress = "joe@bloggs.co.uk" }
```

Creating a new version of a record by using the 'with' keyword

The idea behind this is that you provide a record with the modifications that you want to perform on the record, and F# will then create a *copy* of the record with those changes applied. In this way, you can get the best of all worlds:

- You can provide records to other sections of code without having to worry about their values being implicitly modified without your knowledge.
- You can still easily simulate mutation through copy-and-update.
- If you want to write a function that does modify a record, you have it take in the original version as an argument and return the new version as the output of the function. This is exactly how LINQ works with collections (and it shouldn't come as a surprise to learn that the LINQ feature set is a subset of functional programming for C#).

This way of working is a great fit for event-based architectures, where you record all changes to data over time as immutable events and versions of records.

If you absolutely have to—and this should be the exception to the rule—you can override immutability behavior on a field-by-field basis by adding the `mutable` modifier. You might want to do this if you have a record that will be used in a tight loop, mutating itself thousands of times a second, for example. Because records are reference types (although it's looking increasingly like the next version of F# will allow struct records), every copy-and-update causes a new object to be allocated on the heap, so garbage collector (GC) pressure could cause performance issues in such a situation. But I recommend that the default should be to use immutable data structures initially, test performance, and only if you see an issue, reconfigure the definition of the record. Certainly, in all applications I've written, this has never been an issue for me. Bottlenecks are far more likely to occur with other parts of your application (for example, with database connectivity).

10.2.3 Equality checking

You can safely compare two F# records of the same type with a single = for full, deep structural equality checking.

Listing 10.8 Comparing two records in F#

```
let isSameAddress = (address = addressExplicit)
```
Comparing two records by using the = operator

You can override this behavior with a few attributes that you can place on a record, but I advise you to avoid looking them up unless you really need to, as you then need to fall back to implementing `GetHashCode()` manually. Still, it's worth knowing that there is an escape hatch if needed.

Now you try

Let's practically explore some of these features of records:

1. Define a record type, such as the `Address` type shown earlier.
2. Create two instances of the record that have the same values.
3. Compare the two objects by using `=`, `.Equals`, and `System.Object.ReferenceEquals`.
4. What are the results of all of them? Why?
5. Create a function that takes in a customer and, using copy-and-update syntax, sets the customer's `Age` to a random number between 18 and 45.

6 The function should then print the customer's original and new age, before returning the updated customer record.

Let's wrap up this section by comparing classes and records, as shown in table 10.1.

Table 10.1 Comparing classes and records

	.NET classes	**F# records**
Default mutability of data	Mutable	Immutable
Default equality behavior	Reference equality	Structural equality
Copy-and-update syntax?	No	Rich language support
F# type-inference support?	Limited	Full
Guaranteed initialization	No	Yes

Quick check 10.2

1 At runtime, what do records compile into?
2 What is the default type of equality checking for records?

10.3 Tips and tricks with records

Let's briefly discuss a few extra tips on working with records.

10.3.1 Refactoring

Don't forget that VFPT has support for useful refactoring tools to make life even easier. One such feature enables you to rename refactoring on record fields (F2). Another automatically populates all fields in a record when creating one, which you can then fill in:

1 Start creating an instance of a record.
2 Set at least one field on the record.
3 Move the caret to the *start* of the field declaration and wait for the lightbulb to appear.

QC 10.2 answer

1 Classes.
2 Structural equality.

4   Press Ctrl-period and choose Generate Record Stubs from the pop-up menu, as
shown in figure 10.5.

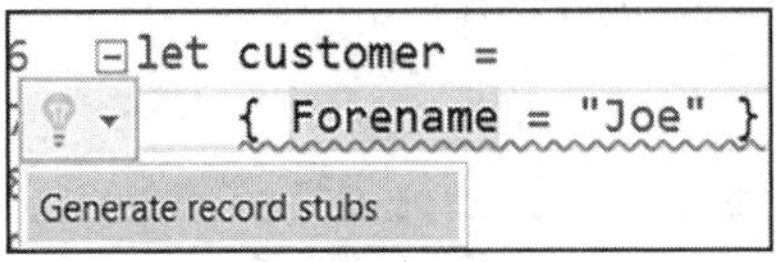

Figure 10.5   Automatically generating record stubs through VFPT

You can configure how to fill in missing fields via VFPT by choosing Tools > Options > F# Power Tools > Code Generation. The dialog box in figure 10.6 opens, displaying your options.

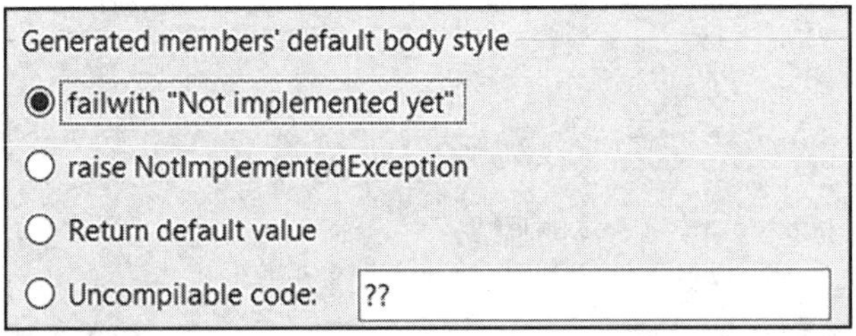

Figure 10.6   Configuring how VFTP autogenerates record stubs

10.3.2 Shadowing

Copy-and-update is a common feature to use in F# when working with records, but it doesn't necessarily feel right to create different names for value bindings every time you update a record. That's why F# allows you to reuse existing named bindings. This feature is called *shadowing*. With shadowing, you can write code as follows:

```
let myHome = { Street = "The Street"; Town = "The Town"; City = "The City" }
let myHome = { myHome with City = "The Other City" }
let myHome = { myHome with City = "The Third City" }
```

Notice here that you're reusing the binding myHome rather than using myHome, myHome1, and myHome2. This *isn't* the same as mutating myHome. Instead, you're reusing the same symbol with a new value. You can observe this in VS by highlighting a symbol and witnessing that the editor highlights references to the instance of the symbol, as shown in figure 10.7.

```
let myHome = { Street = "Th
let myHome = { address with
printfn "%s" myHome.City
let myHome = { address with
printfn "%s" myHome.Street
()
```

Figure 10.7 Visual Studio highlighting referencing to a specific instance of a symbol

10.3.3 When to use records

Records are probably the most common type of data structure in F#. They're more powerful than tuples, with the ability to explicitly name fields as well as using a neat copy-and-update syntax that tuples don't have. For a C# or VB .NET developer, they're a natural fit for all the times you need simple DTOs within your applications. Finally, as records compile down into classes, they can be consumed easily in other .NET languages and systems expecting classes—because that's all they really are; it's just that F# wraps over them with an extremely smart compiler.

Tuples still have their place within F#, particularly when you're working with small bits of short-lived data, and especially if they're used in a context where the data isn't exposed publicly.

Quick check 10.3

1 What is shadowing?
2 When should you use records?

Summary

In this lesson

- You saw the most common data structure in F#, the record.
- You learned the typical use cases that F# records are designed to solve.

QC 10.3 answer

1 The ability to reuse an existing symbol for a new value.
2 For public contracts, typically where tuples aren't a good fit because of the number of fields.

- You saw how type inference works with records.
- You learned about a powerful alternative to working with mutable data, called copy-and-update.

Try this

1 Model the Car example from lesson 6, but use records to model the state of the Car.
2 Take an existing set of classes that you have in an existing C# project and map as records in F#. Are there any cases that don't map well?

BUILDING COMPOSABLE FUNCTIONS

It seems strange to consider that we're on lesson 11 and haven't spent much time talking about functions! But you've already seen (and built your own) functions by now, so you've gained a little exposure to them. You can already do many of the same sorts of things you'd do with methods in C# or VB .NET. This lesson digs into how powerful functions in F# really are:

- You'll gain a proper understanding of F# functions compared to methods.
- You'll learn about a powerful technique called *partial application*.
- You'll learn about two important operators in F# that help build larger pieces of code: pipeline and compose.

Have an energy drink before you start this lesson, as it's probably the one lesson in this book that will throw the most at you in terms of F# features and syntax!

We tend to think of functions and methods as interchangeable terms. But let- bound functions in F# are an entirely different beast compared to methods. These are the sort of functions that you've already been defining so far—bound to a value through the let keyword (you can create classes with methods in F#, although I haven't shown the syntax for this yet). Let's see a quick comparison of methods and functions, as shown in table 11.1.

Table 11.1   Comparing methods and functions

	C# methods	F# let-bound functions
Behavior	Statements or expressions	Expressions by default
Scope	Instance (object) or static (type)	Static (module level or nested function)
Overloading	Allowed	Not supported
Currying	Not supported	Native support

Previous lessons covered some of these points (for example, functions always return something, even if that something is the unit object), but you'll almost certainly be surprised by others. Let's start by discussing the one term in table 11.1 that you might not know yet: *currying*.

 ## 11.1   Partial function application

Partially applied functions are one of the most powerful parts of the function system in F# as compared to C#. These functions open up all sorts of interesting possibilities. Let's start by clarifying something you probably already noticed from previous examples: the following two functions appear to do the same thing, except that one uses brackets (parentheses) and commas for input arguments (like C#), and one doesn't. The former is referred to as *tupled* form and the latter as *curried* form.

Listing 11.1   Passing arguments with and without brackets

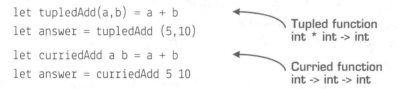

```
let tupledAdd(a,b) = a + b
let answer = tupledAdd (5,10)          Tupled function
                                       int * int -> int

let curriedAdd a b = a + b
let answer = curriedAdd 5 10           Curried function
                                       int -> int -> int
```

Many developers are frightened when they see the explanation of curried functions, and to be honest, you don't need to understand it. To make a long story short, the main differences to take away from listing 11.1 are as follows:

- *Tupled* functions force you to supply all the arguments at once (like C# methods), and have a signature of (type1 * type2 … * typeN) -> result. F# considers all the arguments as a *single object*, which is why the signature looks like a tuple signature—that's exactly what it is.

- *Curried* functions allow you to supply only *some* of the arguments to a function, and get back a *new function* that expects the *remaining* arguments. The following listing shows an example, illustrated in figure 11.1. Curried functions have a signature of `arg1 -> arg2 … -> argN -> result`. You can think of these as a function that *itself* returns a function (please feel free to take a moment to let that sink in).

Listing 11.2 Calling a curried function in steps

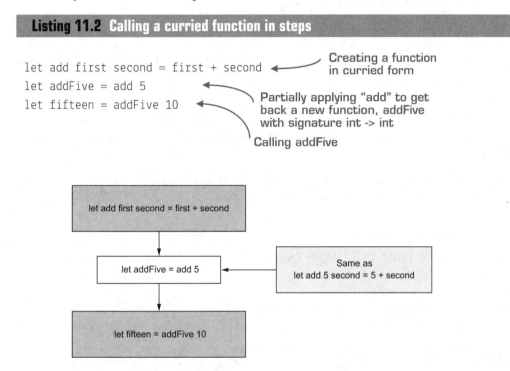

```
let add first second = first + second          Creating a function
                                               in curried form
let addFive = add 5
let fifteen = addFive 10                        Partially applying "add" to get
                                                back a new function, addFive
                                                with signature int -> int

                                                Calling addFive
```

Figure 11.1   Partially applying a function to create a new function

Partial application and currying

You might have heard the terms *curried* and *partially applied* functions before. The two are sort of related. A curried function is a function that itself returns a function. Partial application is the *act* of calling that curried function to get back a new function.

Now that you know what curried functions are, let's have a look at some cases where they offer practical advantages over tupled functions.

Quick check 11.1   What's the difference between a curried function and a tupled function?

11.2 Constraining functions

One easy use for curried functions is in creating a *more constrained* version of a function, sometimes known as a *wrapper* function. You probably use methods like this all the time when you want to make functions easier to call when, for example, a subset of the arguments are the same across multiple calls. Let's look at a simple set of wrapper functions that can create DateTime objects. The first one takes in year, month, and day; the second only the month and day for this year; and the final one only the day for this year and month.

Listing 11.3 Explicitly creating wrapper functions in F#

```
open System
let buildDt year month day = DateTime(year, month, day)
let buildDtThisYear month day = buildDt DateTime.UtcNow.Year month day
let buildDtThisMonth day = buildDtThisYear DateTime.UtcNow.Month day
```

Notice that each function cascades up to a more-generalized version. This is nice, but with curried functions, you can make the two wrapper functions much more lightweight.

Listing 11.4 Creating wrapper functions by currying

```
let buildDtThisYear = buildDt DateTime.UtcNow.Year
let buildDtThisMonth = buildDtThisYear DateTime.UtcNow.Month
```

This code is identical to listing 11.2, except here you don't have to explicitly pass through the extra arguments to the right-hand side; F# automatically does that for you. You wouldn't have been able to do this form of lightweight wrapping with a function in tupled form, because you need to pass all values of the tuple together. Of course, Visual Studio will automatically infer that these are functions, and not simple values, as you can see in figure 11.2.

QC 11.1 answer   A tupled function behaves as a C# function; all arguments must be supplied. Curried functions allow you to supply a subset of the arguments, and get back a new function that expects the remaining arguments.

```
let buildDt year month day = DateTime(year, month, day)
let buildDtThisYear = buildDt DateTime.UtcNow.Year
let buildDtThisMonth = buildDtThisYear DateTime.UtcNow.Month
```

Figure 11.2 Syntax highlighting for curried functions in Visual Studio

It's worth remembering that partially applied functions work from *left to right*: you partially apply arguments starting from the left side and then work your way in. That's why you place year as the first argument: it's the most general argument and the one that you want to partially apply first.

Now you try

Create a simple wrapper function, writeToFile, for writing data to a text file:

1 The function should take in three arguments in this specific order:
   a date—the current date
   b filename—a filename
   c text—the text to write out
2 The function signature should be written in curried form (with spaces separating the arguments).
3 The body should create a filename in the form {date}-{filename}.txt. Use the System .IO.File.WriteAllText function to save the contents of the file.
4 You can either manually construct the path by using basic string concatenation, or use the sprintf function.
5 You should construct the date part of the filename explicitly by using the ToString override—for example, ToString("yyMMdd"). You need to explicitly annotate the type of date as System.DateTime.

If you've done this correctly, your function should have a signature as shown in figure 11.3. It's *really* important to look at the signature of functions like this so that you learn to understand what's happening.

```
let writeToFile (date:DateTime) filename text =
    let path
    File.Wri    val writeToFile : date:DateTime -> filename:string -> text:string -> unit
```

Figure 11.3 Creating a curried function in F#

The body of the function should look something like the following listing.

Listing 11.5   Creating your first curried function

```
open System
open System.IO
let writeToFile (date:DateTime) filename text =
    let path = sprintf "%s-%s.txt" (date.ToString "yyMMdd") filename
    File.WriteAllText(path, text)
```

6   You should now be able to create more-constrained versions of this function.

Listing 11.6   Creating constrained functions

Creating a constrained version of the function to print with today's date

Creating a more-constrained version to print with a specific filename

```
let writeToToday = writeToFile DateTime.UtcNow.Date
let writeToTomorrow = writeToFile (DateTime.UtcNow.Date.AddDays 1.)
let writeToTodayHelloWorld = writeToToday "hello-world"
```

```
writeToToday "first-file" "The quick brown fox jumped over the lazy dog"
writeToTomorrow "second-file" "The quick brown fox jumped over the lazy dog"
writeToTodayHelloWorld "The quick brown fox jumped over the lazy dog"
```

Calling a constrained version to create a file with today's date and "first-file"

Calling the more-constrained version—only the final argument is required

There are many useful applications of curried functions, such as dependency injection at the function level (as you'll see in lesson 12), but curried functions also work well in tandem with another of F#'s functional features: pipelines.

Quick check 11.2   Name at least two differences between C# methods and F# let-bound functions.

QC 11.2 answer   Functions are always static; methods can be instance-level. Functions don't support overloading but do support currying.

11.2.1 Pipelines

Wrapper functions are a nice benefit of curried functions, but they're not the *main* benefit; that's where pipelines come in. Regardless of the language you're in, you'll often need to call methods in an ordered fashion, with the output of one method acting as the input to the next. Let's see an example of a simple set of methods that you want to orchestrate together:

1 Get the current directory.
2 Get the creation time of the directory.
3 Pass that time to the function checkCreation. If the folder is older than seven days, the function prints Old to the console and otherwise prints New.

You might write code that looks like the following listing.

Listing 11.7 Calling functions arbitrarily

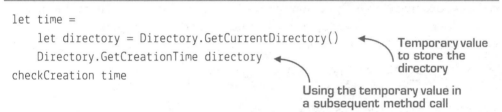

```
let time =
    let directory = Directory.GetCurrentDirectory()       ◄─  Temporary value
    Directory.GetCreationTime directory   ◄─                  to store the
checkCreation time                                           directory
```
Using the temporary value in
a subsequent method call

This isn't bad, but you have a set of temporary variables that are used to pass data to the next method in the call. And if the chain was bigger, it'd quickly get unwieldy. You could try implicitly chaining these methods together, as shown in the following listing.

Listing 11.8 Simplistic chaining of functions

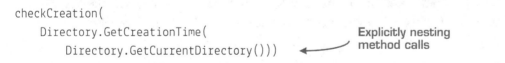

```
checkCreation(
    Directory.GetCreationTime(
        Directory.GetCurrentDirectory()))   ◄─
```
Explicitly nesting
method calls

This is less code, and it's now clear that a specific relationship exists between these functions. But the problem is that the order in which you *read* the code is now the opposite of the *order* of operation. That's definitely not what you want! You want something that looks like figure 11.4.

Figure 11.4 Logical flow of functions

Luckily, F# has a special operator called the *forward pipe* that, much like currying, is a simple yet powerful feature. It looks like this: `arg |> function`. That doesn't mean much, so let's explain it another way:

> Take the value on the *left-hand side* of the pipe, and flip it over to the *right-hand side* as the *last* argument to the function.

In other words, given a function call `addFive x`, instead of calling it as `addFive 10`, you can call `10 |> addFive`. The result is the same; it's simply another way of expressing the same code. The beauty of this is that as long as the *output* of one function matches the *input* of the next one, any function can be chained with another one. This simple rule means that you can rewrite listing 11.8 as follows.

Listing 11.9 Chaining three functions together using the pipeline operator

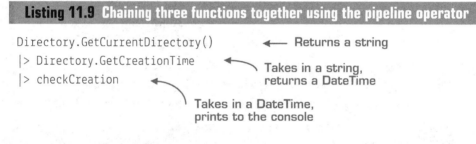

Now your code reads like it operates! Note that you could even have placed the `unit` argument for `GetCurrentDirectory`—the `()` object—at the head of the pipeline, but in this case, I've left it in place.

You'll find that the pipeline is extremely useful for composing code together into a human-readable domain-specific language (DSL). And because pipelines operate on the *last* argument of a function, you can quickly create code that looks like the following.

Listing 11.10 Sample F# pipelines and DSLs

Piped function chain

```
let answer = 10 |> add 5 |> timesBy 2 |> add 20 |> add 7 |> timesBy 3

loadCustomer 17 |> buildReport |> convertTo Format.PDF |> postToQueue

let customersWithOverdueOrders =
    getSqlConnection "DevelopmentDb"
    |> createDbConnection
    |> findCustomersWithOrders Status.Outstanding (TimeSpan.FromDays 7.0)
```

An example DSL for working with customer reports as a pipeline

This might look similar to a feature that already exists in C# and VB: *extension methods*. But they're not quite the same, as you can see in table 11.2.

Table 11.2 Extension methods vs. curried functions

	C# extension methods	**F#**
Scope	Methods must be explicitly designed to be extension methods in a static class with the extension point decorated with the this keyword.	Any single-argument .NET method (including the BCL) and all curried functions can be chained together.
Extension point	First argument in method signature.	Last argument in function.
Currying support	None.	First class.
Paradigm	Not always a natural fit for OO paradigm with private state.	Natural fit for stateless functions.

11.2.2 Custom fonts

Although VS uses Consolas by default, you might want to try the freely available Fira-Code font, a monospace font that supports *ligatures*. This font can represent custom operators much more nicely.

Unfortunately, Visual Studio doesn't support all of the ligatures (unlike VS Code), but most, including the pipeline operator, are rendered correctly, as shown in figure 11.5.

```
customers  ▷  where isOver35
customers  ▷  where (fun customer -> customer.Age > 35)
```

Figure 11.5 Using the FiraCode font in Visual Studio 2015

Let's revisit the simple driving and petrol example from lesson 6 and see whether you can make the code more elegant by using pipelines. Recall that the original code looked something like the following.

Listing 11.11 Review of existing petrol sample

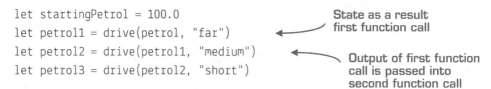

```
let startingPetrol = 100.0
let petrol1 = drive(petrol, "far")
let petrol2 = drive(petrol1, "medium")
let petrol3 = drive(petrol2, "short")
```

State as a result
first function call

Output of first function
call is passed into
second function call

Instead, I now want you to consume this code by using *pipelines*. Notice that in the previous pipeline example, you were working with functions that took only a single argument; this one takes in two arguments: the state (petrol) and the distance travelled. When you want to use pipelining, remember that the *last* argument is the one that gets flipped over to the left side of the pipe. Follow these steps:

1 Take the existing petrol function from listing 6.7 in chapter 6.

2 Convert the function from tupled form to curried form (remove commas and brackets).

3 The data that should be piped through should be the last argument—so in this case, the amount of petrol.

Your code should now look like this listing and can be consumed as follows.

Listing 11.12 Using pipelines to implicitly pass chained state

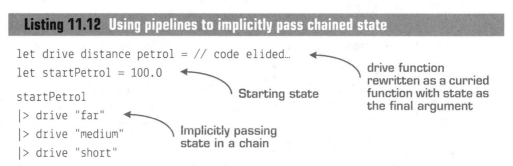

```
let drive distance petrol = // code elided…
let startPetrol = 100.0

startPetrol
|> drive "far"
|> drive "medium"
|> drive "short"
```

drive function
rewritten as a curried
function with state as
the final argument

Starting state

Implicitly passing
state in a chain

When should you use pipelines? Generally, whenever you have a piece of data that logically flows between a set of functions. That's a wooly answer, but an element of this comes with experience (like many features in programming languages), as well as personal preference. Some people prefer to pipeline everything; others use pipelining only if they have at least several functions in the chain. My recommendation is to trust your eyes. What reads better: – customer |> saveToDatabase or saveToDatabase customer? There's no hard-and-fast rule; the choice often depends on context. But the more you code, and the more of other peoples' code that you see, the more confidence you'll gain to experiment with pipelines yourself.

> **Quick check 11.3**
>
> 1   Which argument to a function is one that can be flipped over a pipeline?
> 2   Can you use C# or VB .NET methods with the pipeline?

11.3 Composing functions together

The last element to touch on in this lesson is the somewhat less common *compose* operator (>>), which is useful to be aware of. Compose works hand in hand with the pipeline operator and lets you build a *new* function by plugging a *set* of compatible functions together.

Let's revisit the file-processing pipeline from figure 11.4. If you start thinking about this as a composed functional pipeline, you could name the behavior of this entire pipeline something like checkCurrentDirectoryAge. In this context, the only elements that are of interest are the initial input and the final output. The rest is effectively intermediate state. As such, you could now rewrite the original pipeline chain from listing 11.9 as follows.

Listing 11.13 Automatically composing functions

```
let checkCurrentDirectoryAge =
    Directory.GetCurrentDirectory            Creating a function
                                             by composing a set
    >> Directory.GetCreationTime             of functions together
    >> checkCreation                                 Calling the newly
let description = checkCurrentDirectoryAge()      created composed
                                                 function
```

This code does the same as that in listing 11.9, except you can view this as, "Plug these three functions together, and give me back a *new* function." As long as the result of the *previous* function is the same type as the input of the next function, you can plug them together indefinitely; see figure 11.6.

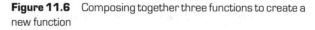

```
let checkCurrentDirectoryAge =
    Director|
    >> Direc     val checkCurrentDirectoryAge : (unit -> string)
    >> check     Full name: Lesson-11.checkCurrentDirectoryAge
```

Figure 11.6   Composing together three functions to create a new function

As you start out with F#, you probably won't find yourself using the compose operator a great deal. But it's worth knowing, and when you get more comfortable with it, it'll allow you to generate extremely succinct and readable code.

> **Quick check 11.4**
>
> 1 What operator do you use for composing two functions together?
> 2 What rule do you need to adhere to in order to compose two functions together?

Summary

Another sizeable lesson! Don't worry—for the next couple of lessons, we'll slow down a little and let you catch your breath! In this lesson

- You learned about the differences between methods and functions in F#.
- You saw the differences between curried and tupled functions.
- You learned about the pipeline operator.
- You learned how F# allows you to natively build larger functions from smaller functions by using the compose operator.

QC 11.4 answer

1 The >> operator is used for composition.
2 The output of the first function must be the same type as the input of the second function.

Try this

Take an existing .NET method in the BCL, or your existing code. Try porting the code to F#, and see what impact it has when the function is curried as opposed to tupled. Then, try looking through an existing project where you are composing methods together manually by calling one method and immediately supplying the result to the next method. Try to create a composed function that does the same thing.

12

ORGANIZING CODE WITHOUT CLASSES

So far you've learned all about relatively low-level elements of F#: language syntax, tuples, records, and functions, but you haven't yet seen how to organize larger amounts of code that should logically be grouped together. In this lesson

- You'll review namespaces in F#.
- You'll cover F# modules, a way to statically group behaviors in a library.
- You'll see how to use both namespaces and modules within a standalone application.

Organizing code elements can be tricky in the OO world, not just in terms of namespacing, but in terms of *responsibilities*. We often spend a lot of time looking at whether classes obey concepts such as single responsibility, or moving methods from one class to another along with associated state. I think that the way things work in F# is much, much simpler. We're not so worried about classes or inheritance or behaviors and state. Instead, because we're typically using stateless functions operating over immutable data, we can use alternative sets of rules for organizing code. By default, follow these simple rules:

- Place related types together in namespaces.
- Place related stateless functions together in modules.

That's pretty much it for many applications. So, the obvious questions are, "What are namespaces in F#?" and "What are modules?" Let's take a look.

12.1 Using namespaces and modules

Let's start by learning about the two core elements in F# for organizing code.

12.1.1 Namespaces in F#

Namespaces in F# are essentially identical to those in C# and VB in terms of functionality. You use namespaces to *logically* organize data types, such as records (for example, a Customer type), as well as *modules*. Namespaces can be nested underneath other namespaces in a hierarchy; again, this should be nothing new to you. You also can open namespaces in order to avoid having to fully qualify types or modules, and you can share namespaces across multiple files. Of course, Visual Studio provides IntelliSense for types as you dot into namespaces, as in C# or VB .NET (see figure 12.1).

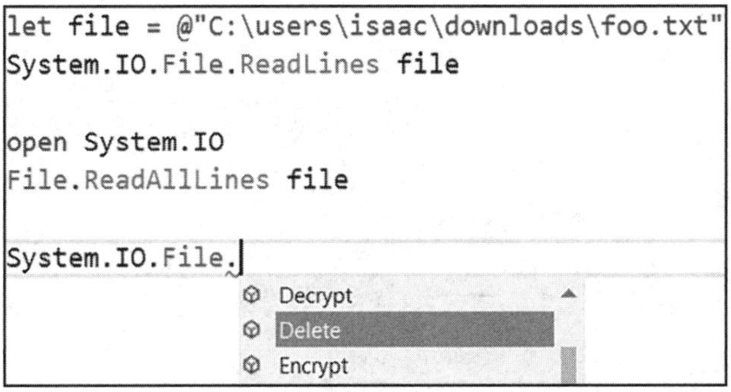

```
let file = @"C:\users\isaac\downloads\foo.txt"
System.IO.File.ReadLines file

open System.IO
File.ReadAllLines file

System.IO.File.|
                    ◎ Decrypt            ▲
                    ◎ Delete
                    ◎ Encrypt
```

Figure 12.1 Accessing the System.IO namespace functionality

You can observe in figure 12.1 that you can manually access functions through a fully qualified namespace, or you can open the namespace, after which you can access the static class File directly. Essentially, this is the same as what you already know in C#.

12.1.2 Modules in F#

One thing that namespaces can't hold are functions—only types. You use modules in F# to hold let-bound functions. But in F#, modules can also be used like namespaces in that they can store types as well. Depending on your point of view, you can think of F# modules in one of two ways:

- Modules are like static classes in C#.
- Modules are like namespaces but can also store functions.

You can create a module for a file by using the module <my module> declaration at the top of the file (for example, module MyFunctions). Any types or functions declared underneath this line will live in the MyFunctions module.

Like static classes, modules can live within an enclosing namespace (which can be nested). It's important to note that in F# you can declare both the namespace and module simultaneously. So module MyApplication.BusinessLogic.DataAccess means that you have a module DataAccess that resides in the MyApplication.BusinessLogic namespace. You don't have to declare the namespace explicitly first.

12.1.3 Visualizing namespaces and modules

Figure 12.2 may be helpful for visualizing the relationship between namespaces and modules in F#.

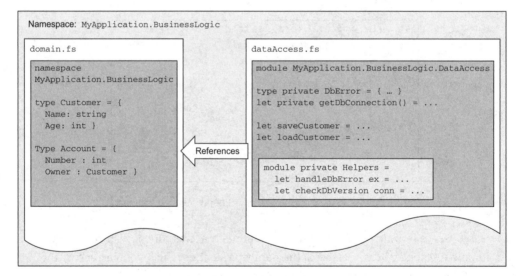

Figure 12.2   Visualizing the typical relationship between namespaces and modules

You can observe several things here. You have two *files* that will be compiled into a single *assembly*, both of which share the same logical namespace, MyApplication.BusinessLogic. Shared domain types are stored in a single file, Domain.fs. Functionality operating on data access is stored in the DataAccess module in the same namespace (which, as mentioned earlier, can be declared inline of the module declaration).

In dataAccess.fs, you don't need to explicitly open MyApplication.BusinessLogic to get access to the Customer and Account types, because the module lives in that namespace anyway, just as you would see with two C# classes living in the same namespace. And, as with C# classes, you won't automatically get access to all types in the entire namespace hierarchy—just to types that live in the same namespace as the module is declared in.

Also, note the nested module, Helpers, which lives inside the DataAccess module. It might help to think of this as an inner (nested) static class. You can use nested modules as a way of grouping functions if you find your modules getting too large; if you're not sure of the full namespace of a module (or function), you can always mouse over it to understand where it lives. Also, notice the private access modifier; see section 12.3.1 for more on this. Figures 12.3 and 12.4 show how functions in both modules and nested modules operate.

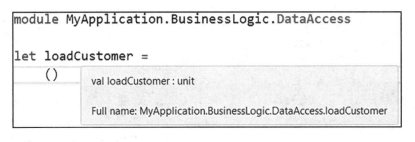

```
module MyApplication.BusinessLogic.DataAccess

let loadCustomer =
    ()
```

val loadCustomer : unit

Full name: MyApplication.BusinessLogic.DataAccess.loadCustomer

Figure 12.3 loadCustomer, a function living in a module that's declared in a namespace

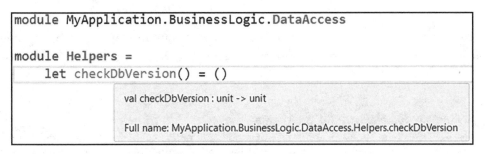

```
module MyApplication.BusinessLogic.DataAccess

module Helpers =
    let checkDbVersion() = ()
```

val checkDbVersion : unit -> unit

Full name: MyApplication.BusinessLogic.DataAccess.Helpers.checkDbVersion

Figure 12.4 checkDbVersion, declared in a nested module

12.1.4 Opening modules

When I first started using F#, I preferred thinking of modules as static classes. Nowadays, I find it more natural to think of them as namespaces that happen to also be able to store functions. One of the reasons for this is that modules can be *opened*, like namespaces.

Using static classes

Something similar to opening modules was added to the latest version of C#, whereby static classes can now be added to a using declaration. In this way, static classes gain a lot of extra flexibility for making more succinct code. Although F#4 can open modules, it currently can't open static classes, although there's an accepted feature request on the F# language design website (https://github.com/fsharp/fslang-suggestions) to add support for this, so hopefully it'll be added in time for the next release.

Opening modules is useful when you don't want to continually refer to the module name in order to access types or functions. Instead, you can call the functions directly as though they were defined in the current module, as shown in the next listing.

Listing 12.1 Opening modules

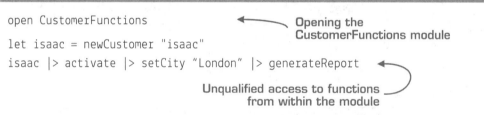

```
open CustomerFunctions                              Opening the
                                                    CustomerFunctions module
let isaac = newCustomer "isaac"
isaac |> activate |> setCity "London" |> generateReport
                                     Unqualified access to functions
                                         from within the module
```

You'll find opening of modules to be a valuable tool in your arsenal when creating simple, easy-to-use DSLs. Callers can open the module with your functions in it and access the behavior directly.

A word on domain-specific languages

Writing DSLs is particularly common in F# because of the syntax of the language (no brackets or braces, pipelining, and so forth). With a few simple functions, you can quickly create a set of behaviors that are human-readable; it's not uncommon to write code that at a top level a business analyst can read and understand. But you should also be careful not to take DSLs too far with, for example, custom operators; it can be difficult to understand what they're doing, and if taken too far, they can sometimes be difficult to learn how to use (while admittedly being extremely powerful).

12.1.5 Namespaces vs. modules

Because modules can be opened, you might think that they're a complete replacement for namespaces, but they're not. Unlike namespaces, a module can't span multiple files. Nor can you create a module that has the same fully qualified name as a namespace in another file. For this reason, you should still use namespaces as in C#, to logically group types and modules. Use modules primarily to store functions, and secondly to store types that are tightly related to those functions.

Quick check 12.1

1 Can you store values in namespaces?
2 Can you store types in modules?

12.2 Moving from scripts to applications

We'll now look at how you can port some existing code from a script into a full-blown project.

Now you try

We discussed in lesson 3 the notion of moving from scripts to projects, and did this for a simple application. You'll try it again now, but this time using modules and namespaces as you learn some features about them along the way:

1 Reopen `MyFirstFSharpApp` that you created earlier, or create a brand-new F# console application.
2 Create a new F# source file called Domain.fs by right-clicking the project and selecting Add New Item, and then selecting Code > Source File, as shown in figure 12.5. This file will hold the types that make up your domain. Recall that .fs files act like .cs files: they live inside a project and are compiled into a full-blown .NET assembly.

QC 12.1 answer

1 No. Namespaces can store only types or modules.
2 Yes. Modules can hold types, values, and nested modules.

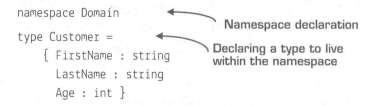

Figure 12.5   Creating a new .fs file in a project

3   Create a second file, called Operations.fs. This will contain the functionality that
    acts on the domain.

4   Go into Domain.fs. You'll see it contains a module declaration, which you can
    delete. Instead, add the declaration for a `Customer` record inside the `Domain` name-
    space. You declare the namespace that code is in by using the `namespace <my
    namespace>` declaration at the top of the file (for example, `namespace MyTypes`). Unlike
    C#, you don't need to add curly braces to live within this namespace (or even the
    F# equivalent—indent your code).

Listing 12.2 Declaring types within a namespace

```
namespace Domain                    ◄──────      Namespace declaration

type Customer =            ◄──────
    { FirstName : string            Declaring a type to live
                                    within the namespace
      LastName : string
      Age : int }
```

Now the `Customer` type lives within the `Domain` namespace. Next, you'll create your module
to contain some functionality that can act on the `Customer`:

1   Open the Operations.fs file. You'll see it already has the module declaration for you.
2   Underneath this, open the Domain namespace.

At this point, you need to watch out for file ordering in the Solution Explorer. Domain.fs must live *above* Operations.fs in order for the Operations module to access it; see figure 12.6. If it's placed below, you can highlight Domain.fs in Solution Explorer and press the Alt-up arrow to move it up the dependency order, or right-click and use the Move Up context menu. If this isn't done, you'll receive the error message shown in figure 12.7.

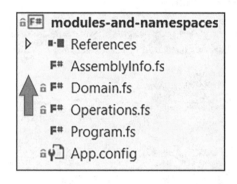

Figure 12.6   Operations.fs must live below Domain.fs to access Domain.fs from Operations.fs.

```
module Operations

open Domain
              The namespace or module 'Domain' is not defined
```

Figure 12.7   Trying to access an inaccessible namespace

3   Create a couple of functions that act on Customer; for example
    a   getInitials gets the initials of the customer.
    b   isOlderThan tests whether a customer is older than a certain age.

Your module should look something like the following listing.

Listing 12.3   Declaring a module that references a namespace

```
module Operations        ◀── Declaring a module
open Domain              ◀── Opening the Domain namespace

let getInitials customer = customer.FirstName.[0], customer.LastName.[0]
let isOlderThan age customer = customer.Age > age
```

Make sure all files are saved; you're now ready to hook them together in Program.fs.

4   Ensure that Program.fs is the last (lowest) file in the project so that it can access both Operations and Domain.

5   You'll notice that you don't have a module declaration in this file. The last file in an application can omit the module declaration and have it taken from the filename (for example, Program).

6   Add open statements for both Domain and Operation.

7   Have the main implementation create a customer, and print out whether the customer is an adult (older than 18) or a child.

Listing 12.4   Declaring a module that references a namespace

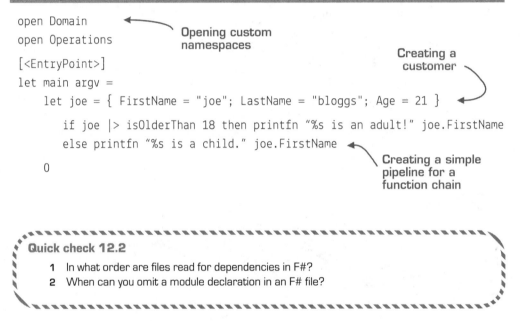

```
open Domain
open Operations                    Opening custom
                                   namespaces
[<EntryPoint>]                                            Creating a
let main argv =                                          customer
    let joe = { FirstName = "joe"; LastName = "bloggs"; Age = 21 }

        if joe |> isOlderThan 18 then printfn "%s is an adult!" joe.FirstName
        else printfn "%s is a child." joe.FirstName
    0                                          Creating a simple
                                               pipeline for a
                                               function chain
```

Quick check 12.2

1   In what order are files read for dependencies in F#?

2   When can you omit a module declaration in an F# file?

QC 12.2 answer

1   Downward—the first file in the project has no dependencies, and the last has no dependents.

2   For the last file in the project.

12.3 Tips for working with modules and namespaces

Let's wrap up by looking at a few miscellaneous features of modules and namespaces.

12.3.1 Access modifiers

By default, types and functions are always public in F#. If you want to use a function within a module (or a nested module) but don't want to expose it publicly, mark it as `private`.

12.3.2 The global namespace

If you don't supply a *parent* namespace when declaring namespaces or modules, it'll appear in the `global` namespace, which is always open. Both `Domain` and `Operations` live in the global namespace.

12.3.3 Automatic opening of modules

You can also have a module automatically open, without the caller explicitly having to use an open declaration, by adding the `[<AutoOpen>]` attribute on the module. With this attribute applied, opening the parent namespace in the module will automatically open access to the module as well. You might use this if you have several modules that contain different functionality within the same namespace and would like to open them all automatically. As long as your program file has access to the containing namespace, you can completely omit the `open` declarations. `AutoOpen` is commonly used when defining DSLs, as you can open a namespace and suddenly get access to lots of functions and operators.

12.3.4 Scripts

Some of the preceding rules work slightly differently with scripts. For starters, you can create `let`-bound functions directly in a script. This is possible because an *implicit* module is created for you based on the name of the script (similar to automatic namespacing). You can explicitly specify the module in code if you want, but with scripts it's generally not needed.

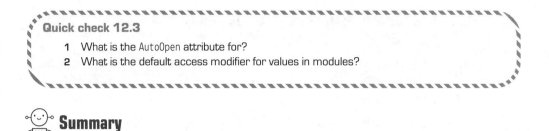

Quick check 12.3

1   What is the AutoOpen attribute for?
2   What is the default access modifier for values in modules?

Summary

That's it for namespaces and modules! In this lesson

- You saw how we typically separate out types and behavior through namespaces and modules.
- You saw how to create and access namespaces in F#.
- You learned about the module system in F#.
- You built a sample application that uses namespaces and modules to separate out functionality, before calling both elements within a program file.

Try this

Create a sample module containing functions that emulate a simple calculator in a module. Experiment with calling the functions from a separate script file. Then, experiment with the [<AutoOpen>] attribute; what impact does it have on the caller's code in terms of succinctness?

13

ACHIEVING CODE REUSE IN F#

We're going to change tack a little in this lesson, and look at using functions (and type inference) in F# to create lightweight code reuse, and to pass functionality (rather than data) *through* a system. If you've used the LINQ framework at all, much of this lesson will be familiar to you. We'll cover

- How we tend to achieve reuse in the OO world
- A quick review of the core parts of LINQ
- Implementing higher-order functions in F#
- Dependencies as functions

We always look to reuse code in our applications, because copy-and-paste is evil— right? Unfortunately, you know as well as I do that reuse at a low cost is sometimes really hard to achieve! There are many types of code reuse that we strive to achieve; this lesson focuses on a common form of reuse, although the outcomes from this lesson can be applied across most forms of reuse.

Let's imagine that you have a collection of customers, and need to filter out some of them based on logic that you don't yet know. In this case, it might be "Is the customer female," but at some point, you might need to write other types of filters, and you don't want to reimplement the logic of "filtering over the customers" every time you need a new filter. What you need is a way to separate out the two pieces of logic, but then combine them together as needed (see figure 13.1).

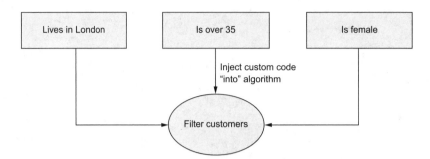

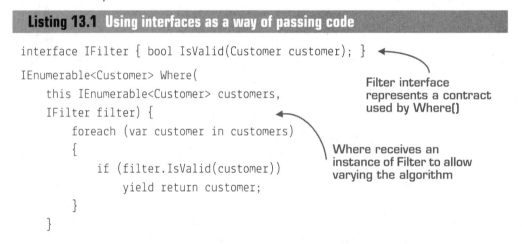

Figure 13.1   Combining a fixed algorithm with varying custom logic

Normally we'd look to inheritance, or perhaps create an interface to represent our filter functionality and use something like the Template or Strategy pattern. I'm not going to get into a debate on the virtues of Template versus Strategy—you can read up on that in your own time—but here's a quick example of the Strategy pattern in C# (in this case, you might also think of it as variant of the Command pattern).

Listing 13.1 Using interfaces as a way of passing code

```
interface IFilter { bool IsValid(Customer customer); }        ◄───
                                                                    Filter interface
IEnumerable<Customer> Where(                                         represents a contract
    this IEnumerable<Customer> customers,                           used by Where()
    IFilter filter) {                          ◄───
        foreach (var customer in customers)
        {                                            Where receives an
            if (filter.IsValid(customer))            instance of Filter to allow
                yield return customer;               varying the algorithm
        }
    }
}
```

You now have an "algorithm" that can be reused—the logic of "filtering over customers"—in your Where method, and a contract by which you can vary it—the IFilter interface. So you can write any arbitrary filter now over customers. Let's see how to consume this design when you want to retain only customers older than 35.

Listing 13.2 Consuming an interface-based design

```
public class IsOver35Filter : IFilter {          ◄─── An instance of an IFilter
    public Boolean IsValid(Customer customer) {
```

```
        return customer.Age > 35;
    }
}
public void FilterOlderCustomers()
{
    var customers = new Customer[0];
    var filter = new IsOver35Filter();
    var olderCustomers = customers.Where(filter);
}
```

Creating an instance of
the IsOver35Filter class

Supplying the
filter to the
Where method

You've had to create a specific class to implement your IFilter interface, and then create
an instance of it later before finally passing it to your Where method.

13.1 Reuse in the world of LINQ

Of course, many methods in the BCL follow the preceding design, particularly from the
early days of .NET, such as IComparable, IComparer, and IEquatable. All of them have a single
method but require the overhead of an interface and class for you to implement them.
Even worse, some have exactly the same signature, but you can't reuse them across both
because in .NET interfaces are *nominal*, not *structural*. Even if two interfaces have the
same structure, they're still treated as two incompatible types; see figure 13.2 for an
example.

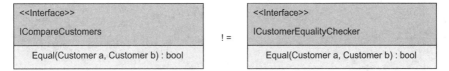

<<Interface>>			<<Interface>>	
ICompareCustomers		!=	ICustomerEqualityChecker	
Equal(Customer a, Customer b) : bool			Equal(Customer a, Customer b) : bool	

Figure 13.2 Nominal types can't be implicitly exchanged for one another even if they
have the same structure.

LINQ and C# 3 introduced a whole raft of features that were inspired by the world of functional programming. One of the biggest takeaways was the pervasive use of *higher-order
functions* (HOF) throughout the LINQ framework. Despite the somewhat technical name, a
higher-order function is a function that takes in another function as one of its arguments.
Let's look at a design similar to LINQ's Where method when acting on customers.

Listing 13.3 Using higher-order functions to reuse code

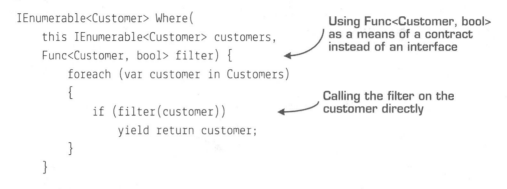

```
IEnumerable<Customer> Where(
    this IEnumerable<Customer> customers,
    Func<Customer, bool> filter) {
        foreach (var customer in Customers)
        {
            if (filter(customer))
                yield return customer;
        }
    }
```

Using Func<Customer, bool> as a means of a contract instead of an interface

Calling the filter on the customer directly

This method looks suspiciously like that in listing 13.1, except here you don't require a specific interface. Instead, you pass in a function that adheres to a contract: it must take in a Customer and return a Boolean—the same signature that the IsValid method has. This is much more flexible than working with interfaces, because any function that has this signature is compatible; it doesn't have to be explicitly designed that way. You can now call it by passing the function directly, as shown in listing 13.4.

To do this even more succinctly, C# 3 also introduced the concept of *lambda expressions*. Although this is another technical-sounding term, in reality, it's just a way of declaring a function inline of a method.

Listing 13.4 Consuming a higher-order function

```
public Boolean IsOver35(Customer customer) {
    return customer.Age > 35;
}
// ...code elided...
var olderCustomers = customers.Where(IsOver35);
var olderCustomersLambda = customers.Where(customer => customer.Age > 35);
```

Creating a function of signature Customer -> bool to check a customer age

Providing the IsOver35 function to the Where higher-order function

Reimplementing IsOver35 as an inline lambda expression

With the lambda-based approach, you've achieved exactly the same logic as you started with, except now it's all achieved in a single line. This is generally a good thing: the code is more readable, less can go wrong, and the code is easier to change. Let's take a moment to review these two methods for achieving reuse; see table 13.1.

Table 13.1   Comparing OO and FP mechanisms for reuse

	Object-oriented	**Functional**
Contract specification	Interface (nominal)	Function (structural)
Common patterns	Strategy/command	Higher-order function
Verbosity	Medium/heavy	Lightweight
Composability and reuse	Medium	High
Dimensionality	Multiple methods per interface	Single functions

Delegates and anonymous methods

One interesting point is that .NET (and C#) has always supported the notion of typesafe function pointers through both delegates (C# 1) and anonymous methods (C# 2). In effect, both are rendered obsolete by the introduction of Func<T> (and lambda expressions), which is a much more lightweight syntax than either of those.

Java's approach to functions

Java introduced the concept of lambda expressions relatively late in the day (Java 8 in 2015). By this time, the single-method interface was so common that the designers of Java opted to make single-method interfaces implicitly compatible with lambda function signatures. In effect, all single-method interfaces are treated as potential lambda expressions. In this way, all existing interfaces were automatically promoted into being usable as lambdas.

Quick check 13.1

1 Name one difference between nominal and structural types.
2 How do we pass logic between or across code in the OO world?
3 How do we pass logic between or across code in the FP world?

QC 13.1 answer

1 Nominal types are defined by their fully qualified type name. Structural types are defined by their signature.
2 We use interfaces to pass logic within a code base in the OO world.
3 We use functions to pass logic within a code base in the FP world.

13.2 Implementing higher-order functions in F#

C# and VB .NET (and the BCL) have a kind of mishmash of both interface and high-order function strategies. You'll see that newer features added to the BCL generally favor lambdas and higher-order functions (for example, the Task Parallel Library), whereas older features usually favor interfaces and classes. Conversely, F#'s built-in libraries almost exclusively focus on higher-order functions; as such, F# makes them extremely easy to work with and create.

13.2.1 Basics of higher-order functions

This section shows how easily you can create simple higher-order functions in F#.

Now you try

You'll start by trying to implement an equivalent of the preceding behavior (filter) in F# to see the difference between both languages and approaches.

Listing 13.5 Your first higher-order function in F#

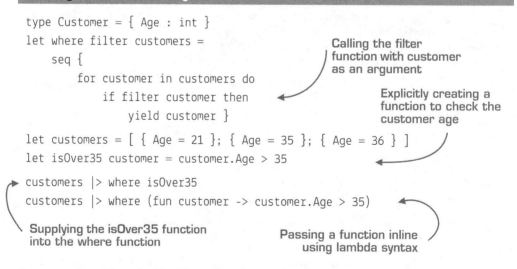

Try executing this code. You'll see that the two last lines return the only Customer who is over 35. In the next samples, you'll see a couple of language features you haven't seen yet:

- The use of the seq { } block—This is a type of *computation expression* in F#, a more advanced topic we'll touch on later for asynchronous programming. Here it's used to express that you're generating a sequence of customers by using the `yield` keyword.

- An F# list, expressed using [; ; ;] syntax—We'll cover this in the next unit.

As in C#, although you can use `let`-bound functions directly as a higher-order function argument, you can also use F#'s lambda syntax. In fact, this code is essentially the same as the C# example, except I've swapped the order of the `filter` and `customer` arguments so that I can pipe `customers` into `where` (remember that |> works by flipping the last argument over to the left).

Our old friend type inference has come into play again, and it's worthwhile spending a little time looking at the type signature of the function, shown in figure 13.3.

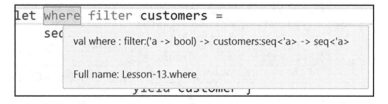

Figure 13.3   F# inferring a higher-order function automatically

As you can see in figure 13.3, `filter` is identified as a function that takes in 'a and returns `bool`:

- The compiler knows it's a function based on usage (`filter customer`).
- It must return a Boolean because the output is used in an `if` clause.
- It takes in any 'a. This is interesting; in our original C# example, you explicitly bound your code to customers, but F# has realized that this function would work just as well over orders or numbers, so it has made it generic.
- A quick way to confirm that `filter` has been correctly identified as a function is to notice that it's colored differently, assuming that F# Power Tools has been configured correctly.

Also, observe that the `customers` value has been identified as a `seq` (F# shorthand for `IEnumerable<T>`) because you use it within a `for` loop.

13.2.2 When to pass functions as arguments

Passing functions as arguments is something you'll do extremely often when working in F# because it's the primary way of achieving reuse. When coupled with F#'s ability to infer, compose, and pipeline functions, passing functions as arguments is easy to achieve without having to write reams of hard-to-read `Func<string,int,bool>`-style type annotations. Although F# has support for interfaces (in some ways, better support than C#), it's certainly not idiomatic to use them except when you're passing many dependencies as a logically grouped set of behaviors (for example, perhaps a set of logging functions or something similar).

It's also easy to create higher-order functions by reverse-engineering them. Start by creating a normal function with the varying element hardcoded into the algorithm. Then, identify all occurrences of that section, replace them with a simple named value that's added as an argument to the function. Figure 13.4 shows a hardcoded version of the "filter customers over 35" function.

```
let whereCustomersAreOver35 customers =
    seq {
        for customer in customers do
            if customer.Age > 35 then
                yield customer }
```

Figure 13.4 A hardcoded function that can be converted into a higher-order function

Observe that this is the same as listing 13.5, except the `filter customer` that was passed in as the first argument has been replaced with the highlighted element of code.

Quick check 13.2

1   Can F# infer the types of higher-order functions?
2   How can you easily identify higher-order function arguments in VS?

13.3 Dependencies as functions

You can easily reference one piece of code from another in F# by using namespaces and modules to reference functions in other files. But at times you'll want to decouple two sections of code from one another, often because you want to be able to swap out the implementation of one without affecting the other. A common use case for this is writing testable code; for example, you might decouple your code from a "real" database so

QC 13.2 answer

1   Yes.
2   Visual F# Power Tools highlights functions in a different color.

that you can mock up data that it reads and writes to. This is known as *dependency injection (DI)*: the class tells you what it requires in the constructor arguments, and you supply those requirements as dependencies. These dependencies often take the form of interfaces that contain the behavior that can be plugged in.

But you've also seen that many interfaces—particularly ones with single methods—can be replaced with functions. Indeed, it's often preferable to explicitly pass in dependencies as functions rather than one larger interface containing dozens of methods, of which you need only one or two. It becomes much easier to understand the relationship between a function and its dependencies. In F#, you can just as easily pass in dependencies, but instead of passing them into constructors of classes, you can pass them into functions directly.

Now you try

Let's see how to write a function that prints a specific message regarding the Customer's age to a variety of output streams, such as the console or the filesystem:

1 Create an empty script file and define a Customer record type (or continue below the existing script you've been working on).
2 Create a function, printCustomerAge, that takes in a Customer and, depending on the Customer's age, prints out Child, Teenager, or Adult, using Console.WriteLine to output text to FSI. The signature should read as let printCustomerAge customer =.
3 Try calling the function, and ensure that it behaves as expected.
4 Identify the varying element of code. For us, this is the call to Console.WriteLine.
5 Replace all occurrences with the value writer. Initially, your code won't compile, as there's no value called writer.
6 Insert writer as the first argument to the function, so it now reads let printCustomerAge writer customer =.
7 You'll see that writer has been correctly identified as a function that takes in a string and returns 'a. Now, any function that takes in a string can be used in place of Console.WriteLine.

Listing 13.6 Injecting dependencies into functions

```
let printCustomerAge writer customer =
    if customer.Age < 13 then writer "Child!"
    elif customer.Age < 20 then writer "Teenager!"
    else writer "Adult!"
```

Specifying your dependency as the writer argument

Calling writer with a string argument

You're now in a position to call this function. First you can confirm it works as before by passing `Console.WriteLine` as the first argument. You can also use the partial application trick to build a constrained version of `printCustomerAge` that prints to the console.

Listing 13.7 Partially applying a function with dependencies

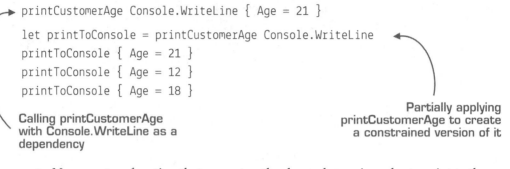

```
printCustomerAge Console.WriteLine { Age = 21 }

let printToConsole = printCustomerAge Console.WriteLine
printToConsole { Age = 21 }
printToConsole { Age = 12 }
printToConsole { Age = 18 }
```

Calling printCustomerAge
with Console.WriteLine as a
dependency

Partially applying
printCustomerAge to create
a constrained version of it

8   Now create a function that can act as the dependency, in order to print to the filesystem instead. You'll use `System.IO.File.WriteAllText` as the basis for your dependency (if the temp folder doesn't exist, create it first!).

Listing 13.8 Creating a dependency to write to a file

```
open System.IO
let writeToFile text = File.WriteAllText(@"C:\temp\output.txt", text)

let printToFile = printCustomerAge writeToFile
printToFile { Age = 21 }
```

Creating a File System
writer that's compatible
with printCustomerAge

9   Read back from the file by using `System.IO.File.ReadAllText` to prove that the content was correctly written out.

You'll notice that I explicitly stated that you should supply dependencies as the *first* argument(s) in a function. This is so you can partially apply the function. You inject the dependencies up front (`Console.WriteLine` in this case), which returns you a new function that requires the remaining argument(s)—in this case, the customer object. This partially applied function might itself then be passed into other functions, which will have no coupling to, for example, Console or File Systems).

Quick check 13.3   What's the key difference between passing dependencies in F# and C#?

 **Summary**

In this lesson, you learned about higher-order functions, the primary way to vary algorithms and pass code in F#, which prepares you for working with the collections modules that you'll look at in lesson 14. In this lesson

- You looked at typical OO designs for extending behaviors through interfaces, and compared them to the functional approach of composing functions together through higher-order functions.
- You gained an understanding of how F#'s type-inference engine makes it extremely easy to reverse-engineer higher-order functions from existing code.
- You saw how to use higher-order functions as a lightweight form of DI.

Try this

Create a set of functions that use another dependency in .NET—for example, working with HTTP data by using WebClient. Write a function that takes in the HTTP client to POST data to a URI. What's the dependency? The WebClient class, or a function *on* the WebClient?

QC 13.3 answer   Dependencies in F# tend to be functions; in C#, they're interfaces.

14

CAPSTONE 2

Before we move on to the next unit—collections—here's another end-of-level bad guy for you to defeat. This time, we'll shift our focus from the basics of coding in F# to the material covered in this unit. In this lesson you'll be expected to

- Develop a standalone F# application in Visual Studio
- Model a domain by using records, tuples, and functions
- Create reusable higher-order functions that can be altered through injected dependencies

That's a lot to do, but if you take this step by step, you'll do fine.

 ## 14.1 Defining the problem

In this exercise, you're going to write a simple bank account system. It needs to have the following capabilities:

1 The application should allow a customer to deposit and withdraw from an account that the customer owns, and maintain a running total of the balance in the account.
2 If the customer tries to withdraw more money than is in the account, the transaction should be declined (the balance should stay as is).

3   The system should write out all transactions to a data store when they're attempted. The data store should be pluggable (filesystem, console, and so forth).

4   The code shouldn't be coupled to, for example, the filesystem or console input. It should be possible to access the code API directly without resorting to a console application.

5   Another developer will review your work, and that developer should be able to easily access all of the preceding components in isolation from one another.

6   The application should be an executable as a console application.

7   On startup, the system should ask for the customer's name and opening balance. It then should create (in memory) an account for that customer with the specified balance.

8   The system should repeatedly ask whether the customer wants to deposit or withdraw money from the account.

9   The system should print out the updated balance to the user after every transaction.

What you *don't* have to worry about is the following:

- Reading data back from the filesystem. The system should store the customer's current balance in memory. If the application is closed, there's no way to resume later.

- Don't worry about opening multiple accounts.

- Don't worry about warning the user if that user tries to overdraw the account. Carry on with the same balance that the user started with.

 14.2 Some advice before you start...

This solution will be larger than the one in the previous capstone. Before you dive in and start writing reams and reams of code, let me give you some simple advice that I always follow when approaching a sizeable chunk of work in F#:

- *Start small.* Resist what will probably be your natural urge to design a complex set of objects and relationships up front. Instead, write simple functions and have each do one thing, and do it well. Trust that you can compose them together later.

- *Plug these functions together*, either by composing them to one another through a third function that calls both, or calling one from another (perhaps via a higher-order function).

- *Don't be afraid of copying and pasting code initially*. You can refactor quickly in F#, especially when using higher-order functions. Instead of prematurely guessing where this might happen, wait until you have evidence of it—and then refactor away!

14.3 Getting started

As usual, start by working with a simple script with types and functions, experimenting and exploring your domain. Once you're happy with what you have, migrate the code over to a full console executable that can be run as a standalone application. If you get stuck, refer to the solution in the code-listings/lesson-14 folder. But try to avoid simply copying and pasting code from it; you'll get much more out of this by trying to do this yourself. Use the suggested solution only as a last resort.

Start by creating a new F# console application named Capstone2, and add an empty .fsx file to the project.

14.4 Creating a domain

You should begin by first trying to model the types in our domain. You'll use F# records for this. You can identify two entities in our domain:

- Customer—A named customer of the bank.
- Account—An account that's owned by a customer. An account should probably have a current balance, a unique ID, and a reference to the Customer that owns the account.

Create two record types that match the preceding definition. Then create an instance of an account in the script directly underneath, to ensure that you're happy with the shape of the account and the fields in it.

14.5 Creating behaviors

You need a couple of functions to model withdrawals and deposits into the account. I'll help by giving you a typical function signature for deposit and a hardcoded implementation that needs replacing.

Listing 14.1 Sample function signature for deposit functionality

```
/// Deposits an amount into an account
let deposit (amount:decimal) (account:Account) : Account =
    { AccountId = Guid.Empty; Owner = { Name = "Sam" }; Balance = 10M }
```

Pure function signature

Just to confirm: this is a pure, curried function that takes in two arguments (amount and account) and returns a new Account (the updated version with the increased balance). Notice that I've explicitly type-annotated this function; this isn't necessary, and you can remove the annotations later. This is just to help you along if needed. Also, notice that I've put the state, account, as the *last* argument to the function. This is so you can pipe data through a chain (for example, account |> deposit 50 |> withdraw 25 |> deposit 10). Remember that you can use copy-and-update syntax in F# (by using the with keyword) to create a new version of a record with updated data.

You also need to create a withdraw function. It'll have an identical signature, but the implementation will be slightly more complex: if the amount is greater than the balance, return the account that was supplied. Otherwise, return an updated account with a reduced balance. Make sure you test your code out in the REPL/script as you go to ensure that you're happy with it.

In the function signature in listing 14.1, I haven't passed in a Customer record. That's because in my model, Customer is a field on Account.

Listing 14.2 Suggested domain model

```
type Customer = { Name : string }          ← Customer record
type Account =
    { AccountId : System.Guid; Owner : Customer; Balance : decimal }
```
Account record with Customer as the Owner field

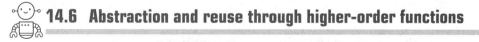 **14.6 Abstraction and reuse through higher-order functions**

The next thing you need to think about is a logging or auditing mechanism. Let's see how to write a couple of simple audit functions, one for the filesystem and one for the console. Both should have the same signature.

Listing 14.3 Creating pluggable audit functions

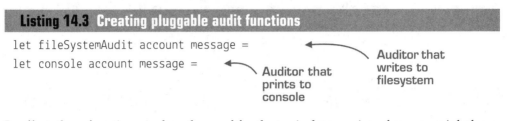

```
let fileSystemAudit account message =
let console account message =
```

Auditor that writes to filesystem

Auditor that prints to console

In effect, these functions replace the need for the typical ILogger interface you might have used in the past that has a single Log() method on it.

For the filesystem auditor, your code should append the contents of message to a file whose path is C:\temp\learnfs\capstone2\{customerName}\{accountId}.txt. You'll probably want to use sprintf as well as some methods within the System.IO.File namespace (for example, do you need to ensure that the directory exists first?)?

The console auditor should print to the console in the format "Account <accountId>: <message>". In this case, you'll probably want to use printfn (for example, "Account d89ac062-c777-4336-8192-6fba87920f3c: Performed operation 'withdraw' for £50. Balance is now £75").

Again, test these functions in isolation in a script to prove you're happy with them; create a dummy account and customer and pass them in, ensuring that the correct outputs occur.

Listing 14.4 Testing functions through scripts

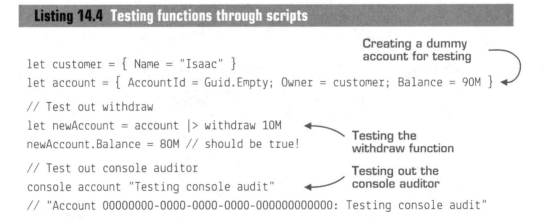

```
let customer = { Name = "Isaac" }
let account = { AccountId = Guid.Empty; Owner = customer; Balance = 90M }

// Test out withdraw
let newAccount = account |> withdraw 10M
newAccount.Balance = 80M // should be true!

// Test out console auditor
console account "Testing console audit"
// "Account 00000000-0000-0000-0000-000000000000: Testing console audit"
```

Creating a dummy account for testing

Testing the withdraw function

Testing out the console auditor

14.6.1 Adapting code with higher-order functions

At this point, notice that your behaviors have little in common. The deposit and withdraw functions have no ability to perform auditing; meanwhile, your audit functions have no knowledge of account behaviors, nor do they create the messages that need to be audited. You need something to wire them up together and create your audit messages (figure 14.1)! You need to create a new function that should do the following:

- Try to perform an arbitrary account operation (withdraw or deposit).
- Audit the details of the transaction (for example, "withdraw £50").
- If the account balance is modified, audit a message with the details of the transaction and the new balance.
- If the account balance isn't modified, audit a message that the transaction was rejected.
- Return the updated account.

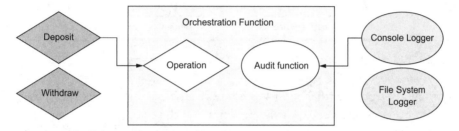

Figure 14.1 Composing disparate behaviors into a single function

This looks nice in principle, but how can you write code to achieve this? Observe that the preceding description is devoid of implementations: operation is either withdraw or deposit; similarly, you don't mention the type of auditor (for example, console or file system). Here's what your signature should look like.

Listing 14.5 Signature for an orchestration of higher-order function

```
let auditAs (operationName:string) (audit:Account -> string -> unit)
    (operation:decimal -> Account -> Account) (amount:decimal)
    (account:Account) : Account =          Sample audit
                                           orchestration function
```

This function should wrap around both an operation (for example, withdraw) and an audit function (for example, console), calling both of them appropriately. Let's review this function signature, one argument at a time:

- operationName—The name of the operation as a string (for example, "withdraw" or "deposit")

- audit—The audit function you want to call (for example, the console audit function)
- operation—The operation function you want to call (for example, the withdraw function)
- amount—The amount to use on the operation
- account—The account to act upon

The function also returns the updated account. Let's compare this function to the signature of one of your operations, deposit, as shown in figure 14.2.

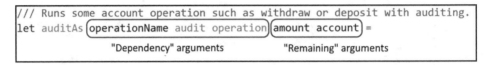

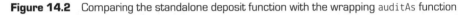

Figure 14.2   Comparing the standalone deposit function with the wrapping auditAs function

It's important to remember that because auditAs is a curried function, you can pass in the first three arguments and get back a *new* function which requires the remaining arguments and that also matches the signature of the original deposit function! Let's see how it works.

Listing 14.6 Partially applying a curried function

Creating an account
and customer

```
let account = { AccountId = Guid.NewGuid(); Owner = { Name = "Isaac" };
  Balance = 100M }

account
|> deposit 100M        ⟵ Calling the "raw" deposit
|> withdraw 50M            and withdraw functions

let withdrawWithConsoleAudit = auditAs "withdraw" consoleAudit withdraw
let depositWithConsoleAudit = auditAs "deposit" consoleAudit deposit

account
|> depositWithConsoleAudit 100M    ⟵ Calling the "decorated"
|> withdrawWithConsoleAudit 50M        versions of deposit and
                                       withdraw
```

Creating new "decorated"
versions of deposit and
withdraw with console
auditing through currying

Create the implementation of the `auditAs` function and test that you can call it correctly. If you struggle to figure it out, first write a version that's tightly coupled to, for example, the deposit function and console logging (it doesn't have the dependency arguments as per the previous figure); then pull those functions out as dependencies one at a time.

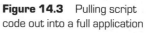

14.7 Writing a console application

Until now, you've only had a single F# script file—not much use as a standalone application. You're now going to pull the code you've written so far into dedicated modules and namespaces so that they can be built into a compiled application, as illustrated in figure 14.3.

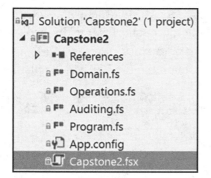

Figure 14.3 Pulling script code out into a full application

Create some .fs F# files in the project as follows:

- *Domain.fs* contains the `Customer` and `Account` record types in the `Capstone2.Domain` namespace.
- *Operations.fs* contains the `deposit`, `withdraw`, and `auditAs` functions in the `Capstone2 .Operations` module.
- *Auditing.fs* contains the `console` and `filesystem` audit functions in the `Capstone2 .Auditing` module.
- *Program.fs* contains the bootstrapper and runner.

14.7.1 Writing the program

The entry point program itself will be fairly simple:

1 Use a combination of `System.Console.ReadLine` and `Console.WriteLine` (or `printfn`) functions to get the user's name and opening balance, and create an `Account` and `Customer` record.

2 Use `Decimal.Parse` to convert from a string to decimal. Don't worry about error handling; you can deal with that another day.

3 Create decorated versions of both the `deposit` and `withdraw` functions that use the console auditor.

4 Use a `while` loop to find out the action that the user wishes to do (deposit/withdraw/exit). Again, use console functions to get user input. See the next section, "Managing the account state," for more details.

5 Depending on input, call the appropriate function (the decorated deposit/withdraw functions) to get an updated account.

14.7.2 Managing the account state

Unfortunately, at this stage you don't know enough about state management to get away without using a mutable value to store the account state. Later in this book, you'll identify ways of writing imperative style code that is normally written as `while` loops with external state. For now, here's a simple scaffold that you can use to fill in the blanks.

Listing 14.7 Simplified main application

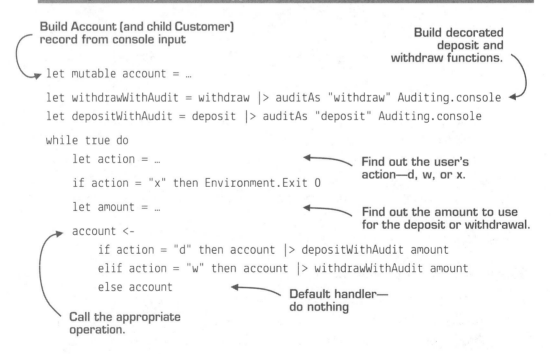

```
                                                        Build decorated
Build Account (and child Customer)                       deposit and
record from console input                               withdraw functions.

let mutable account = …
let withdrawWithAudit = withdraw |> auditAs "withdraw" Auditing.console
let depositWithAudit = deposit |> auditAs "deposit" Auditing.console

while true do
    let action = …                              Find out the user's
                                                 action—d, w, or x.
    if action = "x" then Environment.Exit 0

    let amount = …                              Find out the amount to use
                                                 for the deposit or withdrawal.
    account <-
        if action = "d" then account |> depositWithAudit amount
        elif action = "w" then account |> withdrawWithAudit amount
        else account                     Default handler—
                                          do nothing
Call the appropriate
operation.
```

As in the earlier capstone, use a mutable variable for controlling the overall loop here.

14.8 Referencing files from scripts

As you port code from scripts to full assemblies, you'll often find yourself wanting to access code that you've already ported from a script. Perhaps you're testing new code that interacts with existing code. In this case, it's possible to load an .fs file *into* an .fsx script. This way, you can get the best of both worlds: you can write code that can be accessed from a script, but still run from within; for example, a console application or website. Try the following code listing from an empty .fsx file.

Listing 14.8 Accessing .fs files from a script

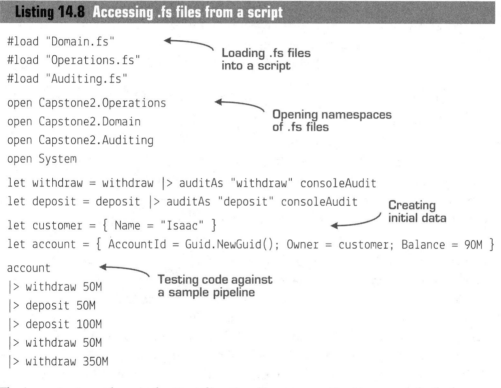

```
#load "Domain.fs"          ◄─────      Loading .fs files
#load "Operations.fs"                  into a script
#load "Auditing.fs"

open Capstone2.Operations  ◄─────
open Capstone2.Domain                  Opening namespaces
open Capstone2.Auditing                of .fs files
open System

let withdraw = withdraw |> auditAs "withdraw" consoleAudit
let deposit = deposit |> auditAs "deposit" consoleAudit      Creating
                                                            initial data
let customer = { Name = "Isaac" }
let account = { AccountId = Guid.NewGuid(); Owner = customer; Balance = 90M }

account   ◄─────      Testing code against
|> withdraw 50M       a sample pipeline
|> deposit 50M
|> deposit 100M
|> withdraw 50M
|> withdraw 350M
```

The important part here is the #load directive. You can use #load to execute both .fsx scripts and .fs files directly into a script as if you had entered the code directly yourself. You need to think about the order of #load commands; you can't load Operations.fs before you load Domain.fs, because the former depends on the latter.

If your code has been implemented correctly, you should see something like the following listing when executing the script.

Listing 14.9 Sample output of running the sample bank account script

```
Account …: Performing a withdraw operation for £50...
Account …: Transaction accepted! Balance is now £40.
Account …: Performing a deposit operation for £50...
Account …: Transaction accepted! Balance is now £90.
Account …: Performing a deposit operation for £100...
Account …: Transaction accepted! Balance is now £190.
Account …: Performing a withdraw operation for £50...
Account …: Transaction accepted! Balance is now £140.
Account …: Performing a withdraw operation for £350...
Account …: Transaction rejected!
```

 **Summary**

I hope that this exercise wasn't too difficult. Don't feel bad if you didn't think of everything up front or had to look at the suggested solution. Developing an instinct for when to use which tools in the language takes time. Also, definitely don't feel frustrated if you thought, "I could have done this with my eyes closed in C#!"

Part of the difficulty nearly every developer goes through when learning F# (or any FP language) when coming from an OO language is to resist the temptation to fall back to the safety net of curly braces and mutation, or to use console runners as a way to iteratively develop an application. In fact, I suspect that other experienced F# developers might have come up with a solution different from mine (notwithstanding the fact that we're not using all the features in F# yet!). As with OO, there are always different ways to solve challenges. But the core features of the application—including immutability, expressions, pure functions, and higher-order functions—would almost certainly all be present.

I recommend that you think up other coding challenges like this one—something that requires you to do a little data modeling and a little functional design, and then try to implement it. The more you do exercises like this, the more your muscle memory will become attuned to all things F#, from basics such as syntax for creating records to more-advanced refactoring and designing higher-order functions.

Collections in F#

One of the difficulties in designing a book such as this is that many of the language and library features overlap with one another, and it's often hard to focus on one specific aspect without introducing others into the mix as well. When I originally planned this book, I envisaged discussing collections a little later—but after thinking about it, I decided to bring it forward.

The reason is that collections in F# are *fantastic*! Combined with the succinct syntax you've already seen, and the possibility of a REPL-based environment, F# allows you to start working with data in all sorts of ways that you might not have considered before. (You'll revisit this in unit 7.)

Part of this unit covers the basic ideas of functional collections, something that, if you've ever used LINQ before, will be quite familiar to you. This part will get you up to speed with the typical, most commonly used collection functions. The latter half of the unit focuses on slightly more advanced tips and tricks; for example, how to use functional collections to work with immutable data to simulate imperative loops and mutation.

WORKING WITH COLLECTIONS IN F#

Something we've touched on only briefly is working with *collections* of data. Nearly everything we've done so far has involved a single record or tuple at a time. Yet F# has excellent capabilities when it comes to working with datasets. Working with data is one of its strongest features, as you'll start to see in the coming lessons. I've set aside this lesson and three more to discuss working with collections. This lesson

- Introduces you to some of the key collection types in F#
- Gets you thinking about transformations in terms of pipelines
- Illustrates how to use immutable F# collections

Simultaneously one of C#'s greatest strengths and weaknesses is that it's become an extremely flexible language, allowing developers to pick any number of ways to approach a problem. This is great in the sense that it can appeal to many types of developers, but it also means—particularly for newcomers—that it can be difficult to get a steer on a consistent, idiomatic way to solve that problem. One great example of that is working with collections. I see this as being divided into three camps:

- *The C# 2 developer*—When thinking about collection operations, the developer thinks in terms of imperative operations: for each loops, accumulators, and mutations. This developer has never found working with LINQ particularly natural or enjoyable.

- *The LINQ developer*—This developer has embraced C# 3 features and uses lambda expressions when working with lists of data for simple operations such as filters, but still uses mutation and imperative code for nonobvious situations. In my experience, these developers often find it easier to make the leap to functional programming.
- *The wannabe FP developer*—This developer has not only embraced LINQ over collections, but has also started to use those features for more general operations, be they accumulating data through aggregations, rules engines, or parallelizable computations. These developers, perhaps without even realizing it, have already started to embrace functional programming.

I'm not suggesting that any one type of developer in this (simplistic) generalization is better or worse than another, but depending on your current viewpoint, you may find more or less of this chapter natural or alien to you! Unsurprisingly, with F# being an FP-first language, you'll find over the next few lessons that collections are used for all sorts of things, and not necessarily just for the typical "filter a list of customers" example.

15.1 F# collection basics

You'll start with a simple challenge. Given a set of football results (that's *soccer* for those of you who aren't European!), you'll try to get an answer to the following question: show me which teams won the most away games in the season. Here's the structure of a single FootballResult record and sample results.

Listing 15.1 A sample dataset of football results

```
type FootballResult =
    { HomeTeam : string
      AwayTeam : string
      HomeGoals : int              Record of
      AwayGoals : int }            input data
let create (ht, hg) (at, ag) =
    { HomeTeam = ht; AwayTeam = at; HomeGoals = hg; AwayGoals = ag }
let results =
    [ create ("Messiville", 1) ("Ronaldo City", 2)
      create ("Messiville", 1) ("Bale Town", 3)
      create ("Bale Town", 3) ("Ronaldo City", 1)
      create ("Bale Town", 2) ("Messiville", 1)
```

Simple helper function to quickly construct a record taking in two (string * int) tuples

An F# list of records starts and ends with [ ].

```
create ("Ronaldo City", 4) ("Messiville", 2)
create ("Ronaldo City", 1) ("Bale Town", 2) ]
```

Now you try

Before you go through some of the alternative solutions available, have a go at trying this yourself in C# or VB .NET (or F# if you like!), using whichever style of programming you feel most comfortable with. The output that you should end up with looks like this:

- Bale Town: 2 wins
- Ronaldo City: 1 win

15.1.1 In-place collection modifications

How did that go? Whichever solution you picked, let's review an imperative style for solving this sort of problem:

1 Create an output collection to store the summary data, perhaps a mutable DTO called Team Summary that has the Team Name and Number of Away Wins.

2 For every result, if the away team scored more goals than the home team, check whether the output collection already contains this team:
  - If it does, increase the count of Away Wins for that entry.
  - If it doesn't, create a new entry with Away Wins set to 1.

3 Implement a sort algorithm to ensure that the results are sorted based on the number of away wins.

Listing 15.2 An imperative solution to a calculation over data

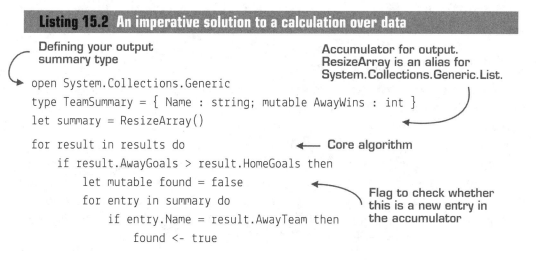

Defining your output summary type

Accumulator for output. ResizeArray is an alias for System.Collections.Generic.List.

```
open System.Collections.Generic
type TeamSummary = { Name : string; mutable AwayWins : int }
let summary = ResizeArray()

for result in results do            ◄── Core algorithm
    if result.AwayGoals > result.HomeGoals then
        let mutable found = false
        for entry in summary do
            if entry.Name = result.AwayTeam then
                found <- true
```

Flag to check whether this is a new entry in the accumulator

```
            entry.AwayWins <- entry.AwayWins + 1
        if not found then
            summary.Add { Name = result.AwayTeam; AwayWins = 1 }
let comparer =
    { new IComparer<TeamSummary> with
        member this.Compare(x,y) =
            if x.AwayWins > y.AwayWins then -1
            elif x.AwayWins < y.AwayWins then 1
            else 0 }
summary.Sort(comparer)
```

Custom IComparer for sorting based on away wins

After executing this code, if you evaluate summary (highlight the value and send it to FSI), you'll see the output. There are a few things to observe here:

- The code follows a flow chart type of design, with branching decisions based on intermediate state.
- It's difficult to see intermediate stages of this code, and there's nothing to suggest that any of it is easily reusable. It's more like you've taken the original objectives and mangled them together into a broth; as such, the final code doesn't reflect the original intent to me insofar as you can't read it at a glance to know what it does.
- You modify in-place (mutate) the summary list when sorting.
- As a side note, you can see one of F#'s nice features for working with interfaces, called *object initializers*. You created an instance of IComparer without having to first define a concrete type!

Let's now compare this with a more declarative style of processing that fits much better with a functional style: expressions over immutable data with pure functions.

15.1.2 The collection modules

At this point, I want to introduce you to the collection modules. Think of is these as F#'s own version of the LINQ Enumerable library (although they're more than that, in reality). There are three modules, each tied to an associated F# collection datatype—List, Array, and Seq—containing functions designed for querying (and generating) collections (you'll see more about those three types in section 15.2). The good thing is that although each module is optimized for the datatype in question, they contain virtually identical surface areas, so after you learn one of them, you can reuse the same skills across the other two. Most of the query functions in these modules are *higher-order functions*, and they follow a similar pattern as per figure 15.1:

1 *Input 1*—A user-defined function to customize the higher-order function
2 *Input 2*—An input list, array, or sequence to apply the function against in some way
3 *Output*—A new list, array, or sequence with the result of the operation

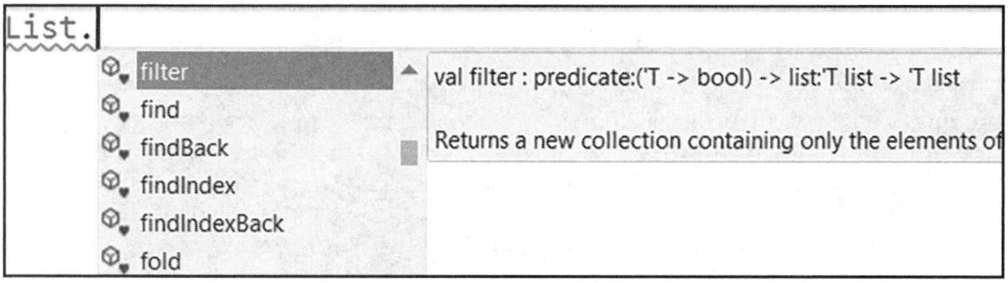

```
List.
   filter                          val filter : predicate:('T -> bool) -> list:'T list -> 'T list
   find
   findBack                        Returns a new collection containing only the elements of
   findIndex
   findIndexBack
   fold
```

Figure 15.1 Exploring the F# List module within an F# script

This follows a similar pattern to LINQ, except whereas in LINQ the input collection is the first argument (in order to play nicely with extension methods), in F# the input collection is always the last argument to the higher-order function (which is curried). This is, once again, in order to play nicely with the pipeline operator; the output (state) of one operation can be chained with the next one, much as LINQ does with extension methods. Let's look at some examples of these higher-order functions for working with collections.

Listing 15.3 Standard pattern for F# collection module functions

Passing a function into Seq.filter to get USA customers

Using an inline lambda function with Array.map

```
let usaCustomers = Seq.filter areFromUSA sequenceOfCustomers
let numbersDoubled = Array.map (fun number -> number * 2) arrayOfNumbers
let customersByCity = List.groupBy (fun c -> c.City) customerList

let ukCustomers = sequenceOfCustomers |> Seq.filter areFromUK
let tripledNumbers = arrayOfNumbers |> Array.map (fun number -> number * 3)
let customersByCountry = customerList |> List.groupBy (fun c -> c.Country)
```

Getting UK customers with Seq.filter and pipeline operator

The second set of function calls are essentially the same as the first except you've flipped the final argument over to the left of the pipe. It's also really important to be able to read and understand the function signatures in IntelliSense; we'll spend time in the next lesson going through some common collection functions so that you gain the skills to figure out the other ones yourself.

LINQ and F#

You can use the standard LINQ functions in F#: open the System.Linq namespace, and all the extension methods will magically appear on any collection. But I strongly urge you to favor F#'s collection libraries. They're designed specifically with F#'s type system in mind and usually lead to more succinct and idiomatic solutions. F# also has a query { } construct that allows use of IQueryable queries. Have a read of them yourself on MSDN; they're extremely powerful.

15.1.3 Transformation pipelines

With the collection modules in mind, let's return to our challenge. Approaching this problem with a functional style needs a slightly different approach: first try to identify simple, isolated functions that you can quickly create, and only then look to compose them together using reusable higher-order functions. Start by thinking about *what* it is you want to do, rather than the *how* that you focused on before:

1 Find all results that had an away win.
2 Group all the away wins by the away team.
3 Sort the results in descending order by the number of away wins per team.

To build this pipeline, you first need to answer the question, "What is an *away win*?" That's easy: whenever the Away Team scores more goals than the Home Team, that's an away win. Start by creating a simple function for that, and then build up a pipeline by using the List module.

Listing 15.4 A declarative solution to a calculation over data

```
let isAwayWin result = result.AwayGoals > result.HomeGoals    ←── A standalone function
                                                                   to calculate whether a
results                                                             result is an away win
|> List.filter isAwayWin
|> List.countBy(fun result -> result.AwayTeam)    ←── Using countBy with an inline lambda
|> List.sortByDescending(fun (_, awayWins) -> awayWins)    expression to return the number of
                                                           rows for each away team
```

Using isAwayWin within
the List.filter HOF

I find it helps to think of a transformation pipeline as a set of dumb workers that take in a set of data and give back a new one. Figure 15.2 illustrates the process. (This also works when working with composed functions operating over a single object.)

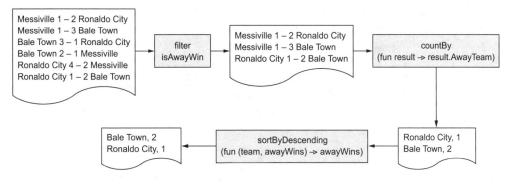

Figure 15.2 Visualizing your transformation pipeline in terms of distinct stages

This pipeline has some interesting properties:

- All stages are composed together with simple functions and pipelines. You could easily add a new stage if you wanted to in the middle.
- Each operation is a pure function that's completely decoupled from the overall pipeline. You can easily test out, for example, isAwayWin in isolation on a single, dummy result to ensure that it works properly. You could also reuse it in any number of other pipelines or sections of code; it's not baked in to the overall query you're carrying out.
- Each stage doesn't affect the input collection. You can repeat any stage a million times, and it will always give the same result.

Not only is the code much, much smaller, and much more readable, but it's also much less likely to have any bugs, because you're deferring probably 90% of the code that you wrote earlier to a set of general-purpose, higher-order functions (filter, grouping, ordering) and varying them by passing in an appropriate bit of code. The trick is to learn the most common higher-order functions so that they become second nature.

Also observe that the three functions you're using—filter, countBy, and sortByDescending— all follow the same function signature as identified earlier, taking in a varying function and an input collection, and returning a *new collection*. You'll often find that pipelines follow three stages, depicted in figure 15.3:

1　Create a collection of some sort.

2　When you're inside the collections world, you can perform one or many transformations on them. You never have to check whether the collection is null or empty, because the collection functions do that for you.

3　You end up with a final collection, or perform an aggregation to leave the collections world (for example, sum, average, first, or last).

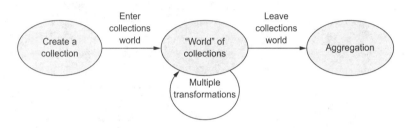

Figure 15.3　Typical stages for a collections pipeline

15.1.4　Debugging pipelines

A side effect of these properties, and F#'s REPL, is that you can opt to execute part of the pipeline and check the output of the pipeline at that stage. This is particularly useful if you have a complex pipeline and aren't getting the correct results at the end. You can execute the pipeline repeatedly, each time going a little further, until you find the error.

Now you try

Let's see how to work through the pipeline that you've just created, as per figure 15.4:

1　To make life easier, before executing each of the next steps, clear the FSI output by right-clicking over FSI and choosing Clear All (*not* Reset!)

2　In the REPL, with the code from listing 15.4 at the ready, execute the first line of the pipeline (results) by using Alt-Enter. You'll see all six results sent to FSI.

3　Repeat the process, but this time highlight two lines so that you execute both results and filter.

4　Do the same again to include countBy.

5　As you execute each subset of the pipeline, building up to the end, compare the results with that of figure 15.2.

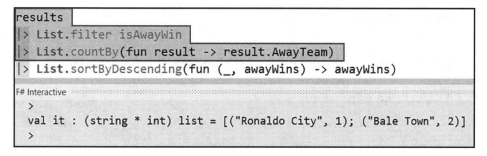

Figure 15.4 Executing a subset of a pipeline for debugging and exploratory purposes

15.1.5 Compose, compose, compose

I believe that one of the most common mistakes people make when implementing a solution for operations such as this is to take a top-down approach. They try to implement loops, manual filters, and sorts over the entire dataset.

Often you'll end up with a far more effective solution by taking a *bottom-up* approach. Solve the simple parts of the problem first by writing small, easy-to-reason-about functions, and then see how to plug them together and reuse them as higher-order functions. Look at the preceding example: you answered the question of what your filter is, but not how to perform the filter itself; that was delegated to the List.filter function.

If you ever find yourself writing a function that takes in a collection and *manually* iterates over it, you're probably doing extra work. You'll see that over the remainder of these lessons.

> **Quick check 15.1**
>
>   1 What are the three main collection modules in F#?
>   2 Why is the input collection the last argument to collection functions?
>   3 What are some of the problems with processing collections imperatively?

QC 15.1 answer

    1 Seq, Array, and List.
    2 This allows easy pipelining of multiple operations through currying.
    3 Difficult to compose behaviors; hard to reason about.

15.2 Collection types in F#

Let's take a more detailed look at the three collection types: sequences, arrays, and lists.

15.2.1 Working with sequences

F# has several collection types, the most common of which is seq (short for *sequence*). Sequences are effectively an alias for the IEnumerable<T> type in the BCL, and for the purposes of this lesson, you can consider them interchangeable with LINQ-generated sequences, in that they're lazily evaluated and (by default) don't cache evaluations. Also, because arrays and F# lists implement IEnumerable<T>, you can use functions in the Seq module over both of them as well.

You can create sequences by using the seq { } syntax, but in my experience this isn't needed that often, so I'm going to skip over it. Instead, focus on the Seq module to consume existing IEnumerable values.

15.2.2 Using .NET arrays

You looked at .NET arrays in one of the first lessons. Like C#, F# has language syntax for arrays. But F# syntax is much more lightweight, and F# also has a nice *slicing* syntax to allow you to extract a subset of an array.

Listing 15.5 Working with .NET arrays in F#

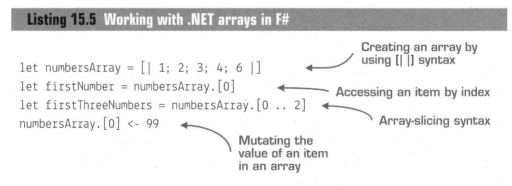

```
let numbersArray = [| 1; 2; 3; 4; 6 |]        ← Creating an array by using [| |] syntax
let firstNumber = numbersArray.[0]            ← Accessing an item by index
let firstThreeNumbers = numbersArray.[0 .. 2] ← Array-slicing syntax
numbersArray.[0] <- 99                         ← Mutating the value of an item in an array
```

You can also iterate over arrays by using for … do syntax as per sequences. Remember that arrays are just standard BCL arrays. They're high performance, but ultimately mutable (although you can safely rely on the Array module functions to create new arrays on each operation).

> **Collection separators in C# and F#**
>
> Watch out! In C#, you separate items in an array with a comma:
>
> ```
> new [] { 1, 2, 3 }
> ```
>
> But in F#, a comma is used to create tuples. You use the semicolon to separate items in an array, sequence, or list:
>
> ```
> [ 1; 2; 3 ]
> ```
>
> If you use commas, you won't get a compile-time error, because this is valid F#. Instead, you'll end up with a *single* tupled item! You can alternatively create a collection by placing each element on a new line, in which case you can omit the semicolon separator entirely.

15.2.3 Immutable lists

F# lists (not to be confused with the System.Collections.Generic.List<T>, a.k.a. ResizeArray) are native to F#. They work in a similar manner to arrays in that they're eagerly evaluated and you can index into them directly. But they have one key difference: F# lists are immutable. After you create a list, you can't add or remove items from it (and if the data inside the list is immutable, it's entirely fixed). Instead, you create *new* lists based on existing lists by using F# language syntax for lists.

Internally, F# lists are linked lists, so it's quick to create a new list with, for example, a single new item at the front of the list. Let's have a quick look at F# list syntax; try working through this sample one line at a time so that you can see the result of each operator.

Listing 15.6 Working with F# lists

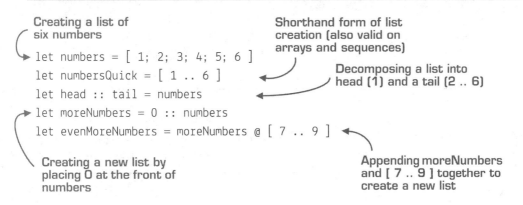

Creating a list of six numbers

Shorthand form of list creation (also valid on arrays and sequences)

```
let numbers = [ 1; 2; 3; 4; 5; 6 ]
let numbersQuick = [ 1 .. 6 ]
let head :: tail = numbers
let moreNumbers = 0 :: numbers
let evenMoreNumbers = moreNumbers @ [ 7 .. 9 ]
```

Decomposing a list into head (1) and a tail (2 .. 6)

Creating a new list by placing 0 at the front of numbers

Appending moreNumbers and [7 .. 9] together to create a new list

You'll see that F# has special operators for working with lists:

1   Create new lists by using the [a; b; c] syntax.
2   Deconstruct a list into a single item (head) and remainder (tail) with the :: operator.
3   Place a single item at the front of a list by using the :: operator.
4   Merge two lists by using the @ operator.

You'll see a warning for the third expression, mentioning something about *pattern matching*. Don't worry about this for now; you'll come back to this in the next unit.

In addition to these language features for working with lists, you have the entire List module at your disposal to perform all manner of useful functions on them, such as sorting and filtering. To be honest, most of this functionality is achievable using the List module, but these operators are sometimes useful, particularly as they can keep code succinct. Don't be surprised if you recoil at this initially. After you learn the operators (and it's really only :: and @), you'll be fine.

15.2.4 Comparing and contrasting collections

Because you can use all three collections almost interchangeably, knowing when to use which one can be difficult. Table 15.1 is a handy reference that quickly distinguishes the features.

Table 15.1   Comparing F# sequences, lists, and arrays

	Seq	List	Array
Eager/lazy	Lazy	Eager	Eager
Forward-only	Sometimes	Never	Never
Immutable	Yes	Yes	No
Performance	Medium	Medium/High	High
Pattern matching support	None	Good	Medium
Interop with C#	Good	Medium	Good

Note that performance is a more complex area. As always, your mileage may vary depending on the context. For example, you can add to the front of a list quickly, but not necessarily to the tail; and sequences have a Seq.cache function that can be used to avoid repeated evaluation. Also, you haven't looked at pattern matching yet—so bear that row in mind!

Quick check 15.2

1 How does `seq` relate to `IEnumerable<T>`?
2 How do higher-order functions relate to collection pipelines?
3 What are the main differences between an imperative and functional approach to working with collections?

Summary

In this lesson, you learned about processing collections in a functional style, and the
benefits that you can gain from doing this. In this lesson

- You explored the three core F# collections.
- You learned about functional collection pipelines.
- You saw a few operations that you might often perform on collections.
- You learned about immutable lists.

In the following lessons, you'll build on this knowledge and gain confidence in working
with collections by working through common operations and functions.

Try this

Find an existing LINQ query that you've written over an in-memory dataset; try to convert it to an equivalent `Seq` pipeline. Or, find an existing query you've written in an imperative style; try to rewrite it to a query pipeline by using a set of chained `Seq` functions.

QC 15.2 answer

1 `seq` is effectively an F# alias for `IEnumerable`, and all functions in the `Seq` module can operate over
   `IEnumerables`.
2 You use higher-order functions to vary collection operations that are then chained together to
   form more-complex functionality.
3 Imperative routines favor modifying collections in place, whereas a functional approach creates
   new collections for each stage of a pipeline. Imperative routines tend to merge all logic together,
   whereas a functional approach tends to view operations as distinct stages that feed into one
   another.

USEFUL COLLECTION FUNCTIONS

Now that you have a reasonably high-level understanding of collections in F#, this lesson focuses on getting your muscle memory trained to use collections in practical situations. This lesson covers the following:

- The most common collection functions across the three types that you've learned about (Seq, List, and Array) with some visualizations and hands-on examples
- A comparison of F# functions with similar LINQ operations
- The differences between imperative and declarative solutions
- Moving between collection types

Each operation we cover has a simple example associated with it, alongside typical use cases and equivalents in both imperative coding and LINQ (if it exists). Go through every example in a script yourself rather than simply reading them; you'll learn these effectively only through practical experience. After that, I'll also point out some other related functions in the collection libraries (denoted by *see also*) that you should look at in your own time.

A quick note: as in LINQ, most of the methods in F# collections operate on empty collections without a problem; you'll get back an empty collection again.

 **16.1 Mapping functions**

Mapping functions take a collection of items and return another collection of items. Usually the mapping can be controlled in some way by the caller, but specialized forms of mapping can be used here as well.

16.1.1 map

The most common collection function you'll ever use is `map`. This function converts all the items in a collection from one shape to another shape, and always returns the same number of items in the output collection as were passed in. At the risk of repeating myself, it's crucial to learn the signatures of collection functions. Here's the signature for `List.map` followed by a sample in figure 16.1:

```
mapping:('T -> 'U) -> list:'T list -> 'U list
```

- `mapping` is a function that maps a *single item* from `'T` to `'U`.
- `list` is the input list of `'T` that you want to convert.
- The output is a list of `'U` that has been mapped.

Figure 16.1   Mapping from a Person list to a String list

The direct equivalent to this in terms of LINQ is `Select()`. A common approach to performing the same operation with a loop is to first manually create an empty output collection, write a `for` loop to iterate over the collection, and manually populate the output collection with the output of every mapped item.

Listing 16.1 `map`

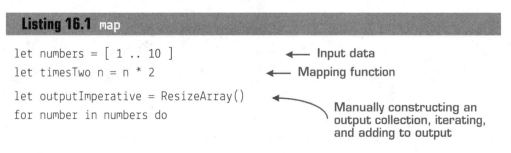

```
let numbers = [ 1 .. 10 ]                    ◄── Input data
let timesTwo n = n * 2                        ◄── Mapping function

let outputImperative = ResizeArray()         ◄──
for number in numbers do                          Manually constructing an
                                                  output collection, iterating,
                                                  and adding to output
```

```
        outputImperative.Add (number |> timesTwo)
let outputFunctional = numbers |> List.map timesTwo
```

Using the List.map higher-order
function to achieve the same output

You can use map for most use cases where the number of input and output elements are the same; for example, loading a set of customers from a list of customer IDs, or parsing a set of strings to decimals. Variants of map include map2, which works by combining two lists of the same type into a new merged list, and mapi, which includes an index item along with the item itself—useful for when you need to know the index of the item.

See also: map2, map3, mapi, mapi2, indexed

Tuples in higher-order functions

F# collection functions make extensive use of tuples as a lightweight way to pass pairs or triples of data items around. F# allows you to "unpack" tuples within lambda expressions directly within a higher-order function, so the following code is perfectly valid:

```
[ "Isaac", 30; "John", 25; "Sarah", 18; "Faye", 27 ]
|> List.map(fun (name, age) -> …)
```

The key part here is the lambda expression in the map call, where the function takes in name and age. This is a form of pattern matching, which automatically deconstructs the object passed in into its constituent parts.

16.1.2　iter

iter is essentially the same as map, except the function that you pass in must return unit. This is useful as an end function of a pipeline, such as saving records to a database or printing records to the screen—in effect, any function that has side effects; see figure 16.2.

```
action:('T -> 'unit) -> list:'T list -> unit
```

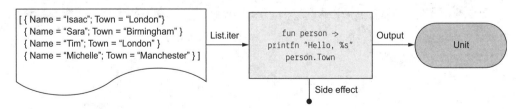

Figure 16.2　Printing the name of a collection of customers

In this example, you're operating over each record and printing a string to the console. This is a side effect, and there's no tangible output for each output—just unit. There's no like-for-like equivalent to iter in LINQ, but you can achieve the same functionality by using a basic for-each loop (or for…in loop in F#). Compare the signature of this function with map and see where the difference is.

See also: iter2, iter3, iteri, iteri2

16.1.3 collect

collect is a useful form of map (in fact, it's the other way around, as you can implement map through collect but not the other way around!). The collect function has many other names, including SelectMany, FlatMap, Flatten, and even Bind. It takes in a list of items, and a function that returns a *new collection from each item in that collection*—and then merges them all back into a *single* list. Sounds confusing, right? Let's take a look at the collect signature first:

```
mapping: ('T -> 'U list) -> list:'T list -> 'U list
```

Now compare it to map:

```
mapping: ('T -> 'U) -> list:'T list -> 'U list
```

See the subtle difference? collect says that the mapping function must return a *list*, rather than a *single value*. Here's an example: let's say that you have a list of customers, and each customer has a list of orders. Let's also assume that you already have a function called loadOrders, which takes in a Customer and returns the orders for that customer (Customer -> Order list). You want to retrieve all of the orders for customers 1, 2, and 5 as a single list, as shown in figure 16.3.

Figure 16.3 A prime candidate for a collect operation

You have a function to load all the orders for a single customer, but how can you use that function to build up a merged set of orders? Unfortunately, if you try to load orders for each customer by using map, you'll end up with the dataset shown in figure 16.4.

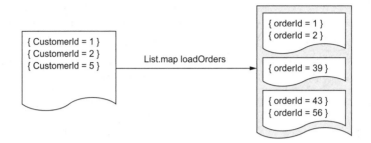

Figure 16.4   Calling `map` against a function that returns a list

The signature of the result of this operation is `Order list list` (or in C# terms, `List<List<Order>>`). Each function call returns a list, so you end up with a list of lists! That's not what you want. This is where `collect` comes in: it expects the higher-order function to return a *collection*, which it calls on each item, just like `map`, but the difference is that it *merges* all the items into a single list, as shown previously in figure 16.3.

Listing 16.2 `collect`

```
type Order = { OrderId : int }
type Customer = { CustomerId : int; Orders : Order list; Town string }
let customers : Customer list = []
let orders : Order list = customers |> List.collect(fun c -> c.Orders)
```

Collecting all orders for all
customers into a single list

Use `collect` to resolve many-to-many relationships, so that you can treat all sibling children as a single concatenated list.

16.1.4   pairwise

`pairwise` takes a list and returns a new list of *tuple pairs* of the original adjacent items, as shown in figure 16.5.

list: `'T list -> ('T * 'T) list`

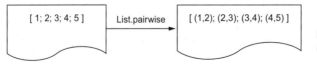

Figure 16.5   `pairwise` operation on a list of numbers

This example shows a list of numbers but can be equally applied to any list of objects that you want to show as adjacent items. `pairwise` operations are useful in many situations—for example, when calculating the "distance" between a list of ordered items such as dates. First, `pairwise` the elements, and then `map` the items.

Listing 16.3 Using `pairwise` within the context of a larger pipeline

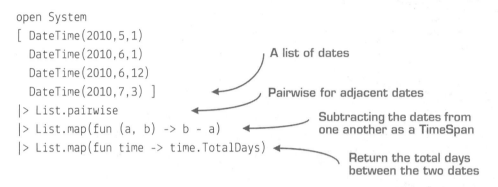

```
open System
[ DateTime(2010,5,1)
  DateTime(2010,6,1)
  DateTime(2010,6,12)
  DateTime(2010,7,3) ]
|> List.pairwise
|> List.map(fun (a, b) -> b - a)
|> List.map(fun time -> time.TotalDays)
```

A list of dates

Pairwise for adjacent dates

Subtracting the dates from one another as a TimeSpan

Return the total days between the two dates

The most common variation of this function is *windowed*. This function is similar to pairwise but allows you to control how many elements exist in each window (rather than fixed at two elements), for example [1;2;3]; [2;3;4]; [3;4;5] and so on.

See also: windowed

Quick check 16.1

1 What is the F# equivalent of LINQ's `Select` method?
2 What is the imperative equivalent to the `iter` function?
3 What does the `pairwise` function do?

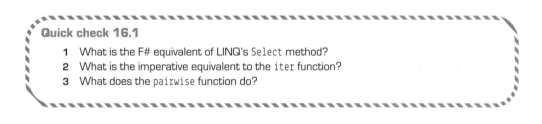

QC 16.1 answer

1 `map` is the equivalent of LINQ's `Select()` extension method.
2 `for-each` loops are the imperative equivalent to `iter`.
3 `pairwise` takes a collection of items and returns a new collection with the items windowed together in pairs.

16.2 Grouping functions

As the name suggests, *grouping functions* perform a logical grouping of data.

16.2.1 groupBy

groupBy works exactly as the LINQ version does (see figure 16.6), except the type signature is much simpler to read than the LINQ equivalent:

```
projection: ('T -> 'Key) -> list: 'T list -> ('Key * 'T list) list
```

The projection function returns a key on which you group all the items in the list. Note that the output is a collection of *simple tuples*. The first element of the tuple is the *key*, and the second element is the *collection of items in that group*. You don't need a custom type for the key/value pairing (such as the confusing IEnumerable<IGrouping<TKey, TSource>> in the LINQ implementation). Also note that each version of groupBy (Seq, Array, and List) ensures that each grouping will be returned in the same type of collection; so groups in Seq.groupBy will be lazily evaluated, but Array and List will not be.

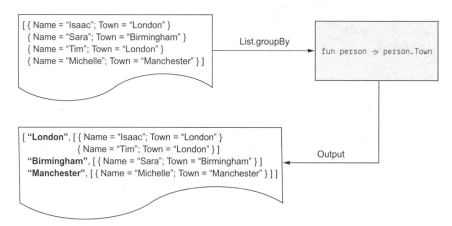

Figure 16.6   Grouping a set of customers by town

16.2.2 countBy

A useful derivative of groupBy is countBy. This has a similar signature, but instead of returning the items in the group, it returns the *number* of items in each group (see figure 16.7):

```
projection: ('T -> 'Key) -> list: 'T list -> ('Key * int) list
```

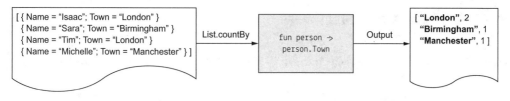

Figure 16.7 Counting customers by town

16.2.3 partition

partition is a slightly simpler version of groupBy. You supply a *predicate* (a function that returns true or false) and a collection; it returns two collections, partitioned based on the predicate:

predicate: ('T -> bool) -> list: 'T **list** -> ('T list * 'T list)

Listing 16.4 Splitting a collection in two based on a predicate

```
let londonCustomers, otherCustomers =
    customers |> List.partition(fun c -> c.Town = "London")
```

Decomposing the tupled result into the two lists

Predicate function to split the list

Note that partition always splits into two collections. This restriction means that you can safely deconstruct the output directly into the two collections, as in listing 16.4. If there are no matches for either half of the split, an empty collection is returned for that half.

See also: chunkBySize, splitInto, splitAt

Quick check 16.2

1   When would you use countBy compared to groupBy?
2   Why would you use groupBy as opposed to partition?

QC 16.2 answer

1   countBy returns the number of elements per group; groupBy returns the elements themselves.
2   groupBy can partition a collection into an infinite number of groups; partition always splits a group into exactly two groups.

16.3 More on collections

You can do lots more with collections in F#. Let's briefly look at some examples.

16.3.1 Aggregates

Both the F# collections and LINQ libraries have many aggregate functions. They all operate on a similar principle: take a collection of items and merge them into a smaller collection of items (often just one). Generally, you'll find that aggregate functions are the last collection function in a pipeline. Here are some examples of aggregate functions in F#; you'll probably be familiar with these functions already.

Listing 16.5 Simple aggregation functions in F#

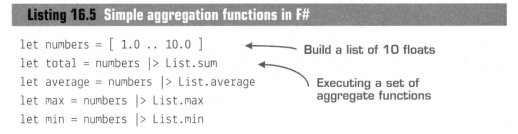

```
let numbers = [ 1.0 .. 10.0 ]          ◄──── Build a list of 10 floats
let total = numbers |> List.sum        ◄──
let average = numbers |> List.average      Executing a set of
let max = numbers |> List.max              aggregate functions
let min = numbers |> List.min
```

All of these functions are specialized versions of a more generalized function called fold; in LINQ, it's called Aggregate(). You'll learn about fold in more detail in the next lesson, as it has many applications aside from just summing numbers.

16.3.2 Miscellaneous functions

This section covers a whole bunch of miscellaneous functions. Many of them have similar LINQ equivalents, so you'll probably already know them. Table 16.1 compares the F# functions to those in LINQ.

Table 16.1 Comparing miscellaneous functions

F#	LINQ	Comments
find	Single()	Equivalent to the Single() overload that takes a predicate; see also findIndex, findback, and findIndexBack.
head	First()	Returns the first item in the collection; see also last.
item	ElementAt()	Gets the element at a given index.
take	Take()	The F# take implementation throws an exception if there are insufficient elements in the collection; use truncate for equivalent behavior to LINQ's Take(). See also takeWhile, skip, and skipWhile.

Table 16.1   Comparing miscellaneous functions (continued)

F#	LINQ	Comments
exists	Any()	See also exists2
forall	All()	See also forall2.
contains	Contains()	
filter	Where()	See also where.
length	Count()	See also distinctBy.
distinct	Distinct()	
sortBy	OrderBy()	See also sort, sortByDescending, sortDescending, and sortWith.

Trying with collections

You might have noticed a whole bunch of functions that start with try (for example, try-Find and tryHead). These are equivalent to the Default methods in LINQ such as FirstOr-Default(). But the F# equivalents all return option types. What are options? For now, think of these as Nullable<T>, although that's not quite accurate. You'll find out more about the Option type in the next unit.

16.3.3   Converting between collections

Occasionally, you'll need to convert between lists, arrays, and sequences. Perhaps you have a function that returns an array and want to pipe the results into another function that expects a list, or you're working with a collection that has specific performance characteristics best suited to an eager array than a lazy sequence. Therefore, each module has functions to easily convert to and from each collection type.

Listing 16.6   Converting between lists, arrays, and sequences

```
let numberOne =
    [ 1 .. 5 ]              ← Construct an int list.
    |> List.toArray         ← Convert from an int list to an int array.
    |> Seq.ofArray          ← Convert from an int array
    |> Seq.head                to an int sequence.
```

As you can see, there are functions in all three modules that begin with `of` or `to` (for example, `ofList` and `toArray`) that perform the appropriate conversion.

Quick check 16.3

1   What is the F# equivalent to LINQ's `Aggregate` method?
2   What is the F# equivalent to LINQ's `Take` method?
3   Give two reasons that you might need to convert between collection types in F#.

Summary

That's about it for this lesson! I hope you're able to see that the F# collection modules have a wide range of powerful functions. At the risk of repeating myself, go through all these examples yourself, executing all the pipelines incrementally; execute just the first line, then the first two lines, and so forth, and observe the outputs in FSI.

It's tempting to fall back to using LINQ for collection operations (indeed, there's nothing to stop you from doing this), but you'll find (especially as you delve into more-advanced features in the coming chapters) that the F# collection modules offer a much better fit for your code. In this lesson

- You saw collection functions that are commonly used in F#.
- You saw how they relate to LINQ's set of collection functions.
- You saw how F#'s native tuple syntax can make the equivalent function signatures much simpler and more consistent than the LINQ equivalents.

Try this

Write a simple script that, given a folder path on the local filesystem, will return the name and size of each subfolder within it. Use `groupBy` to group files by folder, before using an aggregation function such as `sumBy` to total the size of files in each folder. Then, sort the results by descending size. Enhance the script to return a proper F# record that contains the folder name, size, number of files, average file size, and the distinct set of file extensions within the folder.

QC 16.3 answer

1   `fold`
2   `truncate` (not `take`!)
3   Performance reasons, or to match the type signature of a function that you're calling.

MAPS, DICTIONARIES, AND SETS

This lesson should be a fairly easy one as we round off the collection types in F#. So far you've looked at collections that model ordered elements of data in some way— sequences, lists, and arrays—that behave similarly to the BCL `List` or `IEnumerable` types. You'll now spend a little time looking at using other collection types in F#:

- Working with the standard `Generic` dictionary in F#
- Creating an immutable `IDictionary`
- Using the F#-specific `Map` type
- Using the F#-specific `Set` type

 ## 17.1 Dictionaries

F# has several dictionaries available to it. Let's review the main types now.

17.1.1 Mutable dictionaries in F#

You almost certainly already know the `System.Collections.Generic.Dictionary` type from C# or VB .NET. This acts as a standard lookup collection, allowing fast retrieval of values based on a unique key. You'll be happy to know that, as with the majority of the BCL, you can use this class out of the box in F#.

Listing 17.1 Standard dictionary functionality in F#

```
open System.Collections.Generic

let inventory = Dictionary<string, float>()        ◄──── Creating a dictionary

inventory.Add("Apples", 0.33)        ◄──── Adding items to the dictionary
inventory.Add("Oranges", 0.23)
inventory.Add("Bananas", 0.45)
                                     Removing an item
inventory.Remove "Oranges"     ◄──── from the dictionary

let bananas = inventory.["Bananas"]        ◄──── Retrieving an item
let oranges = inventory.["Oranges"]        ◄──── Trying to access an item
                                                  that doesn't exist—
                                                  exception is raised
```

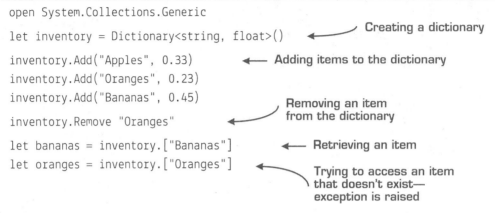

This functionality should be familiar to you. The only thing to remember is that in F#, indexer properties are preceded by a dot (for example, inventory.["Bananas"]). But you can use F#'s syntax to make life easier: like the .NET generic List (or ResizeArray), F# can infer the generic types of a Dictionary, using one of two syntaxes.

Listing 17.2 Generic type inference with Dictionary

```
let inventory = Dictionary<_,_>()        ◄──── Explicit placeholders for
inventory.Add("Apples", 0.33)                  generic type arguments

let inventory = Dictionary()        ◄──── Omitting generic type
inventory.Add("Apples", 0.33)             arguments completely
```

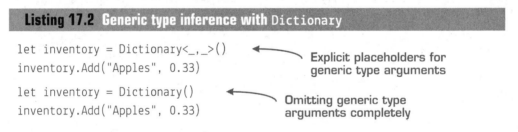

17.1.2 Immutable dictionaries

There's one issue with the standard dictionary: it's mutable, so additions and removals to the dictionary happen in place. In the world of functional programming, we prefer immutable types where possible, so F# has a nice helper function to quickly create an immutable IDictionary, called dict. Because the object that dict returns is immutable, you can't add and remove items to it. Instead, you supply it up front with a sequence of tuples that represent the key/value pairs, which then become the fixed contents of the dictionary for its lifetime.

Listing 17.3 Creating an immutable IDictionary

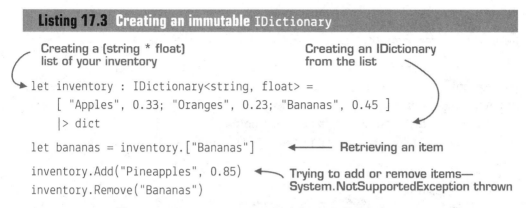

Creating a (string * float)
list of your inventory

Creating an IDictionary
from the list

```
let inventory : IDictionary<string, float> =
    [ "Apples", 0.33; "Oranges", 0.23; "Bananas", 0.45 ]
    |> dict

let bananas = inventory.["Bananas"]          ◄─────── Retrieving an item

inventory.Add("Pineapples", 0.85)   ◄──── Trying to add or remove items—
inventory.Remove("Bananas")              System.NotSupportedException thrown
```

This syntax is lightweight and easy to use, and is especially useful for those situations where you create a lookup and never modify it again. Unfortunately, as you can see in listing 17.3, because it implements IDictionary but is immutable, it has methods on it that you mustn't call (Add, Clear, and Remove), because they'll throw exceptions. That's not so nice; if the type is immutable, it shouldn't be offering those methods! The solution is to use a completely different type: the F# Map.

> **Quickly creating full dictionaries**
>
> The standard Dictionary doesn't allow you to easily create a dictionary with an initial set of data as dict does. But it does allow you to pass in IDictionary as the input—which is implemented by lookups generated by dict! So you can work around this restriction by doing the following:
>
> ```
> [ "Apples", 10; "Bananas", 20; "Grapes", 15 ] |> dict |> Dictionary
> ```
>
> Nice!

Quick check 17.1

1 What sort of situations would you use a dictionary for?
2 How does F# syntax simplify creating dictionaries?
3 Why might you use the dict function in F#?

QC 17.1 answer

1 Typically for fast key/value lookups that can mutate over time.
2 You can omit generic type arguments and use the dict function to help create them.
3 For immutable dictionaries (lookups that can never change).

17.2 The F# Map

The F# Map is an immutable key/value lookup. Like dict, it offers the ability to quickly create a lookup based on a sequence of tuples, but unlike dict, it allows you to safely add or remove items only by using a similar mechanism to modify records or lists. You copy the entries from the existing Map to a new Map, and then add or remove the item in question. You can't add items to an existing Map. Figure 17.1 illustrates the Map operation.

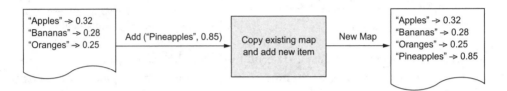

Figure 17.1   Creating a new map from an existing map plus a new item

Let's see how this looks.

Listing 17.4 Using the F# Map lookup

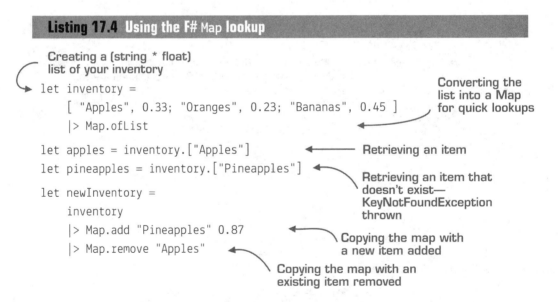

The nice thing with this approach is that you get all the usual benefits of immutability (such as determinism and safety) without the need to give up the ability to (in effect) easily add or remove items from it. Importantly calling Add on a Map that already contains the key won't throw an exception. Instead, it'll replace the old value with the new one as it creates the new Map (the original Map will still retain the original value).

You can also safely access a key in a Map by using TryFind. This doesn't return the value, but a wrapped option. You'll learn about options in the next unit, but keep in the back of your mind that Map plays nicely with them, too.

17.2.1 Useful Map functions

In addition to add and remove, the Map module has other useful functions that are similar in nature to those in the List, Array, and Seq modules and allow you to treat maps as though they were enumerable collections, using the same chained pipelines that you're used to, such as these:

- map
- filter
- iter
- partition

The main difference between the signature of these methods and the equivalents in the other modules is that the Map higher-order functions take in both the key and the value for each element in the map, whereas List, for example, takes in only the value:

- Seq.map: mapping ('T -> 'U) -> source:Seq<'T> -> Seq<'U>
- Map.map: mapping ('Key -> 'T -> 'U) -> table:Map<'Key, 'T> -> Map<'Key, 'U>

Listing 17.5 Using the F# Map module functions

```
let cheapFruit, expensiveFruit =               ◄——————   Two maps, partitioned
    inventory                                            on cost
    |> Map.partition(fun fruit cost -> cost < 0.3)  ◄——
                            Partition higher-order function
                               that receives both key (fruit)
                            and value (cost) as arguments
```

Note that the key and value aren't passed as a tuple but as a curried function, which is why fruit and cost are separated by a space, and not a comma.

Now you try

Now you're going to create a lookup for all the root folders on your hard disk and the times that they were created:

1 Open a blank script.
2 Get a list of all directories within the C:\ drive on your computer (you can use System.IO.Directory.EnumerateDirectories). The result will be a sequence of strings.

3   Convert each string into a full `DirectoryInfo` object. Use `Seq.map` to perform the conversion.

4   Convert each `DirectoryInfo` into a tuple of the `Name` of the folder and its `CreationTimeUtc`, again using `Seq.map`.

5   Convert the sequence into a `Map` of `Map.ofSeq`.

6   Convert the values of the `Map` into their age in days by using `Map.map`. You can subtract the creation time from the current time to achieve this.

Dictionaries, dict, or Map?

Given these three lookup types, when should you use which? My advice is as follows:

- Use `Map` as your default lookup type. It's immutable, and has good support for F# tuples and pipelining.
- Use the `dict` function to quickly generate an `IDictionary` that's needed for interoperability with other code (for example, BCL code). The syntax is lightweight and is easier to create than a full `Dictionary`.
- Use `Dictionary` if you need a mutable dictionary, or have a block of code with specific performance requirements. Generally, the performance of `Map` will be fine, but if you're in a tight loop performing thousands of additions or removals to a lookup, a Dictionary will perform better. As always, optimize as needed, rather than prematurely.

Quick check 17.2

1   What's the main difference between `Dictionary` and `Map`?
2   When should you use `Dictionary` over `Map`?

QC 17.2 answer

1   `Dictionary` is a mutable lookup; `Map` is immutable, creating new maps after each operation.
2   When you need to maximize performance, or are modeling an inherently mutable dataset.

 **17.3 Sets**

Sets are a somewhat rarely used collection type, which is a pity because they allow you to elegantly create solutions to certain problems that would otherwise require several lines of code. As the name suggests, Set implements a standard mathematical set of data:

> *In mathematics, a set is a collection of distinct objects.*
>
> —https://en.wikipedia.org/wiki/Set_(mathematics)

Unlike other collections, Set can't contain duplicates and will automatically remove repeated items in the set for you. F# sets are trivial to use, as they follow the same pattern as the other collection types.

Listing 17.6 Creating a set from a sequence

```
let myBasket = [ "Apples"; "Apples"; "Apples"; "Bananas"; "Pineapples" ]
let fruitsILike = myBasket |> Set.ofList

// val fruitsILike : Set<string> = set ["Apples"; "Bananas"; "Pineapples"]
```

Input data — Converting to a set — Evaluated output shown in FSI

Observe that fruitsILike has only the unique fruits from myBasket, without you needing to explicitly call Distinct. Sets in F# are *especially* useful when you need to perform set-based operations on two sets. Let's assume we have two baskets of fruit and want to combine them to find fruits we both like. Let's compare two approaches: first using List, and then Set.

Listing 17.7 Comparing List- and Set-based operations

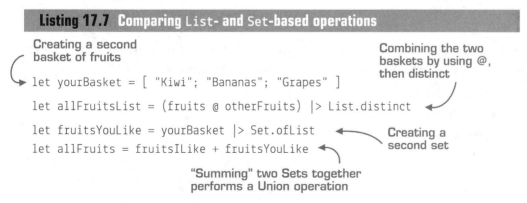

```
let yourBasket = [ "Kiwi"; "Bananas"; "Grapes" ]
let allFruitsList = (fruits @ otherFruits) |> List.distinct
let fruitsYouLike = yourBasket |> Set.ofList
let allFruits = fruitsILike + fruitsYouLike
```

Creating a second basket of fruits — Combining the two baskets by using @, then distinct — Creating a second set — "Summing" two Sets together performs a Union operation

The first two lines should be obvious. The interesting line is the fourth and final expression, fruitsILike + fruitsYouLike, where you seem to be adding two sets together. Can you do this? Yes, you can! This is because the Set module includes operator overloads for addition and subtraction, which internally it redirects to Set.union and Set.difference. As a one-off operation, using List with distinct might suffice, but if you're trying explicitly to model a Set with other set-based behaviors (unions, difference, subset), Set is a much more elegant fit. Here are some more examples.

Listing 17.8 Sample Set-based operations

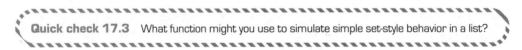

Gets fruits in A that
are not in B

Gets fruits that exist
in both A and B

```
let fruitsJustForMe = allFruits - fruitsYouLike
let fruitsWeCanShare = fruitsILike |> Set.intersect fruitsYouLike
let doILikeAllYourFruits = fruitsILike |> Set.isSubset fruitsYouLike
```

Are all fruits in
A also in B?

What's nice is that although you're using strings here, sets work with any type that supports comparison, which F# records and tuples do by default. You might use sets to find out which products exist in both warehouses, or whether all customers who live in New York are also high-value customers. Of course, sets also have standard functions such as map and filter as well as transformers from/to List, Seq, and Array.

Quick check 17.3   What function might you use to simulate simple set-style behavior in a list?

 **Summary**

That's a wrap! You've now seen all the main types of collections that you'll commonly be dealing with in F#. We reviewed four types of collections:

- Dictionaries
- IDictionary through dict
- Maps
- Sets

QC 17.3 answer   Distinct or DistinctBy

You're almost finished with collections now. All that's left in the next lesson is seeing how to take advantage of some of the more powerful functions in the collection libraries to push things to the limit.

Try this

Continuing from the previous lesson, create a lookup for all files within a folder so that you can find the details of any file that has been read. Experiment with sets by identifying file types in folders. What file types are shared between two arbitrary folders?

18

FOLDING YOUR WAY TO SUCCESS

The preceding few lessons covered the main collection types and how to use them. Here we'll round off with a few scenarios describing how collections can be used in interesting ways to achieve outputs and transformations that you might not think possible through *folding*. You'll look at

- Understanding aggregations and accumulation
- Avoiding mutation through fold
- Building rules engines and functional chains

18.1 Understanding aggregations and accumulators

You're likely already familiar with some of the aggregation functions in LINQ or F# collections, such as Sum, Average, Min, Max, and Count (see figure 18.1). All of these have a common signature: they take in a sequence of elements of type T and return a single object of type U.

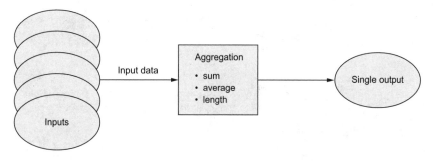

Figure 18.1 High-level visualization of aggregation

You can view this in terms of F# types as follows.

Listing 18.1 Example aggregation signatures

```
type Sum      = int   seq -> int      ◄──── Some example types
type Average  = float seq -> float           of aggregation
type Count<'T> = 'T    seq -> int
```

As you can see, the Sum, Average, and Count functions all share a common theme: they take a *collection* of things and return a *single* other thing.

18.1.1 Creating your first aggregation function

Let's look at how to implement the generic Sum aggregation; for example, calculating the sum of the numbers 1 to 5, or the total value of three customers, or the total cost of 10 orders. Performing any aggregation, or *fold*, generally requires three things:

- The input collection
- An accumulator to hold the state of the output result as it's built up
- An initial (empty) value for the accumulator to start with

See figure 18.2 for a visualization of the generalized aggregation function.

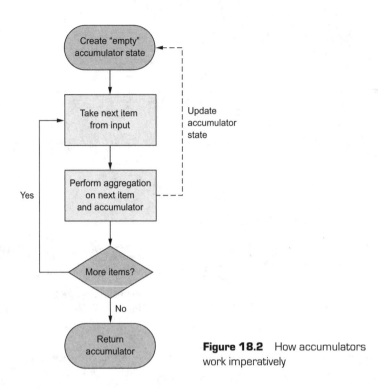

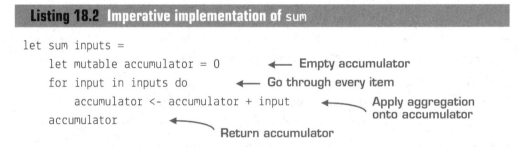

Figure 18.2   How accumulators work imperatively

Let's see how this might work for sum.

Listing 18.2 **Imperative implementation of** sum

```
let sum inputs =
    let mutable accumulator = 0          ◄── Empty accumulator
    for input in inputs do               ◄── Go through every item
        accumulator <- accumulator + input    ◄── Apply aggregation
                                                   onto accumulator
    accumulator          ◄──
                              Return accumulator
```

Interestingly, if you mouse over the sum function, you'll see that it has the exact signature described in listing 18.1: seq<int> -> int. Once again, type inference helps out here by correctly determining that the inputs value is a collection (based on the for loop) and an int based on addition to accumulator.

Now you try

Try to create aggregation functions by using the preceding style for a couple of other aggregation functions:

1 Create a new .fsx script.
2 Copy the code from listing 18.2.
3 Create a function to calculate the *length* of a list (take any list from the previous lessons as a starting point!). The only thing that should change is the line that updates the accumulator.
4 Now do the same to calculate the maximum value of a list.

As you're well aware, though, you're using a mutable variable here for your accumulator, as well as an imperative loop—not particularly composable. A standard answer from a functional programmer would be to rewrite this code by using *recursion*, a style of programming in which a function calls itself as a way of maintaining state. I'm not a massive fan of recursion, because it can be difficult to follow, particularly if you come from an imperative background (see appendix E for a short example). As you'll see, the majority of the time you can get away without recursion; instead, you'll see an alternative, collection-based way to achieve the same code as in listing 18.2, without any mutation and accumulation.

> **Quick check 18.1**
>
> 1 What is the general signature of an aggregation?
> 2 What are the main components of any aggregation?

18.2 Saying hello to fold

fold is a generalized way to achieve the exact sort of aggregations that you've just been looking at. It's a higher-order function that allows you to supply an *input collection* you want to aggregate, a *start state* for the accumulator, and a function that says *how* to accumulate data. Let's look at the argument signature for Seq.fold:

```
folder:( 'State -> 'T -> 'State) -> state:'State -> source:seq<'T> -> 'State
```

> **QC 18.1 answer**
>
> 1 seq<'T> -> 'U.
> 2 A collection to fold over, an accumulator to hold aggregation state, and a start state.

That's a relatively scary-looking signature, so let's break it down step by step:

- folder—A function that's passed into fold that handles the accumulation (summing, averaging, or getting the length, for example)
- state—The initial start state
- source—The input collection

Let's see what it looks like to implement sum by using the fold function.

Listing 18.3 Implementing sum through fold

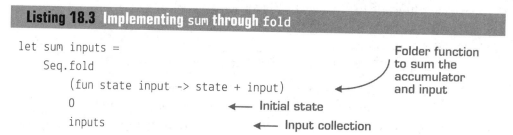

```
let sum inputs =
    Seq.fold
        (fun state input -> state + input)
        0
        inputs
```

Folder function to sum the accumulator and input

◄── Initial state

◄── Input collection

I've put the arguments on different lines here to make each argument somewhat clearer. The key part is the fold function: it takes in the current state (accumulator) value and the next item in the collection; your responsibility is to calculate the *new* state from those two items. If you compare it to listing 18.2, you'll see the same three key elements; the difference is that you don't have to explicitly store an accumulator value or iterate over the collection. All of that is taken care of by fold itself. The next listing adds some logging so you can see exactly what's going on.

Listing 18.4 Looking at fold with logging

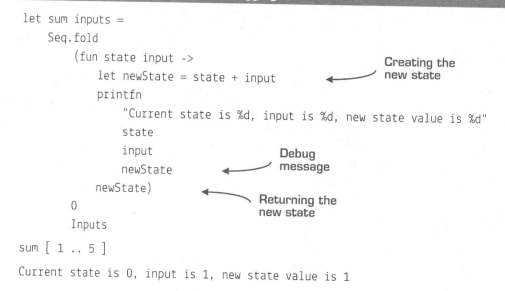

```
let sum inputs =
    Seq.fold
        (fun state input ->
            let newState = state + input
            printfn
                "Current state is %d, input is %d, new state value is %d"
                state
                input
                newState
            newState)
        0
        Inputs

sum [ 1 .. 5 ]

Current state is 0, input is 1, new state value is 1
```

Creating the new state

Debug message

Returning the new state

```
Current state is 1, input is 2, new state value is 3
Current state is 3, input is 3, new state value is 6
Current state is 6, input is 4, new state value is 10
Current state is 10, input is 5, new state value is 15
```

It might help to see this threading of state as a visual diagram, so take a look at figure 18.3.

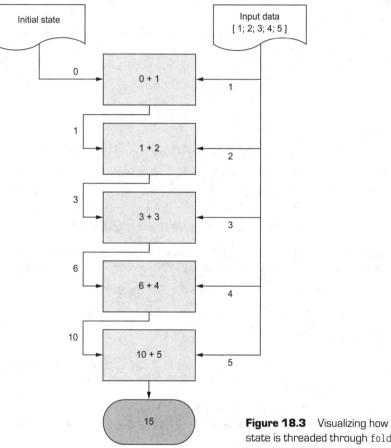

Figure 18.3   Visualizing how state is threaded through fold

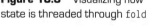

Now you try

Next you'll create a few aggregations of your own to improve your familiarity with fold:

1 Open your script from earlier.
2 Implement a length function by using fold.
3 Implement a max function by using fold.

Some examples of real-world use of aggregations

You probably use aggregations all the time without realizing it. The trick is to spot the signature of "given a collection of items, you get back a single item." Examples include the following:

- Retrieving the total price of a set of orders
- Merging a collection of financial transactions in order to determine whether a customer is high risk
- Aggregating a set of events in an event-driven system over initial data
- Showing a single red/amber/green status on the dashboard of an internal website to indicate whether all back-end systems are functioning correctly

---

18.2.1 Making fold more readable

One thing that I don't find especially nice is the way that the arguments to fold are laid out. You can make them more readable by using one of two tricks: the pipeline operator, which you already know, or the rarely used *double pipeline* operator. The double pipeline operator acts the same as the normal pipeline, but takes in the last *two* arguments and moves them to the front *as a tuple*. Here are three ways of calling the same function.

Listing 18.5 Making fold read in a more logical way

```
Seq.fold (fun state input -> state + input) 0 inputs

inputs |> Seq.fold (fun state input -> state + input) 0

(0, inputs) ||> Seq.fold (fun state input -> state + input)
```

Using pipeline to move "inputs" to the left side

Using the double pipeline to move both the initial state and "inputs" to the left side

Using the double pipe helps me visualize folds. The code now reads to me as, "Here's an initial state of 0 and a collection of input numbers. Fold them both through this function, and give me the answer."

18.2.2 Using related fold functions

In addition to the more specific aggregations such as sum and average, the F# collection library contains variants on fold:

- foldBack—Same as fold, but goes backward from the last element in the collection.
- mapFold—Combines map and fold, emitting a sequence of mapped results and a final state.

- reduce—A simplified version of fold, using the first element in the collection as the initial state, so you don't have to explicitly supply one. Perfect for simple folds such as sum (although it'll throw an exception on an empty input—beware!)
- scan—Similar to fold, but generates the intermediate results as well as the final state. Great for calculating running totals.
- unfold—Generates a sequence from a single starting state. Similar to the yield keyword.

18.2.3 Folding instead of while loops

What if you don't have an up-front collection of data? Perhaps you're waiting on user input, or streaming data from a remote data source. Look at the following example, which streams data from a file and counts the number of characters in the file.

Listing 18.6 Accumulating through a while loop

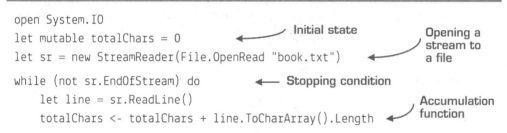

```
open System.IO
let mutable totalChars = 0          ← Initial state          Opening a
let sr = new StreamReader(File.OpenRead "book.txt")  ←        stream to
                                                             a file
while (not sr.EndOfStream) do       ← Stopping condition
    let line = sr.ReadLine()                         Accumulation
    totalChars <- totalChars + line.ToCharArray().Length  ← function
```

There are easier ways to count characters in a file, but the point is that you have an unknown "end" to this stream of data, rather than a fixed, up-front collection. How can you use fold here, which takes in a sequence of items as input? The answer is to *simulate* a collection by using the yield keyword. Let's take a look.

Listing 18.7 Simulating a collection through sequence expressions

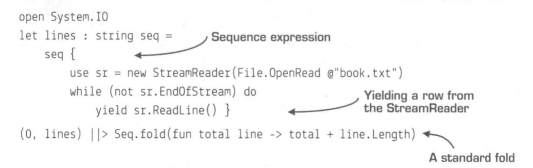

```
open System.IO
let lines : string seq =       ← Sequence expression
    seq {
        use sr = new StreamReader(File.OpenRead @"book.txt")
        while (not sr.EndOfStream) do           Yielding a row from
            yield sr.ReadLine() }   ←           the StreamReader
(0, lines) ||> Seq.fold(fun total line -> total + line.Length)  ←
                                                   A standard fold
```

The `seq { }` block is a form of *computation expression*. I won't talk too much about them in this book, but a computation expression is a special block in which certain keywords, such as `yield`, can be used (there are others, as you'll see in unit 8). Here, `yield` has the same functionality as in C#. It yields items to *lazily generate* a sequence. After you've done that, you can fold over the sequence of strings, as you did earlier.

Quick check 18.2

   1   What's the difference between `reduce` and `fold`?

   2   Which two F# keywords are important in order to lazily generate sequences of data?

18.3   Composing functions with fold

The last element of `fold` that's worth looking at briefly is as a way to *dynamically* compose functions together: given a list of functions that have the same signature, give me a single function that runs all of them together. Let's take the example of a rules engine; you're writing a simple parser and want to validate that a supplied piece of text is valid:

- Every string should contain three words.
- The string must be no longer than 30 characters.
- All characters in the string must be uppercase.

What you don't want to do is hardcode the code that does the parsing and validation. Instead, you want to be able to supply a *collection of rules* and build them together to form a *single rule*. This way, you can add new rules without affecting the main code base. Trying to do this with mutation and imperative loops can be a real pain, so in the interest of space, I'm going to skip that entirely (but feel free to try it yourself!). What you'll see first is how to model such a rules engine, and then how to perform the composition element of it.

Let's start with simple functions to represent your rules. We're not going to bother with interfaces or anything like that. Instead, you'll define a simple function signature for a rule, which you'll also *alias* to a specific type name called `Rule` to make code easier to read later:

```
type Rule = string -> bool * string
```

QC 18.2 answer

   1   `reduce` doesn't require a seed value; it uses the first item in the collection.

   2   `seq` (to create a sequence block) and `yield` (to yield back values).

This signature says, "Give me some text as a `string`, and I'll give you back both a `Boolean` (passed or failed) and a `string` (the error message in case of failure)." You can now use that signature to make a list of rules.

Listing 18.8 Creating a list of rules

```
open System                                           All rules
type Rule = string -> bool * string                   provided
                                   List definition     inline
let rules : Rule list =      ◄─────────┘
    [ fun text -> (text.Split ' ').Length = 3, "Must be three words" ◄
      fun text -> text.Length <= 30, "Max length is 30 characters"
      fun text -> text
                    |> Seq.filter Char.IsLetter
                    |> Seq.forall Char.IsUpper, "All letters must be caps" ]
```

> **Type aliases**
>
> Notice the use of a type alias in listing 18.8: `Rule`. Type aliases let you define a type signature that you can use in place of another one. An alias isn't a new type. The definition it aliases is interchangeable with it, and the alias will be erased at runtime. It's just a way to improve documentation and readability. Note that the compiler won't know which signature to use, so IntelliSense can sometimes show the "full" type rather than the aliased one.

For a larger system, with more-complex rules, you might want to put the rules into a module as proper `let`-bound functions, and then create a list based on those functions. In this case, though, I've defined the rules inline. Notice that you can create a tuple of a *function* with a specific signature and an *error message*. F# infers that `text` is of type `string` because we've said that `rules` is a `list` of type `Rule`.

18.3.1 Composing rules manually

Given the three preceding rules, here's how to manually compose all three into a single "super" rule.

Listing 18.9 Manually building a super rule

```
let validateManual (rules: Rule list) word =
    let passed, error = rules.[0] word        ◄─── Testing the first rule
```

```
if not passed then false, error
else
    let passed, error = rules.[1] word
    if not passed then false, error
    else
        let passed, error = rules.[2] word
        if not passed then false, error
        else true, ""
```

← Checking whether
the rule failed

← Rinse and repeat
for all remaining
rules.

18.3.2 Folding functions together

The approach you've just seen doesn't scale particularly well. An alternative approach is to create a function that when given a list of rules gives back a new rule that runs all the individual rules, using the reduce form of fold. You haven't looked at reduce in detail yet, so refer back to section 18.2.2 for an explanation of it if needed.

Listing 18.10 Composing a list of rules by using reduce

```
let buildValidator (rules : Rule list) =
    rules
    |> List.reduce(fun firstRule secondRule ->
        fun word ->
            let passed, error = firstRule word
            if passed then
                let passed, error = secondRule word
                if passed then true, "" else false, error
            else false, error)

let validate = buildValidator rules
let word = "HELLO FrOM F#"

validate word

// val it : bool * string = (false, "All letters must be caps")
```

← Higher-order function
← Run first rule
← Passed, move
on to next rule
← Failed, return error

Like all our other aggregations, this one goes follows a similar pattern (albeit in this case, 'T and 'U are the same). You can also "explode" the aliased types at the same time:

```
Rule seq -> Rule
(string -> bool * string) seq -> (string -> bool * string)
```

If you're an OO design pattern expert, you might recognize this as the *composite pattern*. What you're doing is the same as in figure 18.3, but rather than the state being an integer, it's a *function* that, on each iteration, covers another rule. Notice also that the signature maps to our original aggregation type: `Rule list -> Rule`.

In effect, this code says, "Given two rules and a word, check the word against the first. If it passes, check against the second one." This is itself returned as a function to `reduce` as a composed rule, which is then used in the next iteration alongside the third rule.

Now you try

You might have found that last bit of code hard to understand at first. Let's explore it so you can better understand what happened:

1 Put `printfn` statements inside the rules themselves (for example, `printfn "Running 3-word rule…"`) so you can see what's happening here. You'll have to make each rule a multiline lambda to do this.
2 Move the rules into a separate module as `let`-bound functions.
3 Add a new rule to the collection of rules that fails if any numbers are in the text (the `System.Char` class has helpful functions here!).

> **Quick check 18.3**
>
> 1 What OO pattern is equivalent to reducing functions together?
> 2 What happens to a type alias after compilation? Is it available at runtime?

Summary

That's the end of collections! You've now looked at a load of aspects of collections in F#. In this lesson in particular, you saw the following:

- Aggregations
- Folding over collections
- Folding over sequences
- Dynamically creating rules engines

QC 18.3 answer
1 The Composite pattern.
2 Type aliases are erased at runtime and revert to the real type that they alias.

You'll use collections throughout the rest of the book, and you'll be introduced to more features of the collection module later. For now, take a breath and get ready for the next unit!

Try this

Create a simple rules engine over the filesystem example from the previous lesson. The engine should filter out files that don't pass certain checks, such as being over a specific file size, having a certain extension, or being created before a specific date. Have you ever created any rules engines before? Try rewriting them in the style we defined in this lesson.

CAPSTONE 3

To round off this unit, you'll dive back into the bank accounts problem you worked on in capstone 2, but this time you'll enhance it with a few new features that will test some of your knowledge of collections, as well as further reinforcing the lessons you picked up earlier in this book. You'll look at

- Creating and working with sequences
- Performing aggregations
- Composing functions together
- Organizing code in modules

19.1 Defining the problem

In this exercise, you'll start from a variant of the code that you ended up with at the end of capstone 2 and enhance it step by step. You designed a basic application that allows you to create an in-memory bank account, and perform withdrawals and deposits into the account. Now you're going to continue that good work with a few enhancements:

- Updating your main command-handling routine to eliminate mutable variables
- Storing a serialized transaction log to disk for each customer
- Rehydrating historical transactions and building an up-to-date account by using sequence operations

219

19.1.1 Solution overview

In the src/lesson-19 folder, you'll see a prebuilt Capstone3.sln solution for you to open. There's also a sample solution in the sample-solution subfolder. As always, use it if you get stuck, but don't use it as a starting point. The whole idea is for you to try to solve this yourself!

19.2 Removing mutability

The first thing you can do with your newfound knowledge of sequences is to remove the dependency on mutable variables for your main driver program. As you may remember from capstone 2, you had to rely on an imperative `while` loop to keep track of the state of the account as you modified the account with deposits or transactions, as shown in figure 19.1.

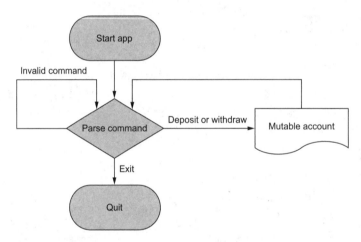

Figure 19.1   Existing imperative main driver loop

19.2.1 Comparing imperative and declarative flows

Although having a mutable variable in a single, isolated place isn't necessarily a problem, you can remove the reliance on it without too much difficulty. Moving from an imperative to a declarative mode of thinking will also provide a more composable way of expressing this logic, and avoid branching logic. There are two ways of avoiding the imperative, mutable model:

- Using recursion, which I've deliberately avoided so far.
- Treating the changes to the account as a *sequence of operations* that are applied against the previous version of the account; when the user decides to quit the application, the sequence stops, and the final account version is the end state (see figure 19.2).

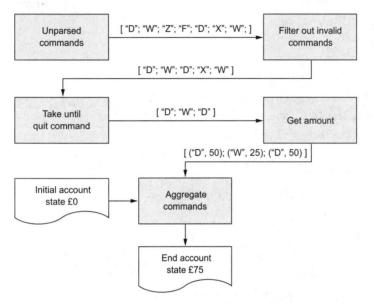

Figure 19.2 Proposed declarative view of commands as a sequence

Given a sequence of commands, you can filter out invalid ones, take until you receive a quit command, apply amounts onto the commands, and finally process them in sequence until you have your final account state.

The problem here, of course, is that your application is interactive. You're asking the user for input, rather than starting with a predefined set of commands. But that's not too difficult to achieve, as you'll see shortly. The easiest thing to do is to start with a preexisting collection of commands in a script and try to build a pipeline that looks exactly like figure 19.2, but in code.

Listing 19.1 Creating a functional pipeline for commands

```
#load "Domain.fs"                                          Initial opening
let openingAccount =                                       account state
    { Owner = { Name = "Isaac" }; Balance = 0M; AccountId = Guid.Empty }
```

```
let account =
    let commands = [ 'd'; 'w'; 'z'; 'f'; 'd'; 'x'; 'w' ]  ◄────

    commands
    |> Seq.filter isValidCommand
    |> Seq.takeWhile (not << isStopCommand)
    |> Seq.map getAmount
    |> Seq.fold processCommand openingAccount  ◄────
```

Set of commands
you want to process

Aggregating the validated
set of commands, using
openingAccount as initial
state

Now you try

Your task, should you choose to accept it, is to implement the functions used in the pipeline in listing 19.1. The descriptions for each function are in the following bulleted list,
followed by stubs in listing 19.2. Start by opening Scratchpad.fsx, which has already
been created for you and has appropriate #load statements to import the .fs files that contain all required types:

- isValidCommand—Checks whether the command is one of (d)eposit, (w)ithdraw, or
  e(x)it.
- isStopCommand—Checks whether the command is the exit command.
- getAmount—Takes in a command and converts it to a tuple of the command and
  also an amount. Your code should check the following:
  - If the command is deposit, return ('d', 50M).
  - If withdraw, return ('w', 25M).
  - Otherwise, return ('x', 0M).
- processCommand—Takes in an account and a (command, amount) tuple. It should
  then apply the appropriate action on the account and return the new account
  back out again.

Listing 19.2   Sample functions for command-processing pipeline

```
#load "Domain.fs"
#load "Operations.fs"

open Capstone3.Operations
open Capstone3.Domain
open System

let isValidCommand (command:char) = if command = 'w' then true else false
let isStopCommand (command:char) = false
```

```
let getAmount (command:char) = command, 0M
let processCommand (account:Account) (command:char, amount:decimal) =
account
```

> **Adapting functions to fit signatures**
>
> Notice that the arguments for processCommand use a hybrid approach of curried and tupled form, so that it plugs into Seq.fold naturally. This isn't uncommon to do, especially when working with higher-order functions. You might ask when is the best time to force a function signature into a particular shape to fit with the caller—and there's not always a great answer. In a way, it's a similar to a question in the OO world of changing the signature of a class to fit into an existing interface: sometimes you'll do it, and other times you'll use an adapter. In F#, an adapter over a function is a lambda (or at worst a let-bound function) that takes in arguments in one shape and maps to another form, so it's probably more common than in the OO world to use the adapter approach.

Now that you have a pipeline, you can test it in the REPL, executing progressively more of the pipeline, one stage at a time. You should see outputs as shown in figure 19.2 for each stage, and end up with an account with a balance of £75.

19.2.2 Moving to user-driven input

Now that you've tested your pipeline in a hardcoded fashion, you can now change to user-driven input. As you'll see, your pipeline stays unchanged; the only difference is that you'll need to replace the hardcoded set of commands with user-generated input, and change the getAmount function to again return user-generated input. First, let's see how to migrate your code into the program.

Now you try

1 Open the Capstone3 solution and navigate to Program.fs.
2 Copy across the helper functions you created in your script above main.
3 Copy across the main pipeline you created based on listing 19.1 in place of the entire // Fill in the main loop here... block.
4 Run the application. You should see the final account printed with a balance of £75.

   Now that you've ported the code, you should start to replace the hardcoded input by using a lazy sequence via the yield keyword.

Listing 19.3 **Creating a sequence of user-generated inputs**

```
let consoleCommands = seq {                    ←——————  A sequence block
    while true do
        Console.Write "(d)eposit, (w)ithdraw or e(x)it: "
        yield Console.ReadKey().KeyChar }   ←——————  Yielding out keys sourced
                                                       from the console
```

This sequence will execute *forever*; every time the pipeline pulls another item from the sequence of commands, it'll loop through, print to the console, and read the key entered. It's important to resist the temptation to filter out invalid commands here. You want this to be a simple stream of keys that you can plug in to the existing pipeline.

5 Next, replace the getAmount function with a new getAmountConsole function. It'll also print to the console to ask the user to enter the amount, before reading a line from the console and parsing it as a Decimal. As this function has the same signature (char -> char * decimal), you can replace the existing call to getAmount in the pipeline with this one.

6 Run the application. With a little bit of care, the output will look something (although probably not exactly) like figure 19.3.

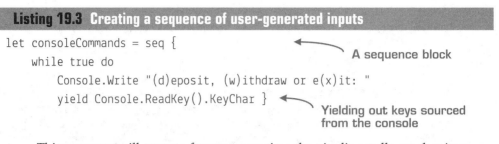

```
■ C:\WINDOWS\system32\cmd.exe

Please enter your name: Sam
Current balance is £0
(d)eposit, (w)ithdraw or e(x)it: d
Enter Amount: 50

Account Sam: deposit of 50 (approved: true)
Current balance is £50

(d)eposit, (w)ithdraw or e(x)it: d
Enter Amount: 25

Account Sam: deposit of 25 (approved: true)
Current balance is £75
```

Figure 19.3 Sample output of our application using a function pipeline over a lazy sequence

What's nice about this approach is that you can treat the *inputs* of data independently of the *processing logic* over that data. You tested some filtering logic and hooked into your existing code base, before replacing a couple of small functions in your pipeline to move from some hardcoded data suitable for testing in a script, to a user-driven console application.

 ## 19.3 Writing transactions to disk

Let's have a little more fun now and see how to add the ability to persist individual account transactions to disk, which will then allow you to reload an account from disk when you restart the application. Recall that so far, you already support the ability to write to both the console and disk. But the format that you emit to disk isn't suitable for what you need. It's just the user-friendly console outputs; you need a structure that's easily machine-readable.

What you need to do is amend your logging functions so that instead of taking in a raw string message to log, they'll take in a Transaction record, which (unsurprisingly) contains the details of the transaction being attempted.

Now you try

1 In Domain.fs, create a new record type, Transaction. It should contain enough detail with which to store what has occurred, such as the amount, whether a deposit or withdrawal (use a string or char field), a timestamp, and perhaps whether the attempt was successful.

2 Open the FileRepository module and change the writeTransaction function so that it takes in a transaction rather than a message.

3 Create a serialized string that represents the transaction record by using basic sprintf functionality; use a custom delimiter so you can easily "split apart" the string again later. You might want to use a third-party serialization framework such as Json.NET, but in the interests of keeping things simple for now, use something like this one.

Listing 19.4 Sample serializer for a transaction record

```
let serialized transaction =
    sprintf "%O***%s***%M***%b"
        transaction.Timestamp
        transaction.Operation
```

```
transaction.Amount
transaction.Accepted
```

In my suggested solution, I've created a module called Transactions in Domain.fs that contains the serialization function, but feel free to put it wherever you want.

4 Your code won't compile, because the console logger (printfTransaction in the Auditing module) no longer matches the function signature of the file logger. Fix it so that it takes in a transaction instead of a message string, and then prints a console message based on the content of the transaction record.

5 You'll also need to fix the auditAs function, which carries out an operation (deposit or withdraw), and logs what happened. You'll need to change it to create a transaction and then pass that to the audit function that's supplied.

6 When that's compiling, make sure in Program.fs to replace the raw calls to deposit and withdraw with the ready-made depositWithAudit and withdrawWithAudit functions.

7 Test the application; you should see that it correctly creates a file in an accounts directory for each transaction made with the serialized contents of each transaction in each file.

19.4 Rehydrating an account from disk

OK, great—you've now managed to get your tool serializing all the transactions to disk. Now, let's go the other way. On startup, instead of creating a blank account with a balance of £0, the tool should search for a folder for that user (by name), and then rehydrate the current status of the account based on their transaction history. This is simple, again, if you break it into small, composable functions.

Now you try

1 Create a function, loadAccount in Operations. This function should take in an owner, accountId, and a list of transactions, and return an account. You'll want to sort the transactions by oldest date first, and then fold them together into an account (pretty much as you've done already in the main program). Depending on whether the transaction was a withdrawal or a deposit, call the appropriate function in Operations.

2 Test this function (you developed the function in the script, right?) so that given a set of transactions that you create in the script, you end up with an account that has the correct balance. When you're happy with it, port it into the application.

3 Now let's deal with pulling back the transactions from disk, which you can then plug into `loadAccount`. Create a `deserialize` function that, given a single `string`, will re-create a `Transaction` record from it. If you created a `Transactions` module, put it in there.

4 Create a function `findTransactionsOnDisk` in `FileRepository` that, given an owner, can retrieve the account ID and all the deserialized transactions from the folder. Several private helper functions are already written in the module to help you along. Because there's a possibility that this is a new user, and this function is an expression, you'll have to cater to that possibility. As you haven't yet learned the "proper" way to do that in F#, return a new `Guid` for the account ID and an empty sequence of transactions by using `Seq.empty`.

5 In Program.fs, instead of starting with a hardcoded empty account, after capturing the account owner's name, you'll want to call `FileRepository.findTransactions-OnDisk` before passing the results to `Operations.loadAccount`. Depending on the signatures of the two functions, you might be able to compose them into one function, but this will depend on whether the output of the first matches the input of the second!

6 Test the application by first creating a new customer and performing several transactions before quitting the application. Then, restarting the application should rehydrate the same account based on the transactions that were already saved.

 **Summary**

And we're done! As always, there's a suggested solution in the repository to give you ideas on what you might have done. You'll come back to this solution later in the book, so you can incorporate other F# language features and libraries as appropriate.

5

The pit of success with the F# type system

We're making progress now! We've covered F# syntax, FP principles, functions, and collections—almost there! This next unit is the last one to focus on core language features in F#—remember that this book covers a core subset of the F# language, after which you'll have some fun writing meaningful applications that use a variety of frameworks and libraries.

A common phrase you'll hear in F# circles is the ability to "make illegal states unrepresentable." In C# and VB .NET, we're used to the notion of proving that an application is correct through, for example, unit tests and console applications. In F#, we still use unit tests, but to a far smaller degree. Part of that, as you know, is because of the REPL. But another reason is that the F# type system allows us to represent business logic as code so that if your application compiles, it probably *just works*. Sounds crazy, right?

In a more tangible sense, this unit is all about modeling program flow, domains, and business logic in F#, covering a set of language features that work together to provide a much more powerful way to reason about what your program does than simple if/then statements and inheritance hierarchies do.

229

20

PROGRAM FLOW IN F#

In C# and VB .NET, we have a variety of ways of performing what I consider *program flow*: branching mechanisms and, to an extent, loops. In this lesson, we'll compare and contrast those features with equivalents in F#, looking at the following:

- `for` and `while` loops
- If/then statements and expressions
- Switch/case statements
- Pattern matching

When you're finished, you'll have a good idea of how to perform all sorts of complex conditional logic much more succinctly than you might be used to.

20.1 A tour around loops in F#

I cover loops briefly in this lesson because the F# side of things has a slightly different syntax compared to C# and VB .NET, with similar behavior. This leaves us more room to focus on branching logic in F#, which is much more interesting. You've already seen examples of these constructs in this book, so you can consider this reference material more than anything.

The main thing to know is that—comprehensions aside—these looping constructs, although officially expressions, are inherently imperative, designed to work with side effects (code that doesn't have any tangible output; for example, printing to the console or saving to the database). In that respect, these loops should be familiar to you (and perhaps unsurprisingly not used as often in F# as C# or VB .NET).

20.1.1 for loops

for-each and for loops can be modeled by using the for .. in construct in F#. for .. in loops also have a handy syntax for creating ranges of data quickly, so although there's a separate construct in F# for simple for loops (known as for .. to), I've ignored it here.

Listing 20.1 for .. in **loops in F#**

```
for number in 1 .. 10 do          ◀── Upward-counting for loop
    printfn "%d Hello!" number

for number in 10 .. -1 .. 1 do        ◀── Downward-counting for loop
    printfn "%d Hello!" number

let customerIds = [ 45 .. 99 ]
for customerId in customerIds do      ◀── Typical for-each-style loop
    printfn "%d bought something!" customerId

for even in 2 .. 2 .. 10 do       ◀── Range with custom stepping
    printfn "%d is an even number!" even
```

20.1.2 while loops

while loops in F# behave just like those that you're used to.

Listing 20.2 while **loops in F#**

```
open System.IO
let reader = new StreamReader(File.OpenRead @"File.txt")    ◀
while (not reader.EndOfStream) do    ◀
    printfn "%s" (reader.ReadLine())
```

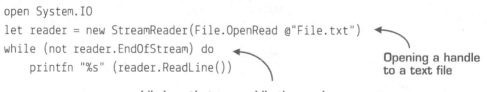

Opening a handle to a text file

while loop that runs while the reader isn't at the end of the stream

Breaking the loop

The main restriction of loops in F# is that there's no concept of the break command, so you can't exit out of a loop prematurely—sorry. If you want to simulate premature exit of a loop, you should consider replacing the loop with a sequence of values that you filter on (or takeWhile), and loop over that sequence instead. In fact, in case you haven't noticed yet, no code you've returned in a function uses "early return"—that's because it's not supported in F#. Again, because everything is an expression, each branch must have an equivalent result.

20.1.3 Comprehensions

Comprehensions are a powerful way of generating lists, arrays, and sequences of data based on for loop–style syntax. The closest equivalent in C# would be the use of the System.Linq.Enumerable.Range() method, except rather than *library* support, F# has native *language* support for this. Here's how comprehensions work.

Listing 20.3 Comprehensions in F#

Generating an array of the letters of the alphabet in uppercase

```
open System

let arrayOfChars = [| for c in 'a' .. 'z' -> Char.ToUpper c |]
let listOfSquares = [ for i in 1 .. 10 -> i * i ]
let seqOfStrings = seq { for i in 2 .. 4 .. 20 -> sprintf "Number %d" i }
```

Generating the squares of the numbers 1 to 10

Generating arbitrary strings based on every fourth number between 2 and 20

You'll find comprehensions useful for quickly generating collections of data based on a set of numbers—for example, calling a SQL stored procedure to load all customers between two date ranges.

Quick check 20.1

1   What restriction does F# place on returning out of loops?
2   What is the syntax to perform `for-each` loops in F#?
3   Can you use `while` loops in F#?

20.2 Branching logic in F#

We're used to using one of two branching mechanisms in C#: if/then and switch/case. The former is used for most general-purpose branching logic; in my experience, the latter tends to be used more rarely. That's unfortunate, because switch/case is a more constrained model than if/then, which operates against a *single value*. This means that it's often a little easier to reason about branching decisions than if/then, but overall it's fairly limited, working only against objects from a few types (integers, strings, and enums). If/then is more powerful, but is completely unconstrained, which means it's relatively easy to write code that's hard to reason about, or branches that accidentally operate over different data.

F# has an entirely different construct for handling branching logic called *pattern matching*. Let's work through an example to illustrate how to improve upon if/else expressions.

20.2.1 Priming exercise—customer credit limits

Let's say you want to write code that calculates a customer's credit limit, based on the customer's third-party credit score, and the number of years that this person has been a customer of yours. For example, if the customer has a credit score of Medium and has been with you for one year, you'd give them a credit limit of $500.

It sometimes helps me to understand a compound condition such as this if I visualize it as a kind of truth table. Let's do that now for the various cases that we want to model; see table 20.1.

Table 20.1 Modeling logic as a truth table

Credit score	Years as a customer	Credit limit
Medium	1	$500
Good	0	$750
Good	1	$750
Good	2	$1,000
Good	<anything else>	$2,000
<anything else>	<anything else>	$250

Even with only two features and a couple of *or* conditions, modeling this with if/then expressions can be a little awkward.

Listing 20.4 If/then expressions for complex logic

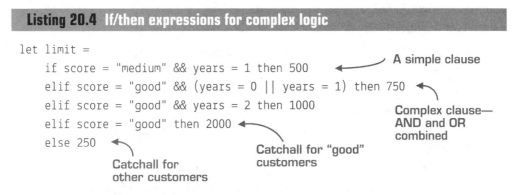

```
let limit =
    if score = "medium" && years = 1 then 500          ← A simple clause
    elif score = "good" && (years = 0 || years = 1) then 750 ←
    elif score = "good" && years = 2 then 1000              Complex clause—
    elif score = "good" then 2000 ←                          AND and OR
    else 250 ←                                               combined
                                         Catchall for "good"
             Catchall for                customers
             other customers
```

You might think that this is standard code, but the truth is, reasoning about the relationships of all the clauses as one unified piece of business logic can be difficult; each clause is completely unrelated. There's nothing to stop you from accidentally comparing against something else instead of score in just one branch, for example. Also, notice that the catchall parts of the code are somewhat implicit; this can lead to all sorts of weird and wonderful bugs, particularly when you have more than just a couple of clauses.

20.2.2 Say hello to pattern matching

F#'s solution to modeling branching logic is an entirely different construct called *pattern matching*. Pattern matching is an expression-based branching mechanism that also allows *inline binding* for a wide variety of F# constructs—in other words, the ability to deconstruct a tuple or record while pattern matching. Perhaps the most apt way that I've heard it described is as *switch*/*case on steroids*; the principles are similar, but pattern matching takes things a whole lot further. Let's take a look!

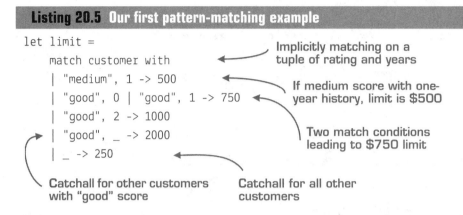

Listing 20.5 Our first pattern-matching example

```
let limit =
    match customer with          ← Implicitly matching on a
    | "medium", 1 -> 500           tuple of rating and years
    | "good", 0 | "good", 1 -> 750  ← If medium score with one-
    | "good", 2 -> 1000             year history, limit is $500
    | "good", _ -> 2000
    | _ -> 250                    Two match conditions
                                  leading to $750 limit
```

Catchall for other customers   Catchall for all other
with "good" score   customers

The syntax is a little different from what you're probably used to (then again, that's par for the course with F#!), but it's also powerful. Some things to note:

- You always test against a single source object, much like switch/case. Unlike if/then, it's impossible to compare against different values across branches.
- You match against *patterns* that represent specific cases. In this example, these patterns are tuples of credit score and years.
- The compiler can automatically infer the type of customer as (string * int) based on the usage within the patterns.
- You're matching here against *constant values*, just like switch/case. But you can also deconstruct a tuple and match against the individual components of it (as you'll see shortly).
- You can model multiple patterns to a single, shared output.
- You can model catchall-style scenarios as well with the wildcard (_) pattern, even on just a subset of the overall pattern.
- Pattern matching is, of course, an expression, so the match returns a value (in this case, the credit limit for the customer). Just like if/then expressions, all the different branches must return the same type—in this case, that's an integer (the credit limit).

20.2.3 Exhaustive checking

One thing that switch/case provides over if/then in C# is that the compiler can give you a little more support (for example, if you switch on the same case twice). Pattern matching has even better compiler support; it provides *exhaustive* checking. Because pattern matches are expressions, a pattern match must *always* return a result; if an input value can't be matched by the code at runtime, F# will throw an exception! To help you out, F# will warn you if you don't cater to all possibilities, as well as telling you about rules that can never be matched.

Now you try

Let's work through a simple example that illustrates how exhaustive pattern matching works:

1 Open a new script file.
2 Create a function getCreditLimit that takes in a customer value. Don't specify the type of the customer; let the compiler infer it for you.
3 Copy across the pattern-matching code from this sample that calculates the limit and return the limit from the function. Ensure that this compiles and that you can call it with a sample tuple; for example, ("medium", 1).
4 Remove the final (catchall) pattern (| _ -> 250).
5 Check the warning highlighted at the top of the match clause, as shown in figure 20.1.

```
let getCreditLimit customer =
    match customer with
    | "med⋮
    | "good    Incomplete pattern matches on this expression. For example, the value '(_,0)' may indicate a case not covered by the pattern(s).
        match years with
```

Figure 20.1 Exhaustive pattern matching

The warning indicates that you haven't considered the case of a customer with an arbitrary credit score and zero years' history.

6 Call the function with a value that won't be matched—for example, ("bad", 0)— and see in FSI that a MatchFailureException is raised.
7 Fill in a new pattern at the bottom of (_, 0) and set the output for this case to 250.
8 Notice that the warning has now changed to say you need to fill in a case for (_, 2), and so forth.

Exhaustive pattern matching is useful here as a reminder to add a catchall, but comes into its own when working with *discriminated unions*, which you'll see later in this unit. Let's now see how F# also warns about *unreachable* patterns:

1 Change the new pattern that you just created to match on (_, 1).
2 Move that clause to be the first pattern.

3 Observe that a warning is now shown against the (medium, 1) case, as shown in figure 20.2.

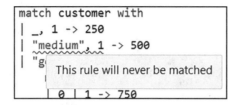

Figure 20.2 F# warns about patterns that can never be matched.

It's important to understand that pattern matching works *top down*. You should always put the most *specific* patterns first and the most *general* ones last.

20.2.4 Guards

F# also provides a nice escape hatch for pattern matching so that you can do any form of check within a pattern rather than just matching against values. This is known as the when guard clause. For example, you could merge two of the preceding patterns into one with the following.

Listing 20.6 Using the when guard clause

```
let getCreditLimit customer =
    match customer with
    | "medium", 1 -> 500
    | "good", years when years < 2 -> 750
    | … // etc.
```

Using the when guard to specify a custom pattern

Notice that you've also bound the number of years that the customer has been with you to the years symbol. As when decomposing a tuple normally, you can choose any symbol that you want. You can also use bound symbols on the right side of the arrow, which is useful if the action for that pattern needs to use input values.

When not to when?

You obviously have a lot of control when using the when clause in pattern matching, but a cost is associated with this: the compiler won't try to figure out anything that happens inside the guard. As soon as you use one, the compiler won't be able to perform exhaustive pattern matching for you (although it will still exhaust all possibilities that it *can* prove).

20.2.5 Nested matches

Just as with if/then (or switch/case), you can nest pattern matches. I recommend doing so only when you have an extreme number of repeated elements. Otherwise, the benefit of removing the repeated element is offset by the cost of the extra code complexity. Here's how the same example would look with nested matches.

Listing 20.7 Nesting matches inside one another

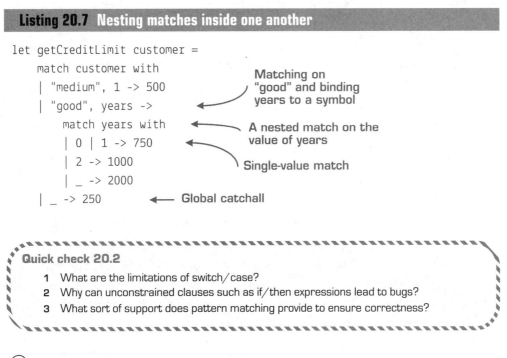

```
let getCreditLimit customer =
    match customer with
    | "medium", 1 -> 500
    | "good", years ->                  Matching on
        match years with              "good" and binding
        | 0 | 1 -> 750                 years to a symbol
        | 2 -> 1000
        | _ -> 2000                   A nested match on the
    | _ -> 250                        value of years
```

Single-value match

Global catchall

> **Quick check 20.2**
> 1 What are the limitations of switch/case?
> 2 Why can unconstrained clauses such as if/then expressions lead to bugs?
> 3 What sort of support does pattern matching provide to ensure correctness?

 ## 20.3 Flexible pattern matching

So far you've seen a couple of types of pattern matching: constant matching (as in listing 20.6) and tuple pattern matching (the ability to deconstruct and match against a tuple of values by using standard F# tuple syntax). But pattern matching can do much more than that; it can also match manyagainst other types of data. This section presents a few common types of matches; you can find a complete list on the F# documentation site at

QC 20.2 answer
1 Limited set of types it can work over; no binding support.
2 It's easy to write branches that are difficult to reason about and inconsistent.
3 Exhaustive pattern matching; binding and construction of tuples and collections.

https://msdn.microsoft.com/en-gb/visualfsharpdocs/conceptual/fsharp-language-reference.

20.3.1 Collections

F# lets you safely pattern match against a list or array. Instead of having code that first checks the length of a list before indexing into it, you can get the compiler to safely extract values out of the list in one operation. For example, let's say you have code that should operate on a list of customers:

- If no customers are supplied (the list is empty), you throw an error.
- If there's one customer, print the customer's name.
- If there are two customers, you'd like to print the sum of their balances.
- Otherwise, print the total number of customers supplied.

Pretty arbitrary logic, right?

Now you try

Let's work through the preceding logic to see pattern matching over lists in action:

1 Create a Customer record type that has fields Balance : int and Name : string.
2 Create a function called handleCustomers that takes in a list of Customer records.
3 Implement the preceding logic by using standard if/then logic. You can use List.length to calculate the length of customers, or explicitly type-annotate the Customer argument as Customer list and get the Length property on the list.
4 Use failwith to raise an exception (for example, failwith "No customers supplied!").
5 Now enter the following pattern match version for comparison.

Listing 20.8 Matching against lists

```
let handleCustomer customers =
    match customers with
    | [] -> failwith "No customers supplied!"          Matching against
                                                        an empty list
    | [ customer ] -> printfn "Single customer, name is %s" customer.Name
    | [ first; second ] ->
        printfn "Two customers, balance = %d"          Matching against a
                                                        list of one customer
```

```
        (first.Balance + second.Balance)
    | customers -> printfn "Customers supplied: %d" customers.Length
handleCustomer []  // throws exception
handleCustomer [ { Balance = 10; Name = "Joe" } ]  // prints name
```

Matching against a list of two customers

Matching against all other lists

One big difference with pattern matching versus manually checking the length of lists first is that here it's *impossible* to accidentally try to access a value in a list that doesn't exist, as the compiler is doing both the length check and expanding the values of the list for you. You're replacing runtime logic for compile-time safety.

An example like this is useful only for small lists; you wouldn't do this for lists of hundreds of items. But you'd be surprised how often you check against lists that have only a few items in them.

20.3.2 Records

You can also pattern match on *records*. What does this mean? Well, here's an example of pattern matching against your fictional Customer type to return a description of records.

Listing 20.9 Pattern matching with records

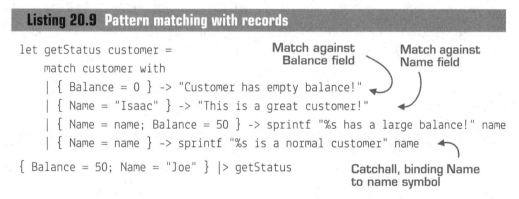

```
let getStatus customer =
    match customer with
    | { Balance = 0 } -> "Customer has empty balance!"
    | { Name = "Isaac" } -> "This is a great customer!"
    | { Name = name; Balance = 50 } -> sprintf "%s has a large balance!" name
    | { Name = name } -> sprintf "%s is a normal customer" name
{ Balance = 50; Name = "Joe" } |> getStatus
```

Match against Balance field

Match against Name field

Catchall, binding Name to name symbol

Notice that you don't have to fill in all the fields, only the ones that you want to match against. But if you want to, you can bind specific fields to symbols so you can use them on the right-hand side—pretty neat!

You can even mix and match patterns. How about checking the following three conditions *all at the same time*:

1   The list of customers has three elements.
2   The first customer is called "Tanya."
3   The second customer has a balance of 25.

No problem!

Listing 20.10 **Combining multiple patterns**

```
match customers with
| [ { Name = "Tanya" }; { Balance = 25 }; _ ] -> "It's a match!"
| _ -> "No match!"
```

Pattern matching
against a list of three
items with specific fields

Quick check 20.3   What collection types can you not pattern match against?

20.4 To match or not to match

With two branching mechanisms at your disposal, which should you use: if/then or pattern matching? My advice is to use pattern matching by default. It's more powerful, easier to reason about, and much more flexible. The only time it's simpler to use if/then is when you're working with code that returns unit, and you're implicitly missing the default branch.

Listing 20.11 **When to use if/then over match**

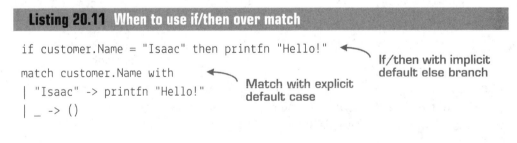

```
if customer.Name = "Isaac" then printfn "Hello!"

match customer.Name with
| "Isaac" -> printfn "Hello!"
| _ -> ()
```

If/then with implicit
default else branch

Match with explicit
default case

QC 20.3 answer   Sequences can't be pattern matched against; only arrays and lists are supported.

The F# compiler is smart enough with if/then to automatically put in a default handler for you for the `else` branch, but the match construct always expects an explicit default handler.

 **Summary**

That's the end of the program flow unit. Let's recap what you looked at:

- You briefly reviewed `for` and `while` loops.
- You saw how to use comprehensions to easily generate collections.
- You compared if/then expressions with switch/case statements.
- You spent most of the lesson looking at pattern matching, a powerful branching mechanism in F#.

We've really only scratched the surface of what's possible with pattern matching. Its real benefit is that it's incredibly expressive, powerful, and yet simple to use—once you know what can be done with it. Don't be surprised if you find it a little unusual; the idea of pattern matching is unlike both branching mechanisms you already know. You'll be using it more and more in the coming lessons in this unit, as it's pervasive within F#, so you'll have more opportunities to get your hands dirty with it.

Try this

Experiment with pattern matching over lists, tuples, and records. Start by creating a random list of numbers of variable length and writing pattern matches to test whether the list

- Is a specific length
- Is empty
- Has the first item equal to 5 (*hint:* use head/tail syntax here with ::)

Then experiment with pattern matching over a record. Continue with the filesystem "Try this" exercise from the previous lessons; pattern match over data to check whether a folder is large, based on average file size or count of files.

21

MODELING RELATIONSHIPS IN F#

Although you've looked at different ways of storing data in F# (tuples, records, and so forth), one thing you haven't looked at much is how to model *relationships* of data together—for example, different types of motor vehicles such as cars, motorbikes, and vans. In this lesson, you'll look at a way of doing this in F#, using a flexible and powerful modeling tool called *discriminated unions*. You'll do the following:

- Briefly review inheritance in the OO world
- Learn what discriminated unions are, and how to use them
- Compare and contrast inheritance and discriminated unions

You're probably familiar with modeling relationships in C# already, through one of two mechanisms: composition and inheritance. The former establishes a *has-a* relationship, whereas the latter typically models the *is-a* relationship; for example:

- A computer *has a* set of disk drives.
- A printer *is a* device.

 **21.1 Composition in F#**

We covered composition in lesson 10, where you created two record types with one referencing the other, but let's quickly recap it with another example.

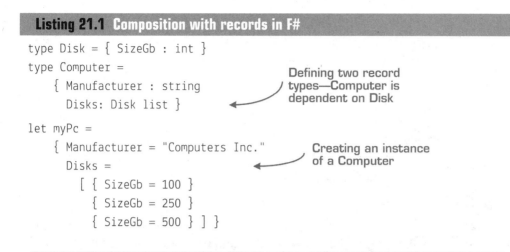

Listing 21.1 Composition with records in F#

```
type Disk = { SizeGb : int }
type Computer =
    { Manufacturer : string
      Disks: Disk list }

let myPc =
    { Manufacturer = "Computers Inc."
      Disks =
        [ { SizeGb = 100 }
          { SizeGb = 250 }
          { SizeGb = 500 } ] }
```

Defining two record types—Computer is dependent on Disk

Creating an instance of a Computer

Units of measure in F#

You'll notice that listing 21.1 has a field called `SizeGb` of type `int`. One of the nice features of F# is units of measure. These allow you to quickly create a specific type of integer—similar to generics—to prevent accidentally mixing incompatible integers together (for example, GB and MB, or meters and feet). In our example, you might have used something like `Size : int<gb>`. We won't be covering units of measure further, but I recommend looking into them in your own time.

In many ways, this code sample is no different from having classes, with one having a property that's an instance of the second class—except that F# records are much more concise, and we don't fall into the dogmatic one-file-per-class approach.

21.1.1 Modeling a type hierarchy

The problem is that so far, we don't have any way of modeling an is-a relationship in F#. For example, if you want to model different types of hard disks in the OO world, it might look something like figure 21.1.

In the OO world, you'll use inheritance here:

- A Hard Disk inherits from Disk.
- You store shared fields in the Disk class.
- You store fields unique to the Hard Disk in the Hard Disk class.
- Common behavior is stored in the Disk class.
- You allow overriding of common behaviors through polymorphism.

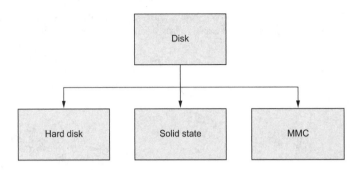

Figure 21.1   An is-a model that might map to an inheritance hierarchy

You might have your common data represented in the Disk type (such as Manufacturer and Size), but have the RPM speed in Hard Disk, and number of pins in MMC. Similarly, you might have a Seek() method on the disk, which might work significantly differently across all three disks. But the ability to seek to a file is a piece of functionality common to all disks, and so might be implemented using *polymorphism*—having an abstract method on the base class, and then overriding that method in the derived class. Callers then couple themselves to only the base class, without having to worry about which implementation they're dealing with.

21.2 Discriminated unions in F#

The standard functional programming answer to modeling is-a relationships is by using a *discriminated union (DU)*. There are other names for it, such as *sum types*, *case classes* in Scala, or *algebraic data types* for people who want to sound smart. The best way to think about them is one of two ways:

- Like a normal type hierarchy, but one that's *closed*. By this, I mean that you define all the different subtypes up front. You can't declare new subtypes later.
- As a form of C#-style enums, but with the ability to add metadata to each enum case.

Let's take a look at a discriminated union for our fictional three-case disk drive hierarchy.

Listing 21.2 Discriminated unions in F#

```
type Disk =                        ◀── Base type
| HardDisk of RPM:int * Platters:int
```
Hard Disk subtype, containing two custom fields as metadata

```
| SolidState
| MMC of NumberOfPins:int
```

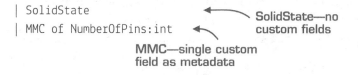

SolidState—no
custom fields

MMC—single custom
field as metadata

Each case is separated by the pipe symbol (as in pattern matching). If you want to attach specific metadata to the case, you separate each value with an asterisk. At this point, it's worth pointing out that you've modeled the equivalent of an entire type hierarchy in four lines of code. Compare this with what you'd normally do in C# with a conventional class hierarchy:

1 Create a separate class for the base type and for each subclass.
2 Best practice (allegedly) dictates that you put each subclass into its own file.
3 Create a constructor for each, with appropriate fields and public properties.

21.2.1 Creating instances of DUs

Let's see how to create, and then use, such a discriminated union in F#.

Now you try

First, start by creating a new script, DiscriminatedUnions.fsx, and copy across the discriminated union definition in listing 21.2. Next, create some different types of disks. Creating an instance of a DU case is simple:

```
let instance = DUCase(arg1, arg2, argn)
```

Start by creating an instance of a Hard Disk with 250 RPM and seven platters, followed by an MMC disk with five pins. Finally, create an SSD disk. Because this disk contains no custom parameters, you can do away with the "constructor call" completely. Let's see how this might look.

Listing 21.3 Creating discriminated unions in F#

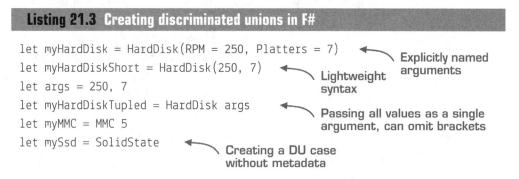

```
let myHardDisk = HardDisk(RPM = 250, Platters = 7)
let myHardDiskShort = HardDisk(250, 7)
let args = 250, 7
let myHardDiskTupled = HardDisk args
let myMMC = MMC 5
let mySsd = SolidState
```

Explicitly named
arguments

Lightweight
syntax

Passing all values as a single
argument, can omit brackets

Creating a DU case
without metadata

How did you do? Note that in our DU, I've assigned specific names to each metadata field. This is optional; you can opt to specify just the types (for example, int * string) but putting in names gives us some documentation, as well as more helpful IntelliSense (as shown in figure 21.2).

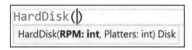

Figure 21.2   Generated DU constructors in F#

Notice also that the values on the left side are all typed as the *base type* (Disk), rather than the specific subtypes, as shown in figure 21.3.

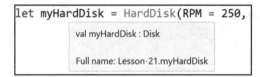

Figure 21.3   Values are assigned as type Disk, not as HardDisk.

21.2.2   Accessing an instance of a DU

Now that you've created your DU, how do you use it? You might try to dot into myHard-Disk and access all the fields. If you try this, you'll be disappointed; you won't get any properties. That's because myHardDisk is of type Disk, and not HardDisk. What you need to do is somehow safely *unwrap* this into one of the three subtypes: HardDisk, SolidState, or MMC. (It's irrelevant that you can see in the code that this is really a HardDisk. As far as the type system is concerned, it could be any one of the three.) How do you safely do this? You use our newfound friend from the previous lesson: pattern matching.

Let's assume you want to make a function that handles your hypothetical Seek() method from earlier. Recall that in an OO hierarchy, you'd make an abstract method on the base class, and provide implementations on each case. In other words, all implementations would live *with their associated type*; there's no one place you'd see all of the implementations. In F#, you take a completely different approach.

Listing 21.4   Writing functions for a discriminated union

```
let seek disk =
    match disk with
    | HardDisk _ -> "Seeking loudly at a reasonable speed!"
    | MMC _ -> "Seeking quietly but slowly"
    | SolidState -> "Already found it!"

seek mySsd
```

Matches on any type of hard disk

Matches on any type of MMC

Returns "Already found it!"

As you know with pattern matching, you can also match on specific values within a match case, so you can enhance the preceding code to match on Hard Disks with an RPM of 5400 and five spindles as per the next listing.

Listing 21.5 Pattern matching on values

```
| HardDisk(5400, 5) -> "Seeking very slowly!"
| HardDisk(rpm, 7) -> sprintf "I have 7 spindles and RPM %d!" rpm
| MMC 3 -> "Seeking. I have 3 pins!"
```

Matching a hard disk with 5400 RPM and 5 spindles

Matching an MMC disk with 3 pins

Matching on a hard disk with 7 spindles and binding RPM for usage on the RHS of the case

This at first glance might appear completely bizarre. You're putting all the implementations in a single place! Every time you add a new type, you have to amend this function! Actually, this is by design and is incredibly powerful. First, you get F# to safely check the type of the subclass for you. You can't accidentally access the RPM field when dealing with a SolidState disk; the type system won't let you until you've matched against the appropriate subtype. Next, not only can you use pattern matching to unbind specific values to variables (as in the second case in listing 21.5 with RPM) but remember that pattern matching enforces exhaustive matching. So, you can use F#'s compiler support to warn you if you've missed a specific case. For example, if you replace the catchall hard disk and MMC match cases in listing 21.4 with those from listing 21.5, you'll see a warning as follows:

```
warning FS0025: Incomplete pattern matches on this expression. For example,
the value 'HardDisk (_, 0)' may indicate a case not covered by the
pattern(s).
```

Similarly, if you decide to add a new disk type—say, UsbStick—the compiler will instantly warn that you're not handling that case here. You can safely add new types without fear of forgetting to handle it. This is all possible because DUs represent a *fixed* type hierarchy; you can't create new subtypes anywhere except where the DU is defined.

Now you try

Let's now see how to write a function that performs pattern matching over a discriminated union:

1 Create a function, describe, that takes in a hard disk.
2 The function should return texts as follows:
   a If an SSD, say, "I'm a newfangled SSD."

b If an MMC with one pin, say, "I have only 1 pin."

c If an MMC with fewer than five pins, say, "I'm an MMC with a few pins."

d Otherwise, if an MMC, say, "I'm an MMC with <pin> pins."

e If a hard disk with 5400 RPM, say, "I'm a slow hard disk."

f If the hard disk has seven spindles, say, "I have 7 spindles!"

g For any other hard disk, state, "I'm a hard disk."

3 Remember to use the wildcard character (_) to help make partial matches (for example, (5400 RPM + any number of spindles), and guard clauses with the when keyword.

Using wildcards with discriminated union matches

It's tempting to use a plain wildcard for the final case in the preceding exercise. But you should always try to be as explicit as possible with match cases over discriminated unions. In the previous example, you should prefer HardDisk _ rather than simply _. This way, if you add a new type to the discriminated union (for example, UsbStick), you'll always get warnings from the compiler to remind you to "handle" the new case.

Quick check 21.1

1 What is the OO equivalent of discriminated unions?

2 Which language feature in F# do you use to test which case of a DU a value is?

3 Can you add new cases to a DU later in your code?

QC 21.1 answer

1 Inheritance and polymorphism.

2 Pattern matching.

3 No. DUs are closed and fixed at compile time.

21.3 Tips for working with discriminated unions

Let's look at a few best practices for working with DUs.

21.3.1 Nested DUs

You can easily create nested discriminated unions—a type of a type. Let's assume you want to create different types of MMC drives and make a nested match on that. How would you do it? First, create your nested DU case, and then add that to the original type hierarchy as metadata on the parent case (in this situation, that's the MMC case of Disk).

Listing 21.6 Nested discriminated unions

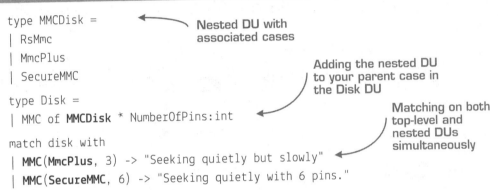

```
type MMCDisk =                    ← Nested DU with
| RsMmc                             associated cases
| MmcPlus
| SecureMMC                       Adding the nested DU
                                  to your parent case in
type Disk =                       the Disk DU
| MMC of MMCDisk * NumberOfPins:int ← Matching on both
                                      top-level and
match disk with                       nested DUs
| MMC(MmcPlus, 3) -> "Seeking quietly but slowly"  simultaneously
| MMC(SecureMMC, 6) -> "Seeking quietly with 6 pins."
```

If you refer back to figure 21.1, what you've done is essentially deepen the hierarchy so that you have three children under the MMC branch.

21.3.2 Shared fields

We haven't yet looked at how to share *common* fields across a DU—for example, the manufacturer name of a hard disk or the size. This isn't supported with DUs; you can't put common fields on the base of the DU (for example, the Disk type). The best way to achieve this is by using a combination of a record and a discriminated union, as shown in figure 21.4. You create a wrapper record to hold any common fields, plus one more field that contains the discriminated union—the varying data.

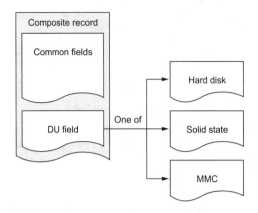

Figure 21.4   Composing shared fields with varying custom data through a record and DU

Here's a code sample that's evolved from the start of this lesson and that models both shared and varying data.

Listing 21.7 Shared fields using a combination of records and discriminated unions

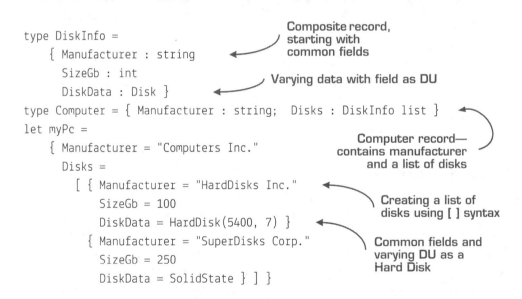

```
type DiskInfo =
    { Manufacturer : string          ← Composite record,
      SizeGb : int                     starting with
                                       common fields
      DiskData : Disk }              ← Varying data with field as DU
type Computer = { Manufacturer : string;  Disks : DiskInfo list }   ←
let myPc =                                      Computer record—
    { Manufacturer = "Computers Inc."         contains manufacturer
      Disks =                                   and a list of disks
        [ { Manufacturer = "HardDisks Inc."   ←
            SizeGb = 100                        Creating a list of
                                                disks using [ ] syntax
            DiskData = HardDisk(5400, 7) }    ←
          { Manufacturer = "SuperDisks Corp."   Common fields and
            SizeGb = 250                        varying DU as a
                                                Hard Disk
            DiskData = SolidState } ] }
```

You can easily visualize this code. Consider how simple it is to map this code directly to figure 21.5.

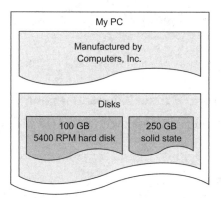

Figure 21.5 Representing your data model visually

> **Active patterns**
>
> F# has an even more powerful—and lightweight—mechanism for classification of data called active patterns. This is a more advanced topic, but I recommend that you check them out in your own time. You can think of them as discriminated unions on steroids.

21.3.3 Printing out DUs

A quick tip: if you ever want to just print out the contents of a DU in a human-readable form, instead of manually matching over all cases and generating a `sprintf` for each one, you can call `sprintf "%A"` on a DU. The compiler will pretty-print the entire case for you!

> **Quick check 21.2**
>
> 1 How do you model shared fields in a discriminated union?
> 2 Can you create one discriminated union with another one?

QC 21.2 answer

1 Through a composite record that contains the common fields and the DU value.
2 Yes, DUs can be embedded (or nested) within one another.

21.4 More about discriminated unions

Let's finish covering DUs with a small comparison against OO hierarchies and enums.

21.4.1 Comparing OO hierarchies and discriminated unions

Let's finish this exploration of DUs by comparing them with OO-style inheritance, as shown in table 21.1.

Table 21.1   Comparing inheritance and DUs

	Inheritance	**Discriminated unions**
Usage	Heavyweight	Lightweight
Complexity	Hard to reason about	Easy to reason about
Extensibility	Open set of types	Closed set, compile-time, fixed location
Useful for plugin models?	Yes	No
Add new subtypes	Easy	Update all DU-related functions
Add new methods	Breaking change	Easy

The hard-and-fast rule is, if you need to have an extensible set of open, pluggable sub-types that can be dynamically added, discriminated unions *aren't* a great fit. Discriminated unions are fixed at compile time, so you can't plug in new items easily.

For DUs with a large number of cases (hundreds) that change quickly, also think carefully. Every time you add a new case, your pattern matches over the DU will need to be updated to handle the new subtype (although the compiler will at least tell you where you need to update your code!). In such a case, either a record or raw functions might be a better fit, or falling back to a class-based inheritance model.

But if you have a fixed (or slowly changing) set of cases—which in my experience is appropriate the vast majority of the time—then a DU is a *much* better fit. DUs are lightweight, easy to work with, and very flexible, as you can add new behaviors extremely quickly without affecting the rest of your code base and get the benefit of pattern matching. They're also generally much easier to reason about; having all implementations in a single place leads to much-easier-to-understand code.

21.4.2 Creating enums

The last point I'll make here is on enums. You can create standard .NET enums in F#
easily enough; the syntax is somewhat similar to a DU:

Listing 21.8 Creating an enum in F#

```
type Printer =        ← Enum type
| Injket = 0
| Laserjet = 1        Enum case with explicit
| DotMatrix = 2       ordinal value
```

The only differences are that you must give each case an explicit ordinal, and you can't
associate metadata with any case. And, although you can pattern match over an enum
easily enough, enums can't be exhaustively matched over, as you can cast any int to an
enum (even if there's no associated enum case!). Therefore, you'll always need to add a
catchall wildcard handler to an enum pattern match in order to avoid a warning. C#
won't warn you about this, so it's easy to forget to do this, which can lead to many
classes of bugs.

> **Quick check 21.3**
>
> 1 When should you not use a discriminated union?
> 2 Why do you need to always place a wildcard handle for enums?

 **Summary**

That's a wrap on this lesson! We covered

- Comparing DUs to class hierarchies
- When and when not to use DUs

QC 21.3 answer

1 For plugin models or for unstable (or rapidly changing), extremely large hierarchies.
2 Any integer value can be cast to an enum without a runtime error.

Discriminated unions are a powerful tool in F#'s arsenal of features to help you model domains quickly and easily. You'll be using them for the next two lessons, so don't worry if it feels a little foreign to you; you're about to get much more comfortable with it!

Try this

Take any example domain model you've recently written in OO and try to model it using a combination of discriminated unions, tuples, and records. Alternatively, try to update the rules engine you looked at earlier in the book, so that instead of returning a tuple of the rule name and the error, it returns a Pass or Fail discriminated union, with the failure case containing the error message.

22

FIXING THE BILLION-DOLLAR MISTAKE

Hopefully, in the preceding lesson, you gained at least an initial appreciation of discriminated unions and how they allow you to quickly and easily model complex relationships. In this lesson, you'll take a look at *one* specific discriminated union that's built into F# and designed to solve a single problem: nothing! Or, more seriously, handling null values. You'll learn about

- Dealing with absence-of-value situations in .NET today
- Working with optional data in F#
- Using helper F# functions to deal with common optional scenarios

22.1 Working with missing values

Imagine you're reading a JSON document from a car insurer that contains information on a driver, including a safety rating that's used to calculate the driver's insurance premiums. Better drivers get a positive score (and lower premium), whereas poor drivers get a negative score, as shown in figure 22.1. Unfortunately, the data is unreliable, so sometimes the JSON document won't contain the safety score for a driver. In such a case, you'll need to send a message to the data provider to request it at a later date again, and assign a temporary premium price of $300. The following listing shows such an example JSON document.

Score < 0		Score 0		Score > 0			No score
$400		$250		$150			$300 + warn

Figure 22.1   Annual insurance premiums on a sliding scale

Listing 22.1 Example JSON document with missing data

```
{ "Drivers" :
    [ { "Name" : "Fred Smith", "SafetyScore": 550, "YearPassed" : 1980 },
      { "Name" : "Jane Dunn", "YearPassed" : 1980 } ] }
```

Driver with a safety
score of 550

Driver without a
safety score

We deal with data like this all the time today. The problem is how you normally reason about this in .NET. Ideally, what you'd like is the ability to encode into your C# class the fact that the Name and YearPassed fields are mandatory, and always populated, whereas SafetyScore might sometimes be missing and is therefore optional. Unfortunately, in C# and VB .NET today, we divide our data into two types, each of which behaves differently in this sense, as described in table 22.1.

Table 22.1   Mandatory and optional values in C# and VB .NET

Data type	Example	Support for "mandatory"	Support for "optional"
Classes	String, WebClient	No	Yes
Structs	Int, Float	Yes	Partial

- *Classes* should always be considered optional, because you can set them to null at any point in time; it's impossible in the C# type system to indicate that a string can never be null.
- *Structs* can never be marked as null, but have a default value instead. For example, an integer will be set to 0 by default. There *are* some ways that we can handle optional data, but these are achieved at the library level, and not within the language and type system.

If you think about it, this is bizarre. Why do we divide the way we can reason about missing data into structs and classes? Surely, we'd like to unify this, so that all types of data can be marked as either mandatory or optional? Before we look at that in further detail, let's discuss classes and structs in a little more detail.

22.1.1 The rise of the billion-dollar mistake

I'm pretty sure that at least 99% of you have seen the window in figure 22.2 many times in Visual Studio.

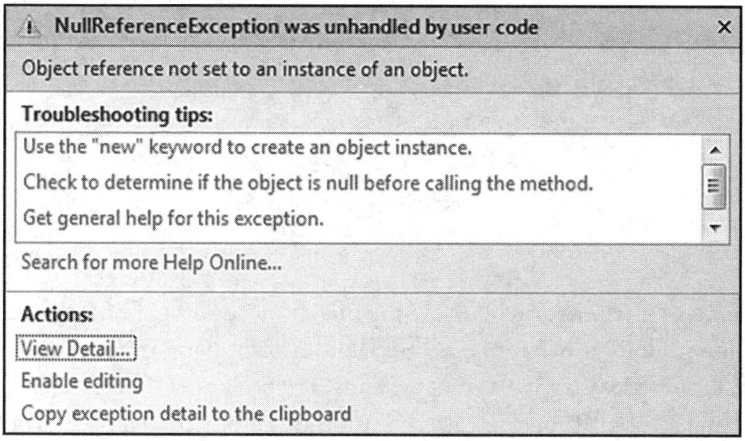

Figure 22.2 A null reference exception dialog box in Visual Studio

We've all seen null reference exceptions before. They crop up in places we never think they should happen and cost us a huge amount of time and effort—not only to fix them, but to diagnose why they happened in the first place. Yet it turns out that the whole concept of null was introduced as a sort of hack into the Algol programming language years ago:

> I couldn't resist the temptation to put in a null reference, simply because it was so easy to implement. This has led to innumerable errors, vulnerabilities, and system crashes, which have probably caused a billion dollars of pain and damage in the last forty years.
>
> —Tony Hoare, https://en.wikipedia.org/wiki/Null_pointer#History

I'd estimate that the cost of null reference exceptions and associated bugs at more than a billion dollars, many times over. And it's not just Sir Hoare. Even members of the C# compiler team have said that they regret putting null into the language. The problem is that now it's in, it's almost impossible to remove. Here's an example of the sort of thing that the .NET type system should be able to prevent.

Listing 22.2 Breaking the type system in .NET

```
string x = null;
var length = x.Length;
```

Creating a null reference to a string

Accessing a property on a null object

We know that this code will fail! But the type system can't help us out here, because in C# or VB .NET, any class object can be assigned null, at any time—so theoretically we should always test before accessing one. Because we can't mark a class object as mandatory, you've probably seen or written code like the following many times.

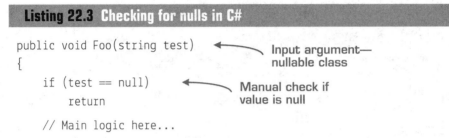

Listing 22.3 Checking for nulls in C#

```
public void Foo(string test)          ◄─────        Input argument—
{                                                    nullable class

    if (test == null)                 ◄─────        Manual check if
        return                                      value is null

    // Main logic here...
```

The problem here is, where do you draw the line at these sorts of null checks? In a perfect world, they should only happen at the boundaries of your application—essentially, only when taking in data from external systems. But we know that it's common to end up with these sorts of null checks scattered throughout our code base. It's not particularly satisfactory, and worse still, it's not safe; you probably won't correctly figure out up front all of the cases where there's really a chance of getting a null reference exception.

> **C# vNext and nulls**
>
> The C# team is putting forth a large effort to introduce some form of null checking support. It'll be some kind of code analyzer that performs branch analysis of your code to "prove" that you can safely access a class object. But this is quite different from F#, which removes the whole notion of nullability from the type system, as you'll see.

22.1.2 Nullable types in .NET

We've seen how the standard class-based system in .NET lets us down. Conversely, structs seem a step in the right direction: by default, they're mandatory. But we obviously need to model optional values as well. How do we do this for integers, for example, when we don't have null? We have a few ways to work around this, from picking a "magic" number that hopefully doesn't clash with genuine values (for example, –1) to having an extra Boolean IsValueSet property on our class that we first need to check before going to the "real" value. Neither choices are satisfactory. In fact, this situation is so common that Microsoft developed the Nullable type in .NET 2 to help. A nullable type is a wrapper that extends around a "real" struct value, which may or may not exist; see figure 22.3.

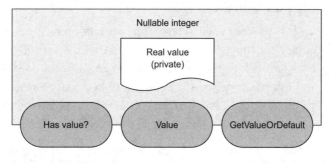

Figure 22.3 Representation of a nullable type

A nullable holds an encapsulated "real" value (which might not be set), and provides a simple API on top of it. You can ask it whether there's a value via the HasValue property, and if that returns true, you can then access the Value property. This is nicer than simple null checking with classes; at least here you can explicitly distinguish between times when a value can never be null (a standard integer) and those that might be missing (a nullable integer). Unfortunately, nullable types can wrap only structs, not classes. Also, although nullable objects add a convenience for us via an API, it doesn't provide us with type safety around them. If you go straight to the Value property without first checking the HasValue property, you still run the risk of getting an exception.

Quick check 22.1

1 Why can't C# prevent obvious null references?
2 How does the nullable type improve matters when working with data that might be missing?

22.2 Improving matters with the F# type system

The simple truth is that the .NET type system itself isn't geared toward allowing us to easily and consistently reason about mandatory and optional data. Let's see how F# addresses these types of data.

QC 22.1 answer

1 The type system doesn't support the notion of non-nullability.
2 Members such as HasValue and GetValueOrDefault provide control over nullable values.

22.2.1 Mandatory data in F#

First of all, unlike the inconsistency with classes and structs, all F# types (tuples, records, and discriminated unions) behave in the same way, in that they're all *mandatory by default*. It is *illegal to assign null* to any symbol that's of an F#-declared type. (This also applies to classes and interfaces defined in F#. Refer to appendix E to see how to create standard OO constructs in F#.) Let's see an example of this based on the computer model from the previous lesson, and how it shows as an error in VS (see figure 22.4).

Listing 22.4 Trying to set an F# type value to `null`

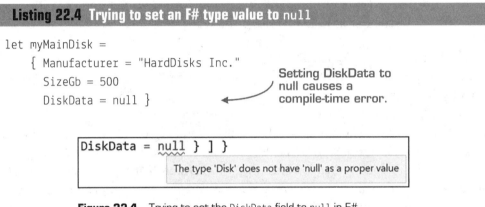

```
let myMainDisk =
    { Manufacturer = "HardDisks Inc."
      SizeGb = 500
      DiskData = null }
```

Setting DiskData to null causes a compile-time error.

```
DiskData = null } ] }
```
The type 'Disk' does not have 'null' as a proper value

Figure 22.4   Trying to set the `DiskData` field to `null` in F#

Recall that records can't be created with only some of the fields assigned, and you can't omit fields when creating discriminated unions. Therefore, any code that uses only F# types *can't* get a null reference exception; there's simply no notion of `null` in the type system.

Beating the F# type system

Corner cases do exist in which you can get null reference exceptions with F# types, using various attributes, and some interoperability scenarios. But 99% of the time, you can forget about null exceptions. In day-to-day programming, they won't be an issue.

F# types at runtime

All three F# types—tuples, records, and discriminated unions—boil down to classes at runtime, and are therefore reference types. But the next version of F# will introduce support to compile them down to value types instead. This has no impact of nullability at compile time, but will be for specific performance and interoperability scenarios.

22.2.2 The option type

We've just established that F# values can never be null and are mandatory by default. But we need some way to deal with operational data such as in listing 22.1, so F# has an *Option type* (also known as *Maybe* in some languages). You can think of this as a kind of nullable, except that it's more flexible (it can work not only on F# types, but also on classes and structs) and has language support to make it easier to more safely work with both "has a value" and "no value" cases. The following shows how to implement optional data in F#.

Listing 22.5 Sample code to calculate a premium

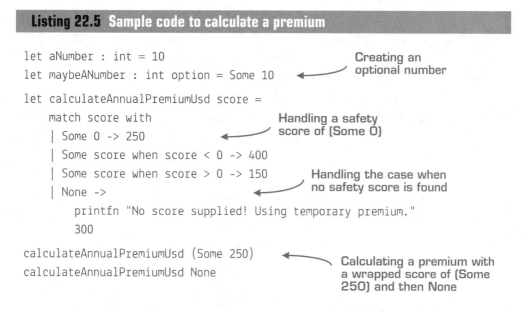

```
let aNumber : int = 10
let maybeANumber : int option = Some 10        Creating an
                                               optional number

let calculateAnnualPremiumUsd score =
    match score with                     Handling a safety
    | Some 0 -> 250                       score of (Some 0)
    | Some score when score < 0 -> 400
    | Some score when score > 0 -> 150    Handling the case when
    | None ->                             no safety score is found
        printfn "No score supplied! Using temporary premium."
        300

calculateAnnualPremiumUsd (Some 250)       Calculating a premium with
calculateAnnualPremiumUsd None             a wrapped score of (Some
                                           250) and then None
```

Option<T> is a simple two-case discriminated union: Some (value) or None. Just as with other discriminated unions, you pattern match over it in order to deal with all the cases, and unlike with null reference checks with classes, here you must explicitly handle both cases (value and no value) up front at compile time; you can't skip the null check.

Also, notice that when you call this function, you can no longer simply pass in 250. You must first wrap it as Some 250 (just as you wrapped the number of pins in an MMC disk in the previous lesson). This is slightly different from working with nullables in C#, where the compiler will silently wrap an integer in a nullable int for you. F# is a little stricter here, and you must explicitly wrap the number yourself.

Now you try

Let's see how to model the dataset from listing 22.1:

1 Create a record type to match the structure of the customer.
2 For the optional field's type, use an option (either `int option` or `Option<int>`).
3 Create a `list` that contains both customers, using `[ a; b ]` syntax.
4 Change the function in listing 22.5 to take in a full customer object and match the `SafetyScore` field on it.

Optional escape hatches

If you dot into an optional discriminated union, you'll see three properties: `IsSome`, `IsNone`, and `Value`. The first two are sometimes useful, but generally you should favor pattern matching or helper functions (see section 22.3). The latter field, `Value`, allows you to go straight to the value of the object without even checking whether it exists. If it doesn't exist, you'll get a null reference exception—exactly what you're trying to avoid! *Don't ever use this.* Instead, use pattern matching to force you to deal with both `Some` and `None` cases in your code up front.

Quick check 22.2

1 Can you get null reference exceptions in F#?
2 How should you safely dereference a value that's wrapped in an option?

22.3 Using the Option module

There are many common scenarios related to working with options, and some associated helper functions that come with F# in the `Option` module. Most of them do the same thing: they take in an optional value, perform an operation (mapping or filtering, for example), and then return another optional value. It may help you to keep that in mind

---

QC 22.2 answer

1 Yes, when working with types declared in C# or VB .NET. Types declared in F# normally don't permit nulls.
2 As `Option` is just a discriminated union, you should use pattern matching to cater to both branches.

as you go through this section that many of these functions are similar to their equivalents in the collection modules.

22.3.1 Mapping

`Option.map` allows you to map an optional value from one kind of option to another by means of a mapping function:

```
mapping:('T -> 'U) -> option:'T option -> 'U option
```

It performs a similar purpose as `List.map`, which you already know:

```
mapping:('T -> 'U) -> list:'T list -> 'U list
```

In other words, it's a higher-order function that takes in an optional value and a mapping function to act on it, but calls `mapping` only if the value is `Some`. If the value is `None`, it does nothing. This is similar to how `List.map` calls the mapper only if there's at least one item in the list. If it's an empty list, nothing happens. And as with `List.map`, the mapping function doesn't have to know about (in this case) options; the act of checking is taken care of for you.

Let's go through an example. Imagine your colleague has written a function, `describe`, that describes the safety score of a driver (for example, Safe or High Risk). It's not designed to work with optional scores, but you want to run it against the optional safety scores from your JSON file. You can either use a pattern match on this, or you can use `Option.map`.

Listing 22.6 Matching and mapping

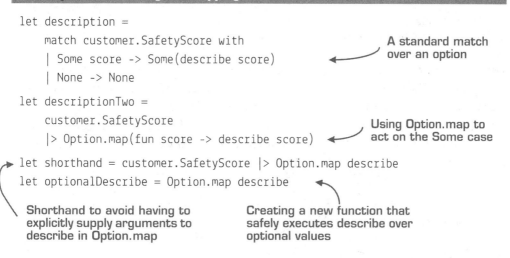

```
let description =
    match customer.SafetyScore with          A standard match
    | Some score -> Some(describe score)     over an option
    | None -> None

let descriptionTwo =
    customer.SafetyScore                     Using Option.map to
    |> Option.map(fun score -> describe score)   act on the Some case

let shorthand = customer.SafetyScore |> Option.map describe
let optionalDescribe = Option.map describe
```

Shorthand to avoid having to explicitly supply arguments to describe in Option.map

Creating a new function that safely executes describe over optional values

All three expressions do the same thing: they run describe only if SafetyScore is Some value, and otherwise do nothing. Option.map is especially useful because you can write entire reams of code without having to worry about optional data. You can then chain them together and wrap them in Option.map to get back a new function that does the option check for you for free. This is known as *lifting* a function.

Also, keep an eye out for Option.map's sibling, Option.iter. As with List.iter, you can use this for functions that return unit, such as printing out an optional customer's name to the screen by using printfn—typically functions that perform side effects.

22.3.2 Binding

Option.bind is the same as Option.map, except it works with mapping functions that *themselves* return options:

```
binder:('T -> 'U option) -> option:'T option -> 'U option
```

Bind is more or less the equivalent of List.collect (or SelectMany in LINQ). It can flatten an Option<Option<string>> to Option<string>, just as collect can flatten a List<List<string>> to List<string>. This is useful if you chain multiple functions together, each of which returns an option.

Listing 22.7 Chaining functions that return an option with Option.bind

```
let tryFindCustomer cId = if cId = 10 then Some drivers.[0] else None
let getSafetyScore customer = customer.SafetyScore
let score = tryFindCustomer 10 |> Option.bind getSafetyScore
```

Two functions that each
return an optional value

Binding both
functions together

Try this one out yourself. Observe that if you replace the call to Option.bind with Option.map, you'll get back an Option<Option<int>>. bind protects you here by doing the *double unwrap* for you: going from Option<Option<int>> to just Option<int>. Getting your head around this double unwrap isn't easy, but as you get more into FP, you'll notice this pattern cropping up all over the place. Even if you don't get it yet, keep it in the back of your mind (or check out one of Scott Wlaschin's many excellent articles on monads if you have some time).

22.3.3 Filtering

You can also *filter* an option by using `Option.filter`. In other words, you run a predicate over an optional value. If the value is `Some`, run the predicate. If it passes, keep the optional value; otherwise, return `None`.

```
predicate:('T -> bool) -> option:'T option -> 'T option
```

Listing 22.8 Filtering on options

```
let test1 = Some 5 |> Option.filter(fun x -> x > 5)   ◄───  test1 equals None.
let test2 = Some 5 |> Option.filter(fun x -> x = 5)   ◄
                                                          test2 is equal
                                                          to (Some 5).
```

22.3.4 Other Option functions

Table 22.2 provides a quick summary of some of the other optional functions. Look at them (and the others in the `Option` module) in more detail in your own time; some of them are handy.

Table 22.2 Optional functions

Function	Description
`Option.count`	If optional value is `None`, returns 0; otherwise, returns 1.
`Option.exists`	Runs a predicate over an optional value and returns the result. If `None`, returns `false`.

Quick check 22.3

1 When should you use `Option.map` rather than an explicit pattern match?
2 What's the difference between `Option.map` and `bind`?

QC 22.3 answer

1 If the `None` case returns `None`, you can replace it with `Option.map`.
2 Bind should be used when the mapping function itself returns an `Option`.

22.4 Collections and options

You might have already noticed that there's a kind of symmetry between the Collection and Option modules. They both have some similar functions such as map, filter, and count. In addition, a set of functions interoperates between them.

22.4.1 Option.toList

Option.toList (and its sibling, Option.toArray) takes in an optional value, and if it's Some value, returns a list with that single value in it. Otherwise, it returns an empty list. This isn't always needed, but it's sometimes handy to be able to treat an optional value as a list (or array).

22.4.2 List.choose

List.choose, on the other hand, is a useful function. You can think of it as a specialized combination of map and filter in one. It allows you to apply a function that might return a value, and then automatically strip out any of the items that returned None:

```
chooser:('T -> 'U option) -> list:'T list -> 'U list
```

Now you try

Let's imagine you have a database of customers with associated IDs, and a list of customer IDs. You want to load the names of those customers from the database, but you're not sure whether all of your customer IDs are valid. How can you easily get back only those customers that exist? Follow these steps:

1 Create a function tryLoadCustomer that takes in a customer ID. If the ID is between 2 and 7, return an optional string "Customer <id>" (for example, "Customer 4"). Otherwise, return None.
2 Create a list of customer IDs from 0 to 10.
3 Pipe those customer IDs through List.choose, using the tryLoadCustomer as the higher-order function.
4 Observe that you have a new list of strings, but only for existing customers.

> **Options, lists, and results**
>
> We're treading dangerously close to the M word (that's monad). If you found this idea of symmetry between lists and options (and of safely working with options) interesting, it's definitely worth your while to read "Railway-Oriented Programming" on the F# for Fun and Profit website (http://fsharpforfunandprofit.com/) by Scott Wlaschin. This website not only goes into more depth on maps, binds, and lifting than here, but also gives a relatively easy-to-understand introduction to working with monads.

22.4.3 "Try" functions

Throughout the collection modules, you'll see functions that start with try, such as try-Find, tryHead, and tryItem. Think of these as equivalent to LINQ's OrDefault functions, except instead of returning null if the function doesn't have any output, these functions all return an Option value: Some value if something was found, and None otherwise.

> **Quick check 22.4**   Why are collection try functions safer to use than LINQ's orDefault methods?

Summary

You saw in this lesson how two features that you learned about earlier in this unit—pattern matching and discriminated unions—can be combined to provide a type-safe, reasonable way of dealing with absence of value, without resorting to nulls. You learned about

- Dealing with absence of value in C#
- Using the option type in F#
- Using the Option helper module

Try this

Write an application that displays information on a file on the local hard disk. If the file isn't found, return None. Have the caller code handle both scenarios and print an appropriate response to the console. Or, update the rules engine code from previous lessons so that instead of returning a blank string for the error message when a rule passes, it returns None. You'll have to also update the failure case to a Some error message!

QC 22.4 answer   try functions return option values, rather than nulls as with defaultOf.

BUSINESS RULES AS CODE

In this last lesson of the unit, you'll see how to use F# language features such as records, options, and discriminated unions to write code that can enforce business rules within code. This lesson covers the following:

- Conventional ways to validate business rules
- Exploring domain modeling in F# more closely
- Exploring single-case discriminated unions
- Encoding business rules through types
- Exception handling

Our code always has some form of business rules within it. Generally, we validate that our code is correct either by running the application and manually seeing whether it does the right thing, or by writing some form of automated test suite that sits alongside our code. This test suite often is as large as the "real" code base itself, and runs tests in code that check the results of the application.

There are, of course, limits to what these tests should and shouldn't do. Because C# is a statically typed language, there are certain tests that we don't need to perform, because the compiler gives us certain *guarantees*. For example

- We don't ever need to check that the Name property on a Person class, which is a string, contains an integer. The type system provides that for free.
- We don't ever need to check that an int is null.

But here are some things that we might want to write automated tests for:

- Ensuring that we don't mix up the AgeInYears and HeightInCm values, both of which are integers
- Checking that an object can never get into an illegal state
- Checking that if we call a method on a class with invalid data, we correctly reject it

This lesson presents examples of these sorts of cases. You'll learn how to model them by using F#'s type system in such a way as to make illegal states *unrepresentable*. Just as C# makes it "illegal" to store an integer in a string field, F# can take this a step further, allowing us to start to model business rules in code, so that it's impossible to represent an illegal state. This means our unit tests are a lot simpler, or ideally can be completely omitted.

You've already seen examples of domain modeling in F# in the preceding few lessons, such as modeling the parts in a computer, or accurately modeling and dealing with the absence of a value. Now you'll take this a step further within the context of a simple scenario. Let's assume that you want to model your customer's contact details in code that adheres to a number of simple rules. You'll take each rule one at a time, and see how your model evolves throughout the code.

23.1 Specific types in F#

Let's start by defining a simple customer record to fulfill the first requirement:

A customer can be contacted by email, phone, or post.

Listing 23.1 A sample F# record representing a sample customer

```
type Customer =
    { CustomerId : string
      Email : string          ←——    Storing all possible
      Telephone : string              contact detail values as
      Address : string }              three separate fields
```

You're using an F# record here, but you could imagine this to be a C# class; it'd look fairly similar. Yet it's not a great fit for the preceding requirements. For example, any of the contact details could be filled in—or all of them—or none! You might say that this is completely reasonable. You might write some unit tests to prove that you never set more than one, and perhaps a get-only property that will tell you which of the three to use later. But fundamentally you're relying on writing code to test other code in the same way a JavaScript developer might write code to "prove" that a string property isn't assigned an integer. How can you more accurately model this?

23.1.1 Mixing values of the same type

One thing that strikes me from the preceding example is that all four fields use the same type: a string. Here's an example of a function that can create a customer.

Listing 23.2 Creating a customer through a helper function

```
let createCustomer customerId email telephone address =
    { CustomerId = telephone
      Email = customerId
      Telephone = address
      Address = email }
let customer =
    createCustomer "C-123" "nicki@myemail.com" "029-293-23" "1 The Street"
```

I hope you caught the errors in that sample: it accidentally mixed up the assignments for a few of the fields! Because you're using the same simple type, string, for all the fields, you get no help here from the compiler. You'd probably find out that you messed up here if you had written some unit tests, or perhaps some days later when you check the database and see you're storing data in the wrong columns. Doh!

23.1.2 Single-case discriminated unions

F# has a nice way of solving this, called *single-case* DUs. What's the point of a DU that has only a single possibility? Because of the simple syntax that DUs provide, you can use them as simple *wrapper classes* to prevent accidentally mixing up values. Here's the syntax for working with single-case DUs.

Listing 23.3 Creating a wrapper type via a single-case discriminated union

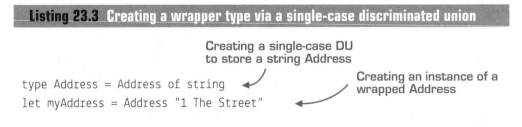

Creating a single-case DU
to store a string Address

Creating an instance of a
wrapped Address

```
type Address = Address of string
let myAddress = Address "1 The Street"
```

```
let isTheSameAddress = (myAddress = "1 The Street")
let (Address addressData) = myAddress
```

Unwrapping an Address into
its raw string as addressData

Comparing a wrapped
Address and a raw
string won't compile

As you can see, compared to multicase DUs, when defining a single-case DU, you can omit the pipe to separate cases—and even put it all on a single line. Because the contents of the discriminated union are obvious, you can also omit the name of the value argument (`string` instead of `address:string`). When you want to create an instance of it, again because it's a single case, you get nice, lightweight syntax of the type name and then the value.

Note that after you've wrapped up a value in a single-case DU, you can't compare a "raw" value with it. You need to either *wrap* a raw value into the Address type, or *unwrap* the Address. You do this in the final line, where the raw string is put into the `addressData` value (notice that because this is a single-case DU, you don't have to bother with pattern matching).

Now you try

Let's see how to enhance your domain model so that you can't accidentally mix and match the values for the different fields:

1 Start with an empty script, creating the `Customer` record and `createCustomer` function (with the incorrect assignments).

2 Create four single-case discriminated unions, one for each type of string you want to store (`CustomerId`, `Email`, `Telephone`, and `Address`).

3 Update the definition of the `Customer` type so that each field uses the correct wrapper type. Make sure you define the wrapper types before the `Customer` type!

4 Update the callsite to `createCustomer` so that you wrap each input value into the correct DU; you'll need to surround each "wrapping" in parentheses (see figure 23.1). If you've done this correctly, you'll notice that your code immediately stops working.

   Interestingly, the compiler error will be generated on the callsite to `createCustomer`. This is a case of "following the breadcrumbs" with type inference; if you mouse over any of the arguments to the function itself, you'll see that this is because you've mixed up the assignments to the wrong fields.

5 Fix the assignments in the `createCustomer` function and you'll see that as if by magic all the errors disappear.

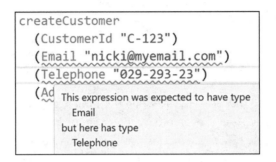

Figure 23.1   A single-case DU can protect you from accidentally assigning values incorrectly.

Listing 23.4 Creating wrapper types for contact details

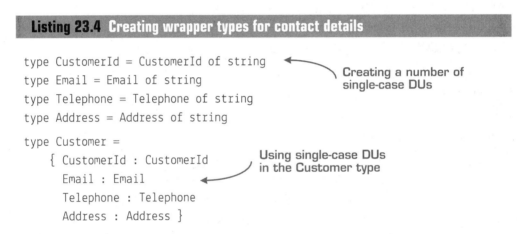

```
type CustomerId = CustomerId of string
type Email = Email of string
type Telephone = Telephone of string
type Address = Address of string

type Customer =
    { CustomerId : CustomerId
      Email : Email
      Telephone : Telephone
      Address : Address }
```

Creating a number of single-case DUs

Using single-case DUs in the Customer type

In addition to obviously trapping this error immediately, there's also another benefit of using single-case DUs: it's now much easier to understand what a value represents rather than, for example, a raw string. You no longer need to rely on the name of a value (for example, theAddress) but can now also use the type itself to indicate the use of the value (a CustomerId or Address, for instance).

> **Give and take with the F# compiler**
>
> Using types to guide the compiler is a much quicker way of getting feedback than writing a unit test or something similar—and it's a much stronger test. A unit test is written by a team of developers; the unit test might be written inconsistently or have mistakes. A compiler is a program that provides consistent behavior—*quickly*. Relying on the compiler here by adding wrapper types gives the compiler much more information about what you're trying to do. In turn, the compiler will be able to help you more by providing more guidance when you've done something you shouldn't have.

Remember to always wrap a value in a DU at the earliest opportunity—for example, when loading in data from a text file or database, along with appropriate validation. After it's "inside" your domain model, you don't have to revalidate it ever again, and you'll only need to unwrap a DU to its raw contents when you need to perform an operation on them. Ideally, you'll have all these related functions in a shared module. For example, you may have a function to create a `Telephone` from a `string`, which performs a regex validation on the raw string before safely returning a `Telephone`.

> **Wrappers with C#**
>
> In truth, you can create similar sorts of functionality in C# or VB .NET by creating a wrapper class for each type (for example, `Telephone`, `Address`, or `CustomerId`). The truth is that we rarely use them because of the overhead of doing this (creating a constructor and a public property on a class in a new file, and so forth). Single-case discriminated unions are much simpler to both create and access, with a much lighter syntax.

23.1.3 Combining discriminated unions

By moving to discriminated unions, you can be sure that you don't accidentally mix up the wrong fields, and at the same time also know that none of your fields can ever be null (because DUs can never be assigned null). But you still haven't solved the task completely: you want to model that *only one* of the contact details should be allowed at any point in time.

Now you try

Merge all three of the single-case DUs into a single three-case DU called ContactDetails and change your Customer type to store that instead of one field for each type of contact detail:

```
type ContactDetails =
| Address of string
| Telephone of string
| Email of string
```

6   Replace the three single-case DUs with the new ContactDetails type.

7   Update the Customer type by replacing the three optional fields with a single field of type ContactDetails.

8   Update the createCustomer function. It now needs to take in only two arguments, the CustomerId and the ContactDetails.

9   Update the callsite as appropriate; for example:

```
let customer =
    createCustomer (CustomerId "Nicki") (Email "nicki@myemail.com")
```

You can now guarantee that one and only one type of contact is supplied (for example, Telephone).

23.1.4 Using optional values within a domain

This next requirement should be fairly simple:

Customers should have a mandatory primary contact detail and an optional secondary contact detail.

Follow these steps:

10   Add a new field to your Customer that contains an optional ContactDetail, and rename your original ContactDetail field to PrimaryContactDetails.

Listing 23.5   Adding an option field for optional secondary contact details

```
type Customer =
    { CustomerId : CustomerId
      PrimaryContactDetails : ContactDetails
      SecondaryContactDetails : ContactDetails option }
```
Adding an optional field for
secondary contact details

11   Update the createCustomer function and callsite as appropriate.

Now you're really starting to make some headway. You'll never have to null check this customer's primary contact details, and have modeled the data in such a way that you can have only one of the three types at once. You've also modeled optional secondary contact details, and would use pattern matching to safely handle both value and absence-of-value cases.

Quick check 23.1

1 What's the benefit of single-case DUs over raw values?
2 When working with single-case DUs, when should you unwrap values?

23.2 Encoding business rules with marker types

That was an easy change. Let's now look at your final change, which is perhaps the most challenging and interesting:

Customers should be validated as genuine customers, based on whether their primary contact detail is an email address from a specific domain. Only when customers have gone through this validation process should they receive a welcome email. Note that you'll also need to perform further functionality in the future, depending on whether a customer is genuine.

A simplistic solution to this might look something like figure 23.2.

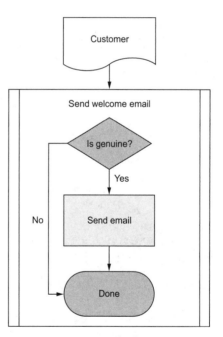

Figure 23.2 A typical procedural piece of logic

And that might work just fine. You'll probably write a couple of unit tests that take in a Customer and ensure that you send the welcome email only for whatever you define as a genuine customer. Maybe you'll even separate the "is a genuine customer" into a helper function so that you can reuse it later. But figure 23.3 shows another way to do this.

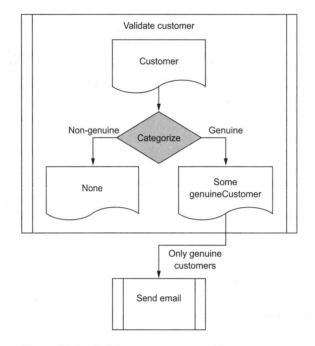

Figure 23.3 Defining custom states with types to prevent illegal cases

In this version, you create a function called ValidateCustomer that takes in a raw, unknown customer, and returns a new, genuine customer, a new type that you can treat differently from the raw one. By doing this, you can distinguish between an unvalidated customer and one that has been confirmed as genuine. As you'll see shortly, this can be useful in numerous ways, but first let's see what that looks like in code.

Listing 23.6 Creating custom types to represent business states

```
type GenuineCustomer = GenuineCustomer of Customer
```

Single-case DU to wrap around Customer

All you do here is create a single-case DU that acts as a *marker type*: it wraps around a standard Customer, and allows you to treat it differently. Here's the code that validates a customer.

Listing 23.7 Creating a function to rate a customer

Custom logic to validate a customer

```
let validateCustomer customer =
    match customer.PrimaryContactDetails with
    | Email e when e.EndsWith "SuperCorp.com" -> Some(GenuineCustomer
    ⟿ customer)
    | Address _ | Telephone _ -> Some(GenuineCustomer customer)
    | Email _ -> None
let sendWelcomeEmail (GenuineCustomer customer) =
    printfn "Hello, %A, and welcome to our site!" customer.CustomerId
```

Wrapping your validated customer as Genuine

The sendWelcomeEmail accepts only a GenuineCustomer as input

This function takes in a normal (unvalidated) Customer, and creates an optional Genuine-Customer as output. Then you create your sendWelcomeEmail function, which allows only a GenuineCustomer as input. This is the key point; it's now *impossible* to call this function with an unvalidated customer, as indicated in figure 23.4.

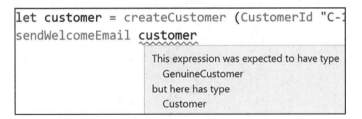

```
let customer = createCustomer (CustomerId "C-1
sendWelcomeEmail customer
```
This expression was expected to have type
GenuineCustomer
but here has type
Customer

Figure 23.4 Making an illegal state unrepresentable

The only way to call it is to create a GenuineCustomer customer, and to do that you need to go past the checks in the validateCustomer function. You can imagine a customer being created and potentially validated (or not!) early in the application, and then used later to send the email—safe in the knowledge that you can't accidentally call it with the wrong type of customer. The email function has no knowledge of how the customer was rated; it simply makes it a requirement through the type system.

You also now no longer have to write unit tests for whether the email code does the correct check on the rating of the customer (or anywhere else you need to split between these types of customers), because the type system protects you; you can send email only for customers of a certain type. In effect, you've made illegal states unrepresentable through types of data.

Breaking the rules?

You might ask what's to stop you from taking a normal customer and then manually wrapping it as a genuine customer, thereby breaking our rules. Well, you *could* theoretically do this. As with many other parts of F#, this is there to guide you to the pit of success, but it won't prevent you from going out of your way to break things! If you want to be safe, you can create signature files (think header files), which can restrict constructors of discriminated unions to a single file, thereby all but guaranteeing reliable construction of a type, but this is usually overkill.

23.2.1 When and when not to use marker types

Creating marker types can be incredibly powerful. You can use them for all sorts of things. For example, imagine being able to define email addresses that have been verified or unverified for your users. Or how about distinguishing between the states of an order in the type system (for example, unpaid, paid, dispatched, or fulfilled)? You could have functions that act on only fulfilled orders and not have to worry about accidentally calling them with an unpaid order! You can also use them at the boundary of your application, performing validation on unchecked data and converting it into checked versions of data, which provide you with security that you can never run certain code on invalid data.

My advice is to start simple: use single-case DUs as wrapper cases to prevent simple errors such as mixing up customer and order IDs. It's cheap and easy to do, and is a massive help in eliminating some awful bugs that can crop up. Taking it further with marker types to represent states is a step up, and definitely worth persevering with. You can eliminate entire classes of bugs as well as eliminate swaths of boilerplate unit tests. But be careful not to take it too far, as it can become difficult to wade through a sea of types if overdone.

23.3 Results vs. exceptions

In F#, you can use exceptions as you would in C#, by using `try .. with` syntax. In the spirit of this book, I'm not showing you that syntax because there's nothing interesting to see (although an example is included in appendix E). But it's interesting to note that exceptions aren't encoded within the type system. For example, let's imagine inserting a customer into a database. The signature might look like this:

```
insertContact : contactDetails:ContactDetails -> CustomerId
```

In other words, given contact details, save them to the database and return their generated customer ID. But this function doesn't cater to the possibility that the database might be offline, or that someone with those contact details might already exist. In fact, someone looking at this code would know this only if there was a try/catch handler somewhere in code, which might be an entirely different area of the code base. This can be thought of as an *unsafe* function.

An alternative to using exceptions is to use a *result*. This is a two-case discriminated union that holds either a *Success* or *Failure*. Here, if the call passes, you return a `Success` with the `CustomerId` generated by the database. If it fails, you'll return the error text from SQL as a `Failure` case.

Listing 23.8 Creating a result type to encode success or failure

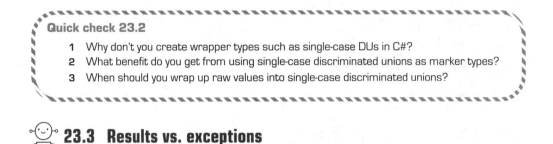

```
type Result<'a> =
| Success of 'a
| Failure of string
```

Defining a simple Result discriminated union

```
insertCustomer : contactDetails:ContactDetails -> Result<CustomerId>

match insertContact (Email "nicki@myemail.com") with
| Success customerId -> printfn "Saved with %A" customerId
| Failure error -> printfn "Unable to save: %s" error
```

Type signature of a
function that might fail

Handling both
success and failure
cases up front

Now, this function clearly states that it might not work, and callers would have to test both success and failure cases in order to safely get to the customer. This pattern is now so common that F# 4.1 will contain a Result type built into the standard library, just like Option. Internally in insertCustomer, you'd execute the code in a try/catch statement; any caught errors would be returned as a failure.

There's a fine line between when to use exceptions and when to use results; I suggest this rule of thumb: if an error occurs and is something that you don't want to reason about (for example, a catastrophic error that leads to an end of the application), stick to exceptions. But if it's something that you *do* want to reason about (for example, depending on success or failure, you want to do some custom logic and then resume processing in the application), a result type is a useful tool to have.

Quick check 23.3

1   What benefit does a result provide over an exception?
2   How should you convert code that throws exceptions into one that returns a result?

Summary

Believe it or not, that was the final language lesson in this book! You did the following:

- Saw how to model business states in code
- Explored some domain modeling step-by-step with F#
- Looked at single-case discriminated unions

QC 23.3 answer

1   Results allow you to clearly state in the type system whether a function can fail.
2   Using a try/with block, converting the exception to a failure.

Another capstone exercise is coming up next to allow you to become more confident working with types and collections. After that, you'll start looking at the applications of F# in various guises.

Try this

Look at an existing domain you've written in C#, and try to see where you might benefit from using options and single-case DUs in your model. Try to port the domain over to F# and see its impact!

CAPSTONE 4

It's back to bank accounts again! This time you're going to apply the lessons you learned on domain modeling into the bank account system. In this exercise, you'll do the following:

- Use options in practical situations
- Use discriminated unions to accurately model a closed set of cases
- Work with collections with more-complex data
- Enforce business rules through the type system

24.1 Defining the problem

When you completed lesson 19, you had a version of a working bank account application that could handle persistence to disk and back again, as well as remove mutation for your command handler. Now you're going to remove some of the "code smells" that have been left lying around by introducing some lovely F# domain modeling. You'll have to do the following:

- Replace the unbounded command handlers with a fixed discriminated union
- Embed options enabling you to cater to situations where you "might not have any data" rather than the arbitrary default values you've used so far
- Consider how you might enforce business rules via some F# types to stop overdrawn customers from withdrawing funds.

24.1.1 Solution overview

As per the previous capstone, src/lesson-24 contains a prebuilt solution for you to use as the basis for this lesson, plus a sample solution with a fully working version for you to learn from. Take a moment to familiarize yourself with the basic solution so that you understand what it's doing; hopefully, it's not too far off from where you ended up in the previous capstone.

 24.2 Stronger typing with discriminated unions

One of the issues with the current version of code for the main program routine is that you're using code to enforce all your rules. "What's wrong with that?" you may ask. After all, isn't that what you're supposed to do? On the one hand, yes. But at the same time, you want to use the F# *type system* as much as possible to save you from any boiler-plate errors.

24.2.1 Reviewing the existing command handler

One area you could improve is in using a simple char value to represent your command. Of course, you need to work with a char to capture the console input, but after you have that value, it continues to be used within the code base. This poses a few smells immediately.

Listing 24.1 The existing command execution pipeline

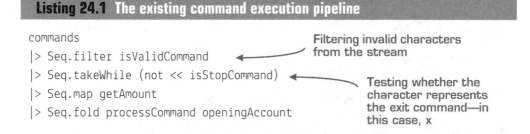

```
commands
|> Seq.filter isValidCommand
|> Seq.takeWhile (not << isStopCommand)
|> Seq.map getAmount
|> Seq.fold processCommand openingAccount
```

Filtering invalid characters from the stream

Testing whether the character represents the exit command—in this case, x

---

Something I'm not fond of here is that you can comment out the Seq.filter line, and the code still compiles; it shouldn't. You want some form of validation layer that can stop you from accidentally missing things like this! Ideally, you want a bounded set of commands that represent actions your application can do, and to go from the weakly typed, essentially unbounded char type into the command type at the earliest possible opportunity, as illustrated in figure 24.1.

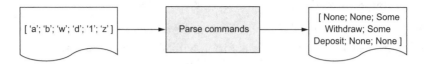

Figure 24.1   Moving from a virtually unbounded type to a strictly bounded command type

Doing this means that within the code, you shouldn't ever be in the situation described in the following listing.

Listing 24.2 Working with unbounded values

```
let processCommand account (command, amount) =
    if command = 'd' then account |> depositWithAudit amount    Using an else
    else account |> withdrawWithAudit amount                   block as a
                                                               catchall case
```

Spot the problem here? You're assuming that if the command isn't the character d, it must be w (for *withdrawal*). Even if you handled the withdrawal case explicitly, there's still the *otherwise* case that needs to be handled. What do you do then? These sorts of smells can initially seem innocuous but can rapidly become the source of awful bugs. Let's see how to stop this from happening now, before it's too late.

24.2.2 Adding a command handler with discriminated unions

Start within scratchpad.fsx to test these tasks. Then move back into Program.fs in the appropriate places:

1   The first thing you'll want to do is create a simple discriminated union called Command to represent your three application commands: Withdraw, Deposit, and Exit. These cases represent all the activities your program can do.

2   Next, you need to write a simple function that can convert a char into a Command. I'd typically use pattern matching here; you can match over the supplied character, and depending on the value, return the appropriate command.

3   Because you can't be sure what value will be provided (it might not be x, w, or d), you'll want to have this function return an Option<Command> to deal with the case that an invalid character is supplied. It's common practice to prefix such functions with the word try (for example, tryParseCommand).

4   Make sure you're happy with that function. Test it in the REPL (for example, does x map to Exit), and then port it into the application.

Now you're ready to hook your new command domain into your code—in the pipeline around line 50 of Program.fs.

5 Replace the code in isValidCommand so that it maps from simple characters into your Command. But because your tryParseCommand function will be returning option values, it's better to use choose rather than map here (lesson 22 covers choose; refer there if needed).

6 You'll notice that the next line in the pipeline immediately doesn't work. That's because it checks against the char x; update it to compare against the Exit command instead (indeed, you might want to put the lambda inline now as the code is obvious to read).

7 Finally, you need to update processCommand. This should pattern match over the command that's supplied; depending on whether it's Deposit or Withdraw, it should call the appropriate function. If it's Exit, it should return the account back out again.

As an extra exercise, you can apply the same technique to the loading of data from the filesystem in Operations.loadAccount, so that instead of an if/then expression against the text withdraw, you can try to parse the text to a Bank Operation discriminated union case first and process that instead.

24.2.3 Tightening the model further

You now have a cleaner domain. It's easier to reason about, because you know that there are only three possible commands, and you don't have to guess what the different characters mean; the DU cases are self-explanatory. Unfortunately, one small smell remains: the match expression in processCommand has to cater to the Exit command as well, even though you know that it should never really be possible (see figure 24.2).

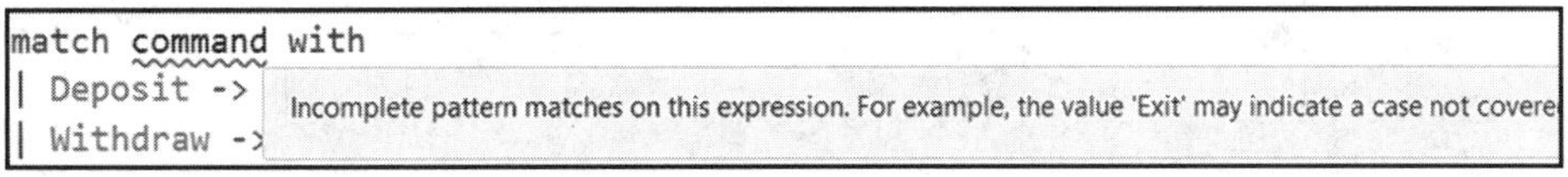

```
match command with
| Deposit ->    Incomplete pattern matches on this expression. For example, the value 'Exit' may indicate a case not covere
| Withdraw ->
```

Figure 24.2 Pattern matching warns that you haven't handled all the cases for your DU.

This is a good example of F# giving you a hint that the current way that you've modeled your domain isn't quite right. You can fix this by enhancing your domain model so that you clearly show that there's a difference between the Exit command and the two bank operations.

Listing 24.3 Creating a two-level discriminated union

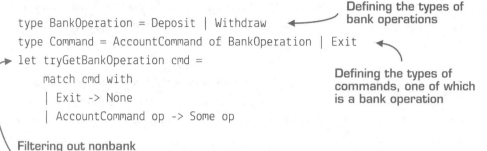

Defining the types of
bank operations

```
type BankOperation = Deposit | Withdraw
type Command = AccountCommand of BankOperation | Exit
let tryGetBankOperation cmd =
    match cmd with
    | Exit -> None
    | AccountCommand op -> Some op
```

Defining the types of
commands, one of which
is a bank operation

Filtering out nonbank
operation commands

What you've done now is create a child DU. A Command is one of the following:

- Exit
- A bank operation (either Deposit or Withdraw)

If you follow this approach (and update the parsing code), you can use tryGetBank-
Operation in the pipeline to convert from a Command to a BankOperation; by the time you get to
the processCommand function, you'll be able to match against BankOperation, which has only
the two cases—exactly what you want. Let's see how that looks in figure 24.3.

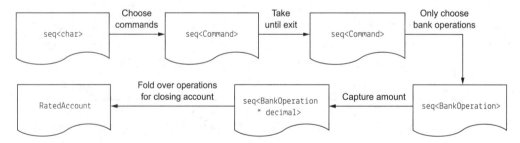

Figure 24.3 Visualizing the updated pipeline

Try testing this pipeline in a script with a set of sample chars, as you did in the previous
capstone!

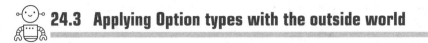 24.3 Applying Option types with the outside world

Let's look at a few situations where it's useful to apply the Option type when dealing with external data that you're not necessarily in control of.

24.3.1 Parsing user input

If the user accidentally types a non-number when entering the amount to withdraw or deposit, the application crashes. Stop that by updating the getAmount function, as shown in the next listing.

Listing 24.4 Safely parsing user input

```
let tryGetAmount command =
    Console.WriteLine()
    Console.Write "Enter Amount: "
    let amount = Console.ReadLine() |> Decimal.TryParse
    match amount with
    | true, amount -> Some(command, amount)
    | false, _ -> None
```

Safely parsing the input from the user

Return output only if the input is a valid decimal.

Invalid input results in no output.

As you can see, F# plays nicely with TryParse methods in the BCL by returning both the Boolean result of the parse operation and the parsed value itself, so you can easily pattern match over it and deal with it as you see fit.

Once again, you've renamed this function to start with try, as it now returns an optional value. You'll need to update the pipeline to use choose rather than map, to skip invalid answers.

24.3.2 Loading existing accounts

In the current implementation of the application, when the program starts up and you've entered your name, the file repository attempts to locate your bank account on disk. If the file repository can't locate the account, it creates a default account and returns that instead. This is nice in a "you don't need to know" kind of way, but it's a bit of a mismatch of responsibilities: the file repository module should retrieve the bank account from disk; if it can't be located, it should be up to the caller to decide what to do next. The call to findTransactionsOnDisk should return an option, rather than a concrete result.

If you dig into the code a bit, you'll find the findAccountFolder function, which is the root of the problem.

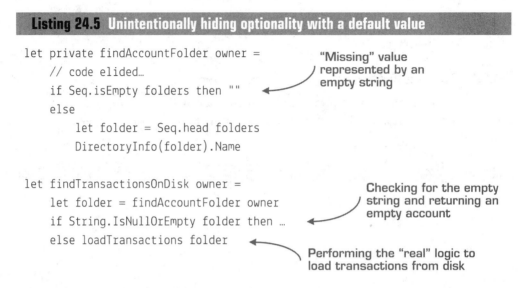

Listing 24.5   Unintentionally hiding optionality with a default value

```
let private findAccountFolder owner =
    // code elided...
    if Seq.isEmpty folders then ""
    else
        let folder = Seq.head folders
        DirectoryInfo(folder).Name
```
"Missing" value represented by an empty string

```
let findTransactionsOnDisk owner =
    let folder = findAccountFolder owner
    if String.IsNullOrEmpty folder then ...
    else loadTransactions folder
```
Checking for the empty string and returning an empty account

Performing the "real" logic to load transactions from disk

Here, you use an empty string to simulate the absence of a value. This is no better than using some magic number of –1 to indicate a missing number. And indeed, the calling findTransactionsOnDisk function has a check for an empty string that's used to indicate that no account exists on disk, and so you create a default account. Fix all this, starting from the ground up:

1   Change findAccountFolder to tryFindAccountFolder. In other words, have it return None if no folder was found, or Some folder name if it was.

2   For bonus points, convert the sequence of directories to a List and pattern match over it instead of the if/else expression.

3   Now fix findTransactionsOnDisk, which will be failing, by removing the empty string check and replacing it with a pattern match against the result of tryFind-AccountFolder.

4   Next, change this function to return an option output:

  a   If no account folder was found, return None.

  b   If an account folder was found, wrap the results of loadTransactions in Some.

24.3.3   Lifting functions to support options

Almost there! You've fixed the low-level file repository: it now returns account details from disk only if they exist. But now Program.fs is broken where you plug together two functions in loadAccountFromDisk, as indicated in figure 24.4.

ransactionsOnDisk >> Operations.loadAccount

> Type mismatch. Expecting a
>   (string * Guid * seq<Transaction>) option -> 'a
> but given a
>   string * Guid * 'b -> Account
> The type '(string * Guid * seq<Transaction>) option' does not match the type 'string * Guid * 'a'

Figure 24.4   Incompatible functions can't be composed together.

Don't be scared by this error! Start by looking at the signatures of the two functions you're trying to compose together:

```
tryFindTransactionsOnDisk: string -> (string * Guid * seq<Transaction>) option
loadAccount: (string * Guid * seq<Transaction) -> Account
```

The output of tryFindTransactionsOnDisk is now an *optional* tuple. The input of loadAccount only accepts a tuple; it doesn't want an optional tuple. Remember, when composing two functions, the type of output of the first *must* match the input type of the second.

The crude solution to this would be to "pollute" loadAccount to take in an optional tuple. Don't do this! A better approach is to create a new function that "lifts" the existing function to handle the optionality.

Listing 24.6   Manually lifting a function to work with an optional input

```
let loadAccountOptional value =
    match value with
    | Some value -> Some(Operations.loadAccount value)
    | None -> None
FileRepository.tryFindTransactionsOnDisk >> loadAccountOptional
```

Wrapping the existing loadAccount function with optionality

Using the newly lifted function in place of the original incompatible one

But there's a much quicker way to do this: anywhere you see this pattern of a match over an option, where the None branch also returns None, you can replace the whole thing with either Option.map or Option.bind. (You use the former if you had to manually wrap the result in the Some branch, as shown here, and the latter if the result from the lifted function was already an Option.)

Listing 24.7 Lifting a function to support options using `Option.map`

```
let loadAccountOptional = Option.map Operations.loadAccount
FileRepository.tryFindTransactionsOnDisk >> loadAccountOptional
```

Lifting a function to support
optionality using Option.map

Composing the newly
lifted function

This will now leave you with the composed `loadAccountFromDisk` with the signature of `string -> Account option`. It may return an account, but *only* if one existed on disk—perfect! At this point, you can rename the function to `tryLoadAccountFromDisk`.

Having done this, the last thing to do is (finally) leave the world of options and create a default account for a new user. The best place to do this is right at the top level, after capturing the user's name and trying to load their account from disk.

Listing 24.8 Creating a default account in the appropriate location

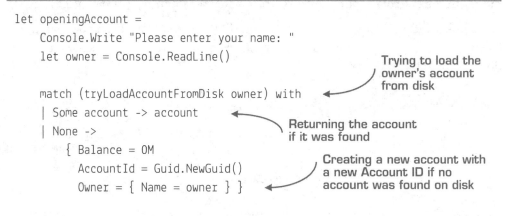

```
let openingAccount =
    Console.Write "Please enter your name: "
    let owner = Console.ReadLine()

    match (tryLoadAccountFromDisk owner) with
    | Some account -> account
    | None ->
        { Balance = 0M
          AccountId = Guid.NewGuid()
          Owner = { Name = owner } }
```

Trying to load the
owner's account
from disk

Returning the account
if it was found

Creating a new account with
a new Account ID if no
account was found on disk

24.4 Implementing business rules with types

This last section touches on how to enforce a slightly higher-level business rule through the type system:

A user can go into an overdrawn state (draw out more funds than they have in their account). But after the account has become overdrawn, the user can't draw out any more funds (although they can still deposit funds). After the balance returns to a non-negative state, the user can withdraw funds once again.

This is something that you could achieve with pattern matching during the withdraw process (replace the current check in `withdraw` so that it checks whether the account is already overdrawn rather than the current behavior of preventing users from being overdrawn at all). But let's try an alternate way: you can enforce this behavior through *types*. First, let's formalize the preceding business rule:

- An account can be in one of two states: *overdrawn* or *in credit*.
- Only an account that is in credit can withdraw funds.
- Any account can deposit funds.

Now model that in F# by enhancing your domain model a little, as in figure 24.5.

Listing 24.9 Modeling a rated account

```
type CreditAccount = CreditAccount of Account
type RatedAccount =
    | InCredit of CreditAccount
    | Overdrawn of Account
```

Marker type for an account in credit

Categorization of account

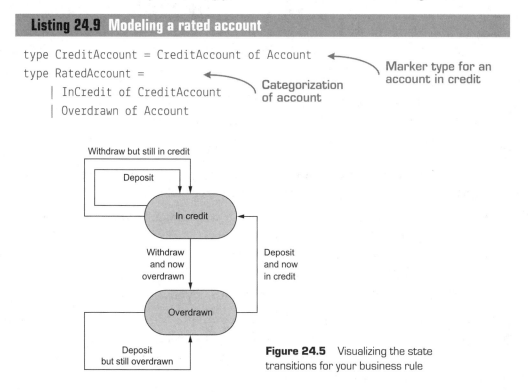

Figure 24.5 Visualizing the state transitions for your business rule

24.4.1 Testing a model with scripts

You've split an account in two paths, and have created a marker, or wrapper, type (`CreditAccount`) to indicate that a specific account is in credit. Now, you can update your core account operation functions.

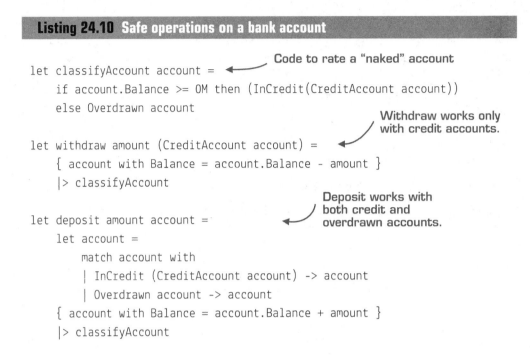

Listing 24.10 Safe operations on a bank account

Code to rate a "naked" account

```
let classifyAccount account =
    if account.Balance >= 0M then (InCredit(CreditAccount account))
    else Overdrawn account
```

Withdraw works only with credit accounts.

```
let withdraw amount (CreditAccount account) =
    { account with Balance = account.Balance - amount }
    |> classifyAccount
```

Deposit works with both credit and overdrawn accounts.

```
let deposit amount account =
    let account =
        match account with
        | InCredit (CreditAccount account) -> account
        | Overdrawn account -> account
    { account with Balance = account.Balance + amount }
    |> classifyAccount
```

I advise you to explore these functions in isolation within a script to get a "feel" for how they work before incorporating them into the code directly. In a nutshell

- classifyAccount is a helper function. It takes in a standard account and categorizes it based on the balance.
- withdraw now takes in only accounts that are in credit. It's not possible to call this function with an overdrawn account.
- deposit accepts both in-credit and overdrawn accounts.

Both withdraw and deposit return a RatedAccount back out; after performing the transaction, they check the current balance of the account, and if it's overdrawn, the account is categorized as Overdrawn, and the whole process begins again. This single function, classify-Account, is the only place allowed to create a RatedAccount.

You can test this easily within a script. As you see in figure 24.6, the compiler blocks you from calling withdraw directly on an account that might be overdrawn. You can get around this by writing a simple wrapper function to assist here that safely tries to withdraw funds and can be used in place of withdraw in the pipeline.

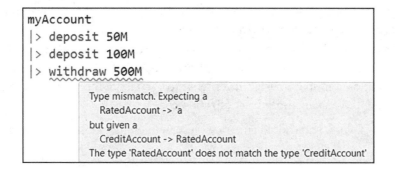

Figure 24.6   Compiler support for enforcing business rules

Listing 24.11   A safe withdrawal wrapper

```
let withdrawSafe amount ratedAccount =
    match ratedAccount with
    | Credit account -> account |> withdraw amount
    | Overdrawn _ ->
        printfn "Your account is overdrawn - withdrawal rejected!"
        ratedAccount // return input back out
```

The point is that you've now provided a barrier around the internal domain. The withdrawal operation doesn't need to perform any validation or checks on balances before carrying it out. Instead, this guarantee is performed by the compiler for you.

24.4.2 Plugging your new model back in

As an exercise, you should now try to plug this code back into the main application. You'll have to watch for several things:

- The loadAccount and processCommand functions need to be updated to work with the new model. Both need to explicitly handle the situation where an attempt is made to withdraw funds from an overdrawn account (rather than blindly passing it through to the underlying code). The nice thing with this approach is that it's now easy to reason about whether an account is overdrawn. You can pattern match over the account (an alternative would be to use an *active pattern*—something you haven't yet looked at, but you could in your own time).
- The auditAs function needs to be updated so that it works for both types of accounts. You need to refactor it carefully so that it works while retaining the ability to work with two types of accounts; take a look at the sample solution if

you get stuck. The `withAudit` composed functions at the top of the program will also need to be updated accordingly.

- You can probably completely remove the `Accepted` property from the `Transaction` record. It's now impossible to attempt a transaction that's rejected from your internal domain, so it doesn't make sense to keep it anymore (this will also mean updating the serialization/deserialization code).

With a little bit of work, you should end up with something that looks similar to figure 24.7.

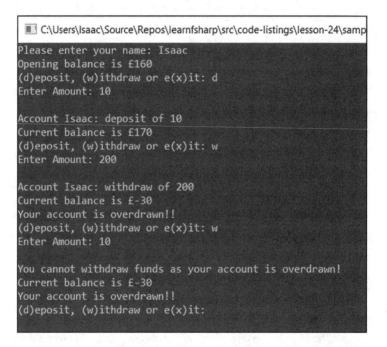

```
C:\Users\Isaac\Source\Repos\learnfsharp\src\code-listings\lesson-24\samp
Please enter your name: Isaac
Opening balance is £160
(d)eposit, (w)ithdraw or e(x)it: d
Enter Amount: 10

Account Isaac: deposit of 10
Current balance is £170
(d)eposit, (w)ithdraw or e(x)it: w
Enter Amount: 200

Account Isaac: withdraw of 200
Current balance is £-30
Your account is overdrawn!!
(d)eposit, (w)ithdraw or e(x)it: w
Enter Amount: 10

You cannot withdraw funds as your account is overdrawn!
Current balance is £-30
Your account is overdrawn!!
(d)eposit, (w)ithdraw or e(x)it:
```

Figure 24.7   Testing the bank account app by using a stronger domain model

The difference as compared to what you had at the start is that the validation layer has been forced "up" above the core domain, and you've now gained extra safety to prevent accidentally calling a function (withdraw) when you shouldn't (when the account is overdrawn).

 **Summary**

That's the end of this capstone. It's probably the hardest one you'll encounter in the entire book, as it focuses on concepts that you probably haven't touched on much in the past, such as using discriminated unions and a rich domain model to enforce business rules. Don't feel too disheartened if you struggled a little!

Living on the .NET platform

You've now finished with the language side of the book! The rest of the units cover areas relating to using those language features in a variety of scenarios, from data access to web programming. You'll focus on using the lessons you've learned so far in F# to perform similar tasks that you're doing today more quickly—and correctly—than you're used to. But don't think that this means there's nothing to learn—far from it!

The first area we'll cover is interoperating with the rest of .NET, which is dominated by C# code bases. You've already worked with the BCL throughout this book, but this unit focuses on larger issues, such as designing applications that work well in a multilanguage solution, as well as under what circumstances to rely on C# or F#. We'll also cover how to use NuGet packages in F# as easily as possible.

CONSUMING C# FROM F#

In the real world, you'll be hard-pressed to write a purely F# application. Not only are most of the NuGet packages out there written in C#, but the entire BCL is too. You've been working with C# types and objects from F# and so you know how to deal with the basics already, but a few extra areas are worth touching upon in order to round off this subject. We'll look at these topics:

- Creating hybrid solutions
- Using Visual Studio tools
- Consuming assemblies from scripts
- Consuming classes and interfaces in F#
- Safely working with nullable objects in F#

25.1 Referencing C# code in F#

In addition to working with the BCL code base, virtually any C# code you write today can be consumed from F#. This includes the following:

- All BCL code
- .NET assemblies including NuGet packages (see lesson 26)
- Sibling projects in the same solution

In other words, you can accomplish the same tasks in F# that you perform today in C#. With that bold statement in mind, let's see how to create a solution that uses both C# and F# code right now!

Dynamic F#

One area with richer support in C#, as compared to F#, is dynamic typing. F# does have *some* support for some dynamic typing through the custom ? operator, which allows you to handle dynamic member access in a similar vein to C#'s dynamic object types, but this feature is rarely used. F# also has meta-programming features such as type providers, which you'll see in the next unit, that somewhat alleviate the need for dynamic typing.

25.1.1 Creating a hybrid solution

Let's start with a simple solution that has some C# utility code that you'll call from an F# project. We'll then expand on this throughout the rest of this lesson.

Now you try

1   Open Visual Studio and create a new F# console application called FSharpProject.
2   Add a new C# class library called CSharpProject to the solution. Add a reference to the CSharpProject from the FSharpProject by using the standard Add Reference dialog box, shown in figure 25.1.

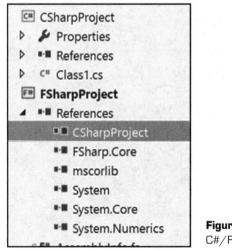

Figure 25.1   A hybrid C#/F# solution

That's it. You can now start to write code in C# and use it in F#! This sort of thing was the original aim of the .NET and CLR teams: to have the ability to mix and match languages across a common runtime, using each language where it fits best in terms of the problem domain at hand. Somewhat disappointingly, somewhere between 1999 and today, this message was more or less replaced with "use C# everywhere."

3 Open the Class1.cs file and replace the contents with a Person class as follows.

Listing 25.1 A simple C# class

```
public string Name { get; private set; }      ←— Public read-only
public Person(string name) {          ←— Constructor
    Name = name; }
public void PrintName() {            ←— Public method
    Console.WriteLine($"My name is {Name}"); }
```

4 Build the CSharpProject.
5 Now let's look at consuming this code from F#. First, replace the contents of the Program.fs file with the following.

Listing 25.2 Consuming C# code from F#

```
[<EntryPoint>]
let main argv =                        Calling the Person
    let tony = CSharpProject.Person "Tony"   ←—  constructor
    tony.PrintName()          ←—  Calling the
    0                              PrintName method
```

6 Run the application.

Quick check 25.1

1 Can you share F# and C# projects in the same solution?
2 Name some types of assets that you can reference from an F# solution.
3 What kind of type is not well supported in F#?

QC 25.1 answer

1 Yes.
2 Assemblies, sibling projects, and BCL code.
3 Dynamic types.

25.2 The Visual Studio experience

Working with multilanguage solutions in Visual Studio is generally a pain-free experience, although not always. Let's look at some common tasks you'll be familiar with, and how they work with hybrid-language solutions.

25.2.1 Debugging

You can debug an application that works across both languages, with no problems. You can set breakpoints in Visual Studio, and even see cross-language call stacks.

Now you try

Now try debugging F# in VS2015:

1   Set a breakpoint inside the definition C# `Person` class constructor.
2   Run the F# console application. Observe that the debugger hits with the `name` value set to `Tony`, as shown in figure 25.2.

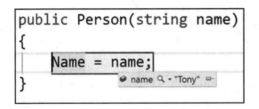

Figure 25.2   Debugging a C# function called from F#

3   Also, observe that the call stack is correctly preserved across the two languages, as shown in figure 25.3.

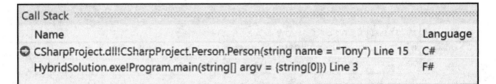

Figure 25.3   A cross-language call stack with both F# and C# stack frames

25.2.2 Navigating across projects

We're used to many of the standard Visual Studio refactoring and navigation features. Visual F# Power Tools adds many of these to F#, including Rename, Find All References, and Go to Definition. Unfortunately, these don't work across languages (my understanding is that this is not an "F#" thing; it's the same across VB .NET and C#, too). For example, Find All References will trap references only in projects of the language that you're currently in; similarly, if you attempt to use the Go to Definition navigation feature on the C# `Person` constructor from F#, you'll instead be taken to the F# metadata view of the C# class, as shown in figure 25.4.

```
namespace CSharpProject

type Person =
    new : name:string -> Person
    member Name : string with get, set
    member PrintName : unit -> unit
```

Figure 25.4 F# metadata view of a C# type

This is unfortunate, but (at least in my experience), it's not a massive show stopper. However, it is something that you should be aware of.

25.2.3 Projects and assemblies

You'll notice that I stressed during the previous exercise to first build the C# project *before* trying to access it from the F# project. That's because Visual Studio doesn't automatically cascade code changes as they're made across languages. You have to first build the dependent assembly before you can see the changes in the client project. If you make a change to code in the C# project, you'll need to explicitly build that project before you can "see" the changes in F#.

25.2.4 Referencing assemblies in scripts

Just as a project file has project and assembly references, so can scripts. The difference is that a project file contains the references embedded within the .csproj or .fsproj file; there's no such notion as a project file for scripts, as they're self-standing. Instead, F# provides a few useful directives in F# scripts, listed in table 25.1.

Table 25.1　F# script commands

Directive	Description	Example usage
#r	References a DLL for use within a script	#r @"C:\source\app.dll"
#I	Adds a path to the #r search path	#I @"C:\source\"
#load	Loads and executes an F# .fsx or .fs file	#load @"C:\source\code.fsx"

Using these directives opens up all sorts of interesting possibilities with scripts when working with third-party code, as you can quickly reference external code and experiment with them in a scratchpad environment. You'll see this in more detail later in this unit. Note that the preceding examples all use absolute paths, but (as you'll see) you can also use paths that are relative to the script location.

Now you try

Now experiment with referencing an assembly within a script:

1　Create a new script as a new solution item called Scratchpad.fsx.

2　Open the script file and enter the following code.

Listing 25.3　Consuming C# assemblies from an F# script

```
#r @"CSharpProject\bin\debug\CSharpProject.dll"

open CSharpProject
let simon = Person "Simon"
simon.PrintName()
```

Standard F# code to utilize the newly referenced types

Referencing the CSharpProject from an F# script. Relative references work relative to the script location.

3　Execute the code in the script by using the standard Send to F# Interactive behavior. Notice the first line that's output in FSI:

```
--> Referenced 'C:\[path elided]\CSharpProject\bin\debug\CSharpProject.dll'
(file may be locked by F# Interactive process)
```

You use @ to treat backslashes as literals. Note that if your script lives in a different location, the #r line might not work. If that's the case, navigate to where it is in Windows Explorer in order to identify the correct path.

25.2.5 Debugging scripts

Visual Studio also allows you to debug F# scripts! I've purposely steered away from this because debugging can, in my opinion, be a costly way to identify issues as opposed to designing small, simple functions with minimal dependencies. But sometimes it's necessary, particularly if you're using your script as a harness with which to test, for example, C# code.

Now you try

Let's debug the script that you already have open to see how it operates in VS2015:

1. With the script from listing 25.3 still open, right-click line 3 (the constructor call line) with your mouse.
2. From the pop-up menu, choose Debug with F# Interactive.
3. After a short delay, you'll see the line highlighted, as shown in figure 25.5. From there, you can choose the regular Step Into code as usual.

```
open CSharpProject
let simon = Person "Simon"
simon.PrintName()   ≤ 3,532ms elapsed
```

Figure 25.5   Debugging an F# script in Visual Studio 2015

4. You can also do the same by using the keyboard shortcut Ctrl-Alt-Enter.
5. When you've finished debugging, you can click Stop from the toolbar, or press Shift-F5 to stop the debugging session.

Quick check 25.2

1. Can you debug across languages?
2. Can you go to a definition across languages?
3. How do you reference a library from within a script?

QC 25.2 answer

1. Yes. This works out of the box in Visual Studio 2015.
2. Partially. Visual Studio will show you metadata for the defined type in the language you've just come from.
3. Using the #r directive.

25.3 Working with OO constructs

Let's move away from looking at Visual Studio tooling features now, and back to some language-level concerns, by seeing how F# improves on standard C# object-oriented constructs such as constructors and interfaces. Notice in listing 25.3 that that you don't need to bother with the `new` keyword when calling constructors (or supply brackets for single-argument constructors). That's because F# considers a constructor to be a function that, when called, returns an instance of the type (in this case, `Person`), so you can use constructors in the same way as any function. For example, let's say you want to create five `Person` objects by using a list of names. Here are two ways you can do this.

Listing 25.4 Treating constructors as functions

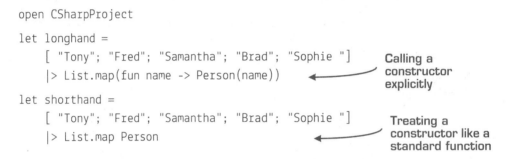

```
open CSharpProject

let longhand =
    [ "Tony"; "Fred"; "Samantha"; "Brad"; "Sophie " ]
    |> List.map(fun name -> Person(name))
let shorthand =
    [ "Tony"; "Fred"; "Samantha"; "Brad"; "Sophie " ]
    |> List.map Person
```

Calling a constructor explicitly

Treating a constructor like a standard function

The first version would have been typical code in F# 3, but since F# 4 you can use the shorthand second version. The `Person` constructor is a function taking in a string, which is the single argument used in `List.map` here, so you can omit the argument entirely.

25.3.1 Working with interfaces

Like classes, interfaces are a fact of life in the .NET framework. They can sometimes be useful in F# as well, particularly when working with pluggable pieces of code that need to change at runtime. As such, F# has good support for implementing them, both at the language and at the tooling level.

Here's how to create a simple instance of a standard BCL interface in F#: the `System.Collections.Generic.IComparer` interface. This interface enables you to tell whether one object is greater than, less than, or equal to another object of the same type. Let's see how to create, and consume, an instance of this interface in F#.

Listing 25.5 Treating constructors as functions

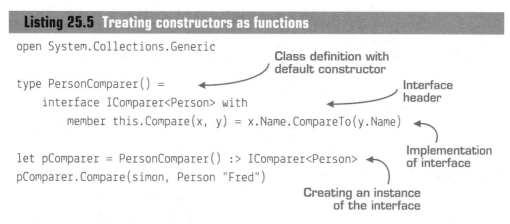

```
open System.Collections.Generic
                                              Class definition with
                                              default constructor
type PersonComparer() =
    interface IComparer<Person> with                        Interface
                                                            header
        member this.Compare(x, y) = x.Name.CompareTo(y.Name)

                                                        Implementation
let pComparer = PersonComparer() :> IComparer<Person>   of interface
pComparer.Compare(simon, Person "Fred")
                                           Creating an instance
                                           of the interface
```

The first few lines of this snippet are reasonably self-explanatory, although one point of interest is that the Compare function doesn't need any type annotations for x and y. These are inferred in F# by the generic type argument <Person>. It's important to note, however, that you have to explicitly upcast from your PersonComparer type to IComparer<Person> by using the :> operator. This is because F# implements interfaces *explicitly*, so without this cast, you wouldn't be able to call the Compare method. You can also define explicit interface implementations in C#, but it's generally not used. If you haven't used explicit interfaces before, see https://docs.microsoft.com/en-us/dotnet/articles/csharp/programming-guide/interfaces/explicit-interface-implementation for more details (they're a fully supported feature of C#).

Now you try

F# Power Tools comes with a handy refactoring to implement an interface for you:

1 Enter the first three lines from listing 25.5.
2 Remove the with keyword from the third line.
3 Move the caret to the start of IComparer in the same line.
4 You'll be presented with a smart tag (figure 25.6). Press Ctrl-period to open it.
5 Try both forms of generation. The first (nonlightweight) will generate an implementation with fully annotated type signatures; the latter will omit type annotations if possible and place method declarations with stub implementations on a single line.

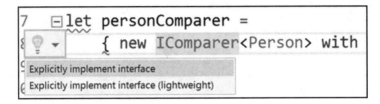

Figure 25.6   The VFPT Implement Interface refactoring

25.3.2 Object expressions

F# has another trick up its sleeve for working with interfaces, called *object expressions*. Object expressions let you create an instance of an interface without creating an intermediary type. Sounds impossible, right? Here's what it looks like.

Listing 25.6 Using object expressions to create an instance of an interface

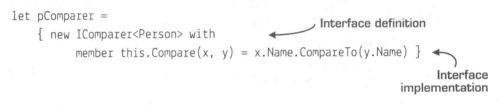

```
let pComparer =
    { new IComparer<Person> with
        member this.Compare(x, y) = x.Name.CompareTo(y.Name) }
```

The type of pComparer here is IComparer<Person>. Its "real" name is generated by the compiler, and you can never see this (unless using reflection). Using object expressions allows you to skip over the need to manually construct a type to hold the implementation. You can create the implementation of the interface as an *object* in one step!

25.3.3 Nulls, nullables, and options

You saw in lesson 19 how to work with options. The problem is that C# classes and structs don't work natively with options. How do you marry these two worlds? Well, since F# 4, you also have a few handy combinators in the Option module that allow you to easily jump between F# options and classes, which are always potentially null, and structs that are wrapped as nullables.

Listing 25.7 Option combinators for classes and nullable types

```
open System

let blank:string = null
let name = "Vera"
let number = Nullable 10
```
Creating a selection of null and non-null strings and value types

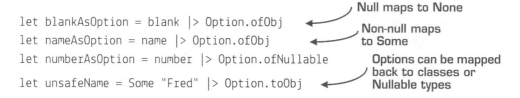

```
let blankAsOption = blank |> Option.ofObj
let nameAsOption = name |> Option.ofObj
let numberAsOption = number |> Option.ofNullable
let unsafeName = Some "Fred" |> Option.toObj
```

Null maps to None

Non-null maps to Some

Options can be mapped back to classes or Nullable types

In this way, you can safely map from other applications or libraries (which return data that may or may not be null) into a "safe" F# domain that allows you to more easily reason about nullability of data. Then, when leaving F# and going back to the C# or VB .NET world, you can use Option.toObj to go back to the "unsafe" world of potentially null classes.

Quick check 25.3

1 What is an object expression?
2 How do you convert between a nullable and an option in F#?

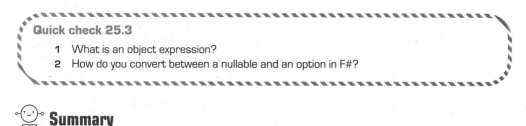

Summary

Hopefully, that was a relatively gentle introduction to the second half of this book! You learned about the following:

- Multilanguage .NET solutions
- Visual Studio tooling support
- Tricks for working with scripts
- F# language features that allow you to easily work with C# constructs

Try this

Take any existing C# / VB .NET solution that you have, add an F# class library project to it, and reference your C# library (alternatively, create an F# script and reference the C# DLL by using the #r directive). Try to create some of your C# types from F#. If your application has some form of console runner, try to rewrite it as an F# console application. Explore driving your existing OO code from F#.

QC 25.3 answer

1 An F# language feature that allows you to create instances of interfaces without a formal implementation type.
2 Using the Option.ofNullable and Option.toNullable helper functions.

26

LESSON

WORKING WITH NUGET PACKAGES

In the preceding lesson, you spent time working with non-F# projects from F#, as well as learning a few tricks on working with scripts. In this lesson, you'll move on to working with dependencies within scripts and projects, rather than writing standalone scripts. You'll see

- How to work with NuGet packages in F#
- Tips and tricks when working with scripts
- What the Paket dependency manager is

 26.1 Using NuGet with F#

The good news is that NuGet packages work out of the box with F# projects in Visual Studio. There's no difference compared to working with C#!

26.1.1 Working with NuGet with F# projects

Let's first see how NuGet packages work with F#.

Now you try

You're going to download a NuGet package from the main public NuGet server and use it within an F# class library:

1   Create a new F# class library in Visual Studio called NugetFSharp.
2   Using the standard Manage NuGet Packages dialog box, add the Newtonsoft .Json package to the project.
3   You'll see that the package is downloaded and added as a reference, as in your C# project. You can now use it directly from your F# source files.
4   Change the contents of the Library1.fs file to the following code.

Listing 26.1   Using Newtonsoft.Json in F#

```
module Library1

open Newtonsoft.Json                                    Defining an
type Person = { Name : string; Age : int }              F# record

let getPerson() =
    let text = """{ "Name" : "Sam", "Age" : 18 }"""
    let person = JsonConvert.DeserializeObject<Person>(text)
    printfn "Name is %s with age %d." person.Name person.Age
    person                                              Using
                                                        Newtonsoft.Json to
      Sample JSON text that                             deserialize the object
      matches your record structure
```

Here are some interesting points to note:

- You use triple-quoted strings here to allow you to use single quotes within the string without the need to prefix with a backslash.
- Newtonsoft.Json works out of the box with F# record types! It'll automatically map JSON fields to F# record fields, as with C# class properties.

The main takeaway from this, though, is that you can use virtually any NuGet package with F#. You can benefit from all of the existing libraries out there, while still using the stronger type system, more succinct syntax, and powerful compiler of F#.

26.1.2 Experimenting with scripts

One of the nicer things that you can do with the F# REPL is to use it in conjunction with NuGet packages to quickly and easily explore and test a new NuGet package, or to put together a quick proof of concept that you're working on. Let's see what I'm talking about.

Let's imagine that you need to test a new NuGet package that your team has decided to start using on an existing project. You'll probably look on the website of the package (if there is one), skim through the Getting Started section of the documentation (again, if there is one), and then download the package to your solution. Finally, you'll try to embed this package within the context of your application. This is a common approach, but usually one fraught with problems. For example, testing the package within the context of your application might be difficult. What if that code is called in only specific circumstances that are difficult to reproduce?

Alternatively, perhaps you'll use unit tests or a console application to prove how it works, but we've already discussed how those are poor ways to experiment and explore. It's much more productive to use a script to test how a package works—in isolation—so that you can learn how to use it properly; only then, after you're confident in how it works, do you add it to your code base.

Now you try

Next you'll add another NuGet package to your project, and work with both this and Newtonsoft.Json from within a script:

1 Add the Humanizer NuGet package to the project. This package can take arbitrary strings and try to make them more human-readable.
2 Open Script1.fsx, which was already added to the project on creation.
3 Reference the Humanizer assembly in your script by using the #r directive you saw earlier in this unit. The simplest option is to open the References node in Solution Explorer, shown in figure 26.1, get properties of the Humanizer DLL, copy the entire path into the clipboard, and then enter the following code

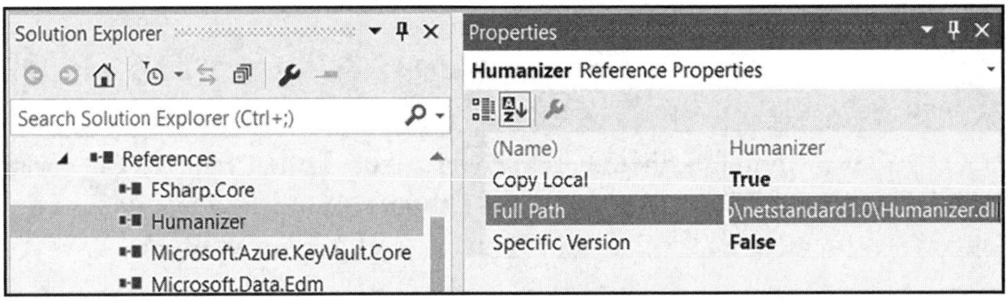

Figure 26.1   Determining the full path of an assembly from a NuGet package

Listing 26.2 Referencing an assembly from a NuGet package

```
#r @"<path to Humanizer.dll>"
open Humanizer
"ScriptsAreAGreatWayToExplorePackages".Humanize()
```

Referencing an assembly by using #r

4 Execute the code; the output in FSI should be `Scripts are a great way to explore packages`.

5 Explore the overloads of the Humanize method in the REPL (for example, one takes in a `LetterCasing` argument).

The main point to see here is that you've used a script to quickly get access to a NuGet package that you've downloaded, and started to explore how it works in an isolated and safe environment. It's much quicker to do this in a script, as you get immediate feedback in the REPL for what's going on. Plus, because you're working in a script file, you can save the script and use it again later, or use it as a form of documentation to show other developers how to use a dependency correctly!

> **Sending references to FSI**
>
> You can also right-click any assembly and choose the Send to F# Interactive option, which sends #r directly to FSI. But your scripts won't "know" about the reference and so won't give you IntelliSense, and you'll need to redo it every time you reset FSI. Explicitly adding #r to your scripts is a much better option.

26.1.3 Loading source files in scripts

Next you'll use the code you wrote earlier in listing 26.1 within a script.

Listing 26.3 Loading a source file into a script with a NuGet dependency

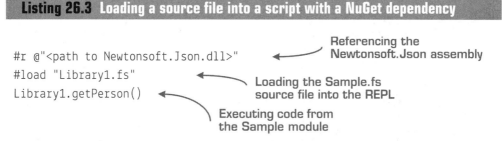

```
#r @"<path to Newtonsoft.Json.dll>"
#load "Library1.fs"
Library1.getPerson()
```

Referencing the Newtonsoft.Json assembly

Loading the Sample.fs source file into the REPL

Executing code from the Sample module

Here, you load the Library1.fs source file and call a function exposed by it. An important point to note here is that you have to explicitly reference the Newtonsoft.Json assembly before loading the script; this is required, as Library1.fs uses the Newtonsoft namespace. If you comment out the line that references Newtonsoft.Json, you'll see an error, as shown in figure 26.2.

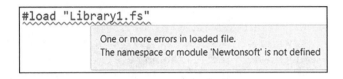

Figure 26.2 Trying to load a source file without having referenced a required dependency

Also be aware that if you #load an .fs file into a script, any other .fs files that it depends on will need to be loaded first!

26.1.4 Improving the referencing experience

The way you're referencing assemblies here has a couple of problems. First, you're copying the full absolute path, which is useless if you're going to share a script with other developers on your team. Second, a load of repetition exists in the paths for both Humanizer and Newtonsoft.Json. You can fix that as follows.

Listing 26.4 Loading a source file into a script with a NuGet dependency

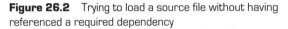

```
#I  @"..\packages\"
 #r @"Humanizer.Core.2.1.0\lib\netstandard1.0\Humanizer.dll"
 #r @"Newtonsoft.Json.9.0.1\lib\net45\Newtonsoft.Json.dll"
```

Add the "..\packages\" folder to the   Simplified NuGet
search list by using a relative path.   package reference

You've moved to using a relative path to the script location (..\packages\) rather than an absolute path. This means you can share this script with the rest of the team; in addition, you've used the #I directive so you don't have to retype that in every #r directive. You also could have not bothered with the #I directive, and copied that to the start of both the #r directives.

> **NuGet and project references**
>
> The way NuGet interacts with .NET projects is going through something of a redesign in the next version of the .NET project system; projects might even be able to reference the NuGet package directly (rather than assemblies in those packages). Similarly, there's talk of a #nuget directive that might be added to F# scripts, but that's speculation at this point.

26.1.5 Using autogenerated references

Even when using the #I trick, maintaining the list of dependencies in a script (in the correct order!) can be a pain. Thankfully, F# Power Tools has a solution to the issue of referencing project and source files.

Now you try

Now use the autogenerated references from Power Tools to see how it can help matters:

1 Right-click the References node of the project and select the Generate References for F# Interactive option.

2 A new folder, scripts, is created in the project, along with two files: load-references and load-project, as shown in figure 26.3.

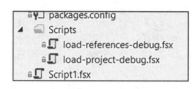

Figure 26.3 Generated script files from Visual F# Power Tools

3 Open the two files. You'll see that the former contains #r directives for all referenced assemblies, and the latter contains #load for every source file in the project (and calls the references file too!).

4 Remove all the #r and #load directives from the script you created, and replace them with a single `#load @"Scripts\load-project-debug.fsx"`.

What's especially good about this is that the files are regenerated whenever new dependencies or files are added to the project, so you don't have to maintain them manually.

> **When can't I use autogenerated references?**
>
> If you're sticking with Visual Studio and F# projects, autogenerated references files work fine. But if you have a C#-only solution and still want to use F# scripts for exploration (which is not uncommon), you have two options. First, although you can use standalone F# scripts in a C# project (or as a solution item), you won't get the autogenerated reference scripts, as these are available to create only in F# projects. The alternative is to create an F# project that contains nothing but your exploratory scripts, and within which you can also create the autogenerated reference scripts.

26.2 Working with Paket

NuGet is a great tool. It simplifies sharing dependencies across .NET projects and acts as a central repository for reusable .NET components. But it has several shortcomings, partly due to the way in which it first came into being, and partly due to design decisions that were made over the years.

Paket is an open source, flexible, and powerful dependency management client for .NET that aims to simplify dependency management in .NET. It's backward-compatible with the NuGet service, so you can continue to use existing NuGet packages, but it provides an alternative client-side application that replaces the existing NuGet client and that also adds a whole host of new features. It's written in F# but is fully compatible with C#, VB .NET, and F# projects and solutions. (Disclaimer: I'm one of the contributors to the Paket project.)

There's another reason I'm showing you Paket: if you look at virtually any F# open source project, or start to read any F# examples online, virtually all of them will use Paket rather than NuGet. Therefore, it's definitely worth your while to get up to speed with Paket sooner rather than later.

26.2.1 Issues with the NuGet client

Here are a few issues you've probably come up against in the past with NuGet:

- *Invalid references across projects*—NuGet doesn't prevent you from adding the same package, but with different versions, to two projects. You may have a reference to Newtonsoft.Json version 6 in Project A, and version 7 in Project B within the same solution. You won't get a compile error, but might get a runtime error, depending on any number of factors.

- *Updates project file on upgrade*—Every time you update a NuGet dependency, the project file changes, because NuGet packages store the version in the physical path. This can cause merge conflicts as well as unnecessary changes to the project file.

- *Hard to reference from scripts*—Because the physical path is stored in the packages folder, scripts are tightly coupled to packages. If you update a package, your scripts will break (unless you're using the generated references file from VFPT).

- *Difficulty managing*—NuGet is difficult to reason about on large solutions (or multiple solution-sharing projects), because NuGet doesn't have a unified view of dependencies across all projects or solutions (although, admittedly, NuGet 3 did put in some UI tricks to make this experience a little better). How often have you worked on a large solution or project and deliberately put off upgrading NuGet packages because you're afraid that upgrading will somehow break something?

26.2.2 Benefits of Paket

Paket addresses all of the preceding issues, as well as adding several new features, including these:

- *Dependency resolver*—Paket understands your dependencies across all projects in your solution (or repository), and will keep all your dependencies stable across all projects. It won't allow you to accidentally upgrade a version of a dependency for only a part of your solution.

- *Easy to reason about*—You don't have to worry about child dependencies of NuGet packages. Paket allows you to focus on the top-level dependencies, while it internally manages the children for you without your needing to worry about them.

- *Fast*—Paket is extremely fast, with an intelligent resolver and caching mechanism so that restoring packages occurs as quickly as possible.

- *Lightweight*—Paket is a command-line-first tool. It has an extension for Visual Studio as well, but this is essentially a wrapper around the command-line tool, rather than the other way around. You don't need a GUI to add packages to your solution or project; the configuration files are plain text, lightweight, and easy to maintain.

- *Source code dependencies*—You can have a dependency on, for example, a specific commit of a GitHub file. This is extremely useful when working with tiny dependencies (for example, helper or utility modules or the like) that don't justify creating a NuGet package.

Why am I showing you Paket here? One of the things you'll notice if you start working with any F# open source projects in the future is that virtually all of them use Paket rather than NuGet. It not only has many advantages over NuGet, but also plays much more nicely with F#. Scripts work more easily with Paket-sourced dependencies, and it doesn't couple you to Visual Studio if you decide you want to, for example, use Visual Studio Code (or any other IDE for that matter).

Now you try

In this exercise, you'll convert your existing package from NuGet to Paket:

1 In the existing solution, add the WindowsAzure.Storage NuGet package.

2 Open the packages.config file. Observe that it has approximately 50 NuGet packages. Which package is dependent on which? Why are you seeing 50 packages when you asked for only three (Humanizer, Newtonsoft.Json, and Windows-Azure.Storage)?

3 Navigate to the latest Paket release and download the Paket.exe application (https://github.com/fsprojects/Paket/releases/latest) to the root folder (alongside the solution file).

4 Delete the entire packages folder.

5 Open a command prompt and navigate to the root folder of the solution.

6 Run `paket convert-from-nuget`. Paket converts the solution from NuGet tooling to Paket. Observe the following:

   a All packages are downloaded in the packages folder but without version numbers. Paket doesn't include version numbers in paths. This makes referencing NuGet packages much easier from F# scripts!

   b Two new files have been created: paket.dependencies and paket.lock. The former file contains a list of all top-level dependencies and is designed to be human readable and editable; the latter contains the tree of interdependencies.

   c Your project is updated so all NuGet packages reference the new (version-free) paths.

7 Run `paket simplify`. This parses the dependencies and strips out any packages from the paket.dependencies file that aren't top-level ones. Observe that the dependencies file contains only two dependencies: Humanizer and Windows-Azure.Storage (Json is a dependency of WindowsAzure.Storage). The lock file still maintains the full tree of dependencies.

8 You can now open Script1.fsx; observe that the references are currently broken. Rebuilding the solution regenerates the references script to point to the correct locations. Notice that the paths no longer have the version numbers in them. In the future, updating NuGet dependencies in Paket won't break scripts that reference assemblies simply because the version changed.

There's tons more to learn about Paket than I've shown you here, so it's well worth looking on the Paket website at its documentation. It contains guidance on all the features and quick starts, and it has a responsive team that will answer questions on GitHub or Twitter.

26.2.3 Common Paket commands

Here are some common Paket commands:

- `paket update`—Updates your packages with the latest versions from NuGet. By default, Paket selects the highest version of any package available and intelligently ensures that the latest versions are compatible across all your dependencies.
- `paket restore`—Brings down the current version of all dependencies specified in the lock file. Useful for CI processes to ensure repeatable builds.
- `paket add`—Allows you to add a new NuGet package to the overall set of dependencies (for example, `paket add nuget Automapper project NugetFSharp` gets the latest version of the `Automapper` NuGet package and adds it to the `NugetFSharp` project).
- `Paket generate-load-scripts`—Generates a set of .fsx files that call #r on all assemblies in a package and their dependencies.

There's also a Visual Studio extension for Paket (available in Visual Studio Extensions and Updates), which provides much of this functionality directly within Visual Studio.

Paket as an example of open source collaboration

Paket is a good example of how open source, community-led projects can work. What started as a small project with a couple of developers now has dozens of contributors and is used in many organizations. It's a good example of how a set of developers saw what they felt was room for improvement in the existing NuGet story, and were able to rapidly create a new tool that fits the needs of many developers. Many of the features in Paket were originally thought to be unimportant by the NuGet team, but now there are signs that some of those features might be introduced into NuGet at some point.

⫸

(continued)

I should point out that this hasn't always been a pain-free journey. The Paket and NuGet teams haven't always had the most positive relationship (although this has improved over time). Also, if you're used to the somewhat lethargic pace of NuGet updates, you might be in for a shock with Paket. It's not unusual to have intra-day updates and fixes to the tool!

Quick check 26.2

1   Why can it be difficult to work with NuGet packages from F# scripts when using the NuGet tool?
2   What does the paket.dependencies file contain?

Summary

In this lesson, you got your hands dirty with NuGet and F#. You did the following:

- Saw how to, and why you might want to, use NuGet packages within F# scripts
- Learned tips for how to make working with scripts even easier through Visual F# Power Tools
- Got a brief introduction to the Paket dependency manager

Try this

Take an existing .NET solution you've been working on. Try first to create an F# project in the solution, referencing the same NuGet packages as the C# project. Then, generate a references script to the project and see whether you can start to work with those NuGet packages from your own script! Try converting the solution from NuGet to Paket. You might even find that Paket refuses to convert if discrepancies exist in your NuGet configuration (such as different versions of the same package)!

QC 26.2 answer

1   NuGet uses the version number of the package within the path of the package, so every time you update a package, your F# scripts will break.
2   The set of top-level dependencies for your solution.

27

EXPOSING F# TYPES AND FUNCTIONS TO C#

In this unit (and indeed throughout this book), you've concentrated on how to consume C# from F#. But it's common to also go the *other* way, and write libraries in F# and consume them in C#. For example, you might create a data access layer in F# underneath a C# GUI, or write a general-purpose NuGet package in F# that can be consumed in both C# and F#. This lesson covers the following:

- F# data types
- Namespaces and modules
- F# functions
- Gotchas when consuming F# code from C#

Even in an existing code base that's mostly C#, you'll still want to work with F# in some cases. We'll cover more of this in the coming lessons, but it's not that unusual—particularly when working on larger projects or with existing code bases. The following section provides some examples of interoperating between F# and C#.

27.1 Using F# types in C#

We're fortunate that the F# team spent time looking at the situations that arise when exposing data created in F# to C#, because they've done a great job in nearly all common cases. As you'll see, F# data types all boil down to primitives that you already know; it's simply that the F# language allows us to work with those same primitives at a higher level. Let's first look at the common F# data types we discussed in the first half of the book.

27.1.1 Records

Records map extremely well in C#. They appear as regular classes, with a nondefault constructor that takes in all fields exposed in the record. A default constructor *won't* normally be generated, so it won't be possible to create the record in an uninitialized (or partially initialized) state. Each field will appear as a public getter-only property, and the class will implement various interfaces in order to allow structural equality checking. Also, although I've not shown it in this book, you can create member functions on a record. These are exposed as methods in C#.

Now you try

Let's see how to create a mixed solution, which you'll use to create a number of F# types and explore how they render in C#:

1 Create a new solution in Visual Studio, Interop.

2 Create an F# class library, FSharp-Code.

3 Create a C# console application, CSharpApp.

4 Reference the FSharpCode project from the CSharpApp project so that you can access the F# types from the C# project, as shown in figure 27.1.

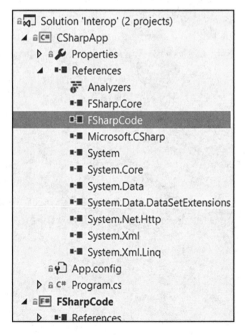

Figure 27.1 Creating a mixed-language solution and referencing F# from C#

5 Open Library1.fs, remove the sample class definition, and rebuild the solution.

6 In Library1.fs, create a simple record type to model a car, taking care to change the namespace as shown in the following listing

Listing 27.1 An F# record to be accessed from C#

```
namespace Model

/// A standard F# record of a Car.
type Car =
    { /// The number of wheels on the car.
      Wheels : int
      /// The brand of the car.
      Brand : string }
```

Record definition using lightweight triple-slash comments

7 Now that you've created the type, go to Program.cs and within the Main() method, try typing Model to get IntelliSense for the namespace. You'll see that nothing appears! This is because C# and F# projects can (currently) see changes in code only after you've compiled the child project—in this case, the F# project.

8 Go ahead and rebuild the solution. You'll see that you can now create an instance of the F# record type, although it appears as a class to C#, as shown in figure 27.2.

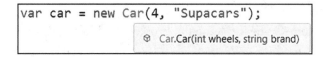

```
var car = new Car(4, "Supacars");
                    ⊙  Car.Car(int wheels, string brand)
```

Figure 27.2 Creating an F# record from C#

9 Notice that you can access getter-only properties on the car that map to the fields. Also observe that the triple-slash comments show in tooltips.

10 Try to use Go To Definition (F12) from the C# project when the caret is over the Car type. Observe that a C# rendering of the F# type, based on its IL metadata, is shown. Also notice the interfaces that are implemented for structural equality (for example, IEquatable<T> and IComparable<T>), as well as override Equals and Get-HashCode.

27.1.2 Tuples

Tuples in F# are instances of the standard System.Tuple type, so they appear as such when consumed from C#, with standard Item1, Item2, and ItemN properties. The standard .NET tuple type supports up to only eight items, so F# has a trick up its sleeve here: if you have a tuple wider than eight items—let's say ten items—the eighth element of the tuple will itself be another tuple that has the last three items. But I strongly recommend avoiding *ever* getting into a situation where you have a tuple more than three items wide. Stick to records for such a case.

Tuples in C# 7

C# 7 will almost certainly have language support for tuples, much as F# currently has. But this will be a brand-new type (most likely called `System.ValueTuple`) that, unlike `System.Tuple`, is a value type. To seamlessly interoperate with this, the next version of F# will introduce a new `struct` keyword, which you'll use to tell the F# compiler to also use `System.ValueTuple`, so that exposing this to C# should allow you to take advantage of C# language support as well. For now there's nothing to worry about.

27.1.3 Discriminated unions

Remember that discriminated unions in F# are roughly equivalent to a class hierarchy in C#, except that they're a *closed* set of classes. And, sure enough, if you try to consume a discriminated union from F#, that's exactly what you'll see: a set of classes (one per case), along with a set of static helper methods to allow you to both easily check which case the value is, and to create instances of a case yourself.

But be aware that there's one fundamental problem with using discriminated unions in C#. Without any support for pattern matching (something that will be partially rectified in C# 7—it'll probably have support matching over type checks), you'll quickly find that it can be painful to reason about a discriminated union in C#. Remember that in C# with inheritance, behaviors are part of the class, and you use polymorphism to access different implementations through virtual dispatch. Discriminated unions don't have behaviors on them, but rather separate standalone functions that operate over all *cases* through pattern matching.

Now you try

Let's see how to enhance your solution to illustrate tuples and discriminated unions:

   1 Update Library1.fs as follows.

Listing 27.2 Creating tuples and discriminated unions in F#

```
/// A standard F# record of a Car.
type Car =
    { /// The number of wheels on the car.
      Wheels : int
      /// The brand of the car.
      Brand : string
      /// The x/y of the car in meters
      Dimensions : float * float }
```
← A property on the record that's a tuple

```
/// A vehicle of some sort.
type Vehicle =
    /// A car is a type of vehicle.
| Motorcar of Car
    /// A bike is also a type of vehicle.
| Motorbike of Name:string * EngineSize:float
```
← A discriminated union using both record and inline arguments

2 Rebuild the F# project, and then correct the C# to create a Car. You need to pass in a Tuple<Float, Float> for the new argument—for example, Tuple.Create(1.5, 3.5).

3 Notice that if you access the Dimensions property on the car, you'll get Item1 and Item2 for X and Y.

Let's now look at discriminated unions. You created a discriminated union in listing 27.2 that has two cases: Motorcar and Motorbike.

4 In IntelliSense, navigating to Model.Vehicle is shown in figure 27.3.

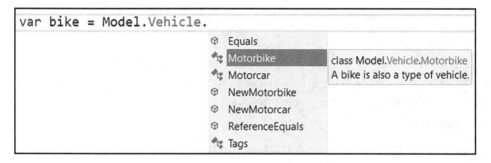

```
var bike = Model.Vehicle.
```
- Equals
- **Motorbike**   class Model.Vehicle.Motorbike
- Motorcar   A bike is also a type of vehicle.
- NewMotorbike
- NewMotorcar
- ReferenceEquals
- Tags

Figure 27.3 Creating cases of a discriminated union from C#

You can see both cases as nested types underneath the `Vehicle` type. Beware: there are no constructors available for either case. Instead, you're provided with *builder* methods such as `NewMotorbike` that allow you to create instances of the cases.

5 Create an instance of a `Motorbike`.

6 The type of value returned will be `Vehicle`—not `Motorbike`! In order to test which type the variable is, you need to use the `IsMotorbike` and `IsMotorcar` properties on the vehicle instance, and then cast it as appropriate. Only then will you be able to access the properties on the `Motorbike` itself.

This forces you to adopt a clear separation between data and behavior, and use type-based pattern matching (which in C# 6 means resorting to casts or the `as` keyword) to access the "real" data.

Quick check 27.1

1 How are records represented in C#?

2 Why are discriminated unions sometimes difficult to reason about in C#?

27.2 More on F# interoperability

Let's quickly run through other interop scenarios for F# and C#.

27.2.1 Using namespaces and modules

You've seen how to use namespaces and modules to logically group types and functions together in F#. How are they exposed in C#, though?

F# namespaces in C#

Namespaces in F# are not only logically the same as in C#; they're essentially exactly the same thing. If you make a type within a namespace in an F# assembly, you can reference it in C# by using the exact same namespace. Easy.

Modules in C#

A module is rendered in C# as a static class. Any simple values on the module such as an integer or a record value will show as a public property. Functions will show as

---

methods on the static class, and types will show as nested classes within the static class. As you can see, there's a pretty good mapping for these. You probably won't even know that you're accessing an F# module from C#!

27.2.2 Using F# functions in C#

As you know, functions in F# come in two forms: *tupled* and *curried*. F# will render both to C# as though they were tupled, so all arguments will be required at once, unlike curried functions in F#, where you can pass in just a subset to return a new function. There's one exception where this breaks down: if you expose an *already partially curried* function to C#, it'll look pretty strange. If you can avoid trying to read the IntelliSense, it works reasonably well, but it's completely nonidiomatic C#.

Now you try

Next, experiment with F# functions firsthand to see how they render in C#:

1 Enter the following code at the bottom of Library1.fs.

Listing 27.3 Exposing a module of functions to C#

```
module Functions =
    /// Creates a car
    let CreateCar wheels brand x y =        ← Function in curried form
        { Wheels = wheels; Brand = brand; Dimensions = x, y }
    /// Creates a car with four wheels.
    let CreateFourWheeledCar = CreateCar 4  ← Partially applied function
```

2 Rebuild the F# project.

3 Call the `Model.Functions.CreateCar` function from C#. It appears as a normal static method.

4 Call the `Model.Functions.CreateFourWheeledCar` function from C#. It appears as a property of type `FSharpFunc`, which has an `Invoke` method on it that takes in a single argument. (You need to add a reference to `FSharp.Core` to see this. Take the newest one you can find, which is 4.4.0.0 at the time of writing.)

5 Observe that calling `Invoke` will return another propety with another `Invoke` method! Each call relates to one constructor argument (except the first, which has been supplied in the F# code already!).

Listing 27.4 Calling F# functions from C#

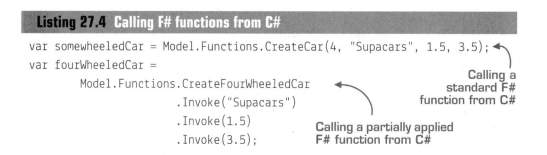

```
var somewheeledCar = Model.Functions.CreateCar(4, "Supacars", 1.5, 3.5);
var fourWheeledCar =
        Model.Functions.CreateFourWheeledCar
                .Invoke("Supacars")
                .Invoke(1.5)
                .Invoke(3.5);
```

Calling a standard F# function from C#

Calling a partially applied F# function from C#

To cut a long story short, try to avoid providing partially applied functions to C#. If you absolutely must, wrap such functions in a "normal" F# function that explicitly takes in all arguments required by the partially applied version, and supplies those arguments manually.

Quick check 27.2

1   How are modules declared in F# rendered in C#?
2   Can you use F#-declared curried functions in C#?

27.3 Summarizing F# to C# interoperability

Table 27.1 roughly summarizes how well (or not) different elements operate in C#.

Table 27.1 Summarizing F# to C# interoperability

Element	Renders as	C# compatibility
Records	Immutable class	High
Tuples	System.Tuple	Medium/high
Discriminated unions	Classes with builder methods	Medium/low
Namespaces	Namespaces	High
Modules	Static classes	High
Functions	Static methods	High/medium

QC 27.2 answer

1   As static classes.
2   Yes, although they can be unusual in C# to work with.

27.3.1 Gotchas

This section covers a few edge cases where you might need to do something a little different in order to use a specific type in C#.

Incompatible types

A few types in F# don't exist in C#. Generally, this is because there's no CLR support for them, and they're erased at compile time. The two main elements are unit of measure (which we haven't touched on) and type providers (which we'll deal with in the upcoming lessons).

CLI Mutable

On rare occasions, you'll need to create an F# record from C# in an uninitialized state (without having provided all fields to a constructor), or without getter-only properties. Primarily, this is important for interoperating with third-party libraries that create objects by using reflection. These libraries typically create an uninitialized object first, and then set each property one at a time (MongoDB and Azure Web Jobs SDKs are two examples). By default, these libraries won't work with F# records, so to get around this, you can place the [<CLIMutable>] attribute on a record. This doesn't change anything from an F# point of view, but affects the underlying IL that's emitted so that C# code can access a default constructor, and properties have setters.

Options

You can consume F# option types in C#, after you add a reference to FSharp.Core. But as with other discriminated unions, they're not particularly idiomatic to work with in C#. Adding a few well-placed extension methods that remove the need for supplying type arguments can help, though, so it's worth looking at this if you want to use F#'s Option type in C#.

Accessibility modifiers

F# also supports accessibility modifiers, just like C#—for example, public, private, and internal. Unlike C#, things are public by default in F#, but if you want to make a function or value hidden from C# code, mark it as internal.

Collections

F# arrays are standard .NET arrays, so they work without a problem. Likewise, sequences appear as IEnumerable<T> to C# code. But the F# list isn't the same type as the standard .NET generic list (known in F# as ResizeArray). Again, without pattern matching (and the List module), it's of limited use, although as it implements IEnumerable<T>, you can use LINQ on it. My advice is to avoid exposing it to C# clients. Arrays and sequences work fine, and you won't place a dependency on the FSharp.Core assembly on callers with those.

Quick check 27.3

1   What do tuples render as in C#?
2   What is the purpose of the [<CLIMutable>] attribute?

Summary

In this lesson, you looked at exposing code from F# to C#:

- You saw how records, tuples, and discriminated unions can be consumed in C#.
- You saw how to work with namespaces, modules, and functions.
- You learned what parts of F# don't map well into the mostly OO C# language.
- You saw how to help smooth interoperability issues for certain common cases.

Try this

Take an existing application that you already have that's written in C#. Try to port your domain model from C# to F# and then reference it from C#. Try doing a simple mapping, without using any advanced F# modeling features, before trying a more complex model that uses, for example, discriminated unions and options. Then try moving business logic from C# to F# and functions on modules, rather than stateful classes.

QC 27.3 answer

1   The System.Tuple type.
2   CLIMutable provides a nondefault constructor and public setters for all properties.

28

LESSON

ARCHITECTING HYBRID LANGUAGE APPLICATIONS

This final lesson of this unit presents all the elements we've discussed so far within the context of a larger, cohesive element. This lesson doesn't have specific step-by-step exercises, as we'll be reviewing a prebuilt code base. After this lesson, a capstone exercise will build on this information in the context of the banking application you've been writing throughout this book. This lesson covers

- Crossing the boundaries from F# and C#
- Playing to the strengths of a language
- Case study—driving a WPF application from F#

28.1 Crossing language boundaries

We touched on this briefly earlier in this unit, but it's worth reviewing this point in more depth. Although beneath the covers F# and C# share the same runtime, at compile time F# affords us much more safety, thus allowing us to focus on solving business problems rather than checking for nulls and so on throughout our code base. Let's look briefly at how to work between the two languages in an attempt to get the best of both worlds, taking advantage of the F# type system while still being friendly to C#.

28.1.1 Accepting data from external systems

It's extremely useful to use the F# type system to model your domain effectively. But when interoperating with other systems (or languages), an impedance mismatch may occur between F# and the other side. For example, F# features such as discriminated unions (sum types) and non-nullability by default don't exist in C#. As such, at times you'll want to model something in such a way that you need to choose one of two approaches to take.

On the one hand, if you expose data structures that are foreign to C# developers, you make your API tricky to consume. On the other hand, using a simple data model that's usable everywhere means giving up features in F#. And this is about more than exposing APIs to C#. Sometimes you'll be forced to deal with "dirty" data from external sources (for example, JSON, CSV, or HTTP endpoints)—data that you don't trust to adhere to a particular schema, or that doesn't allow defining domains as richly as F#.

A good way around this is to define an *internal* F# domain that contains all the niceties that you've seen throughout this book (discriminated unions, option types, records, and so forth) while also using a *public* API designed to be easy for consumers to work with (such as C# developers). When you move in and out of the F# world, you marshal data *between* the two formats. This is particularly important when going from the weakly typed external shape to the internal, stricter F# shape. Going from data structures that can't encode rich schema information into the F# world is shown in figure 28.1.

> **SQL and C#—an impedance mismatch of types**
> The designers of SQL got one thing spot on: they allowed any data type to be marked as either null or non-nullable. In the early days of C#, there was no concept of Nullable<T>, so when reading, for example, nullable ints from a database, you needed to pick a default integer value to map to in case there was no value on the database.

In listing 28.1, let's see an example of working with a simple domain that you want to use from C# from a public API point of view, but want to do all the calculation from within F#. This model represents a simple order system. An order has an ID, a customer name, the set of items to order, plus an optional way to contact the customer to provide updates of shipping progress.

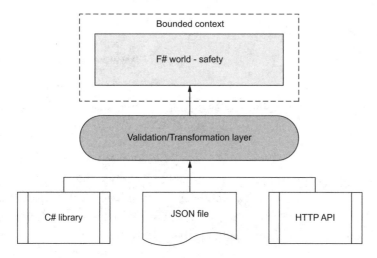

Figure 28.1 Providing a gateway into the F# world as a means of ensuring type safety

Listing 28.1 A simple domain model for use within C#

```
type OrderItemRequest = { ItemId : int; Count : int }
type OrderRequest =
    { OrderId : int
      CustomerName : string // mandatory
      Comment : string // optional
      /// One of (email or telephone), or none
      EmailUpdates : string
      TelephoneUpdates : string
      Items : IEnumerable<OrderItemRequest> } // mandatory
```

A mandatory string through convention

An optional string

A set of related properties

Even a relatively simple domain model such as this has a set of implicit rules that are documented through code comments and the like. You're using records here, as they're extremely lightweight and work well in C#, but there are better ways to model this in F#.

Listing 28.2 Modeling the same domain in F#

```
type OrderId = OrderId of int
type ItemId = ItemId of int
type OrderItem = { ItemId : ItemId; Count : int }
type UpdatePreference =
```

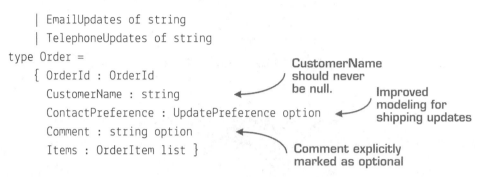

```
     | EmailUpdates of string
     | TelephoneUpdates of string
type Order =
     { OrderId : OrderId
       CustomerName : string
       ContactPreference : UpdatePreference option
       Comment : string option
       Items : OrderItem list }
```

CustomerName should never be null.

Improved modeling for shipping updates

Comment explicitly marked as optional

It's relatively simple to go from a weaker model to a stronger model. At the entrance to your F# module, you accept the weak model, but immediately validate and transform it over to your stronger model. Once in this shape, you no longer have to check for nulls or otherwise invalid data and can immediately benefit from the improved modeling capabilities.

Listing 28.3 Validating and transforming data

```
{ CustomerName =
     match orderRequest.CustomerName with
     | null -> failwith "Customer name must be populated"
     | name -> name
  Comment = orderRequest.Comment |> Option.ofObj
  ContactPreference =
     match Option.ofObj orderRequest.EmailUpdates, Option.ofObj
     ➥orderRequest.TelephoneUpdates with
     | None, None -> None
     | Some email, None -> Some(EmailUpdates email)
     | None, Some phone -> Some(TelephoneUpdates phone)
     | Some _, Some _ -> failwith "Unable to proceed - only one of telephone
     ➥ and email should be supplied" }
```

Simple null check

Explicitly marking an optional string

Safely creating a discriminated union from flattened data

In this (simplified) example, you perform these checks before entering your "safe" F# world:

- Null check on a string.
- Convert from a string to an optional string.
- Confirm that the source request has a valid state; if the incorrect mix of fields is populated, the request is rejected.

Working with strings in F#

In F#, I prefer to be explicit about nullable fields. Sadly, it's not possible in F# to make strings non-nullable, as they come from the BCL (the same as any other C# class). Every string could be null, even if you know it never would be. So although theoretically you should wrap all reference types in F# options in order to be completely safe, I tend to take a more pragmatic approach:

- If you know that a string field could conceivably be null, convert it to an option type by using `Option.ofObj`.
- If it shouldn't ever be null, check at the F# boundary and reject the object if it's null; if it's not null, leave it as a string.

In this way, you still gain a safety net, and can model the distinction between optional strings and mandatory strings, while not incurring the cost of placing option types throughout your code base.

28.1.2 Playing to the strengths of a language

At the start of this book, I briefly distinguished between features that are natural to F# and those in C#—for example, mutability and expressions. At times, you'll still want to use C# in a large system, either because of tooling or the domain at hand. Here are some examples:

- *ASP .NET MVC GUIs*—C# has rich support with Razor syntax for creating HTML GUIs on the server. There are third-party templates (downloadable directly from within Visual Studio) that allow you to create an MVC application in F#, but a low-frills way to get going is to create all your views and web hosts in a C# project, and delegate to F# for your controllers (or core business logic) onward. Given the stateless nature of web applications, F# is a great fit, and you'll see in a couple of units' time how simple this is to do.
- *Windows Forms GUIs*—C# again benefits from code generation for GUIs, but more than that, local client GUIs are generally mutable by nature. Again, this isn't necessarily an idiomatic fit for F# (although you can do it). Some good third-party libraries such as Fody make binding C# classes to WPF applications with MVVM easy. I know of developers who use F# for the entire WPF stack, including code-behind views, through the ingenious FsXaml and FSharp.ViewModule projects, others that leave code-behind as C# but use F# for view models, and still others who have their view models in C# but services and below in F#. There's no

right answer here; experiment with different blends of F# and C# to see what feels more natural to you.

- *Dynamic code*—When working with truly dynamic data structures, F# isn't a great fit. There are two options: using the ? operator, which allows you to perform a limited amount of dynamic coding, or using type providers. Again, see the next unit for this.

- *Entity Framework*—I have to say, since working with F#, I've gone completely off Entity Framework, because F# has far better data access libraries for most use cases. Nonetheless, if after working through the next unit, you still want to use EF, I'd exercise caution about defining your code-first models in F#. EF is designed to work with inherently mutable classes, using virtual methods, and so on—things that you can definitely model in F#—but again it's probably a better fit for C#.

Quick check 28.1

1 What features from the F# type system might be missing for simpler domains such as JSON or CSV?
2 Why should you consider having a rich internal, and simpler external, domain?
3 Can you name a scenario for which C# might be a better fit than F#?

28.2 Case study—WPF monopoly

Let's look at a slightly larger application that uses a combination of C# and F# projects to provide a cohesive end-to-end experience for a WPF application that models most of the rules of the classic Monopoly game. Rather than writing all the code yourself, you can download the source code from https://github.com/isaacabraham/monopoly (you can use HEAD, but if you prefer, the specific commit that I've written this lesson against is 092c53d). Go ahead and download, build, and open the MonopolyStats solution. Now let's take a look at some of its aspects.

QC 28.1 answer

1 Basic types, but also features such as discriminated unions and custom records.
2 Richer domain allows for better modeling internally, while a simple external domain can make life easier for consumers coming from simpler type systems.
3 Systems where code generation is essential or important; frameworks or libraries that are inherently mutable or designed for C#.

28.2.1 Application overview

Monopoly is a board game: players take turns throwing dice to move around a board of land properties, buying and selling them while also making money by renting properties when other players land on them. Although our application doesn't model the entire game, it does model the core parts:

- All of the board pieces
- Rules regarding rolling on special places such as Chance and Go to Jail
- Rules such as throwing consecutive doubles

The application allows you to roll dice randomly, either one at a time, or repeatedly roll the dice hundreds (or thousands) of times, accumulating statistics on which properties on the board are landed on the most. A sample of the application can be seen in figure 28.2.

The interesting parts of this application center around how the application is modeled in F#, and then how you interact with it from C#.

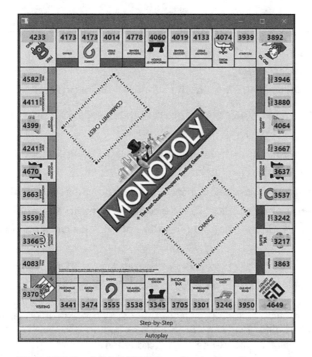

Figure 28.2 A C# WPF GUI application running on top of an F# back end

28.2.2 Separating UI concerns from domain logic

The application is separated into four real components: a core domain written in F#, as well as three clients—the WPF application you see here, plus an F# script used during development, and a simple F# console application. It might be interesting to note that the WPF GUI was written last. The code base was developed by using the REPL and script first, before adding a console and WPF application afterward. All of them rely on the same code base, though, as illustrated in figure 28.3.

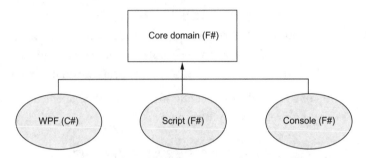

Figure 28.3 A core domain that can service multiple consumers

The core domain is set in three files in the MonopolyStats project:

- *Types.fs*—Contains the various domain types used in Monopoly, such as the board pieces and decks of cards.
- *Data.fs*—Contains the entire data model based on the defined types—the layout of the board and the two decks of cards.
- *Controller.fs*—Contains the application logic and rules to drive the main program, and represents your public API. The code is split into a module with your stand-alone, stateless functions and a (simpler) public class for consumption in C#.

Active patterns

In Controller.fs, you'll see two examples of active patterns—a lightweight form of discriminated unions. In the first one, you classify a number of doubles as either `ThreeDoubles` or `LessThanThreeDoubles`, which you can then pattern match over later. This can improve readability and enables simple reuse of classifications.

The Test.fsx script contains simple operations that you can perform on the game logic, including experimenting with standalone functions before testing the full Controller class to play a game. It's worth looking through this code in your own time, but there are some key points to note, which I'll address now. Have the solution open as you go through this!

28.2.3 Expressions at the core

The logic for the game is handled in the Monopoly.Functions module, such as moveBy (given a current board position, moves by a specific distance), playTurn (plays a single move), and tryMoveFromDeck (optionally moves the player when landing on a card deck). Observe that all of these functions are *expression-based*, operating on state that's supplied to them and returning a new state. Even the overall playGame function returns a list of all the moves that occurred; it builds the history up through scan (itself a derivative of fold). No mutation is involved.

These functions aren't all guaranteed to be entirely pure. (Some of them use functions that may be impure; for example, rollDice has a signature unit -> int * int.) Nevertheless, you can call each function directly from a script with repeatable results and no hidden dependencies, which is crucial for easy testing and exploration. Remember, it's relatively easy to dumb down an expression-based API to become statement-based, but it's very difficult to go the other way. You should always strive to start with expressions if possible.

28.2.4 C# interoperability

When called from C#, I've wrapped the calls to the Functions module into a Controller class with a single method on it, PlayGame(). (Notice the Pascal casing, which is also C#-friendly.) This class exposes an OnMoved event that's fired whenever a move occurs (so that they can be shown in the GUI as they happen). Notice that this event is decorated with the CLIEvent attribute, which is needed to expose events to the C# world; unfortunately, you can't have CLIEvents on modules.

28.2.5 WPF and MVVM

The entire WPF and MVVM layer has been implemented in C#. The application has two commands: one to play 50,000 turns in succession, and the second to play one turn at a time. The commands both set up event handlers to the OnMoved event from the Controller class, and use that to update the GUI with the number of times a position was landed on. There's nothing here that should be unfamiliar to a C# WPF developer; the only difference is that you're calling F# to drive your view models rather than C#. Here's a snippet from the `AutoPlayerCommand` class that shows you calling F# from the C# class `AutoPlayCommand`.

Listing 28.4 Calling F# from a C# view model

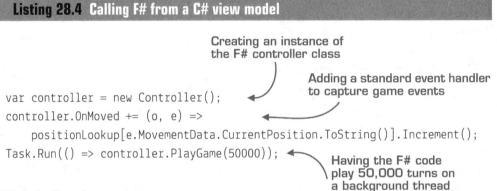

Creating an instance of
the F# controller class

Adding a standard event handler
to capture game events

```
var controller = new Controller();
controller.OnMoved += (o, e) =>
    positionLookup[e.MovementData.CurrentPosition.ToString()].Increment();
Task.Run(() => controller.PlayGame(50000));
```

Having the F# code
play 50,000 turns on
a background thread

28.2.6 Randomness

The last point of interest from an FP point of view is how to handle randomness within the application. In the "real" application, you use the `System.Random` class to generate dice throws and pick Chance cards. But when testing and exploring, you want to have repeatable, deterministic results. Looking at the `playTurn` function, you can see the first two higher-order functions it takes in are to roll dice and pick a card. Both are simple functions that have no dependency on `System.Random`. By doing this, you can now easily test this function from a script as follows.

Listing 28.5 Using deterministic functions for exploration

```
let rollDice() = 3, 4          ←—— Always roll 3, 4.
let pickCard() = 5             ←—— Always pick card 5.
let startingPosition = { CurrentPosition = Go; DoubleCount = 0 }
let move = Functions.playTurn rollDice pickCard ignore startingPosition
```

Play from Go using
these functions.

Note that if you can't decouple yourself from `Random`, you can also achieve deterministic random behavior by passing in a seed value when creating the `Random` object. Again, observe that you have a pure (or mostly pure!) F# domain using specific F# types, but have wrapped it up with a simplified façade of a class with an event record to make it more C# friendly.

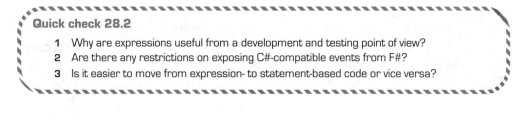

 ## Summary

In this lesson, you looked at an example exposing F# to C# within the context of a slightly larger application. This lesson covered the following:

- Working with *dual* domains: one F# for internal modeling, and a simplified one for consumption by, for example, C#
- Creating a hybrid application that uses WPF/MVVM in C# with an F# engine
- Separating deterministic behavior from nondeterministic functions such as System.Random

Try this

Try enhancing the Monopoly application by recording the cost of landing on each property and adding that to the state of the application. Alternatively, add support for saving the state of the game to and from disk. Finally, if you're a WPF expert, look at how you could port the application from C# to F# by using the FsXaml F# library.

QC 28.2 answer

1 They enable repeatable results on functions in a deterministic manner.
2 You can't expose C#-compatible events from an F# module.
3 It's easy to move from expressions to statements, but not the other way around.

29

CAPSTONE 5

Now that you've finished this unit, let's wrap up by applying these lessons back to the Bank Accounts application that you've been working on. You'll see how to

- Integrate your existing F# code base with a C# WPF application
- Use third-party NuGet libraries within your F# code base
- Observe how F# domains resolve up to C# in a real solution

29.1 Defining the problem

The objective of this capstone is to plug a C# Windows Presentation Foundation (WPF) GUI on top of the existing F# code base, replacing the console program runner with an event-driven UI. The system will provide the same Withdraw and Deposit commands as the console, as well as an updating transaction history. You can see how this looks in figure 29.1.

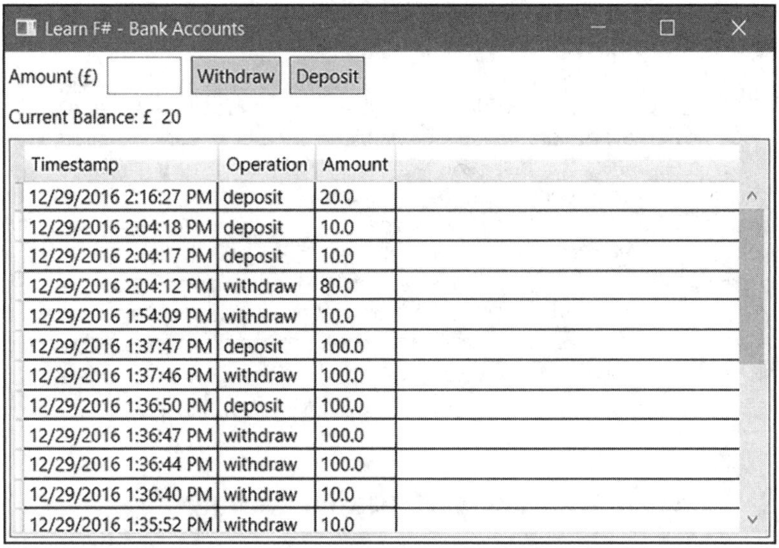

Figure 29.1 Sample WPF GUI for the Bank Accounts application

> **I don't know WPF!**
>
> Because you may not be familiar with WPF (or even GUI programming at all), you'll find a prebuilt GUI solution here using the Model-View-ViewModel (MVVM) design pattern. If you're a WPF whiz, feel free to scrap the supplied solution and start again! But the objective of this capstone isn't to get bogged down in the depths of WPF (and if you've done any WPF or Silverlight in the past, you'll know just how complex things can get). Instead, you want to focus on the integration of the C# and F# worlds from a language point of view, as well as how the OO and FP paradigms work together.

29.1.1 Solution overview

src/code-listings/lesson-29 has both a starting solution and a completed version in the sample-solution folder. There are two projects: the F# core application, and the WPF C# front end. The latter depends on the former. (If you're a fan of the dependency inversion principle, you'll know that this breaks that pattern, but for the purposes of this lesson, it's overkill to add it in.)

I've also changed the F# project from a console application to a class library, although I've left the old Program.fs code in there for you to reuse if you wish. By the end of this capstone, you'll be able to remove that file completely.

Can't you do WPF in F#?

You can definitely write WPF applications in F#. Admittedly, the out-of-the-box experience is a bit of a let-down, as Visual Studio won't do any of the code generation that you get with C#. But two excellent libraries are available on NuGet that make using WPF in F# relatively pain-free. First, there's FsXaml [https://github.com/fsprojects/FsXaml], a library that removes the need for the code-behind code generation through a type provider (see unit 7). Second, if you're a fan of the MVVM pattern, you might want to check out the FSharp.ViewModel project, which allows you to quickly and easily create view models that support `INotifyPropertyChanged` and command bindings [https://github.com/fsprojects/FSharp.ViewModule]. I'm deliberately avoiding them in this lesson, but I use both libraries all the time and can definitely recommend looking into them to enable 100% F# solutions (if that's what you want).

29.2 Plugging in a third-party NuGet package

Let's start with a fairly lightweight change to your F# code. In the previous incarnation of your app, you wrote a simplistic serialization routine for persisting bank transactions to disk. Now you're going to update that to work with the Newtonsoft.Json library.

Now you try

1 Add a NuGet package reference to the Core F# project for Newtonsoft.Json, as shown in figure 29.2. It shouldn't be too hard to find, as it's the most popular package on NuGet.

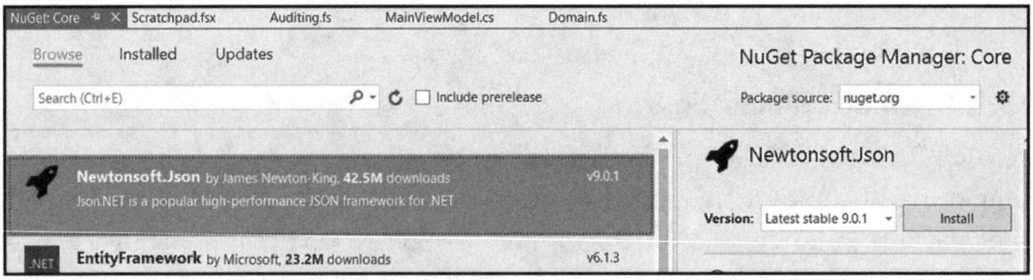

Figure 29.2 Adding Newtonsoft.Json to an F# project

2   Open scratchpad.fsx and add a #r reference to the Newtonsoft.Json package, or use VS to generate a load references script and #load that in instead (this is what listing 29.1 uses).

3   Create a dummy transaction record and serialize it to a string by using the `Newtonsoft.Json.JsonConvert.SerializeObject` method. What's nice is that (as with any nongeneric, single-argument method) you can use this method natively with the pipeline operator.

4   Observe that the string that's emitted looks like plain, standard JSON.

5   You can use the `DeserializeObject` method to go back to an F# record again.

Listing 29.1   Using JSON .NET with F# records

```
#load @"Scripts/load-project-debug.fsx"

open Capstone5.Domain
open Newtonsoft.Json
open System

let txn =
    { Transaction.Amount = 100M             Serializing an F#
        Timestamp = DateTime.UtcNow           record into a      Deserializing a
        Operation = "withdraw" }              plain string       string back into
                                                                 an F# record
let serialized = txn |> JsonConvert.SerializeObject
let deserialized = JsonConvert.DeserializeObject<Transaction>(serialized)
```

6   Now that you know how to use JSON.NET with F#, you can replace the implementation of the serialization functions in the `Domain.Transactions` module with new ones that use JSON.NET.

29.3   Connecting F# code to a WPF front end

Now let's move on to the main event—connecting your F# bank account code to C# WPF.

29.3.1   Joining the dots

You'll find a module in the F# project, Api.fs. This module contains a set of functions that act as your façade over the top of the real bank account code base. This code should provide the same functionality that lives inside Program.fs, except for anything to do with command handling and parsing. You need to implement four functions:

- LoadAccount — This should return a full account object based on the current state of the transactions for an owner, similar to what tryLoadAccountFromDisk does.
- Deposit — This should perform the same logic as the depositWithAudit function in Program.fs.
- Withdraw — As per withdrawWithAudit, you'll have to manually unwrap creditAccount into an account in order to get at the AccountId and Owner fields.
- LoadTransactionHistory — You should try to find any transactions on disk for the owner. Note that you want to return only the transactions, not the owner or account ID, so although you can use tryFindTransactionsOnDisk, you'll need to be selective about what parts of the function output you pass back out.

You'll notice that, unlike the original F# code, all the functions here work off Customer, and not Account. The rationale behind this is that before performing any operation, you should load the latest version of the account from disk rather than using an in-memory account that's provided to you. Doing this guarantees that the UI can't repeatedly pass you the same version of an account and withdraw funds using it. The easiest way to load in the account from disk is for the last three functions to call LoadAccount as the first thing that they do.

Also, be aware that both LoadAccount and LoadTransactionHistory should return absolute values rather than option types. Both of them will either have to pattern match or use defaultArg to return a default value if the account doesn't yet exist on disk.

After you've implemented the API, you should test it in a script to make sure it works as expected. Then, after you're happy with the way it's working, you should be in a position to run the app!

29.3.2 Consuming the API from C#

Let's briefly look at how to consume the API from C#. Again, don't worry too much about the intricacies of WPF and MVVM, but how the F# API sits within C#.

First, observe that you can create an instance of a Customer record within C#, no problem. It appears as though it's a normal class, and you can use it as a property on the view model, as seen in figure 29.3.

```
public MainViewModel()
{
    Owner = new Customer("isaac");
```

Figure 29.3 Creating an F# record from C#

The API itself also appears to C# as though it was a normal static class, and even though the functions are in curried form in F#, they show as regular methods in C#; see figure 29.4.

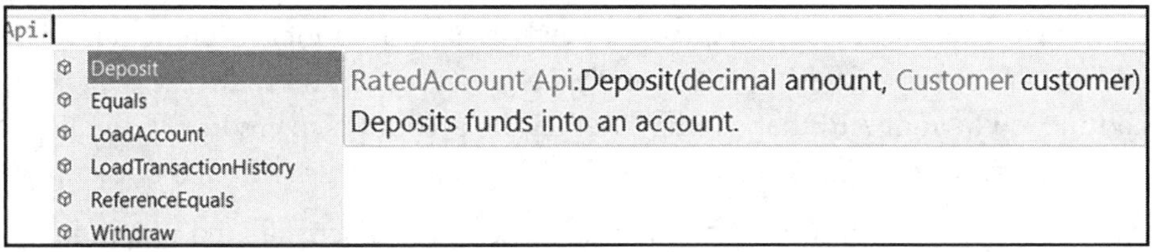

Figure 29.4 Accessing an F# API from C#

So far, so good.

7 Let's now confirm that you also have IntelliSense comments from the F# triple-slash declarations shown here in C#. Ensure that you have the XML Documentation File selected in the Build tab of the Properties pane of the F# project, as shown in figure 29.5.

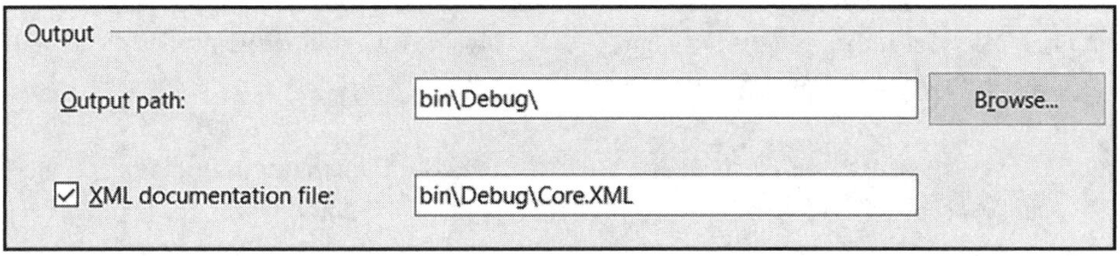

Figure 29.5 Turning on XML comments for a .NET project in Visual Studio 2015

When it comes to displaying the Transaction records onscreen, it *just works*. You create an ObservableCollection in the ViewModel (a collection that also emits events for item changes that WPF can listen to and force rebindings of the UI). This is then bound in XAML to CollectionViewSource, which in turn is connected to the DataGrid UI control. If this doesn't mean anything to you, don't worry. But if you have used WPF or Silverlight before, this should be standard fare.

29.3.3 Using types as business rules in C#

You've spent some time looking at business rules in code, using types to distinguish between overdrawn and in-credit bank accounts. Can you do the same in C#? Well, not really. C# 7 will have a limited form of pattern matching that you'll be able to use to match an object against different types—but not much more.

But in this case, you can use the properties that F# emits with compiled discriminated unions to simplify a rule for your GUI: whether or not to enable the Withdraw button. This button should be available only if the bank account is in credit. How do you do this?

One option is to duplicate logic in C# to check whether an account is in credit (alarm bells should be ringing as soon as I mentioned *duplication of logic*). Alternatively, you could add a function to your API that checks whether the account is in credit. Or, finally, you could always enable the button and leave the API to handle this (which it does anyway).

But you can go one better: remember that RatedAccount is a discriminated union that's either Overdrawn or InCredit, and only when the account is of type InCredit do you want to enable the button. If you right-click RatedAccount and choose Go to Definition from Main-ViewModel.cs, you'll see it's represented as a base class, with Overdrawn and InCredit as two subclasses.

Listing 29.2 Viewing a discriminated union from C#-generated metadata

```
public abstract class RatedAccount {          ◄─── Base class
    public Boolean IsInCredit { get; }        ◄─── Runtime type check tags
    public Boolean IsOverdrawn { get; }
    public class InCredit : RatedAccount {     ◄─── InCredit subclass
        public CreditAccount Item { get; }
    }
    public class Overdrawn : RatedAccount {     ◄─── Overdrawn subclass
        public Account Item { get; }
    }
}
```

And handily for us, F# also generates properties to allow you to easily check which subclass a rated account is. Let's look at the C# code for the Withdraw command object, which is the code that's called whenever the user clicks the button, as well as a parse function (to parse the textbox into an integer) and a function that indicates whether the button should be enabled.

Commands in WPF

I'm deliberately skimming over the WPF side of things here, but it's worth understanding what a command in WPF is. A standard command contains two methods: Execute() and CanExecute(). The former is called whenever the control that it is bound to is activated; for example, a Button click. The latter is called by WPF to determine whether to enable the control—for example, to disable a Button so it can't be clicked.

Listing 29.3 Using F# types to enforce UI rules

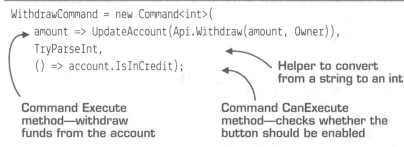

```
WithdrawCommand = new Command<int>(
    amount => UpdateAccount(Api.Withdraw(amount, Owner)),
    TryParseInt,
    () => account.IsInCredit);
```

Helper to convert
from a string to an int

Command Execute
method—withdraw
funds from the account

Command CanExecute
method—checks whether the
button should be enabled

What's absolutely beautiful here is how you check whether the button should be enabled. You check the IsInCredit tag that's generated by F#. If this account is of the type InCredit, you enable the Withdraw button! You're not running any code to check bank balances; you're using the type system to enforce a business rule! And because you refresh the command after every transaction occurs, this will automatically refresh as needed. Lovely.

 ## 29.4 Common fields on discriminated unions

One thing you want to do in the app is display the balance of the account. Unfortunately, to do this, you'd normally have to first pattern match on whether the account is Overdrawn or InCredit, pull out the Account, and then get the Balance. In F#, this is more or less bearable, but in C#, it'd be awful. To work around this, you can add a *member property* to RatedAccount, which will do the work for you.

Listing 29.4 Creating a member field on a discriminated union

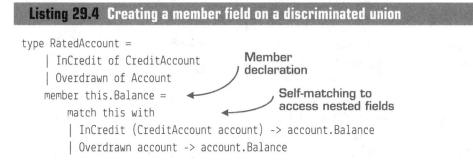

```
type RatedAccount =
    | InCredit of CreditAccount
    | Overdrawn of Account
    member this.Balance =
        match this with
        | InCredit (CreditAccount account) -> account.Balance
        | Overdrawn account -> account.Balance
```

Member
declaration

Self-matching to
access nested fields

If you add this code to the RatedAccount code in F# and recompile, you'll see that a Balance property is now visible from C#, and you can uncomment the line in the UpdateAccount()

method so that the balance is correctly shown in the GUI. (In the full solution, I've created a generic `GetField` helper member to get any property that's common to both sides of the DU.) You haven't seen member properties before; they're occasionally useful but generally not necessary for many F# workloads.

29.5 Polishing up F# APIs for consumers

Here are a few more tasks that you can complete in order to make the experience even better from a C# perspective.

29.5.1 Encapsulation

We haven't bothered much with this so far, but when exposing an API to external consumers, it's common to hide internal implementation details. Not only does this stop developers from accidentally taking dependencies on things you might change in the future, but it also makes things simpler for external developers. They can much more easily explore an API if only a limited subset is made visible. Currently, if you dot into Capstone5, you'll see that all the F# modules and namespaces are available, as in figure 29.6.

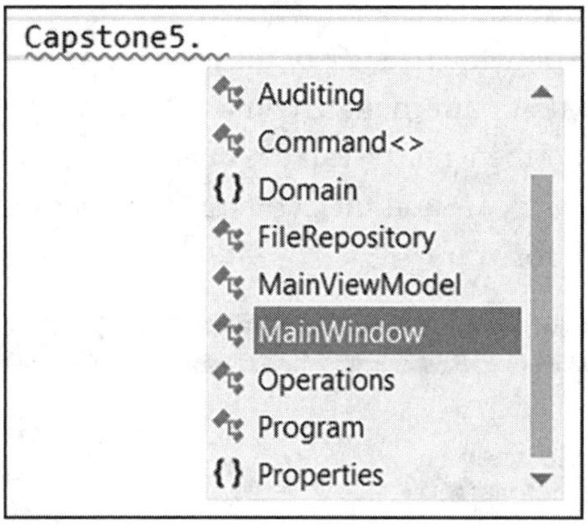

Capstone5.

- **⁺ᵗ** Auditing
- **⁺ᵗ** Command<>
- **{}** Domain
- **⁺ᵗ** FileRepository
- **⁺ᵗ** MainViewModel
- **⁺ᵗ** MainWindow
- **⁺ᵗ** Operations
- **⁺ᵗ** Program
- **{}** Properties

Figure 29.6 Unnecessarily showing internal implementation modules to consumers

8 You can easily rectify this by placing the `internal` or `private` modifier for any module that you don't want to show (for example, `module internal Capstone5.Operations`). Recompile, and you'll see in C# that these modules no longer show up.

29.5.2 Naming conventions

9   Although in F# it's common to use camel casing for functions (for example, `classify-Account`), in C# we use Pascal casing (for example, `ClassifyAccount`). If you're exposing code publicly to C# callers, make the effort to adhere to this naming convention. Alternatively, decorate the function with the `[<CompiledName>]` attribute to change the function name post-compile—for example, `[<CompiledName "ClassifyAccount">]`.

29.5.3 Explicit naming

In F#, we occasionally omit argument or field names from types—such as fields on a case on a discriminated union, or when we compose functions together. This doesn't render so well in C#. Unnamed DU fields will be rendered as `Item1`, `Item2`, and so on, and unnamed function arguments will be named `arg1`, `arg2`, and so forth. In such cases, try to explicitly name function arguments.

29.6 Working with pure functions in a mutable world

This final section briefly discusses issues to be aware of when mixing OO and GUI worlds with the FP world. How do you mix stateless functions with mutable data on a GUI? The answer is ultimately more complex—and subjective—than we can completely discuss here, but here in a nutshell are my thoughts.

First, I recommend by default trying to work with a stateless F# layer, and threading state between the GUI and back-end layers from one call to the next. Each call to the F# layer takes in a state and returns a new state. In this project, this really doesn't hold true, but in effect you're generating new versions of the Account and Transaction History after every action. In other words, instead of mutating a stateful Account after each action, you generate a new Account after every API call, as shown in figure 29.7.

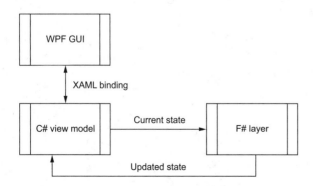

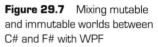

Figure 29.7 Mixing mutable and immutable worlds between C# and F# with WPF

On the other hand, there's obviously a performance cost associated with rebinding everything to a GUI on every call. You'll need to be cautious about this sort of approach if you're working with a GUI that's sending thousands or millions of events a second to a stateless F# layer. In this case, you might, for example, design your F# API to return only changes to state from the previous state, and then manually apply those changes to the GUI.

There's no hard-and-fast rule. I tend to believe that you should do the simplest thing first and optimize only if there's good reason to.

 **Summary**

Hopefully that wasn't too bad! You've now spent some time trying to hook up a C# WPF application to an F# code base, as well as adding some NuGet packages into the mix. You've seen that F# can interoperate with the rest of the .NET ecosystem easily and effectively.

Working with data

Working with data is (in my opinion!) one of the most exciting sections of this book. It focuses on working with external data sources such as JSON, CSV, and SQL while narrowing the impedance mismatch between data sources and writing code in a way you've probably never seen before, through type providers. If you've been working with C# for a reasonable amount of time, you'll remember the "aha" moment when you first saw LINQ. Type providers provide a similar shift in the way you work with code and data, only magnified by 100. When combined with the REPL and scripts, F# opens up entirely new opportunities for ad hoc data processing and analytics.

Remember—free your mind!

30

INTRODUCING TYPE PROVIDERS

Welcome to the world of data! The first lesson of this unit will

- Gently introduce you to type providers
- Get you up to speed with the most popular type provider, FSharp.Data

After this lesson, you'll be able to work with external data sources in various formats more quickly and easily than you've ever done before in .NET—guaranteed!

30.1 Understanding type providers

Type providers are a language feature first introduced in F# 3.0:

> *An F# type provider is a component that provides types, properties, and methods for use in your program. Type providers are a significant part of F# 3.0 support for information-rich programming.*
>
> —https://docs.microsoft.com/en-us/dotnet/articles/fsharp/tutorials/type-providers/index

At first glance, this sounds a bit fluffy. You already know what types, properties, and methods are. And what does *information-rich programming* mean? The short answer is to think of type providers as T4 templates on steroids—a form of code generation, but one that lives *inside* the F# compiler. Confused? Read on.

Let's look at a somewhat holistic view of type providers first, before diving in and working with one to see what the fuss is all about. You might already be familiar with the notion of a compiler that parses C# (or F#) code and builds IL from which you can run applications, and if you've ever used Entity Framework (particularly the earlier versions) or old-school SOAP web services in Visual Studio, you're familiar with the idea of code generation tools such as T4 templates. These are tools that can generate C# code from another language or data source, as depicted in figure 30.1.

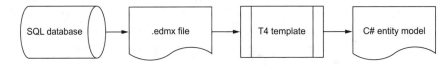

Figure 30.1   Entity Framework database-first code generation process

In this example, Entity Framework has a tool that can read a SQL database schema and generate an .edmx file—an XML representation of a database. From here, a T4 template is used to generate C# classes that map back to the SQL database.

Ultimately, T4 templates and the like, although useful, are awkward to use. For example, you need to attach them into the build system to get them up and running, and they use a custom markup language with C# embedded in them; they're not great to work with or distribute.

At their most basic, type providers are just F# assemblies (which anyone can write) that can be plugged into the F# compiler, and can then be used at edit time to generate entire type systems for you to work with *as you type*. In a sense, type providers serve a similar purpose to T4 templates, except they're much more powerful, more extensible, more lightweight to use, and extremely flexible. They can be used with what I call *live* data sources, and also offer a gateway not just to data sources but also to other *programming languages*, as shown in figure 30.2.

Unlike T4 templates, type providers can affect type systems without rebuilding the project, because they run in the background *as you write code*. Dozens, if not hundreds, of type providers are available, from ones that work with simple flat files, to relational SQL databases, to cloud-based data storage repositories such as Microsoft Azure Storage or Amazon Web Services S3. The term *information-rich* programming refers to the concept of bringing disparate data sources into the F# programming language in an extensible way.

Don't worry if that sounds a little confusing. You'll take a look at your first type provider in just a second.

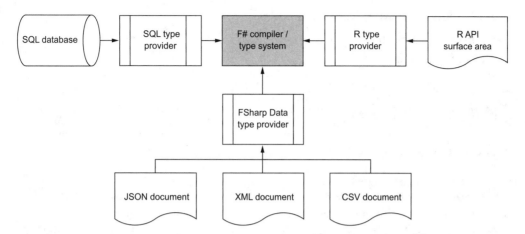

Figure 30.2   A set of F# type providers with supported data sources

Quick check 30.1

1 What is a type provider?
2 How do type providers differ from T4 templates?
3 Is the number of type providers fixed?

30.2 Working with your first type provider

Let's look at a simple example of a data access challenge, not unlike what you looked at in lesson 13. You'll work with soccer results, except that rather than working with an in-memory dataset, you'll work with a larger, external data source—a CSV file, located in learnfsharp/data/ FootballResults.csv. You need to answer the following question: which three teams won at home the most over the whole season?

QC 30.1 answer

1 A flexible code generation mechanism supported by the F# compiler.
2 Type providers are supported within the F# compiler directly, and allow edit-time type generation; there's no code generation as with T4 templates.
3 No. Type providers can be written, downloaded, and added to your applications as separate, reusable components.

30.2.1 Working with CSV files today

Let's first think about the typical process that you might use to answer this question, as shown in figure 30.3.

Figure 30.3   Steps to parse a CSV file in order to perform a calculation on it

Before you can even begin to perform the calculation, you need to *understand* the data. This usually means looking at the source CSV file in Excel or a similar program, and then designing a C# type to match the data in the CSV. Then, you do all of the usual boilerplate parsing: opening a handle to the file, skipping the header row, splitting on commas, pulling out the correct columns, and parsing into the correct data types. Only after doing all of that can you start to work with the data and produce some business value. Most likely, you'll use a console application to get the results, too. This entire process is more akin to typical software engineering—not a great fit when you want to explore data quickly and easily.

30.2.2 Introducing FSharp.Data

You could quite happily perform the preceding steps in F#; at least using the REPL affords you a more exploratory way of development. But that process wouldn't remove the whole boilerplate element of parsing the file, and this is where your first type provider comes in: FSharp.Data.

FSharp.Data is an open source, freely distributable NuGet package designed to provide generated types when working with data in CSV, JSON, or XML formats.

Using scripts for the win

At this point, I'm going to advise you to move away from heavyweight solutions and start to work exclusively with standalone scripts; this fits much better with what you're going to be doing. You'll notice in the code repository a build.cmd file—run it. This command uses Paket to download NuGet packages into the packages folder, which you can then reference directly in your scripts. This means you don't need a project or solution to start coding—you can simply create scripts and jump right in. I recommend creating your scripts in the src/code-listings/ folder (or another folder at the same level, such as src/learning/) so that the package references shown in the listings here work without needing changes.

Working with CSV files

Let's look at our first experiment with a type provider, the CSV type provider in FSharp.Data, and perform the analysis that we discussed at the start of this section.

Now you try

You'll start by doing some simple data analysis over a CSV file:

1 Create a new standalone script in Visual Studio by choosing File > New. You don't need a solution here; remember that a script can work standalone.
2 Save the newly created file into an appropriate location as described in "Scripts for the win."
3 Enter the following code.

Listing 30.1 Working with CSV files using FSharp.Data

Referencing the
FSharp.Data assembly

Connecting to the CSV file
to provide types based on
the supplied file

```
#r @"..\..\packages\FSharp.Data\lib\net40\FSharp.Data.dll"
open FSharp.Data
type Football = CsvProvider< @"..\..\data\FootballResults.csv">
let data = Football.GetSample().Rows |> Seq.toArray
```

Loading in all data from
the supplied CSV file

That's it. You've now parsed the data, converted it into a type that you can consume from F#, and loaded it into memory. Don't believe me? Check out figure 30.4.

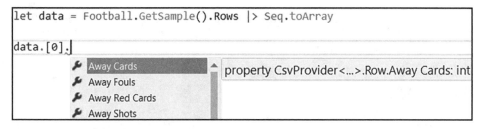

Figure 30.4   Accessing a provided type from FSharp.Data

You now have full IntelliSense to the dataset. That's it! You don't have to manually parse the dataset; that's been done for you. You also don't need to figure out the types; the type provider will scan through the first few rows and infer the types based on the contents of the file! Rather than using a tool such as Excel to understand the data, you can now begin to use F# as a tool to both understand *and* explore your data.

Backtick members

You'll see in figure 30.4, as well as from the code when you try it out yourself, that the fields listed have spaces in them! It turns out that this isn't a type provider feature, but one that's available throughout F# called *backtick members*. Just place a double backtick (``) at the beginning and end of the member definition, and you can put spaces, numbers, or other characters in the member definition. Visual Studio doesn't correctly provide IntelliSense for these in all cases (for example, `let`-bound members on modules), but it works fine on classes and records. You'll see some interesting uses for this when dealing with unit testing.

Visualizing data

While we're at it, let's also look at an easy-to-use F#-friendly charting library, XPlot. This library provides access to charts available in Google Charts as well as Plotly. You'll use the Google Charts API here, which means adding dependencies to XPlot.GoogleCharts (which also brings down the Google.DataTable.Net.Wrapper package):

1 Add references to both the XPlot.GoogleCharts and Google.DataTable.Net.Wrapper assemblies. If you're using standalone scripts, both packages will be in the packages folder after running build.cmd. Use #r to reference the assembly inside one of the lib/net folders.

2 Open the XPlot.GoogleCharts namespace.

3 Execute the following code to calculate the results and plot them as a chart, as shown in figure 30.5.

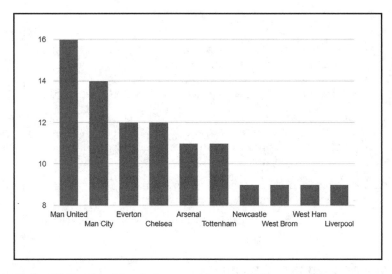

Figure 30.5   Visualizing data sourced from the CSV type provider

Listing 30.2   Charting the top ten teams for home wins

```
data
|> Seq.filter(fun row ->
    row.``Full Time Home Goals`` > row.``Full Time Away Goals``)
|> Seq.countBy(fun row -> row.``Home Team``)
|> Seq.sortByDescending snd
|> Seq.take 10
|> Chart.Column
|> Chart.Show
```

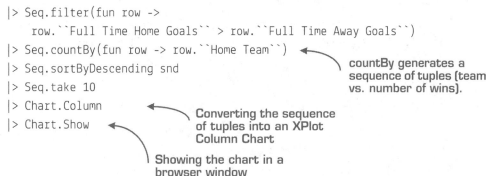

countBy generates a sequence of tuples (team vs. number of wins).

Converting the sequence of tuples into an XPlot Column Chart

Showing the chart in a browser window

In a few lines of code, you were able to open a CSV file you've never seen, explore the schema of it, perform an operation on it, and then chart it in less than 20 lines of code—not bad! This ability to rapidly work with and explore datasets that you haven't even seen before, while still allowing you to interact with the full breadth of .NET libraries that are out there, gives F# unparalleled abilities for bringing in disparate data sources to full-blown applications.

Type erasure

The vast majority of type providers fall into the category of *erasing* type providers. The upshot of this is that the types generated by the provider exist only at *compile* time. At runtime, the types are erased and usually compile down to plain objects; if you try to use reflection over them, you won't see the fields that you get in the code editor.

One of the downsides is that this makes them extremely difficult (if not impossible) to work with in C#. On the flip side, they're extremely efficient. You can use erasing type providers to create type systems with thousands of types without any runtime overhead, because at runtime they're of type `Object`.

Generative type providers allow for runtime reflection, but are much less commonly used (and from what I understand, much harder to develop).

30.2.3 Inferring types and schemas

One of the biggest differences in terms of mind-set when working with type providers is the realization that the type system is driven by an external data source. This schema may be inferred, as you saw with the CSV provider. Let's see a quick example of how this can affect your development process:

1 In your script, change the data source for the CSVProvider from FootballResults .csv to FootballResultsBad.csv. This version of the CSV file has had the contents of the Away Goals column changed from numbers to strings.

2 You'll immediately notice a compile-time error within your query, as shown in figure 30.6.

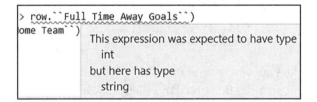

Figure 30.6   Changes in inferred schema cause compile-time errors.

This is because the type provider has inferred the types based on the contents of the sheet.

This point is crucial to grasp, within the context of not only a script, but also a full-blown application. Imagine you're compiling your application off a CSV file provided by your customer, and one day that customer provides you with a new version of the format. You can supply the new file to your code and instantly know where incompatibles in your code are; any breaking changes won't compile. This sort of instant feedback is much quicker than either unit tests or runtime errors. Instead, you're using the compiler and type system—the earliest possible stage—to show you exactly where code breaks. Also, in case you're wondering, type providers support the ability to redirect from one file to another so that you can compile against one but run against another. You'll deal with this in the coming lessons.

Finally, note that when it comes to schema inference, some type providers work differently from others. For example, FSharp.Data allows you to manually override the schema by supplying a custom argument to the type provider. Others can use some form of schema guidance from the source system. For example, SQL Server provides rich schema information from which a type provider doesn't need to infer types at all.

Writing your own type providers?

Sorry—but this book doesn't cover how to write your own type providers! The truth is that they're not easy to develop—particularly testing them while you develop them—but a few decent resources are worth looking at, such as the Starter Pack [https://github .com/fsprojects/FSharp.TypeProviders.StarterPack], as well as online video courses. If you're interested in learning how to write your own, I strongly advise you to look at some of the simpler ones to start with, or try to contribute to one of the many open source type providers; this is probably the best way to learn how they work.

Quick check 30.2

1 What are erased types?
2 What are backtick members?

QC 30.2 answer

1 Erased types are types that exist at compile-time only; at runtime, they're "erased" to objects.
2 Backtick members are members of a type surrounded with double backticks, which allow you to enter spaces and characters that would normally be forbidden in the name.

Summary

In this lesson, you took your first look at type providers. The remainder of this unit will introduce you to other forms of type providers and give you an idea of how far they can go. In this lesson

- You saw what type providers are at a high level and learned about some of their uses.
- You explored the FSharp.Data package and saw how to work with CSV files.
- You saw the XPlot library, a charting package that's designed to work well with F#.

Try this

Find any CSV file that you have on your PC. Try to parse it by using the CSV type provider and perform simple operations on it, such as list aggregation. Or download a CSV containing data and from the internet and try with that!

Alternatively, try creating a more complex query to compare the top five teams that scored the most goals and display it in a pie chart.

31

BUILDING SCHEMAS FROM LIVE DATA

Hopefully, you enjoyed using type providers in the previous lesson; this lesson builds on that one. You'll explore the notion of building types from live data sources that exist outside your code base. You'll learn about

- Creating schemas from type providers from remote data sources
- Mixing local and remote data sources
- Avoiding issues when working with remote data sources

 31.1 Working with JSON

In this section, we'll cover the basics of working with JSON data files with type providers.

31.1.1 Live and local files

In the previous lesson, you saw how to work with a type provider operating against a *local* data source—a CSV file placed on the local filesystem. As it turns out, many type providers also offer the ability to work against *remote* data sources; indeed, some providers are designed to work against remote data sources as the primary way of working.

These may be resources that you own, but they might as easily be publicly available resources that you don't own and aren't in control of. A good example of this can be

365

seen when working with JSON data. You might use JSON as a local storage mechanism—for example, as configuration files or local data storage. But JSON is also commonly used as a data transfer format for HTTP-enabled APIs, particularly RESTful APIs, as shown in figure 31.1.

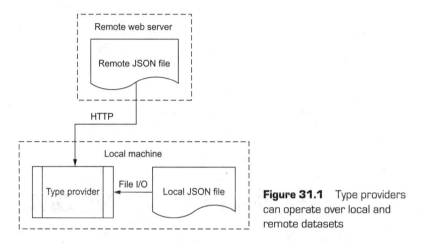

Figure 31.1 Type providers can operate over local and remote datasets

Let's see how to access data from a remote JSON resource quickly and easily—in this case, using publicly available TV listings from the United Kingdom's BBC website.

Listing 31.1 Opening a remote JSON data source

```
#r @"..\..\packages\FSharp.Data\lib\net40\FSharp.Data.dll"      Referencing
open FSharp.Data                                                FSharp.Data
type TvListing =
JsonProvider<"http://www.bbc.co.uk/programmes/genres/comedy/schedules/
   upcoming.json">
let tvListing = TvListing.GetSample()
let title = tvListing.Broadcasts.[0].Programme.DisplayTitles.Title
```

Creating an instance
of the type provider

Creating the TVListing
type based on a URL

The type provider will pull down the resource over HTTP for you, parsing it as though it were a local file. As you dot into the tvListings value, you'll see that you're presented with a full type hierarchy representing the entire JSON document. The JSON provider automatically infers schema based off the full document content. There's no need to manually download data locally to start to use it in F#—you can point to a public, remote resource (as in figure 31.1) and instantly start to work with it.

> **DUs and records in type providers**
>
> One of the (current) restrictions on type providers is that they can't generate discriminated unions. This does somewhat limit the ability of generated schemas. For example, if the JSON type provider sees different types of data across rows for the same field, it'll generate a type such as `StringOrDateTime`, which will have both optional `string` and `DateTime` properties, one of which will contain `Some` value. A more idiomatic way to achieve this in F# is to use a discriminated union with two cases, `String` and `DateTime`.

31.1.2 Examples of live schema type providers

Here are some examples of type providers that can work off of public data sources:

- *JSON type provider*—Provides a typed schema from JSON data sources
- *HTML type provider*—Provides a typed schema from HTML documents
- *Swagger type provider*—Provides a generated client for a Swagger-enabled HTTP endpoint, using Swagger metadata to create a strongly typed model
- *Azure Storage type provider*—Provides a client for blob/queue/table storage assets
- *WSDL type provider*—Provides a client for SOAP-based web services

Now you try

Next you'll try use the HTML type provider to visualize some Wikipedia data, to show the number of films acted in over time by Robert DeNiro. Given an HTML page, this type provider can find most lists and tables within it and return a strongly typed dataset for each of them. It handles all the HTTP marshaling as well as type inference and parsing (although given the inconsistent nature of HTML, it doesn't work on all pages). The HTML type provider is already included in the FSharp.Data package, so there's nothing more to download:

1 Within the script you already have opened, add references to the Google.Data-Table.Net.Wrapper and GoogleCharts DLLs. You can find them in the packages folder.
2 Open the XPlot.GoogleCharts namespace.
3 Create a handle to a type based on a URL that contains an HTML document:

```
type Films =
HtmlProvider<"https://en.wikipedia.org/wiki/Robert_De_Niro_filmography">
```

4 Create an instance of `Films` called `deNiro` by calling `Films.GetSample()`.

5   If you browse to the URL in your web browser, you'll see tables in the document, such as Film, Producing, and Directing. These tables map directly to types generated by the provider, and each table has a Rows property that exposes an array of data; each row is typed to represent a table row (see figure 31.2).

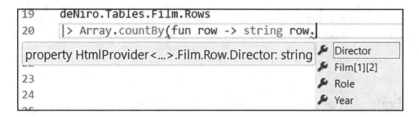

Figure 31.2   Accessing a generated type based on an HTML table

6   Write a query that will count the number of films per year and then chart it. First, use the Array.countBy function to count films by Year. This will give you a sequence of tuples, which are used by the chart as X and Y values. You'll want to convert the Year property to a string (rather than an int) so that the chart will create the correct number of elements in the x-axis.

7   Pipe the result into the Chart.SteppedArea function, and then into Chart.Show.

The output should look something like figure 31.3, although, of course, as this is taken from live data, the results may be slightly different! If you couldn't write the query, don't worry. A complete example is included in the code samples.

In a few lines of code, you retrieved data from a remote HTML resource over HTTP and parsed the data into a strongly typed object, before performing some simple analysis of it. Bear in mind that although you're using a script, this approach would work equally well over a fully compiled console, web, or Windows application. Even better, if the source data changed schema, you'd know it instantly. The next time you open Visual Studio, you'd immediately have red "squigglies" under your code. You wouldn't even need to run the application and wait for a deserialization exception to know that there was a problem; the compiler does that for you. This is because every time you open the solution, the VS editor effectively uses the F# compiler to validate the code (and provide IntelliSense), which in turn will connect to the data source. And finally, you now know how to use Wikipedia as a database directly from within F#!

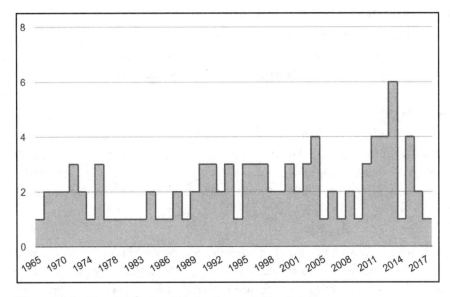

Figure 31.3 Charting the results taken from a Wikipedia table

Quick check 31.1

1   Which type provider would you use to read data from a SOAP service?
2   Which package do the JSON and HTML type providers live in?

31.2   Avoiding problems with live schemas

On the one hand, working directly with remote data to generate schemas allows you, with a few lines of code, to instantly start working with data; you don't have to download anything locally, or simulate an external service. But working with remote schemas does raise a few interesting issues, primarily because a type provider links the compilation of your code to a remote data source that you might not control. Let's look at some of these issues.

QC 31.1 answer

1   The WSDL type provider.
2   FSharp.Data.

31.2.1 Large data sources

One obvious problem is, what do you do if you need to work with a relatively large dataset (for example, 500 MB)? Do you need to load the entire dataset in order for the type provider to work? Won't that be slow or memory-intensive?

31.2.2 Inferred schemas

Another problem occurs when inferring schemas. What if you have a CSV file with a field that's missing for the first 9,999 lines and is populated in only the final line? Does the type provider need to read through the entire dataset in order to infer that type? Or if there are many resources, all of which follow the same schema, which one should you use?

31.2.3 Priced schemas

Some data sources charge you for every request you make. This occurs, for example, when accessing data from one of the two major cloud vendors (Microsoft Azure or Amazon Web Services). Both vendors charge you (admittedly, tiny amounts) for reading data from cloud storage—even just listing the files that are stored in them! The Azure type provider provides the ability to dot into your cloud storage, so you can navigate through blobs of data directly from within Visual Studio. Unfortunately, doesn't this mean that you'll be paying every time you dot into a container?

31.2.4 Connectivity

Here's one last issue: if you're working against a remote resource, you need to have the ability to connect to that resource in order to generate types. Let's assume you lose internet connectivity for a while. What happens then? The type provider won't be able to connect to the data source, which in turn will prevent the compiler from generating types from which you can develop against.

Capabilities that are built into many type providers can help with these sorts of problems. For example, many type providers allow you to limit the number of lines that the data source runs against for schema inference, so you might want to use the first 50 lines to generate types for a CSV file, even though it has 1 million lines in it. Alternatively, some type providers such as the CSV Provider allow you to pass in a string that defines the headers (for example, `"Name,string;Age,int;Dob,DateTime"`). But there's another way of solving these sorts of problems once and for all, which you'll look at next.

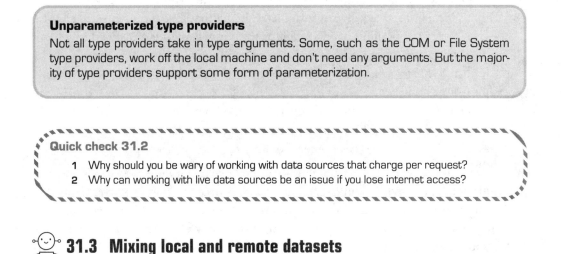

Unparameterized type providers

Not all type providers take in type arguments. Some, such as the COM or File System type providers, work off the local machine and don't need any arguments. But the majority of type providers support some form of parameterization.

Quick check 31.2

1 Why should you be wary of working with data sources that charge per request?
2 Why can working with live data sources be an issue if you lose internet access?

31.3 Mixing local and remote datasets

It's important at this point to realize that type providers have two phases of operation: *compilation* and *runtime,* as illustrated in figure 31.4.

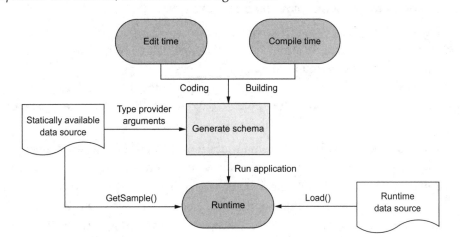

Figure 31.4 Understanding the relationship between edit, compile, and runtime with type providers

- The *compile* phase generates types based off a point-in-time schema (whether that's local or remote is irrelevant); this is the bit that gives you red squiggles if you mistype something. Think of this as the equivalent of the custom tool phase of T4 templates, if you've ever had to work with them before. The phase kicks in both at *edit time* (when you're typing code into VS) and at *compile time* (when you perform a build).
- The *runtime* phase uses the previously compiled types to work with data that matches that schema. This might be the same data that was used to generate the schema, but it can also be another (possibly remote) data source.

When either *coding* (editing in Visual Studio) or *building* (compiling code in VS or even MSBuild), the type provider will use the static data source to generate a schema and push that into the type system. Later, at runtime, you might use another data source with the same schema against the type provider; we'll look at that next. The main point is that you can use a local sample dataset for development and compilation, while redirecting to a potentially larger, real-world dataset at runtime, which solves the problems raised in section 31.2.

31.3.1   Redirecting type providers to new data

You'll notice with the type providers that you've used so far that you generate a type provider instance by using the GetSample() function on the type. What this means is, load in all data from the file that you used to generate the schema as the data source. But, there's nothing to stop you from repointing a type provider at a secondary data source that has the same schema. You'll often do this to overcome the issues I mentioned earlier. For example

- You use a local CSV file with a small subset of data used for schema generation, but you point the CSV provider to a larger file when working with data.
- You use a small, local JSON file that you create to guide the JSON type provider to infer types correctly, but you point to a real remote file when working with data.
- You use the local Azure storage emulator when developing with the Azure Storage type provider—thus saving you money and time—but point to a real storage account at runtime.

In other words, you use a local data file, typically one that's committed into source control, as part of your compile-time source code. This data file represents the schema, and is used by the type provider for type generation, but isn't necessarily the data that you'll work with.

Later in this unit, we'll talk more about working with type providers in full-blown applications, dealing with things such as securing connection strings, so relax if you're worrying about how to use these within the context of, for example, CI servers or live applications.

> ### Local and live data mismatches
>
> There's one issue with working with local data sources for schema, and separate sources for live data: you run the risk that the shape of the live data will change and you won't update your local schema file. In such a case, you'll be back in the world of runtime errors (which in itself is no worse than the world we currently live in). To be honest, that's a sacrifice you might have to make, and if you own the live data endpoint (for example, an internally hosted REST service), you won't have to worry about the case that a schema changes without your knowledge.

Now you try

Let's see how to use the NuGet website as a data source to work with NuGet package statistics and the HTML type provider, which is able to parse the HTML tables that contain per-package download statistics (see figure 31.5). You'll use a local copy of a web page to give you a schema—and enable you to develop offline—but then redirect it to a live page to retrieve the data:

1 Create an instance of the HTML type provider that points to sample-package .html in the data folder (if you use a relative path, make sure it's correct). If you open this, you'll see it's a sample of the NuGet package details page.
2 Using the GetSample() method, you can interrogate the Tables property to discover that there's a Version History property, which has members that reflect the equivalent table located in the HTML.

Version History		
Version	Downloads	Last updated
NUnit 3.5.0 (this version)	**36,334**	**04 October 2016**
NUnit 3.4.1	314,342	30 June 2016
NUnit 3.4.0	40,367	25 June 2016
NUnit 3.2.1	268,165	19 April 2016

Figure 31.5 A Version History table from the NuGet website

3 Now, instead of using GetSample(), use the Load() method to load in data from a live URI. This takes in a string URI for the "real" data:

```
let nunit = Package.Load "https://www.nuget.org/packages/nunit"
```

4 Repeat the process to download package statistics for the Entity Framework and Newtonsoft.Json packages. The URI is the same as in the preceding step, but use entityframework or newtonsoft.json in place of nunit.

Now that you have package statistics for all three packages, you can find the most popular specific versions of all of three packages combined.

5 Retrieve the Version History rows for all three packages and combine them into a single sequence; use Seq.collect to combine a sequence-of-sequences into a flattened sequence. Notice that this is the exact same code you'd use with "normal" records or values; you can use provided types in exactly the same way.

Listing 31.2 Merging sequences of provided values

```
[ entityFramework; nunit; newtonsoftJson ]
|> Seq.collect(fun package -> package.Tables.``Version History``.Rows)
```
Creating a list of   Merging all rows from each
package statistics values   package into a single sequence

6 Sort this combined sequence in descending order by using the Downloads property.
7 Take the top 10 rows.
8 Map these rows into tuples of Version and Downloads.
9 Create a Chart.Column that's then piped into Chart.Show; the results should look similar to figure 31.6.

You use a local file for your schema (which in this case is taken directly from a web browser), but download multiple datasets by using the same type provider instance. You could equally do the same for JSON or CSV. Then you merge the data into a simple shape from which you can graphically represent it.

Quick check 31.3   What does it mean to redirect a type provider at runtime?

QC 31.3 answer   Redirecting a type provider is the act of using a different data source at runtime from the one used at compile time.

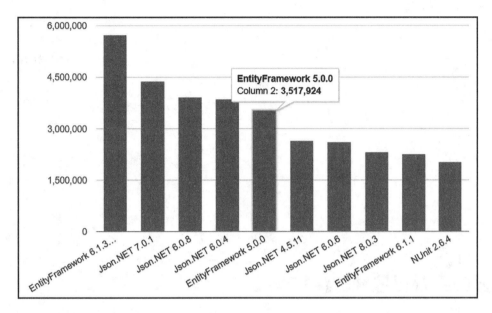

Figure 31.6 Identifying the most popular NuGet release across multiple packages

Summary

That's a wrap for this lesson. You worked with more type providers and learned about the distinction between schema and data and the different phases of type providers. In this lesson

- You worked with the HTML and JSON type providers.
- You learned about some of the issues that arise when working with schemas that point to live data sources.
- You saw how to distinguish between schema and data by generating types from a static, local schema but point to live sources for data.

Try this

Using the HTML type provider and the Wikipedia page listing all music tracks by the band Dream Theater (https://en.wikipedia.org/wiki/List_of_songs_recorded_by_Dream_Theater), calculate the year that they released the most albums. Visualize this as a line chart showing the number of tracks they released per year.

WORKING WITH SQL

In this lesson, you'll learn to use type providers with a database that you're probably familiar with, Microsoft SQL Server. You'll see how to

- Quickly and easily execute queries and commands against a SQL database
- Insert data quickly and easily
- Work with reference data in code

In my experience, .NET developers working with SQL Server typically use frameworks that fall into one of two categories:

- A full-blown object-relational mapper (ORM) tool, such as Entity Framework or NHibernate. These tools attempt to provide a layer of abstraction over the top of a relational DB by mapping relational tables into .NET hierarchical object models. They also typically provide features such as state tracking and conversion from IQueryable queries into (occasionally well-optimized) T-SQL.
- Query/command patterns using either ADO .NET or a Micro ORM wrapper, such as Dapper or PetaPoco. These provide you with the ability to write direct SQL against a database, and automatically map the results against a DTO that you've created. They tend not to provide complex state tracking but are designed to be lightweight, high-performing, and simple to use.

Both approaches have pros and cons. I'm not about to be drawn into another debate about which one you should go with; plenty of resources and opinion pieces are available online that you can read up on. Instead, I'll show you how F# fits in with the data access story, particularly with type providers, and then let you make up your own mind.

> **What's SQL?**
>
> Don't worry if you're not an expert—or even a beginner—in SQL. This lesson covers relatively basic areas of SQL and focuses on the F# side of the story. Even if you've never used SQL, you'll still find this a useful lesson—particularly as it shows how type providers can effectively bridge the gap between a foreign language and F#—in this case, T-SQL, which is Microsoft's query language for SQL Server (based on the SQL standard).

 32.1 Creating a basic database

In this lesson, you'll first create a simple database with pre-populated data that you'll then work with in the remainder of this lesson. The database, Adventure Works Light, is a simple order management database that you'll use to experiment with. Don't worry; you don't need to install the full-blown SQL Server (or even SQL Express)! Instead, you'll use the lightweight LocalDB, a free, lightweight in-process SQL database that's perfect for developing against.

Now you try

First you'll deploy a sample database locally that you'll use for the remainder of the lesson:

1 In Visual Studio, navigate to the SQL Server Object Explorer (View menu).

1 Expand the SQL Server node.

2 You should see a node underneath that begins with (localdb). I can't tell you which one it'll be, as the SQL team keeps changing the format with each release, but it'll look something like (localdb)\ProjectsV12 or (localdb)\MSSQLLocalDB.

3 If you don't see any (localdb) nodes, you probably need to install SQL Server Data Tools (SSDT). This lightweight installer should be directly available from within Extensions and Updates in Visual Studio.

4   Now, import a database onto the server. Right-click the Databases node within the localdb server instance and choose Publish Data-Tier Application, as shown in figure 32.1.

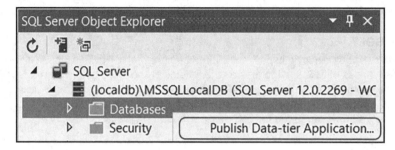

Figure 32.1   Publishing a DACPAC to SQL Server

5   In the dialog box that appears, set the File on Disk option to the adventureworks-lt.dacpac file from the data folder of the code repository, and set the Database Name to AdventureWorksLT.

6   Click Publish (ignore any warnings that may appear about overwriting data). Within a few seconds, Visual Studio will create a new database and populate it for you to test.

That's it. You now have a local database that you can experiment with. You can explore the database from within Visual Studio directly by right-clicking any table and choosing View Data. Of course, you don't want to rely on point-and-click GUIs, but on using F# as a way to view the data directly without needing to leave the code editor!

32.2 Introducing the SqlClient project

Let's start by looking at the open source and free SqlClient package, a data access layer designed specifically for MS SQL in the Micro ORM school of thought that contains several type providers, each of which have several tricks up their sleeves that make them much more powerful than, for example, Dapper. Since I started using this library, I've completely moved away from ORMs in general.

32.2.1 Querying data with the SqlCommandProvider

Let's now look at getting your hands dirty with the first type provider in the package, the SqlCommandProvider.

Start by connecting to the database that you just created and running a simple query to retrieve some data from it:

1 Open a new script and add a reference to the assembly in the FSharp.Data.Sql-Client package. This is located in the packages folder, and you can manually #r the DLL. If using a full solution, you can opt to download the package from NuGet and generate a references script through VFPT (see lesson 25).

2 Open the FSharp.Data namespace.

3 Enter the following code.

Listing 32.1 Querying a database with the SqlCommandProvider type provider

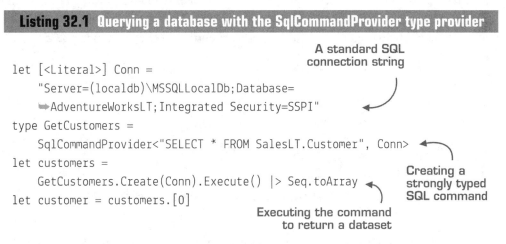

A standard SQL connection string

```
let [<Literal>] Conn =
    "Server=(localdb)\MSSQLLocalDb;Database=
    ➥AdventureWorksLT;Integrated Security=SSPI"
type GetCustomers =
    SqlCommandProvider<"SELECT * FROM SalesLT.Customer", Conn>
let customers =
    GetCustomers.Create(Conn).Execute() |> Seq.toArray
let customer = customers.[0]
```

Creating a strongly typed SQL command

Executing the command to return a dataset

A few things are happening here, so let's go through them one at a time:

- First, you create a value to hold the connection string to SQL so that you can reuse it (rather than passing it inline to the type provider). This value is also marked with the [<Literal>] attribute, to mark it as a compile-time constant, which is needed when passing values as arguments to type providers. (Also notice that the value is Pascal-cased; it's best practice to do this for literals.)
- Next, you generate a strongly typed command, GetCustomers, based off the connection string and an embedded SQL query. I imagine that right now most likely you're recoiling in horror at this. Don't worry; we'll talk about this in more detail shortly.
- Finally, you execute the query, again passing in the connection string. This time, though, the connection string is used as the runtime data source, rather than for compile-time schema generation. The latest versions of the SqlCommandProvider

don't allow you to implicitly reuse the static connection string, to protect you from accidentally pointing to, for example, a development database at runtime, so you *have* to pass in a connection string when executing a query (even if, as in your case, it's the same one). It's as if there were no `GetSample()` function for the CSV provider, and you had to always use `Load()`. I'm not particularly fond of this decision, but I understand why it was made.

Now let's address the most obvious question: isn't embedding SQL directly into your application inherently bad? Leaving aside the point that you can pass in a path to a .sql file instead of embedding it in—no, in the case of the SqlCommandProvider, it's not a bad thing to do at all. That's because the SQL you've entered in there isn't just a magic string— it's actually used by F# in various ways to provide *compile-time* safety. First, the TP automatically generates a type based on the result set from SQL, for free; as you dot into `customer`, you're presented with IntelliSense that suggests properties, as shown in figure 32.2.

Figure 32.2 Working with data supplied from SQL by the SqlCommandProvider

Because SQL has a type system (with non-nullability across all types, unlike C#), there's also no need to try to infer the type based on a sample of data—you can use the schema from SQL and cascade it into F# directly. So, for example, if you navigate to the `MiddleName` property, you'll see that this has been rendered as a `string option` type, because it's a `varchar null` in SQL. And the type provider goes even further than this, as you're about to find out:

1 Write some code to print the text `<firstname> <lastname> works for <company name>` for the `customer` value. You'll need to either use `%A` for `CompanyName`, or use `defaultArg` to safely unwrap the value from an option.

2 Change the SQL to read `SELECT TOP 10 FirstName, LastName FROM SalesLT.Customer`. Observe that your code now no longer compiles, as the SQL outputs only `First-Name` and `LastName`. Also, notice that the error occurs in the exact place you'd expect, where the `CompanyName` field is accessed.

3 Change the table name in the SQL query from `Customer` to `Foo`. Observe that the query itself now no longer compiles, with the error `Invalid object name 'SalesLT.Foo'`.

Change the query to read `SELECT * FROM SalesLT.Customer WHERE CompanyName = @CompanyName`. This time, you'll see that the compiler breaks on the next line: the `Execute()` method now expects you to pass in the `CompanyName` as an argument as required by the query!

How does the type provider know which table names are valid in your database? How does it know to create a method taking in a value matching the parameter specified in the SQL? This is possible because the type provider validates the SQL against the SQL server itself while generating types (at compile time only; it doesn't happen at runtime). If the SQL is invalid, it automatically cascades the errors as a compiler error. Similarly, it uses this information in order to understand what arguments the SQL query expects, and then cascades them to the generated types.

> **SQL restrictions in the type provider**
> The SQL you can use here can be far more complex than simple `SELECT` statements; you can use joins, common table expressions, stored procedures—even table valued functions. But there are a few SQL commands that the TP doesn't support; have a look at the official documentation at http://fsprojects.github.io/FSharp.Data.SqlClient/.

32.2.2 Inserting data

You can insert data with the SqlClient package in two ways. The first is to generate insert or update commands and execute them as indicated previously. An alternative is to use a handy wrapper around good old .NET data tables; if you've been using .NET since before the days of LINQ, you'll remember these.

Now you try

Next you'll add some data to the Product Categories table. You'll use a second type provider included in the SqlClient package, called `SqlProgrammabilityProvider`:

1 Create a new `AdventureWorks` type by using the code:
   `type AdventureWorks = SqlProgrammabilityProvider<Conn>`.
2 Create an instance of the `ProductCategory` table type in F#. You can navigate to this via `AdventureWorks.SalesLT.Tables`; it's just a regular class.

In fact, this type is a standard DataTable, except it has added provided members on it, such as a strongly typed AddRow() method.

3 Add three items to the table by using the AddRow() method:

   a Mittens (Parent Category ID 3)

   b Long Shorts (Parent Category ID 3)

   c Wooly Hats (Parent Category ID 4)

   As the parent category ID is nullable on the database, you'll have to wrap the ID as an option; for example, Some 3.

4 You can then call the Update() method on the table. This does all the boilerplate of creating a DataAdapter and the appropriate insert command for you.

5 Back in SQL Server Object Explorer, check that the new items have been added by right-clicking the table and selecting View Data. You should see the extra rows added at the end of the table.

A BulkInsert() method also is added to data tables. This allows you to insert data by using SQL Bulk Copy functionality, which is extremely efficient and great for large one-off inserts of data. You can also use the data table for updates and deletes, or via T-SQL commands.

32.2.3 Working with reference data

One last area that the SqlClient package addresses is working with reference data. Normally, in any data-driven application, you'll have static (or relatively stable) sets of lookup data— categories, country lists, and regions that need to be referenced both in code and data. You'll normally have a C# enum (or perhaps a class with constant values in it) that matches a set of items scripted into a database. Obviously, you'll need to be careful to keep them in sync; for example, whenever a new item is added, you have to add it to the enum and also to the database with the same ID.

The type provider introduces SqlEnumProvider to help you by automatically generating a class with values for all reference data values based on an arbitrary query. Here's an example of that for product categories.

Listing 32.2 Generating client-side reference data from a SQL table

```
type Categories = SqlEnumProvider<"SELECT Name, ProductCategoryId
  FROM SalesLT.ProductCategory", Conn>      ◄——    Generating a Categories type
let woolyHats = Categories.``Wooly Hats``    ◄——    for all product categories
printfn "Wooly Hats has ID %d" woolyHats
```

Accessing the Wooly Hats integer ID

What's interesting is that you've now bound your F# type system to the *data inside a remote system*. If you were to delete the Wooly Hats row from the database and then close and reopen the script in Visual Studio (to force the compiler to regenerate the provided types), you'd see that the code no longer compiles. In this way, it's impossible at compile time for your code and data to become out of sync. Of course, if you deploy the application and then delete the data from the DB, you're out of luck; remember that type providers are a compile-time-only feature.

Quick check 32.1

1 How does the SqlCommandProvider remove the risk of "stringly-typed" queries?
2 In addition to manually creating INSERT statements, how else does the SqlClient package let you perform data insertion?

 ## 32.3 Using the SQLProvider

I'm aware that not everyone is a fan of the sort of low-level SQL queries that the Sql-Client library forces us down. Personally, I'm a big fan of them, as the sort of stateless model is a good match with FP practices, is a good fit for many applications, and completely avoids many of the antipatterns that you can end up with when using large ORMs. Nonetheless, a fantastic type provider called SQLProvider (http://fsprojects .github.io/SQLProvider/) offers an alternative way to work with SQL databases. I should also point out that SQLProvider isn't bound to SQL Server only—it also works with Oracle, SQLite, Postgres, MySQL, and many ODBC data sources. Let's see how to achieve the same sort of functionality as with the SqlClient package.

32.3.1 Querying data

As an ORM, SQLProvider supports the IQueryable pattern. Like many IQueryable providers, it's not 100% complete, but it's powerful enough to do the things you'll need on a day-to-day basis—and a lot more. Here's an example of an F# query expression to get the first 10 customers.

QC 32.1 answer

1 By providing edit- and compile-time validation of the query against a live SQL database.
2 Through DataTable support, which provides Insert and BulkInsert functionality.

Listing 32.3 Querying data by using the SQLProvider library

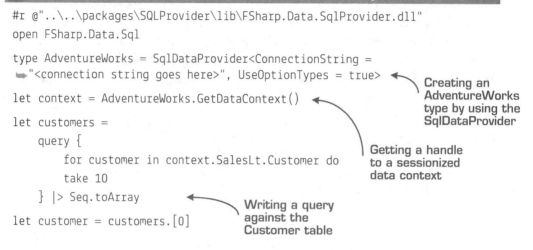

```
#r @"..\..\packages\SQLProvider\lib\FSharp.Data.SqlProvider.dll"
open FSharp.Data.Sql

type AdventureWorks = SqlDataProvider<ConnectionString =
    "<connection string goes here>", UseOptionTypes = true>

let context = AdventureWorks.GetDataContext()

let customers =
    query {
        for customer in context.SalesLt.Customer do
        take 10
    } |> Seq.toArray

let customer = customers.[0]
```

Creating an AdventureWorks type by using the SqlDataProvider

Getting a handle to a sessionized data context

Writing a query against the Customer table

Again, let's quickly review this. Having referenced the SQLProvider assembly, you create a provided type for the database. Notice that this type provider takes in further parameters—in this case, whether to generate option types for nullable columns (otherwise, a default value will be generated instead). Next, you create a handle to a *Data-Context*. If you've used Entity Framework before, you'll know what a data context is—a stateful handle to a database within which client-side operations can be tracked and then a set of changes sent back to the database. Finally, you write a query expression to take the first 10 customers from the database.

More on query expressions

F# query expressions are another form of computation expression, similar to what you saw earlier with seq { } (and will see again in the next unit with async { }). A query expression can be thought of as equivalent to a LINQ query in C#: they operate in a similar way, with an expression tree parsed by a specific provider to convert the tree into another language (in this case, T-SQL). Unlike the LINQ query syntax, which is fairly limited, F# query expressions have a large set of operations, such as sortBy, exists, contains, and skip; see https://docs.microsoft.com/en-us/dotnet/articles/fsharp/language-reference/query-expressions for the full list. Query expressions can be used in F# over any IQueryable data source, so you can use them anywhere you'd write a LINQ query in C#.

You're not restricted to using the table entities either. You can project results to your own custom records or use tuples (remember that F# doesn't have anonymous types).

Listing 32.4 Projecting data within a more complex query

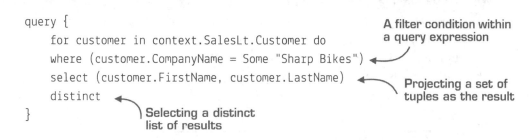

```
query {
    for customer in context.SalesLt.Customer do
    where (customer.CompanyName = Some "Sharp Bikes")
    select (customer.FirstName, customer.LastName)
    distinct
}
```

A filter condition within a query expression

Projecting a set of tuples as the result

Selecting a distinct list of results

One of the nicest things about SQLProvider is that, unlike SqlClient, you get full Intelli-Sense on the tables and columns within it. This makes it excellent for exploration of a database, because you don't have to leave F# to understand the database contents; you get everything through IntelliSense.

32.3.2 Inserting data

Adding data to the database is simple. You create new entities through the data context, set properties, and then save changes—basically the same pattern that you use with Entity Framework.

Listing 32.5 Inserting new data

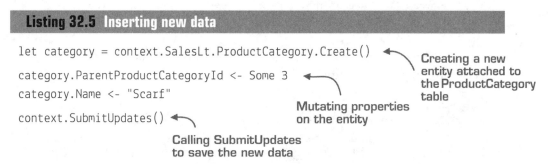

```
let category = context.SalesLt.ProductCategory.Create()
category.ParentProductCategoryId <- Some 3
category.Name <- "Scarf"
context.SubmitUpdates()
```

Creating a new entity attached to the ProductCategory table

Mutating properties on the entity

Calling SubmitUpdates to save the new data

It's worth running this yourself. Observe that all entities track their own states and have a _State property on them. If you create a new entity, you'll see that its initial state is Created, but after calling SubmitUpdates(), its state changes to Unchanged. It's also interesting to note that unlike SqlClient, SQLProvider uses a data context, which by its very nature is stateful. Updates are performed by first loading the data from the database, mutating the records, and then calling SubmitChanges().

32.3.3 Working with reference data

Working with reference data with the SQL Provider is incredibly easy thanks to a feature called *individuals*. Every table on the context has a property called Individuals, which will generate a list of properties that match the *rows in the database*—essentially the same as the Enum Provider. You also have subproperties underneath that allow you to choose which column acts as the "text" property (for example, As Name or As ModifiedDate), as shown in figure 32.3.

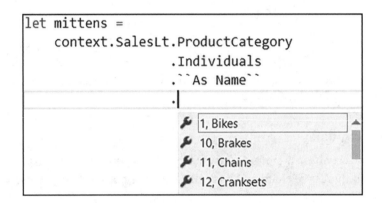

Figure 32.3   Navigating through reference data by using Individuals by Name

Again, like the SqlClient, the items in this list are based on the database contents, so if data is removed, you'll instantly know that your application is out of sync.

> **What about Entity Framework?**
>
> I don't want to rule out Entity Framework (EF) as a data access technology for F#; I simply don't feel it's as powerful or useful as either of the preceding type providers, both of which give you much stronger type checking than EF in different ways, and allow you to start exploring databases much more quickly—in just a few lines of code, as you've seen. Furthermore, to create entities that work with EF requires creating types that have mutable virtual properties and the like—the complete opposite of the kinds of types that F# makes it easy to use. For these reasons, I suggest using one of the preceding technologies (or similar) rather than EF. If you *must* use EF, I recommend creating a C# layer for your entity model and accessing that from F#.

Quick check 32.2

1   What's the key distinction between SqlClient and SQLProvider?
2   Is SQLProvider coupled to just MS SQL Server?

Summary

In this lesson, you saw how to use two type providers to work with relational data stores, and how simple they can make your life. They fit especially well with the exploratory nature of scripts, and give you much stronger typing than you might be used to when working with SQL and .NET. In this lesson

- You saw the SqlClient library, a lightweight wrapper on top of ADO .NET that gives you strongly typed and validated SQL commands directly within F#.
- You then saw the SQLProvider, an alternative type provider that uses an ORM-style data context model for exploring and working with SQL.
- You learned about F# query expressions, another form of computation expression that allows you to model queries against data.
- You saw how type providers can be used to bring data into the type system directly with, for example, reference data and individuals.

Try this

Connect to a database that you already have. Experiment with using both type providers against the data source. Also, look at reference data tables that you have in your application layer; see if you can replicate this using both type providers and compare this to the approach you've currently taken.

QC 32.2 answer

1   SqlClient is a low-level type provider in which you write your own SQL. The SQLProvider is an ORM that generates queries and commands based on query expressions.
2   No, the SQLProvider works with several other SQL databases.

33

CREATING TYPE PROVIDER-BACKED APIS

So far in this unit, you've looked at various types providers; hopefully, you now get the gist of how they typically operate as well as the sorts of features and pitfalls to be aware of so that you can explore and try out other ones yourself. This lesson shows how to quickly create APIs driven by type providers that other components can easily consume. You'll learn

- How coupling to type providers can affect your application
- How to create APIs over type providers
- When to create decoupled APIs

Just so that we're on the same page here, let's recap what I mean by a *type provider–backed API*. So far, you've looked at using type providers in an *exploratory* mode—for example, analyzing data within a single script. But there's nothing to stop you from integrating type providers within the context of a *standalone application* as well—be they console applications or web apps, whether 100% F# or hybrid language applications. There are, however, some things that are worth being aware of before trying to integrate a type provider into an application.

At their most basic, type provider APIs are no different than standard data-oriented APIs that you create; these typically follow the Gateway, Facade, or Repository design patterns, by providing a simple layer on top of a lower-level data access layer. Even if you don't know what those design patterns are, you've probably done this sort of thing a hundred times before with data access technologies such as Entity Framework or ADO .NET to provide a layer of abstraction between your application and the underlying, for example, SQL, database, as shown in figure 33.1.

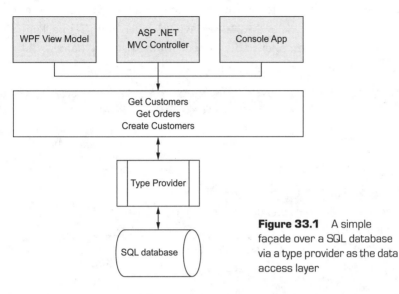

Figure 33.1   A simple façade over a SQL database via a type provider as the data access layer

33.1 Creating a tightly coupled type provider API

In this section, you'll create a simple API that follows from a previous lesson—one that can provide statistics on NuGet packages. You'll create a simple API to do the following:

- Retrieve the total number of downloads for any given package
- Retrieve details for a specific version of a NuGet package
- Retrieve details of the latest stable release of a NuGet package

33.1.1 Building your first API

Start by building your first API, which directly exposes data and types generated by a type provider.

Now you try

1 Create a new F# console project and add the FSharp.Data NuGet package.
2 Create a script file called NuGet.fsx in which you'll write the API. You'll port this into an .fs file later, but for now you'll stick with a script and the REPL while you're in exploration mode.

3   Reference FSharp.Data within the script by either using `#reference` manually or a Power Tools-generated script and `#loading` it.

4   Open the FSharp.Data namespace and create an instance of the HTML type provider that points to sample-package.html that you looked at earlier in this unit.

5   Create a function, `getDownloadsForPackage`, which, given a NuGet package name, will return the total number of downloads for the package name.

6   Your code should look something like the following listing.

Listing 33.1   Creating your first type provider–backed API function

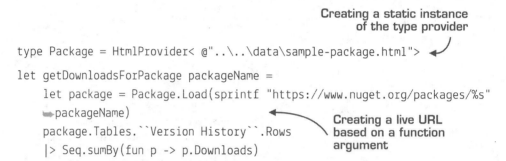

Creating a static instance
of the type provider

```
type Package = HtmlProvider< @"..\..\data\sample-package.html">

let getDownloadsForPackage packageName =
    let package = Package.Load(sprintf "https://www.nuget.org/packages/%s"
    packageName)
    package.Tables.``Version History``.Rows
    |> Seq.sumBy(fun p -> p.Downloads)
```

Creating a live URL
based on a function
argument

That was easy! The most important part is that you're dynamically building up the URL for the "live" HTML Provider endpoint based on the package name that's supplied, after which you perform a simple in-memory query. You'll notice that the function has a simple signature of `string -> decimal`. There's no clue for the caller that they're using a type provider:

7   Try calling this function from the script for a set of packages (for example, Entity-Framework and Newtonsoft.Json).

8   Now try the next API function. Create a new function, `getDetailsForVersion`. It should download the package as before, except this time the query will be different—you'll try to find the row where the Version *contains* text that will be provided as an argument. You can use `find` or `tryFind` in the `Seq` module for this (essentially the F# equivalents to LINQ's `First` and `FirstOrDefault`).

9   Notice that this function returns a strange-looking type called `HtmlProvider<…>` `.VersionHistory.Row` (and if you used `tryFind`, as a wrapped `option`). This is the *static name* of a *provided type* that represents Version rows; you're exposing this type directly outside your API. Now, that's not necessarily a problem, but it *is* something we'll discuss again later in this lesson.

33.1.2 An exercise in refactoring

At this point, let's take a quick detour and see how to do a little refactoring of the code to get some reuse across both functions, as they both do something similar. A basic refactor might be to create a helper function that loads the package by name so that you can call it from both functions—something like this.

Listing 33.2 Trying to gain code reuse across multiple functions

Creating a helper function to load package data

```
let getPackage packageName =
    packageName |> sprintf "https://www.nuget.org/packages/%s" |>
    Package.Load
let getDetailsForVersion versionText packageName =
    let package = getPackage packageName
    package.Tables.``Version History``.Rows |> Seq.tryFind(fun p ->
    p.Version.Contains versionText)
```

Using the helper function in a higher-level function

That's not bad, but you can do better. Here's a more tightly refactored version that uses function composition to reduce the size of your API functions to the bare essentials.

Listing 33.3 Further refactoring an API implementation

Retrieves package data

Navigates to the Version History rows

```
let getPackage =
    sprintf "https://www.nuget.org/packages/%s" >> Package.Load
let getVersionsForPackage (package:Package) =
    package.Tables.``Version History``.Rows
let loadPackageVersions = getPackage >> getVersionsForPackage
let getDownloadsForPackage =
    loadPackageVersions >> Seq.sumBy(fun p -> p.Downloads)
let getDetailsForVersion versionText =
    loadPackageVersions >> Seq.tryFind(fun p -> p.Version.Contains
    versionText)
```

Composes the first two functions together

Uses the composed function at the API level

A refresher on pipelines and composition

Before you go too much further, let's quickly recap the three core features of functions in F# (refer to lesson 11 if you need to):

- Piping (|>) pipes a value through a set of functions in sequence and returns the resulting value.
- Composing (>>) combines several functions into a new function. When called with a value, the resulting function will pipe the value through those functions in sequence.
- Partial application, or currying, is the ability to call a function and supply only a subset of the inputs; a new function is returned that takes the remaining arguments as inputs.

Let's go through this step by step. First, you can simplify the getPackage function by using *function composition*. Remember the >> operator? Well, you can use it here to eliminate the explicit packageName argument being passed in—in other words, sprint "…%s" can itself be thought of as a function that takes in a string and returns another string, which you then connect as the input for the Package.Load function. And because the input of Package .Load is a string, the signatures are compatible.

Next, you create a simple helper function, getVersionsForPackage, that navigates to the rows of the VersionHistory.Rows collection of a given package. You could've written this as an inline lambda, but I think that this is more readable.

Third, you compose those two functions together to build an even bigger function, load-PackageVersions. Again, compare the inputs and outputs, as shown in figure 33.2.

Figure 33.2 Composing functions together to build progressively more complex behaviors

You can compose getPackage and getVersionsForPackage together because the *output* of the first is the same type as the *input* of the second function. The composed function takes in the same type as the input of the first function, and returns the same type as the output of the last function. This leaves the main two API functions, which you compose *again* (!)—

this time using the appropriate query function that you wanted to use before. In this way, you can start to build up tiny composable and reusable behaviors quickly and easily (refer to lesson 11, or for the official reference, to https://docs.microsoft.com/ en-us/dotnet/articles/fsharp/language-reference/functions/index).

10 Create the final function, `getDetailsForCurrentVersion`. This should do the same as `getDetailsForVersion`, except that the text you're looking for is always the same: `"(this version)"`. You should be able to create this function by calling `getDetails-ForCurrent-Version` and supplying only the first argument (the version text to search for).

Although this mini-exercise you've just gone through doesn't have anything to do specifically with type providers, it's a good lesson in composing small functions together to build more complex ones that can be used as the basis for an API (or indeed any DSL).

> **Quick check 33.1**
>
> 1 Can you build APIs from type providers?
> 2 What rule must be followed in order to compose two functions together?
> 3 Can we reference provided types statically in function signatures?

33.2 Creating a decoupled API

What you've done will work just fine. But sometimes, exposing provided types directly as an API won't be suitable or even possible. In this case, you need to manually construct types (such as F# records and discriminated unions) and then map from the provided types to these manually created types. In this case, you create a truly decoupled API from the type provider in the sense that you expose no types at all from the type provider to callers.

QC 33.1 answer

1 Yes, by using the provided types as the domain.
2 The output of the first function must be the same type as the input of the second.
3 Yes.

33.2.1   Reasons for not exposing provided types over an API

Here are issues you might come across when working with type providers and reasons that you might want to decouple yourself from provided types within your application code base:

- The business domain may not fit exactly with the data supplied by a type provider (particularly providers that don't allow you to reshape, or *project*, the data in any way), so you may need to map between the two.
- Remember that (at the time of writing) provided types can't create records or discriminated unions. This limits the richness of the types that can be emitted from a type provider, which may in turn lead to writing extra code to compensate for this. It might be better to map to a richer domain earlier, which will simplify the rest of your code base.
- Provided types generally can't be consumed outside F#. If you have a hybrid language solution, you can forget about consuming an API such as the preceding one from C#, because in two of the methods, you expose provided types in your public API.
- Most type providers create types that are erased at runtime. You can't reflect over them, and therefore any code that uses reflection or something similar to generate outputs won't work. You wouldn't be able to use the SQL Provider directly with a framework like Newtonsoft.Json to create JSON from provided types, because at runtime there are no types to reflect over; everything's just a System.Object.

> **Working with provided types at runtime**
>
> Authors of type providers use a few workarounds to get around the erasing types runtime issue. One is to create generative type providers, which emit "real" types at runtime that can be reflected over. This approach has pros and cons; some type providers are specifically designed to be erasing as they carry no runtime overhead in terms of types. The alternative is that some type providers expose a weakly typed dictionary of key/value string pairs for the properties that can be accessed at runtime.

33.2.2   Enriching a domain by using F# types

Let's see how to create a slightly more expressive domain for your NuGet packages for your API. Here's a set of F# types that represents your domain more expressively than what you're getting back from the HTML type provider.

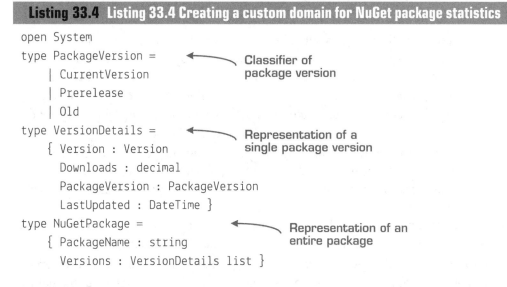

Listing 33.4 Listing 33.4 Creating a custom domain for NuGet package statistics

```
open System
type PackageVersion =              ◄            Classifier of
    | CurrentVersion                            package version
    | Prerelease
    | Old
type VersionDetails =              ◄            Representation of a
    { Version : Version                         single package version
      Downloads : decimal
      PackageVersion : PackageVersion
      LastUpdated : DateTime }
type NuGetPackage =                ◄            Representation of an
    { PackageName : string                      entire package
      Versions : VersionDetails list }
```

This model has some nice properties compared to the original model. For example, you no longer have the package name repeated through every version; it's now stored only once at the top of the package. In addition, each version is now no longer just a string, but has a proper System.Version as well as a classification of whether this version is a prerelease, current, or historical package. With this model, you could more easily reason about the versions in a package, so it would be easy (and much safer!) to find out the current version of a package, or to determine whether there have ever been any beta versions.

33.2.3 Mapping between provided types and F# domains

Of course, now you actually need to write the code to map from your provided types to this rich domain! I encourage you to have a crack at doing this yourself. I've also supplied a sample solution next (and in the source code sample repository).

Now you try

Now try to create the code to map from the provider types to your strongly typed F# domain:

1 Write a function, parse. This function should take in a single string representing the Version property of a NuGet VersionHistory row, and return a tuple of a System .Version object (based on the version in the supplied string) and the classification

of PackageVersion. So, the string "Json.NET 8.0.3" should return (8.0.3, Old), and
"9.0.2-beta1" should return (9.0.2, Prerelease).

2 You can split the string on both a space and - to determine the sort of version it is,
   and then use pattern matching on the resultant array to identify the sort of string
   it is. Watch out when splitting strings because package names can have spaces in
   them (for example, F# Data 2.2.3). You can use either standard array indexing
   logic or pattern matching. You might struggle with pattern matching, so you can
   refer to my suggested solution for that. There are two cases:

   a If the string ends in "(this version)", the package name is all words except the
      last three words, which will be, for example, "2.2.3 (this version)".

   b Otherwise, the package name will be all words except for the last word, which
      will be the version.

3 Write a function, enrich, that takes in a sequence of VersionHistory.Row objects (from
   the type provider) and returns NuGetPackage (your new domain model).

4 To determine the package name, take the package name from the first row in the
   collection (again, you'll need to do some work to parse to just get out the name
   part). Assume that it's repeated across all rows, so it's safe to use the first row.

5 You can create the Version list by creating a VersionDetails record for each row,
   copying across the Downloads and LastUpdated fields, and parsing the Version field.

Here's a sample solution for the parse function if you got stuck! The rest of the solution is
provided in the source code samples.

Listing 33.5   Creating a custom domain for NuGet package statistics

Inner function to parse
version number from a string

```
let parse (versionText:string) =
    let getVersionPart (version:string) isCurrent =
        match version.Split '-', isCurrent with
        | [| version; _ |], true
        | [| version |], true -> Version.Parse version, CurrentVersion
        | [| version; _ |], false -> Version.Parse version, Prerelease
        | [| version |], false -> Version.Parse version, Old
        | _ -> failwith "unknown version format"
    let parts = versionText.Split ' ' |> Seq.toList |> List.rev
    match parts with
    | [] -> failwith "Must be at least two elements to a version"
```

Converting
an array of
strings to a
reversed list

```
| "version)" :: "(this" :: version :: _ -> getVersionPart version true
| version :: _ -> getVersionPart version false
```

Matching on two cases of strings to parse version number and identify current/old version

This is more complex pattern matching than you've previously seen. Looking at the lowest pattern match (not the one in getVersionPart), you do two things:

1 Split the string on spaces, convert it to a list, and then reverse it.

2 Pattern match on the list of strings. You can also match on arrays, but one of the nice things you can do with lists is to decompose part of a list.

3 The first match says that if it's an empty list, you'll fail with an error.

4 The next match clause says that the list must contain at least three elements, the first two of which must be "version)" and "(this", and the third part will bind to the symbol version. The remaining elements are ignored.

5 Otherwise, you say that the first element of the list is bound to version, and then ignore the rest.

You do similar pattern matching for the helper function, which parses the version string to get out the version number and the pre-release/current version status. Notice that when you're pattern matching here, you match against a bounded array, one that has a known length at compile time, by using [|a;b;c;|] syntax (with lists, it's [a;b;c;]). Previously, you checked against an unbounded list by using [a::b::c::_]. This unbounded syntax works only for lists, and unbounded lists work *forwards-only*, so you reverse the list before matching.

The benefit of using pattern matching for this sort of parsing rather than list/array indexing is that you use the F# *language* to get to individual parts of the array. With this approach, you can much more concisely and precisely state what you want to check rather than using things such as array length values and so on. It's also impossible to "accidentally" index into an item that doesn't exist when using pattern matching against an array or list.

33.2.4 Updating your API with a new domain

Finally, now update your API to use a new domain. It's very natural to do in F#, thanks to both function composition and type inference.

Listing 33.6 **Listing 33.6 Updating your API with your latest domain model**

```
let loadPackageVersions = getPackage >> getVersionsForPackage >> enrich >>
    (fun p -> p.Versions)
let getDetailsForVersion version = loadPackageVersions >> Seq.find(fun p ->
    p.Version = version)
let getDetailsForCurrentVersion = loadPackageVersions >> Seq.find(fun p ->
    p.PackageVersion = CurrentVersion)

let details =
    "Newtonsoft.Json" |> getDetailsForVersion (Version.Parse "9.0.1")
```

Adding your enrich
function into the
existing pipeline

Getting details for a
specific version of
Newtonsoft.Json

As you can see, it's not a great deal of code. The main work is to add the enrich function into loadPackageVersions, and then add a small inline function that returns the versions. You could have left that last part out, but then all callers would need to do it. Then, you simply fix the compiler errors. In the case of getDetailsForCurrentVersion, it involves more or less a total rewrite because it can no longer reuse the getDetailsForVersion function, but when a total rewrite of a function consists of half a line of code, that's not a massive problem.

> **Saving data with type providers**
>
> You're seeing in this unit how effective type providers are at reading data. What about saving data back out? Some type providers support this, although because of their nature, it's probably not the standard behavior. Often you'll need to look at putting the data into records and then persisting them manually.

33.2.5 Converting to a standalone application

The last part of this lesson will quickly port your code over to a full-blown application. It's pretty simple!

Now you try

You'll now convert your script to a standalone application:

1 Rename the file to an .fs file.
2 Remove any #load or #references you have.

3 Remove any code in the file that doesn't relate to the API itself.

4 Place a module declaration at the top (for example, `module NuGet`)

5 Ensure that the following remains:

   a Open the FSharp.Data namespace.

   b Create the type provider type.

   c Define your custom domain model.

   d Mark all functions as private except those that you want to expose in the API.

6 From Program.fs, you should be able to call your API; for example:

```
getDetailsForCurrentVersion "entityframework" |> printfn "%A"
```

Quick check 33.2

   1 Give one reason you might use a decoupled API over type providers.
   2 What benefit does pattern matching over lists give you versus indexing in directly?
   3 What does the :: symbol mean in the context of pattern matching over lists?

 **Summary**

This lesson showed you how to start using type providers within the context of a running application, rather than simply within scripts. In this lesson

- You created a simple API façade over a type provider.
- You learned about times when provided types aren't always suitable for use within an application, and where you may prefer to use a richer domain model instead.
- You created a rich F# domain and mapped from provided types to it.
- You practiced refactoring code by using composition and type inference.
- You saw an example of more advanced pattern matching to parse strings.

QC 33.2 answer

   1 Richer types (for example, DUs), as well as improved interoperability with C#.
   2 Compile-time safety.
   3 Splits a list into a head and tail.

Try this

Building on a previous "Try this," create an API that can return the songs for any given Dream Theater album by using Wikipedia as a data source. Try returning strings to start with; then build up to creating an explicit domain model for Albums and Tracks, hydrating the model from the provided HTML provider types. Then, expose this as a WPF application written in C#.

34

USING TYPE PROVIDERS IN THE REAL WORLD

This is the final lesson on type providers. So far, you've looked at various providers in the data space. You understand how and where to use them, what their strengths are, and when and where you might not use them. In this lesson, you'll wrap up by working specifically with type providers in a real-world development process. You'll learn about

- Working with configuration files
- Manually redirecting type providers
- Using type providers in a continuous integration (CI) environment

34.1 Securely accessing connection strings with type providers

You've already looked at how to point to live data sources in a type provider, by redirecting from a static data source to a remote one at runtime. Sometimes this works quickly and easily—as you saw with public sources such as the public NuGet feed—but occasionally you'll need to point to a secure resource, which means you'll need to pull in a secret key at runtime in order to access the "real" data. This could be a NuGet key, a SQL connection string, or a username and password—it doesn't matter. The question is, how can you provide that secret value safely to the type provider? You certainly don't want to hardcode your secret connection string into the application, so what can you do?

34.1.1 Working with configuration files

One option that many type providers offer is the ability to use *application configuration files* to source a connection string, rather than having to supply it directly within code as a literal value (which is what you've done so far). This provides immediate benefits:

- Config files are a well-understood concept in .NET and will be familiar to you.
- Config file values can be replaced at deployment or runtime without any changes to your application code or binaries.
- No secure strings reside in your code base.

Now you try

Now you're going to quickly use the configuration file support within the SQL Client type provider to see how to easily use configuration files:

1 If you haven't yet done so, run build.cmd in the root directory of the source listings to ensure you have the SQL Client type provider NuGet package on disk.
2 Open the ready-made TypeProviderConfig solution in src\code-listings\lesson-34. This contains a simple console application, SqlDemo, that retrieves the first 50 customers from the database and prints their company and names to the console.
3 Observe that the connection string is hardcoded into the application in order to create the Command type.
4 Observe that the same connection is used in order to execute the query (line 8).
5 Open the app.config file in the project and locate the AdventureWorks connection string element.
6 Set the value of the connectionString attribute to the connection string being used in Program.fs.
7 Remove the connection string symbol (Conn) from F# and update the GetCustomers definition as follows.

Listing 34.1 Supplying connection details to a type provider via config

```
type GetCustomers = SqlCommandProvider<"SELECT TOP 50 * FROM
SalesLT.Customer", "Name=AdventureWorks">
```
⟵ Supplying the connection string name to the SQL Client type provider

8 Remove the explicit Conn value being supplied to the GetCustomers.Create() call, as it's no longer needed. (Note: this is a specific design decision of the SQL Client type provider.)

You've now removed the hardcoded connection string from code and replaced it with a *reference* to a connection string in a configuration file.

9   Go back into the app.config file and deliberately change the connection string to something invalid (for example, "XXX").

10 Rebuild the solution. Observe that your solution no longer compiles. You'll have to correct the connection string in the configuration file first.

34.1.2 Problems with configuration files

Configuration files are a familiar way to store connection strings. They're well supported in the .NET ecosystem, with dedicated support for connection strings as well. But a couple of issues may arise with configuration files that can make it difficult to work with them and type providers, particularly when you use configuration files as the source for both compile-time and runtime data.

The most important issue is that working with configuration files from within scripts is a real pain. By default, the app.config file that the script will be bound to isn't your project's config file, but rather one that's used to host F# Interactive—FSI.exe (see figure 34.1)! Visual Studio's REPL (FSI) is just a standard .NET application and has its own app.config file.

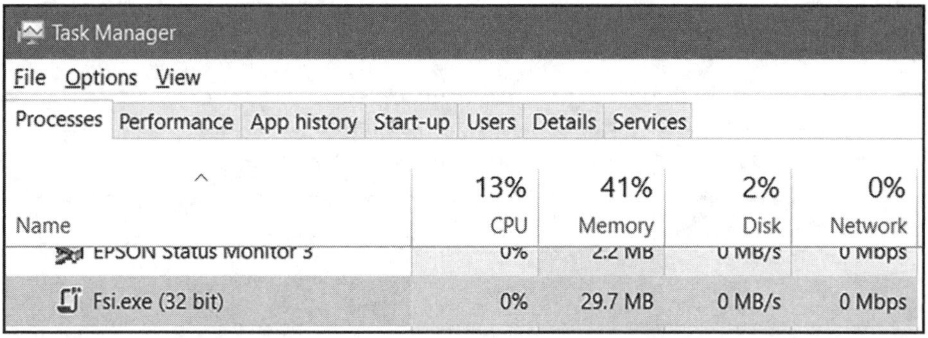

Figure 34.1 FSI.exe is a standard .NET application that can be viewed in Task Manager.

Thus, if you try to bind to a type provider that's driven from a connection string from within a script (or #load a file that contains code that does this), there's a good chance that the type provider will try to search within FSI.exe.config rather than your application config file. This almost certainly isn't what you want, especially when working on a team of developers, as each one will need to remember to do this in their own environment. If they forget, they won't get errors when compiling (as compile time will correctly use app.config in the project!), but when #loading the same code from within a script, they will get errors. Take it from me: it will end in tears; don't do it.

> **SQL Client and configuration files**
> The SQl Client package does support some form of redirection here, and you can override the default behavior and supply a specific path to an app.config at compile time so that a different config file is used. But it's complicated to manage and confusing to reason about. Which config file is being used at compile time? What about at runtime?

If you're working on a large project, with many developers, and you want to retain the ability to #load code that performs data access with type providers through scripts, be aware of the limitations. There's nothing to prevent you from saying that any code you #load through scripts can't connect to a database directly, and that data (or functions that return data) must be supplied via higher-order functions. In other words, code that *operates* on data should never be responsible for directly *retrieving* that data itself. It may be supplied by a function that loads data, but this is done in a decoupled manner. This is a good practice in some ways, as it reduces coupling between your business application and the source of data for them, which in turn makes testability easier.

> **Quick check 34.1**
> 1 Can you use connection strings with type providers?
> 2 Name one benefit of using connection strings with type providers.
> 3 When should you not use connection strings with type providers?

> **QC 34.1 answer**
> 1 Yes.
> 2 Ease of use.
> 3 When you want to decouple code from a data source, especially with scripts.

34.2 Manually passing connection strings

What other options are there? The second choice is more akin to what we've discussed previously in this unit: using a static, hardcoded connection to a public/local data source for compile-time code, and redirecting to a secure connection at runtime (see figure 34.2)

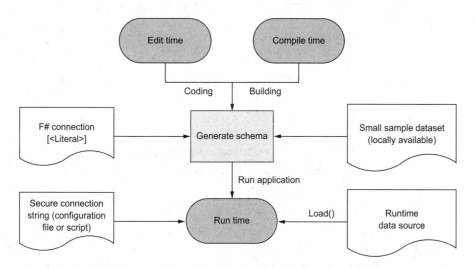

Figure 34.2 Using different data sources and connections at compile time and runtime

In this way, you can control your application at compile time through a well-known sample dataset—perhaps just enough rows of data to allow you to compile the application and for the type provider to infer schema. Then, at runtime, you (optionally) redirect to another data source. This might be a test database, or integration server, or a private feed of data that contains secure information. This is passed in to the type provider as an override. (In the context of, for example, FSharp.Data, you'll use Load() rather than GetSample(); in the case of SQL Client, it means passing in a connection string when calling Create().)

Now you try

Let's see how to adapt your code to work with a supplied override connection string sourced from a configuration file:

1 Replace Program.fs with the following code.

Listing 34.2 **Separating retrieval of live connection string from application code**

```
open System.Configuration

[<EntryPoint>]
let main _ =
    let runtimeConnectionString =
        ConfigurationManager
            .ConnectionStrings
            .["AdventureWorks"]
            .ConnectionString
    CustomerRepository.printCustomers(runtimeConnectionString)
    0
```

Retrieving a connection string from the configuration file manually

Supplying that connection string to the data access layer

CustomerRepository is a module that contains the same code that you wrote earlier in Program.fs, except it now expects a connection string to be supplied to it for use at runtime. In the case of your console application, you can retrieve this from the app.config file by using the standard .NET Configuration Manager.

2 Open the DataAccessThroughScript.fsx file and execute the code in it.

3 Observe that this file does the same thing as Program.fs, except rather than read from a configuration file, you've hardcoded a connection string in the script and supplied it in, but this could conceivably come from anywhere (a text file, config file, or a web service, for example).

The main takeaway here is that you've decoupled your data access code from the retrieval of the connection string to the data source. Your console application uses the app.config file to retrieve the connection string, but your script wasn't forced to use that as well. This sort of decoupling is crucial when developing larger applications, because being able to quickly and easily "jump in" to a specific, arbitrary source file through a script and test it quickly and easily is a key benefit of working with scripts and a REPL.

Quick check 34.2   Why is it good practice to decouple your data access code from a connection string?

QC 34.2 answer   Scripts can more easily access production code against any data source.

34.3 Continuous integration with type providers

Let's now talk a little about working with continuous integration (CI) and continuous deployment (CD) processes. Both terms relate to the automation of your application being compiled, tested, and optionally deployed whenever you make changes to the source code. You may already be using systems such as Team City, Jenkins, AppVeyor, or Visual Studio Team Services for this. Even if you aren't using them today, they're growing in popularity all the time, and it's worth knowing how type providers work with them.

34.3.1 Data as part of the CI process

You already know that type providers generate types at compile time not through a custom tool (as in the case of T4 templates), but through the F# compiler. Whenever you perform a build of code, the type provider kicks in, accessing the data source from which it generates types that are used later in the compilation process.

Of course, CI servers build your code too—not just Visual Studio! Your build server will need access to a valid data source in order to compile your code. For some data sources, this won't be a problem (for example, CSV or JSON data); include a static sample file in your solution and compile off that. But what about other data sources, such as SQL Server or Azure Storage? What then? The answer is, as usual, that it depends. Some data sources have local emulators that can run on a build server (such as Azure Storage), or may already host lightweight processes that can be used for compilation (SQL Server has LocalDB). Other systems may not have such a rich tooling environment, and you might need to have a "real" data source service available for your CI server to use in order to build code.

34.3.2 Creating a build process with a SQL type provider

Figure 34.3 contains an example of how to achieve this sort of approach when using a SQL type provider. The key is to be able to quickly and easily create an *isolated* database on the CI server itself (or at least, on a database server that the CI server can easily reach). This is relatively easy to achieve by using SQL Server LocalDB (the same database service you used earlier in this unit) and Microsoft's DACPAC technology. Many CI servers support LocalDB out of the box, including AppVeyor and Microsoft's own Visual Studio Team Services.

Once the CI database is built, the application points to it for compilation (and potentially unit testing or integration testing). Then, after the build and test phases are completed, a separate configuration value is used to direct the *runtime* connection string that's set to point to the live database server. The build database is then destroyed; when a new commit into source control occurs, a clean database using the latest database schema is created and the whole process starts again.

Using this approach, it's extremely difficult to get into a situation where your source code and the latest database schema get out of date. If you make changes to the database and commit it without testing against the latest source code, the compile will fail if the schema changes are incompatible with your F#. You won't even need to run integration tests!

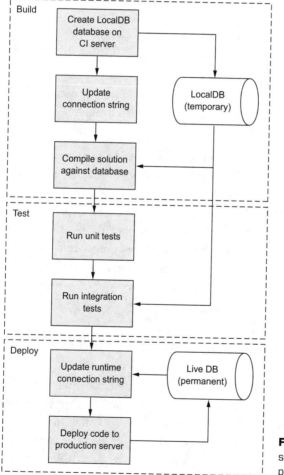

Figure 34.3 Building a solution using a SQL type provider through a CI server

Quick check 34.3 Why is creating a CI process sometimes more work when using type providers?

Best practices

You've seen alternative mechanisms for configuring type providers in this lesson. It's important to always remember that type providers nearly always have two modes of operation—*compile time* and *runtime*—and that you can usually redirect type providers to a different data source at runtime.

Things get trickier when mixing scripts as a driver against production code, especially if you throw configuration files into the mix. Be careful when making choices as to whether to use configuration files. My advice is summarized in table 34.1.

Table 34.1 Configuring type providers

Compile time	Runtime	Effort	Best for
Literal values	Literal values	Very easy	Simple systems, scripts, fixed data sources
app.config	app.config	Easy	Simple redirection, improved security
Literal values	Function argument	Medium	Script drivers, large teams, full control

I advise you to start with using simpler configuration mechanisms, as you may be fine using, for example, literal values for many use cases. But for larger teams—and where you want to be able to hook into your F# code base through arbitrary scripts—manually passing connection strings in your application gives you the most control, at the cost of greater effort.

QC 34.3 answer You need to ensure that data sources required by type providers are available as part of the CI process in order to perform a build of your application..

 **Summary**

In this lesson

- You saw some ways to replace type provider configuration data to allow working with private connection strings.
- You saw the pros and cons of various approaches to working with connection strings.
- You worked with type providers within the context of a CI process.

That's the end of the "Working with Data" unit! You've seen how easy it is to explore data within the context of F#, using the REPL in conjunction with type providers to rapidly investigate data sources, perform operations, and then visualize them. You've also seen tips and exercises for incorporating type providers within a standalone .NET application as well as some of the concerns for working with connection strings in a secure fashion.

Try this

Perform a build by using your CI tool of choice (Team City, for example). Build an F# application by using a type provider with a local data source for compiling, but a remote one for execution.

35

LESSON

CAPSTONE 6

Before you leave the world of data, let's apply some of what you learned in this unit to the Bank Accounts solution you've been working on. In this lesson, you'll plug in a SQL Database layer to the application instead of the file-based repository that you've been using until now.

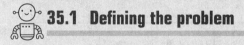

35.1 Defining the problem

This capstone is an exercise in hooking in a different data source to an existing code base, but it also explores challenges you might face with configuration and state in modules, particularly from an interoperability perspective—working with type providers in multilanguage solutions. You'll then work on performing SQL queries and commands, configuration, and finally making a pluggable repository layer.

35.1.1 Solution overview

src/code-listings/lesson-35 has both a starting and a completed solution; there are three projects: the two from the previous (slightly modified) capstone, plus a new SQL database project. You'll be deploying this locally before connecting the application to it. I've also added a binding redirect to the WPF application's app.config file to ensure that you always look for F# 4's FSharp.Core (4.4.0.0) rather than the F# 3.0 version (4.3.0.0).

35.2 Hooking up a SQL database

The first thing you'll be doing is creating your SQL database. Look in the BankAccount-
Db project; there's already a BankAccountDb.publish.xml file that you can double-click
from within Visual Studio to get to a prefilled dialog box, shown in figure 35.1. Click the
Publish button to deploy the database.

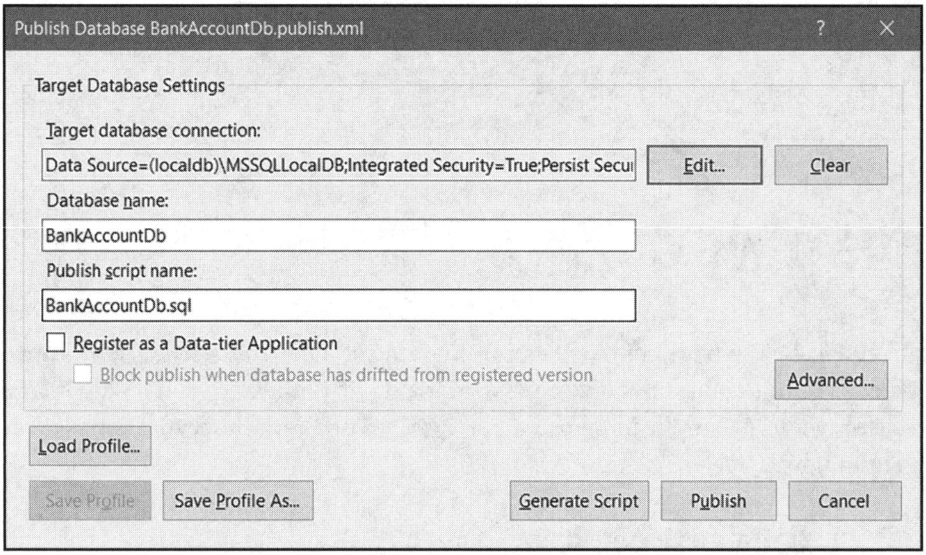

Figure 35.1 The Publish Database dialog box in Visual Studio for a database project

Note that I've already done a couple of things to save you some time working with SQL:

- The FSharp.Data.SqlClient package to handle data access is already installed.
- The app.config file is already configured to use a SQL connection string.

The database itself contains three tables:

- A table for Account information (the account ID and owner), dbo.Account.
- A table that contains details of every transaction that occurred, dbo.Account-
  Transaction.
- A lookup table for the two operation types (Withdraw or Deposit), dbo.Operation.
  This is commonly known as *reference data*—static (or slowly changing) data that
  acts as a lookup for other tables.

After you've deployed the database, you can compile the solution to ensure that it builds. If it doesn't, it's because the database you deployed to doesn't match the connection string in the configuration file. Update it by republishing the DB if required.

35.3 Creating a SQL data access layer

Now that the database is deployed, you can look at the code needed to interact with the database. For this exercise, you'll be using the `FSharp.Data.SqlClient` package, but to help you along, I've created a standalone scratchpad.fsx script in the solution that's set up with example queries for you to test and explore as you go; keep this handy!

35.3.1 The SQL repository

Once again, don't worry if you're not a SQL guru. The solution already contains the SQL queries you'll need. This `SqlRepository` module contains two functions that will replace the calls to the existing `FileRepository`:

- `getAccountAndTransactions` tries to find the account and transaction history of a customer (replaces `tryFindTransactionsOnDisk`).
- `writeTransaction` saves a single transaction to the database.
- If you look at both the SQL and File repositories, you'll notice that the functions in both modules have identical signatures, so all you need to do is to implement the SQL ones before switching over.

35.3.2 Working with SQL to retrieve account history

Reading the account history (`getAccountAndTransactions`) has the following signature:

```
owner:string -> (Guid * seq<Transaction> option)
```

Given an owner, this function should optionally return the Account ID (the `Guid` in the preceding code line) and a sequence of transactions for the account. You need to implement this function; you'll notice three prewritten SQL queries in the `SqlRepository.DB` submodule. These are there to perform all the heavy lifting, leaving you to compose them together:

- `GetAccountId` returns the Account ID for a given owner (if they exist).
- `FindTransactions` returns the list of all transactions for a given `AccountId`.
- `FindTransactionsByOwner` returns the list of all transactions for a given Owner, along with the account ID for each row.

You could implement getAccountAndTransactions in one of two ways. The first is to call both the GetAccountId and FindTransactions queries separately; if the first query returns None, this is a new account; return None. Otherwise, find any transactions for that Account ID and return them together with the Account ID as Some; see figure 35.2.

You can test out the queries by opening the SQL Server Object Explorer pane, locating the server and database, and right-clicking to choose New Query. From here, you can paste in a query and click the Execute button on the query toolbar. Alternatively, if you want to test this query in a script, you can reuse one of the scripts from earlier in the unit (be sure to use the connection string from the app.config file!).

	AccountId
1	8E7A7909-5667-4CFB-8726-AC3C083EA621

	Timestamp	OperationId	Amount
1	2016-12-30 17:02:53.757	2	10
2	2016-12-30 17:02:54.337	2	10
3	2016-12-30 17:02:54.510	2	10
4	2016-12-30 17:02:57.203	2	50
5	2016-12-30 17:02:57.377	2	50
6	2016-12-30 17:02:59.487	1	100
7	2016-12-30 17:03:02.533	2	24
8	2016-12-30 17:03:04.220	1	1

Figure 35.2   The result of calling two SQL queries to locate Account and Transaction history

Observe that the GetAccountId query returns a Guid option, and not an array of Guid. This is because you've supplied the SingleRow = true argument to the type definition in F#.

Listing 35.1 Calling GetAccountId to try to retrieve account details

```
type GetAccountId = SqlCommandProvider<"SELECT TOP 1 AccountId FROM
dbo.Account WHERE Owner = @owner", Conn, SingleRow = true>
let accountId : Guid option =
  GetAccountId.Create(connection).Execute("tony")
```

Defining a query to
retrieve the Account ID
for an owner

Executing the query,
passing in a specific owner
name

But the problem with this is that you perform two SQL queries here. The second, more efficient way would be to call a single query that returns all the data in one go, and that's what FindTransactionsByOwner does.

FindTransactionsByOwner performs a join across both tables and returns a single result set, with AccountId replicated across all rows. As you can see, although this works, the "shape" of your data has changed. Now, you have a single result set, with AccountId replicated across all rows, as per figure 35.3.

AccountId	Timestamp	OperationId	Amount
8E7A7909-5667-4CFB-8726-AC3C083EA621	2016-12-30 17:02:53.757	2	10
8E7A7909-5667-4CFB-8726-AC3C083EA621	2016-12-30 17:02:54.337	2	10
8E7A7909-5667-4CFB-8726-AC3C083EA621	2016-12-30 17:02:54.510	2	10
8E7A7909-5667-4CFB-8726-AC3C083EA621	2016-12-30 17:02:57.203	2	50
8E7A7909-5667-4CFB-8726-AC3C083EA621	2016-12-30 17:02:57.377	2	50
8E7A7909-5667-4CFB-8726-AC3C083EA621	2016-12-30 17:02:59.487	1	100
8E7A7909-5667-4CFB-8726-AC3C083EA621	2016-12-30 17:03:02.533	2	24
8E7A7909-5667-4CFB-8726-AC3C083EA621	2016-12-30 17:03:04.220	1	1

Figure 35.3   The result of a single query that joins across both Account and Transaction tables

There are three possibilities here:

- There's no existing account for the owner, in which case you should get back no rows at all.
- There's an existing account for the owner, but no transactions, in which case you should get back a single row with only the Account ID populated (figure 35.4).

AccountId	Timestamp	OperationId	Amount
8E7A7909-5667-4CFB-8726-AC3C083EA6D1	NULL	NULL	NULL

Figure 35.4   The result of a query for an account holder with no transactions

- There's an existing account for the owner with some transactions, in which case you should get back at least one row with all fields populated (as shown previously in figure 35.3).

The SqlCommandProvider is smart enough to figure out that the join might not be successful, so the provided type generated from the query is a mandatory Account ID, but the remaining three fields are *optional*. As a result, you'll have to map this into a

`<Guid * Transaction seq>` option. This is a classic *impedance mismatch* between a relational database model (rows and columns) and a type system such as F# that allows complex types and non-two-dimensional models.

. . . .

Now you try

1 Implement the `getAccountAndTransactions` function by using one of the two preceding approaches.
2 If you elected the more efficient, second option, you could use a pattern match over the records (once converted to a list):
   a If it's an empty list, there's no account holder.
   b If it's a single-item list and the three columns are blank, it's an account holder with no transactions.
   c Otherwise, it's an account with a proper transaction history.
3 As you construct the `Transaction` records, you'll need to set the `Operation` field by mapping from the SQL field `OperationId` (an int) to a `BankOperation` (an F# discriminated union). For now, hardcode it to `Deposit`.

35.3.3 Working with reference data

Setting the `Operation` field of the `Transaction` needs a simple mapping from the `OperationId` on the database to the discriminated union `BankOperation`. The usual process for doing this would be to manually create an enum in code that "happens to match" the database structure, and map between them. The type provider can't do the mapping for you, but it can at least remove the need for you to manually create and maintain an enum. You can use the following code to easily map from one type to another without any hardcoding.

Listing 35.2 Using a provided enum to safely map into an F# domain model

```
let toBankOperation operationId =
    match operationId with
    | DbOperations.Deposit -> Deposit
    | DbOperations.Withdraw -> Withdraw
    | _ -> failwith "Unknown DB Operation case!"
```

The `DbOperations` type is an enum type that's generated by the type provider, and contains both bank operation cases (based on the contents of the Operations table in SQL). This provides a fairly strong guarantee that you can safely create Bank Operation DUs (although I've still kept an explicit failure handler just in case), without the need for magic numbers.

Using provided types in a domain model

You'll notice that you have to map from the generated provided types into a "pure" F# domain model. Partly this is because your solution involves C#, and provided types don't necessarily play well in a non-F# environment. But there's also a question of whether you would want to tightly couple your domain model with data that's directly generated from SQL. I certainly wouldn't rule out the possibility of doing that. Indeed, it's an extremely rapid way to get up and running, but in a larger-scale application, it wouldn't be uncommon to decouple your domain model from the data store completely.

35.3.4 Inserting data into SQL

When it comes to implementing the writeTransaction function, you have a couple of options. You can either manually create an INSERT SQL statement, or use the data table support that the type provider offers. I've opted to go with the latter, but feel free to write your own insert statement if you want.

Either way, you'll have one issue to contend with: when you insert a transaction, you also need to insert the owner/account information, but *only* if this is a new account. You could decide to make this a decision supplied to the repository—that callers have to know whether this is a new account—but a simpler option is to do one of the following:

- Check whether there's already a record for this account in the database; if there isn't, insert a new record.
- Always try to insert the account/owner record, and if it fails, swallow the exception that's raised as a result.

You can write code as follows to create a data table, insert a row into it, and then persist it to the database.

Listing 35.3 Creating a data table with a row for insertion into SQL

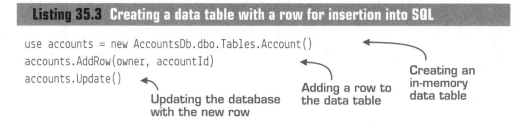

```
use accounts = new AccountsDb.dbo.Tables.Account()
accounts.AddRow(owner, accountId)
accounts.Update()
```

Creating an in-memory data table

Adding a row to the data table

Updating the database with the new row

You can use the existing GetAccountId query to check whether there's an existing account ID for the supplied owner, and match on the result to test whether to create an account. Alternatively, you could elect to always try to perform the insert, and catch the exception if it's a SqlException where the text contains Violation of PRIMARY KEY constraint.

Listing 35.4 Pattern matching over an exception

```
try codeThatMightThrow()          ←—— Executing code in a try/with block
with
| :? SqlException as ex when ex.Message.Contains "Violation of PRIMARY KEY
↪constraint" -> ()  ←
| _ -> reraise()  ←
                    Rethrowing       Checking against a type with
                    the current      the :? operator in conjunction
                    exception        with a when clause
```

The :? operator is analogous to a safe form of type cast; if the exception is a SqlException, you bind it to the symbol ex and can then use it within the when clause. This sort of functionality is being brought into C# 7 as a limited form of pattern matching.

It's worth bearing in mind that the writeTransaction function is a function in your system that returns unit; it's writing to a database and gives back nothing. This makes it somewhat difficult to reason about, because you've encoded the error into an exception. A more functional approach might be to return Result<unit>; at least this explicitly states that the save was successful, even if you don't have any payload with that success.

When performing the save, you'll be mapping backward, and taking the fields from a Transaction record into a function call that takes primitives (strings, ints, and so forth), including the integer for the OperationId on the database. You can use another pattern match to map from the BankOperation to the DbOperations enum value, essentially inverting listing 35.2 (a clean approach might be to make a dedicated helper submodule to store both conversion functions).

With your SQL data access layer now written, all you have to do is plug it in. The simplest option is to replace the calls in the Api to any functions in the FileRepository module with those in the SqlRepository module. They should be drop-in replacements, as the function signatures match exactly! Do this, and test the application to prove it works end to end.

35.4 Making a pluggable data access layer

Let's look at ways to improve the architecture of the application.

35.4.1 Pluggable data access repositories

Coming from an OO background, your instinct at this point might be to wonder why you're tightly coupling the service layer (the orchestration logic in API) with the data layer (the SQL repository). Can't you decouple the two of them—perhaps using some form of dependency injection with an IoC container? You bet!

It's beyond the scope of this lesson to do that in detail, but in the sample solution, you'll see how it's done. You can do it yourself without too much difficulty, as you'll see next.

Now you try

1   Inside Api.fs, everywhere you see a hard reference to `SqlRepository`, remove that and pass in the function (`writeTransaction` or `getAccountAndTransactions`) as a higher-order function.

2   Note that because both `Withdraw` and `Deposit` load up the account from the DB before performing the write, they have dependencies on both read and write SQL functions!

3   Now the caller to the API needs to pass in the SQL-dependent functions—the view model code in the client. Compiling the app will show you exactly where you need to pass in the functions. You'll also have to make the SQL repository code public again, because the view model will need to inject it into the API calls.

35.4.2 "Reusing" dependencies across functions

The problem with this solution is that you now have to repeatedly pass in the SQL dependencies for every function call, every time you call an API function—not great. In a purely functional solution, you'd partially apply those functions with the relevant dependencies within a bootstrapper of some sort. (I believe the current trendy term to use these days is *composition root*) and then pass the partially applied versions into the app.

But it's sometimes useful to "group up" a list of functions into a single, logical bundle. In this case, it's especially useful because all of the functions (read and write to database) use the same dependencies (the calls to the read and write functions). In F#, it's not possible to parameterize a module with arguments, so in this case you can fall back to using an interface that represents your API.

Listing 35.5 Representing functions through an interface rather than a module

Name of the interface   Members of
                                                         the interface

```
/// Represents the gateway to perform bank operations.
type IBankApi =
    abstract member LoadAccount : customer:Customer -> RatedAccount
    abstract member Deposit : amount:Decimal -> customer:Customer ->
RatedAccount
    abstract member Withdraw : amount:Decimal -> customer:Customer ->
RatedAccount
    abstract member LoadTransactionHistory : customer:Customer ->
Transaction seq
```

You can now create an instance of this interface, which takes in the dependencies as function arguments.

Listing 35.6 Creating a factory function for the Bank API

Factory function taking in   Implementations
varying dependencies as   with access to
function arguments   dependencies

```
let buildApi loadAccountHistory saveTransaction =
    { new IBankApi with
        member this.LoadAccount(customer) = // code elided
        member this.Deposit amount customer = // code elided
        member this.LoadTransactionHistory(customer) = // code elided
        member this.Withdraw amount customer = // code elided }
```

Using this, you can easily make a SQL or File bank API. There's a fully working example in the sample solution, but here are a few things to note:

- You pass in the read and write functions as function arguments.
- In the function body, you create an instance of IBankApi. (F# allows you to create anonymous objects from interfaces; there's no need to formally declare a type.)
- The implementations of the member functions can all access the read and write dependencies. In effect, you're partially applying all the member functions with both dependencies simultaneously!

This approach to viewing interfaces is an interesting one. In the OO world, we tend to think of interfaces as objects that have a list of member methods on them to fulfill the interface; in the FP world, you can flip this on its head and think of interfaces as a group of functions that can be *looked up* by name. In that sense, rather than using an interface, you could as easily have used an F# *record of functions*.

Listing 35.7 Using a record instead of an interface

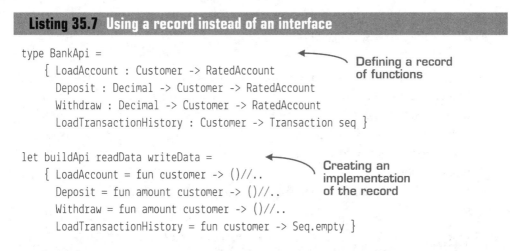

```
type BankApi =
    { LoadAccount : Customer -> RatedAccount                    Defining a record
      Deposit : Decimal -> Customer -> RatedAccount             of functions
      Withdraw : Decimal -> Customer -> RatedAccount
      LoadTransactionHistory : Customer -> Transaction seq }

let buildApi readData writeData =
    { LoadAccount = fun customer -> ()//..              Creating an
      Deposit = fun amount customer -> ()//..           implementation
      Withdraw = fun amount customer -> ()//..          of the record
      LoadTransactionHistory = fun customer -> Seq.empty }
```

I personally prefer to use interfaces in such situations; it's a well-known pattern. But using records in this way does offer some advantages, such as better support for type inference.

35.4.3 Handling SQL connection strings directly

As you observed earlier in this unit, using application configuration files is a quick way to get up and running with SQL, but moving to an explicit connection string gives you more flexibility and control; plus it makes it much easier to work with SQL in scripts. The final thing you'll want to do is migrate from the implicit connection strings that using a configuration file offers, to working explicitly with a connection string.

Now you try

1 For all functions in the SQL Repository module, take in an extra string argument called connectionString and pass that into all calls that connect to the DB—for example, GetAccountId.Create() for reads.

2 Do the same for the `Update()` calls, except you need to manually create a `Sql-Connection` object first (and remember to `Open()` it!).

Listing 35.8 Creating a SQL Connection object

```
open System.Data.SqlClient
use connection = new SqlConnection(connectionString)
connection.Open()
```
Opening the connection before using it

Creating a SQL connection object in a using block

3 Where the `IBankApi` is created, you'll need to pass a `connectionString` into both the higher-order function calls. You can opt to get a handle to the connection string here, or take the connection string in as an argument.

4 Either way, either in the ViewModel or the factory function, you need to get a handle to the connection string. First, add a reference to the System.Configuration assembly.

5 You can then use the `ConfigurationManager` static class to pull out the connection string.

Listing 35.9 Retrieving a connection string from the configuration system

```
open System.Configuration
ConfigurationManager.ConnectionStrings["AccountsDb"].ConnectionString
```
Using ConfigurationManager to retrieve the AccountsDb connection string

Now that you've done this, you've completely decoupled the API layer from the data access layer, while you've also removed the dependency on the application configuration from the SQL layer.

 **Summary**

That's another capstone done! You've successfully integrated a SQL data access layer into the application by using a type provider to quickly and easily give you strongly typed access to a database. You also had a look at a practical example of creating a pluggable interface from F# in tandem with higher-order functions in order to decouple an API from a data access layer.

Web programming

You can't have any programming language and platform these days without having a decent story for web programming! Luckily, F# is a great fit for working on the web, with a great set of libraries and frameworks that it can use. This unit covers both creating and consuming web-based resources. You'll use a set of technologies that exist in the general .NET ecosystem—ones that you're probably already familiar with—and some cool F#-specific technologies as well.

36

ASYNCHRONOUS WORKFLOWS

The past few units have focused almost exclusively on libraries and frameworks that work with F#. This first lesson of the unit briefly hops back to the language side of things and introduces an important language feature in F# called *asynchronous workflows*, which allow you to orchestrate asynchronous and multithreaded code in a manageable way. These provide ways to parallelize code more easily, allowing you to create high-performing and scalable applications. You'll see

- Why asynchronous programming is important
- What async workflows are
- A comparison of async programming in F# and C#
- Computation expressions in general

36.1 Comparing synchronous and asynchronous models

Although there's a decent chance that you're already aware of multithreading and asynchronous programming (especially if you've been working with C# 5), it's worth quickly covering these terms and why they're important for the web. I'm going to slightly simplify things by talking about synchronous and asynchronous work. The former represents work that happens in a single, sequential flow of execution—essentially, all the code you've written thus far. Asynchronous work represents the notion of doing work

425

in the background, and when it completes, receiving notification that the background work has finished, before consuming the output and continuing.

Why might you want to perform background work? The most obvious reason is performance, because doing work in the background allows you to perform multiple tasks at the same time. You can kick off several tasks in the background, each working with its own pieces of data, and then when they're all done, carry on with the main program. Efficiency concerns exist as well, particularly when it comes to communicating with external systems such as databases or other web servers. Using asynchronous APIs can free up threads in the application while they wait for the external resource to return, so that the web application can effectively handle more requests from more users at the same time. An example comparing both approaches is shown in figure 36.1.

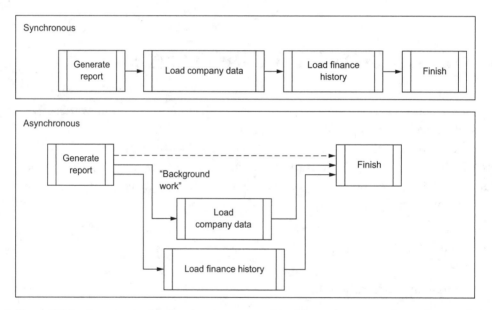

Figure 36.1 An example of performing the same work both in synchronous and asynchronous fashion

36.1.1 Threads, tasks, and I/O-bound workloads

There are several (perhaps too many!) ways of performing background work in .NET. I'm not going to devote too much time to this, but rather give you a brief overview; many great resources are available for you to read up on this elsewhere in painful detail.

Threads

The lowest primitive for allocating background work is the *thread*. A .NET application has a thread pool with a finite number of threads; when you execute work on a background thread, the thread pool assigns a thread to carry out the work. When the work is finished, the thread pool reclaims the thread, ready for the next piece of background work.

Tasks

Introduced in .NET 4, *tasks* are a higher-level abstraction over threads. They're much easier to work with and reason about, with good support for cancellation and parallelism, and so effectively became the de facto type in C# and VB .NET to use for performing background work.

I/O-bound workloads

Both threads and tasks can be thought of as supporting *CPU-bound* workloads—work that's carried out in the current process. I/O-bound workloads are background tasks that you want to execute that *don't* need a thread to run on. These are typically used when communicating and waiting for work from an external system to complete. Instead of using a thread from the pool (which both the thread and task models do), the operating system provides a low-level callback that .NET monitors; when the external system returns with data, .NET picks up the response and resumes work. These sorts of methods are truly asynchronous; they don't block any threads while running. Table 36.1 shows some example I/O- and CPU-bound workloads.

Table 36.1   Examples of I/O- and CPU-bound workloads

Type	Example
CPU	Calculating the average of a large set of numbers
CPU	Running a set of rules over a loan application
I/O	Downloading data from a remote web server
I/O	Loading a file from disk
I/O	Executing a long-running query on SQL

Why is asynchronous code important with regard to web applications in particular? The main reason is *throughput*. A web application may be receiving hundreds, or even thousands, of requests from different users per second, and processing those requests as quickly as possible is usually extremely important. Because a .NET process has only a finite number of threads, it's important to use those threads as effectively as possible—

and this means eliminating times that a thread is blocked, idling—for example, waiting for SQL to return some data. That's why, where possible, you should try to work with asynchronous code.

36.1.2 Problems with asynchronous models

From a programming perspective, a few difficulties arise when working with asynchronous code. Reasoning about several background items working concurrently (at the same time) is hard, particularly with things like synchronization of multiple work items or exception handling.

In the spirit of this book, I'm not going to go over the same ground that's been covered in depth many times before (particularly since C# 5 came into being). Suffice it to say that writing truly asynchronous code by using what's called *continuation passing style* is very hard to get right. In order to solve this, the F# team came up with a brilliant solution: *asynchronous workflows*.

> **What about async/await?**
>
> If you've used a relatively recent version of C# (basically C# 5 onward), you're almost certainly aware of the async/await pattern. Great! Then a lot of this lesson will feel natural to you. That's because the async/await pattern is based on F#'s asynchronous workflows—although as you'll see, async/await isn't quite as flexible.

Quick check 36.1

1 What's the preferred type to use in .NET when executing work in the background?
2 What's the difference between CPU- and I/O-bound workloads in terms of their activity on a thread?

QC 36.1 answer

1 `System.Threading.Tasks.Task.`
2 CPU-bound workloads consume a thread while working; I/O ones shouldn't.

36.2 Introducing asynchronous workflows

Whereas threads and tasks are library features to schedule background work, the async workflow is a *language*-level feature to achieve the same thing.

36.2.1 Async workflow basics

The gist of async workflows is easy: wrap any code block that you want to execute in the background in an `async { }` block. As you'll see, this can range from something as simple as a single value to doing a complex set of calculations. Let's look first at how you might schedule work in the background by carrying out the same piece of work synchronously and asynchronously; execute both blocks separately in a script to observe the differences in behavior.

Listing 36.1 Scheduling work with async blocks in F#

```
printfn "Loading data!"                         A conventional,
System.Threading.Thread.Sleep(5000)             synchronous sequential
printfn "Loaded Data!"                          set of instructions
printfn "My name is Simon."

async {
    printfn "Loading data!"                     Wrapping a portion of
    System.Threading.Thread.Sleep(5000)         code in an async block
    printfn "Loaded Data!" }
|> Async.Start                                  Starting the async block
printfn "My name is Simon."                     in the background
```

The first version executes a set of code instructions that block the thread for five seconds (simulating loading data from an external system) before printing someone's name. The problem is that you can't print the final line until the first three are completed (and FSI will be completely blocked for you while it executes).

The second version wraps the long-running portion of code into an `async { }` block, and fires it off in the background by using the `Async.Start` method. The difference is that now the person's name is printed immediately, while the asynchronous block executes in a background thread.

Let's now look at another example. This time, unlike the previous example, which was a fire-and-forget one, you'll see how to asynchronously execute code that *returns* a value.

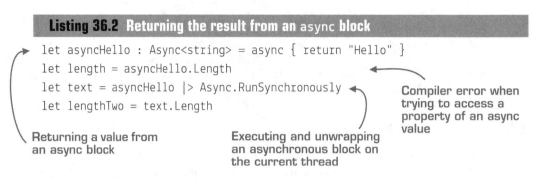

Listing 36.2 **Returning the result from an** async **block**

```
let asyncHello : Async<string> = async { return "Hello" }
let length = asyncHello.Length
let text = asyncHello |> Async.RunSynchronously
let lengthTwo = text.Length
```

Returning a value from
an async block

Executing and unwrapping
an asynchronous block on
the current thread

Compiler error when
trying to access a
property of an async
value

Try this out yourself, executing one line at a time. As you can see, by wrapping the text Hello in an async block, rather than getting back a string, you get back an *async* string. This means, "When you start this async workflow, it will at some point in the future return a string." You can't dot into an async workflow to, for example, get the length of a string; you first need to *unwrap* the value. A couple of other points worth noting are

- Unlike normal expressions, the result of an async expression must be prefixed with the return keyword.
- You can unwrap an Async<_> value by calling Async.RunSynchronously. This is roughly equivalent to Task.Result; it blocks the current thread until the workflow is completed.

One other important distinction is that creating an async block doesn't automatically start the work in the block; you have to explicitly start it. One way is to use one of the methods on the Async class—for example, RunSynchronously or Start (see section 36.5.3 for a full list of useful methods). Also, unlike Task.Result, if you repeatedly call RunSynchronously on an async block, it will re-execute the code every time.

36.2.2   More-complex async workflows

You can do more than simple one-liners in an async block. If you want to delegate work that does more than output hello world, that's no problem; you can wrap entire function calls and blocks of code within them. Here's an example of a more complex async workflow that calls a nested function.

Listing 36.3 **Larger** async **blocks in F#**

```
open System.Threading

let printThread text = printfn "THREAD %d: %s"
Thread.CurrentThread.ManagedThreadId text

let doWork() =
```

A standard function
that simulates a long-
running piece of work

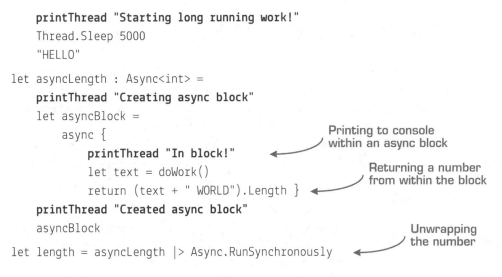

```
    printThread "Starting long running work!"
    Thread.Sleep 5000
    "HELLO"

let asyncLength : Async<int> =
    printThread "Creating async block"
    let asyncBlock =
        async {
            printThread "In block!"          ←  Printing to console
                                                within an async block
            let text = doWork()              ←  Returning a number
            return (text + " WORLD").Length }    from within the block
    printThread "Created async block"
    asyncBlock                               ←  Unwrapping
                                                the number
let length = asyncLength |> Async.RunSynchronously  ←
```

If you execute this code in one chunk, you'll see the following output:

```
THREAD 1: Creating async block
THREAD 1: Created async block
THREAD 5: In block!
THREAD 5: Starting long running work!
```

It's important to realize that no work occurs until you execute the *final line* in the script; everything up until that point compiles the code but doesn't start the background work. You can create async blocks easily, pass them around your application without problems, and then execute them at a time of your choosing by calling Async.RunSynchronously.

Quick check 36.2

1. What extra keyword must you use in async blocks to return a value?
2. Do async workflows immediately execute on creation?

QC 36.2 answer

1. return.
2. No. You should start them explicitly by using Async.Start or RunSynchronously.

36.3 Composing asynchronous values

`async` blocks like those you've seen so far are already useful in their own right. You can easily reason about what you want to run asynchronously, and then pass that code around as a simple value. But you've seen that to unwrap an asynchronous value, you need to call `Async.RunSynchronously`. This blocks the current thread until the async workflow has executed—which is a real shame! What's the point in passing around code that can run in the background if you need to block the current thread to get at the result? Luckily, F# has a built-in way to continue when a background workflow completes, called `let!`.

Listing 36.4 Creating a continuation by using `let!`

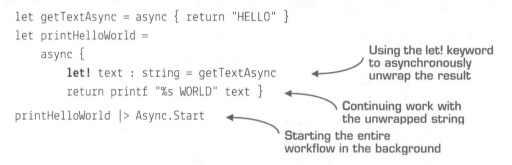

```
let getTextAsync = async { return "HELLO" }
let printHelloWorld =
    async {
        let! text : string = getTextAsync
        return printf "%s WORLD" text }
printHelloWorld |> Async.Start
```

Using the let! keyword to asynchronously unwrap the result

Continuing work with the unwrapped string

Starting the entire workflow in the background

A few things are happening here, so let's take it step by step. First, you create an `async` block. Inside that block, you execute the `getTextAsync` computation and *wait* for the string result by using the `let!` keyword (if you've used C# 5's async/await before, think of this as loosely equivalent to `await`). This keyword is valid only when inside the `async` block; you can't use it outside. Now, notice that the value `text` is a type string—not an async string! Essentially, `let!` waits for `asyncWork` to complete in the background (it doesn't block a thread), unwraps the value for you, and then continues. Try replacing `let!` with just `let` and see what happens. Finally, you close the block and then start this composed async workflow in the background by using `Async.Start`. `Async.Start` is perfect if you want to kick off a workflow that has no specific end result, as in this case where the workflow prints out something to the console.

`async` blocks also allow you to perform try/with blocks around a `let!` computation; you can nest multiple computations together and use .NET IDisposables without a problem.

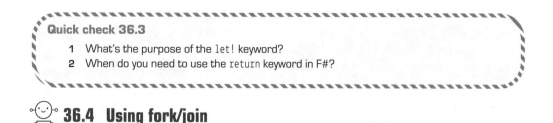
36.4 Using fork/join

One thing that's extremely easy to achieve with `async` blocks is to perform a *fork/join*: you launch several async workflows in the background, wait until *all* of them are completed, and then continue with all the results combined. In F#, you use `Async.Parallel` to collate a *collection* of async workflows into a *single*, combined workflow. Note that it doesn't start the new workflow; instead , it creates a *new* workflow that represents the result of all the individual workflows collated together (see figure 36.2).

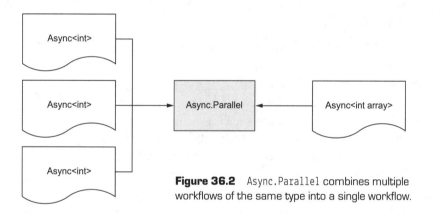

Figure 36.2 `Async.Parallel` combines multiple workflows of the same type into a single workflow.

Here's how you might asynchronously generate and work with 50 random numbers.

Listing 36.5 Looking at fork /join with `Async.Parallel`

```
let random = System.Random()
let pickANumberAsync = async { return random.Next(10) }
let createFiftyNumbers =
    let workflows = [ for i in 1 .. 50 -> pickANumberAsync ]
```

Creating 50 asynchronous computations

```
    async {
        let! numbers = workflows |> Async.Parallel
        printfn "Total is %d" (numbers |> Array.sum) }
createFiftyNumbers |> Async.Start
```

Executing all computations in parallel and unwrapping the collated results

Again, try this yourself; the important thing to note here is the use of `Async.Parallel`. Remember that this handy function goes from `Array<Async<T>` to `Async<Array<T>>`—see figure 36.2. In this case, this means going from `Array<Async<int>>` to `Async<Array<int>>`, which can be awaited (incidentally, this is similar to `Task.WhenAll`).

Now you try

Now try downloading data from HTTP resources—using a BCL method that supports F#'s async feature natively. It'll use .NET's native async support so that you can download data much more efficiently:

1 Write a function, `downloadData` that takes in a single string URL and asynchronously returns the number of bytes in the contents. It should have a signature of `string -> Async<int>`:

   a You can use the standard `System.Net.WebClient` object to perform the download.

   b You can use a handy method on the `WebClient` designed to work specifically with async workflows, called `AsyncDownloadData`. (You'll have to create a `System.Uri` from the string to work with this function.)

3 You can use `let!` to unwrap the `async<byte[]>` into a `byte []`.

4 You can then return the `Length` of the byte.

5 Within your script, create an array of three URLs:

   a http://www.fsharp.org

   b http://microsoft.com

   c http://fsharpforfunandprofit.com

4 Use standard `Array.map` in conjunction with your `downloadData` function to map the array of `string` into an array of `Async<int>`.

5 Use `Async.Parallel` to execute the workflows in parallel and return all the results as one.

6 Use `Async.RunSynchronously` to block until you have the results.

7 Sum the results by using standard `Array.sum` to get the total number of bytes downloaded.

Your code should look like something like this.

Listing 36.6 Asynchronously downloading data over HTTP in parallel

```
let downloadData url = async {
    use wc = new System.Net.WebClient()
    printfn "Downloading data on thread %d" CurrentThread.ManagedThreadId
    let! data = wc.AsyncDownloadData(System.Uri url)
    return data.Length }

let downloadedBytes =
    urls
    |> Array.map downloadData
    |> Async.Parallel
    |> Async.RunSynchronously

printfn "You downloaded %d characters" (Array.sum downloadedBytes)
```

> **Quick check 36.4** What does `Async.Parallel` do?

36.5 Using tasks and async workflows

Since .NET already has the `Task` type, let's spend a few minutes comparing it with `Async`.

36.5.1 Interoperating with tasks

The `Async` type isn't something pervasive in .NET—instead, there's a good chance that any libraries you use work with the `Task` type. Luckily, F# has a couple of handy combinators (or transformation functions) that allow you to go between `Task` and `Async`, similar to how `Option` has combinators for `Nullables`:

- `Async.AwaitTask` converts a task into an async workflow.
- `Async.StartAsTask` converts an async workflow into a task.

QC 36.4 answer `Async.Parallel` allows fork/joins of multiple `Async` values.

Now you try

Let's see how to change the preceding code so that it uses the task version of Download-DataTaskAsync, rather than the F#-specific AsyncDownloadData version:

1 Starting from listing 36.7, replace the call to AsyncDownloadData with one to Download-DataTaskAsync.

2 Your code won't compile. You can only unwrap an Async<_> inside an async block, but you have a Task here. So, pipe the Task into the Async.AwaitTask function to convert the Task into an Async. Your code will compile again.

3 Replace the call to Async.RunSynchronously with a call to Async.StartAsTask. Observe that downloadedBytes is no longer an int[] but a Task<int[]>.

4 In the call to the printfn expression, rather than printing out downloadedBytes, print out downloadedBytes.Result.

Listing 36.7   Replacing calls to and from Async with Task-bound methods

```
let downloadData url = async {
    let! data =
        wc.DownloadDataTaskAsync(System.Uri url) |> Async.AwaitTask
    return data.Length }
let downloadedBytes =
    urls
    |> Array.map downloadData
    |> Async.Parallel
    |> Async.StartAsTask

printfn "You downloaded %d characters" (Array.sum downloadedBytes.Result)
```

Using the AwaitTask combinator to convert from Tasks to Async

Using the StartAsTask combinator to convert from Async to Task

36.5.2   Comparing tasks and async

Let's take a quick look at table 36.2 at some of the distinctions between .NET's Task and F#'s Async types, as well as the async/await pattern.

Table 36.2   Tasks and async compared

	Task and async await	F# async workflows
Native support in F#	Via async combinators	Yes
Allows status reporting	Yes	No
Clarity	Hard to know where async starts and stops	Very clear

Table 36.2 Tasks and async compared (continued)

	Task and async await	F# async workflows
Unification	Task and Task<T> types	Unified Async<T>
Statefulness	Task result evaluated only once	Infinite

The venerable Tomas Petricek has a great post on async/await versus async workflows, with several excellent examples of where async/await breaks down. I recommend you read this in your own time (see http://tomasp.net/blog/csharp-async-gotchas.aspx/), particularly around the notion of where async starts and stops.

In general, internally in your F# code I recommend using async workflows wherever possible. At times you might want to use tasks instead, but that's unusual. One case is for interop purposes; another is for extremely large numbers of CPU-bound items, where Task is more efficient. Async was originally designed for asynchronous work rather than, for example, huge numbers of tiny CPU-bound work items.

Of course, it's not unusual to rely on libraries that themselves expose tasks (including many within the BCL), but generally you'll immediately convert them to asyncs so you can use let! on them within an async block.

36.5.3 Useful async keywords

Table 36.3 provides a quick list of most of the common Async keywords and functions that you'll be using.

Table 36.3 Common Async commands

Command	Usage
let!	Used within an async block to unwrap an Async<T> value to T
do!	Used within an async block to wait for an Async<unit> to complete
return!	Used within an async block as a shorthand for let! and return
Async.AwaitTask	Converts Task<T> to Async<T>, or Task to Async<unit>
Async.StartAsTask	Converts Async<T> to Task<T>
Async.RunSychronously	Synchronously unwraps Async<T> to <T>
Async.Start	Starts an Async<unit> computation in the background (fire-and-forget)
Async.Ignore	Converts Async<T> to Async<unit>
Async.Parallel	Converts Async<T> array to Async<T array>
Async.Catch	Converts Async<T> into a two-case DU of T or Exception

Some of these you haven't seen yet, but it's good to know that they're there. Experiment with them on a scratchpad in order to see how they work.

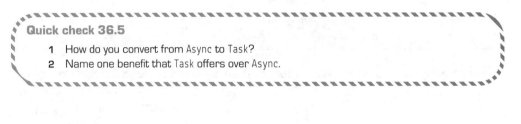

Quick check 36.5

1 How do you convert from Async to Task?
2 Name one benefit that Task offers over Async.

 **Summary**

You've now completed the async lesson. In this lesson

- You were introduced to the async expression.
- You learned how to use it to easily compose multiple async blocks together.
- You learned to execute multiple async workloads in parallel.

Try this

- Write an application to demonstrate the differences in terms of performance and threads between synchronous, multithreaded, and asynchronous parallel downloading of 10 HTTP resources.
- Then, try using the Async methods included in FSharp.Data for downloading JSON data from a remote resource.
- Finally, try to handle an exception raised in an async block by using the Async.Catch method.

QC 36.5 answer

1 Using Async.StartAsTask.
2 Tasks allow you to report on the progress of a work item. Tasks are also more efficient when working with large groups of work items.

37

EXPOSING DATA OVER HTTP

In this lesson, you'll look at ways to create HTTP-enabled APIs by using F# on the .NET platform. First, you'll do this by using the well-known Microsoft ASP .NET framework, using the Web API component; you'll then move on to looking at an alternative web technology, Suave. You'll learn about

- Working with the ASP .NET Web API and F#
- Reasoning about HTTP response codes in F#
- Working with `Async` and ASP .NET
- Using Suave, an F#-first web application model

37.1 Getting up and running with the ASP .NET Web API

Let's jump straight into this lesson and dispel any fears that your ASP .NET applications are somehow not compatible with F# by creating an ASP .NET application, in F#! You'll look at two hosting mechanisms: web projects and console apps.

37.1.1 Web projects with F#

Exposing data over HTTP in .NET is most commonly done by using Microsoft's ASP .NET framework; if you've done any form of web programming on .NET, it's a safe bet that you've used it in some form, be it using the old-school Web Forms, its replacement MVC, or its API-focused sibling Web API. The most common and popular way to host an ASP .NET application in .NET is as a *web project*. These projects bootstrap into IIS (or its little sibling, IIS Express), with a web.config file providing configuration information to .NET (rather than an app.config).

Here's the bad news out of the way: within the F# world, out of the box, Visual Studio has no tooling support for web projects. Now here's the good news: the F# community has fixed this with some excellent third-party templates that are available within Visual Studio.

Problems with F# and web projects

The basic lack of support for web projects boils down to Visual Studio not understanding how to resolve a web project with F# tooling. You can manually create a web project by creating a standard F# console application and changing the project GUID in the .fsproj file, but that leaves you with another problem: the Add New Item dialog box won't work, so you'll never be able to add a new file to the project. Thankfully, a registry fix can be applied, and will automatically be done when you install the F# MVC template.

Now you try

You're now going to create a basic ASP .NET Web API 2 application with F#:

1 Open Visual Studio and choose the standard New Project.
2 In the New Project dialog box, choose Online > Templates > Visual F# > F# MVC 5.
3 From the next dialog box, choose Web API 2.2 and Katana 3.0 (Empty). You'll now have an empty Web API project with no controllers. Although larger, ready-made templates are available with ready-made controllers, start with an empty one so that you can see the basics first (you'll also notice a non-Katana Web API project, which uses the older global.asax-based web projects). In case you're unaware of Katana: it's a middleware layer that allows you to plug lightweight OWIN-compliant web applications into IIS.
4 Build the solution to pull down any NuGet packages required.
5 Run the solution. You'll see that a website is created on IIS Express, and a browser page opens with an error page. Of course, there's nothing to see yet!

At this point, let's take a look at what you have in the solution: a single F# file, Startup.fs. This file acts as the bootstrapper of your application and is similar to what you'd have with the equivalent empty project in C#. A Startup class contains two methods: one to configure the ASP .NET app builder, and another to configure the Web API.

6   Delete the two serialization lines (you'll come back to them shortly).

7   Add a new file to the project, Controllers.fs, and enter the following code into the file. This file will implement a simple ASP .NET controller class that can respond to HTTP GET requests to the api/animals route.

Listing 37.1 Your first Web API controller

```
namespace Controllers
open System.Web.Http                          Creating a type
                                              from which to
type Animal = { Name : string; Species : string }   expose data

[<RoutePrefix("api")>]
type AnimalsController() =                     Setting the Web
    inherit ApiController()                    API route prefix

    [<Route("animals")>]                       Setting the Web API route
    member __.Get() =
        [ { Name = "Fido"; Species = "Dog" }   Creating a
          { Name = "Felix"; Species = "Cat" } ]  GET handler
```

This should be similar to what you've done in the past with the Web API in C#; in fact, this is a standard .NET class, although the syntax looks a little different from C#. If you haven't used the Web API before, the RoutePrefix and Route attributes identify the path that the HTTP request should come from (for example, api/animals). I've elected to use explicit Attribute routing here rather than set up conventions in the bootstrapper, but you could've just as easily done that, too. Notice that you've defined a standard F# record here and are exposing an F# List of Animals—nothing special there!

8   Run the application again and navigate to api/animals. Depending on what browser you're using, the result will either be opened directly in the browser or downloaded. Using Chrome or Firefox, you'll see output that probably looks something like figure 37.1.

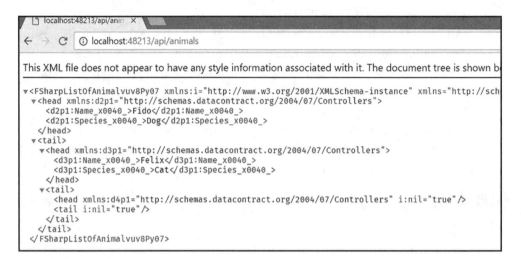

Figure 37.1   Default XML output when using ASP .NET

9   Ugh—XML! That's not what you want. You'd like some JSON data, right? Let's turn off the XML formatter. In the `RegisterWebApi` method, add the following line:

```
config.Formatters.Remove(config.Formatters.XmlFormatter) |> ignore
```

10   Rerun the application and refresh the browser, as shown in figure 37.2.

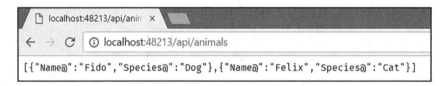
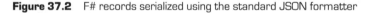

Figure 37.2   F# records serialized using the standard JSON formatter

11   OK, this is looking better, as you're now getting back JSON—except all the fields have @ post-fixed on them. This is a side-effect of the way F#'s fields are compiled, and one you can easily fix by replacing ASP .NET's JSON formatter with one that comes with JSON.Net. Back in `RegisterWebApi`, add the following line:

```
config.Formatters.JsonFormatter.SerializerSettings.ContractResolver <-
    Newtonsoft.Json.Serialization.DefaultContractResolver()
```

12   Rerun the application and refresh the page, as shown in figure 37.3.

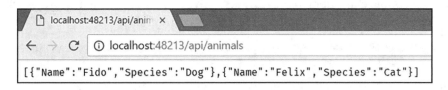

Figure 37.3 F# records are correctly serialized by using the Newtonsoft.Json formatter.

Job done! You've now created an ASP .NET Web API controller that uses the standard .NET web project. Remember that Web API isn't tied to C# or VB .NET, so any other feature in ASP .NET such as filters can be used (and implemented) in F#, as well as the other features of Web API's routing engine.

CLIMutable for F# and JSON

A common misconception in the F# community is that you must use the [<CLIMutable>] attribute on F# records in order to make them compatible with JSON serialization. This isn't true, and hasn't been for some time now; just use the DefaultContractResolver.

37.1.2 Using OWIN host with F#

An alternative mechanism for working with Web API is to use the OWIN host for Web API, a lightweight host for ASP .NET that allows you to create a web host as part of any application (for example, a console application, Windows service, or WPF application). Another benefit of this approach is that you remove the reliance on custom tooling (Visual Studio project templates); there's just a standard .NET console/service and a couple of library calls, and you can more easily see what's happening—there's no "magic" happening behind the scenes.

Now you try

Now you'll try to create an F# console app that uses the OWIN host to host your Web API app:

1 Create a standard F# console application.
2 From the project properties, set the target framework to .NET 4.5.2.
3 Install the `Microsoft.AspNet.WebApi.OwinSelfHost` NuGet package.
4 Copy across the Controllers and Startup files from the previous web project.

5 Replace the entry point of Program.fs with the following. It starts up a listener on your machine, using the Startup class for configuration.

Listing 37.2 Using the OWIN host to run a web application from a console

```
open Microsoft.Owin.Hosting

[<EntryPoint>]
let main _ =
    use app = WebApp.Start<Startup>(url = "http://localhost:9000/")
    printfn "Listening on localhost:9000!"
    Console.ReadLine() |> ignore

    0 // return an integer exit code
```

Launching the web app host within the console application

Blocking the console from quitting

6 Try browsing localhost:9000/api/animals. The result should be the same as before.

Quick check 37.1

1 Can you create F# web projects in Visual Studio?
2 Do you need to use CLIMutable to serialize records in JSON for ASP .NET?

37.2 Abstracting the Web API from F#

One thing about the Web API is that you have to expose controllers as classes. This isn't necessarily a terrible thing, but it does go against the grain of everything you've done thus far (using modules as the primary method for grouping functions together). In my experience, it's not uncommon to separate out the implementation of a controller to a module, and have the controller as a simple mapper that's responsible for marshalling data in and out of the web app. This way, you can write your application code without worrying about HTTP response codes. In some ways, this isn't so different from working with mixed C#/F# applications, but here we're talking about JSON and HTTP responses as the output, rather than C# classes.

QC 37.1 answer

1 Yes, but only via the third-party F# web templates.
2 Not when using Newtonsoft's standard JSON serializer.

37.2.1 Abstracting HTTP codes from F#

Let's take a simple example and consider basic HTTP results to be one of a few different values:

- Success with a certain payload (HTTP 202)
- Invalid (HTTP 400)
- Not found (HTTP 404)
- Internal error (HTTP 500)

One thing you wouldn't want to do is force your internal F# code to be polluted with HTTP codes. A much better way is to abstract this away from your internal domain. Table 37.1 and figure 37.4 provide a sample mapping from HTTP return codes to a simple F# domain model that models the first three cases using a nested discriminated union.

Table 37.1 Mapping HTTP return codes from F# types

HTTP code	F# type	Example
202 (Accepted)	Some Success	Some(Success { Animal = "Cat"; Name = "Felix" })
400 (Bad Request)	Some Failure	Some(Failure "You must provide a valid name")
404 (Not Found)	None	None
500 (Internal Error)	Exception	SQL connection exception

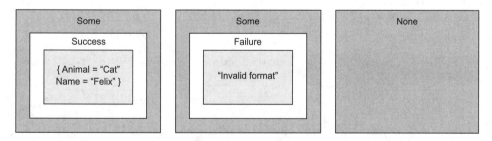

Figure 37.4 Modeling both success/failure and absence of value with DUs

Let's see how this maps to your real code; start by abstracting away the implementation from the controller into a standalone module like the following. (I've also added a second function to try to find a specific animal by name.)

Listing 37.3   Listing 37.3 Moving Web API logic to a standalone module

```
module AnimalsRepository =
    let all =
        [ { Name = "Fido"; Species = "Dog" }
          { Name = "Felix"; Species = "Cat" } ]
    let getAll() = all
    let getAnimal name = all |> List.tryFind(fun r -> r.Name = name)
```

The getAnimal function returns an Option<Animal>. The next task is to write a simple mapper function to go from this to an HttpResponseCode object that ASP .NET understands, and update the controller class as well.

Listing 37.4   Mapping between F# and HTTP domains

Helper function to map
from Option to
HttpResponseCode

```
[<AutoOpen>]
module Helpers =
    let asResponse (request:HttpRequestMessage) result =
        match result with
        | Some result -> request.CreateReponse(HttpStatusCode.OK, result)
        | None -> request.CreateReponse(HttpStatusCode.NotFound)

[<RoutePrefix("api")>]
type AnimalsController() =
    inherit ApiController()

    [<Route("animals/{name}")>]
    member this.Get(name) =
        AnimalsRepository.getAnimal name |> (asResponse this.Request)
```

Mapping from
Option<Animal> to
an HttpResponseCode

You now have a function that can take in any result, in this case, either Some result or None, and map it to an appropriate HttpResponseMessage. Notice that rather than manually creating an HttpResponseMessage, you're using the CreateResponse method on the Request object that you get for free when inheriting from ApiController and passing that in (this is all created for you by the ASP .NET Controller Factory). Also, notice the explicit type annotation on the createReponse argument. Because HttpRequestMessage isn't an F# type, type inference won't be able to figure it out for you as usual.

Now you try

Next, enhance the application to handle success/failure cases more cleanly:

1 Run the application, hitting the route api/animals/Felix, and observe that the route returns HTTP 202 with the correct result.

2 Browse the route api/animals/Toby; the result will be 404 with no response payload.

So far, you've accounted for two of the four cases from table 37.1. Now you'll account for the next one, HTTP 400, which is often used, for example, for validation errors (invalid requests).

3 Create a new discriminated union type, Result. This type can store one of two cases: either a successful payload, or a failure with a string explaining the error:

```
type Result<'T> = Success of 'T | Failure of error:string
```

4 Update the implementation of getAnimal so that if the name supplied contains any nonletters, a failure case is raised with an appropriate error. Refer to table 37.1 if you need help with the syntax to create a nested discriminated union (Option<Result<Animal>>).

5 You'll also have to lift the result of the existing call to tryFind into a Success case so that the types of both cases match.

6 Update the asReponse function so that it caters to Some Failure and Some Success cases instead of just Some.

7 Run the application and test that all three cases are working.

Because the Web API automatically cascades exceptions to response codes of 500, you don't have to do anything there. But you can test it out by adding logic to your getAnimal function so that if it takes in a special string (for example, "FAIL"), it raises an exception by using the failwith function.

Error handling in F#

To reiterate, it's not always considered best practice to include exceptions as a standard part of your application. Instead, use something like Result to raise failure cases that you can account for. This way, they're included in the type system, and you can more easily reason about them through pattern matching. Again, Scott Wlaschin's excellent series on railway-oriented programming is an in-depth look at how to model failure cases, as well as how to reason about them succinctly.

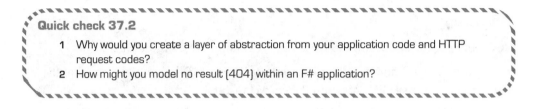

37.3 Working with Async

The Web API has native support for working with tasks. Your controllers can return data asynchronously (and therefore wrapped as Task<T>), and the Web API will happily unwrap this automatically in the background for you. Let's see how to work with asynchronous data in F# by using F#'s Async type, and yet still interoperate with the Web API's support for tasks, as shown in figure 37.5:

1   Wrap the implementation of getAnimal in an async { } block (remember to explicitly return the result of the match expression!). Obviously, in this example no real asynchrony is occurring; you're just pushing this work to a background thread, but the principle is the same.

2   The controller method will break, because you're trying to push an Async<Option<Result <Animal>>> into asResponse, which expects an Option<Result<Animal>>; you need to unwrap the async somehow. The simple thing to do would be to call Async.RunSynchronously, but this defeats the whole purpose of using asynchronous code within a web app. Instead, you can make the controller method itself asynchronous.

Listing 37.5 Creating an asynchronous Web API controller method

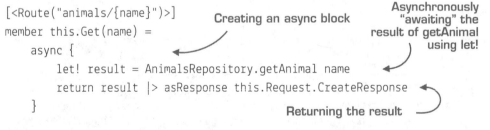

```
[<Route("animals/{name}")>]                                    Asynchronously
member this.Get(name) =            Creating an async block       "awaiting" the
    async {                                                     result of getAnimal
        let! result = AnimalsRepository.getAnimal name              using let!
        return result |> asResponse this.Request.CreateResponse
    }                                          Returning the result
```

3 Notice that the result of the controller method is now an `Async<HttpResponseMessage>`.

4 You're still not there. The Web API doesn't know how to work with F# `async` blocks, only Tasks. Run the application and try to access the route; you'll always get back an HTTP 200 with an empty payload.

5 However, Web API can natively unwrap `Task<T>`. Convert the async to a `Task` by pipelining the async workflow that's returned by the `Get(name)` method into `Async.StartAsTask`. The result of the controller method will now be `Task<HttpResponseMessage>`.

6 Rerun the application and observe that the results are once again correct.

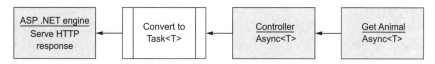

Figure 37.5   Moving from an F# `Async<T>` to `Task<T>` as needed by ASP .NET

Your code now will run entirely asynchronously, yet still play nicely with the Web API framework's support for `Task`.

Quick check 37.3   How do you return F# results wrapped in async blocks over ASP .NET?

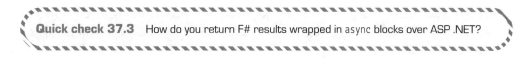

37.4   Introducing Suave

Suave is an F#-first web library designed to allow you to model your web applications by using an entirely functional-first model. It's lightweight, and after you get your head around the concepts it introduces (which, admittedly, are different from those you'll know from ASP .NET), you can rapidly create powerful applications in a lightweight fashion.

37.4.1   Modeling web requests as functions

One thing about ASP .NET is that it (unsurprisingly) pushes you into an object-oriented model. You have controllers that inherit from base controllers; controllers are objects

QC 37.3 answer   Convert from `Async` to `Task` via the `Async.StartAsTask` combinator.

with methods on them, and so forth. In reality, web applications are a great fit for functional programming and F#:

- Web apps are by nature nearly always stateless; you take in an HTTP request and give back an HTTP response.
- Web apps often need to use asynchronous programming, which F# has excellent support for.
- Web apps—particularly the back end—are often data-centric; another great fit for F#.

Suave takes a different approach to ASP .NET: every request is handled by a *web part*, which itself is built up of other, smaller web parts. A web part is a function with a simple signature:

```
HttpContext -> Async<HttpContext option>
```

This means that given an HTTP context (the details on the request/response), a web part must asynchronously return either of the following:

- Some context—typically, the context that was passed in, perhaps along with an updated response payload
- Nothing

A web part can be composed of other, smaller web parts, each working together to create a pipeline that builds up to a final response. You can think of these as similar to filters or visitors. For example, one web part may convert an object to JSON. Another might check whether the supplied route is a GET or POST request, and so forth. The following code provides a simple Suave pipeline that mirrors your existing Web API controller; also see figure 37.6. Table 37.2 shows some common web parts.

Listing 37.6 A simple Suave pipeline

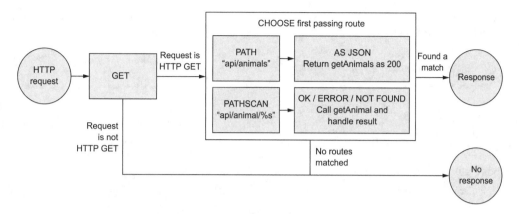

Figure 37.6   A simple Suave pipeline

Table 37.2   Common Suave web parts

Web part	Description
OK	Returns a string response as HTTP 200.
GET	Checks the incoming request. If it's a GET, it passes the context along; otherwise, returns nothing.
CHOOSE	Takes in several web parts, trying each of them sequentially. The first one to return a valid response is returned; otherwise, returns nothing.
PATH	Scans the request URI. If it matches the specified URL, it passes the context along; otherwise, returns nothing.

This model of composing web parts is powerful, as you can rapidly build up arbitrary pipelines based on small, reusable functions. But the syntax and model are very different from what you're probably used to. For example, a custom >=> operator is used to connect two web parts together, as well as the underlying nature of Suave—basically, a purely functional pipeline.

What's nice about Suave is that it's extremely lightweight. No code-gen is needed, nor is there any requirement for custom projects. It can live as a console application or service and is easy to start—just a single line of code, in fact: `startWebServer defaultConfig app`, where `app` is your overall composed web part. The code sample has a full example that shows how you might adapt the existing code into Suave. If you like what you see, it's worth checking out some of the excellent resources (both online and paper-based) to learn more about it.

Quick check 37.4

1 What's a web part in Suave?
2 What does Suave's GET web part do?

Summary

That's a wrap for creating web applications in F#! In this lesson

- You learned how to create ASP .NET Web API applications in F# and Visual Studio.
- You got F# to work smoothly with ASP .NET.
- You marshaled data between F# and ASP .NET domains.
- You worked with the Suave F# web programming library.

Try this

Enhance the sample application so that it handles POST requests as well as GETs. Alternatively, create a web application in F# by using ASP .NET that serves data sourced from the FootballResults.csv file in the data folder from the source code repository. Try to use the CSV type provider as the data access layer!

QC 37.4 answer

1 A function that takes in an HTTP context and may return a new context, asynchronously.
2 If the request is an HTTP GET, passes the context back out; otherwise, returns nothing.

CONSUMING HTTP DATA

Having seen how to serve HTTP data by using ASP .NET in F#, you're now going to look at the other side of the fence: consuming HTTP data quickly and easily by using various F# libraries. You'll learn about

- How you might access HTTP endpoints today
- Using FSharp.Data to work with HTTP endpoints
- HTTP.fs, a lightweight F# library for HTTP access
- The Swagger type provider

Let's start by quickly considering a few common situations you might encounter today.

You've written an ASP .NET Web API application and deploy it to an environment ready for testing. Quickly, the test team gives you feedback about some issues: some data doesn't match as expected. And under certain circumstances, the APIs don't seem to respond at all. You need to set up a way to easily explore these cases as they come, possibly even in a repeatable way.

Here's another one. You need to consume an HTTP endpoint from an external supplier. The problem is that there's no SDK to consume the API; you need to do it all yourself. The API is complex. You need to first authenticate with a time-limited token, before exploring the API (we don't cover this in detail in this lesson, but an example is in the code samples for this lesson).

What options do you have for these sorts of situations? One is to use a tool such as Fiddler or Postman. These are either dedicated Windows or web applications that allow you to test endpoints by sending example request payloads to an endpoint, getting the response back in the browser, and analyzing the responses. But this isn't necessarily the most effective tool; you have to leave your development IDE and context switch to another tool. And, if you want to do anything with the response, you need to copy the information manually into an IDE to experiment with the data. To get around this, another option is to go straight to the `System.Net.WebClient` (or related classes) to start hitting the endpoints directly. Doing this is often painful to do, particularly with a console application.

F# provides libraries for working with HTTP data quickly and easily. In this lesson, you'll explore three options, each with different benefits.

38.1 Using FSharp.Data to work with HTTP endpoints

FSharp.Data's JSON type provider works well at consuming HTTP endpoints that expose JSON data quickly and easily.

Now you try

You're going to test this by using the HTTP API that you created in the previous lesson:

1 Open the Web API project from the previous lesson and start the Web API endpoint. Note that the following code samples assume a port of 8080, but you can find the correct port from the Web tab of the project's properties pane (see figure 38.1).

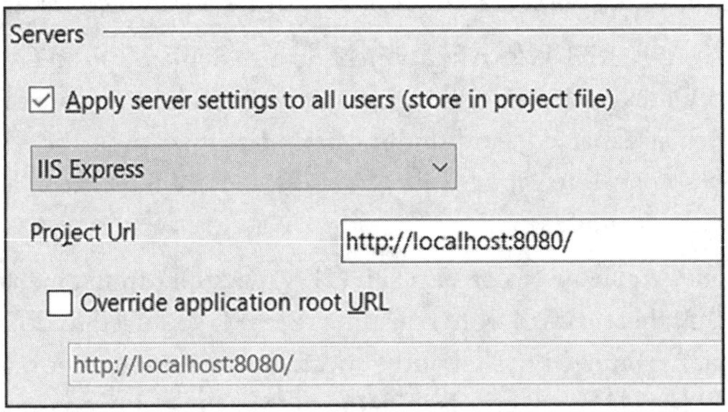

Figure 38.1   Identifying the host URI of IIS Express for Web API in Visual Studio 2015

2 Create a new .fsx script and reference the FSharp.Data NuGet package.

3 Enter the following code to retrieve the names of all animals.

Listing 38.1 Using FSharp.Data to access an HTTP endpoint

```
#I @"..\..\..\packages"
#r @"FSharp.Data\lib\net40\FSharp.Data.dll"
open FSharp.Data
type AllAnimalsResponse =
    JsonProvider<"http://localhost:8080/api/animals">
let names =
    AllAnimalsResponse.GetSamples()
    |> Seq.map(fun a -> a.Name)
    |> Seq.toArray
```

Creating a type that matches the api/animals route

Retrieving all animals

Accessing the JSON in a strongly typed fashion

As you can see in figure 38.2, you can get IntelliSense over the payload of a route, as it's simply JSON (this is similar to what you did in the Data unit when accessing the NuGet API). You can also easily make a parameterizable function to get a specific animal.

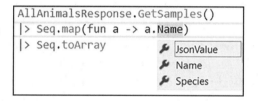

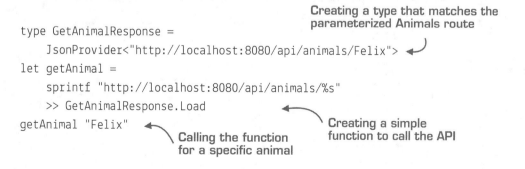

Figure 38.2 IntelliSense from FSharp.Data and an HTTP route

4 Enter the following code.

Listing 38.2 Creating a parameterizable function to access a route

Creating a type that matches the parameterized Animals route

```
type GetAnimalResponse =
    JsonProvider<"http://localhost:8080/api/animals/Felix">
let getAnimal =
    sprintf "http://localhost:8080/api/animals/%s"
    >> GetAnimalResponse.Load
getAnimal "Felix"
```

Creating a simple function to call the API

Calling the function for a specific animal

Unfortunately, using FSharp.Data does have a few restrictions. First, it doesn't give you total control over things such as HTTP headers and the like, and second, it works only with JSON data (obviously). Finally, it doesn't provide any built-in way of handling various response codes (for example, 400, 404, or 500). You need to write code that can wrap any call within a try/with block and convert into a discriminated union (for example, Result<'T>).

Listing 38.3 Writing a simple try/with converter to Result

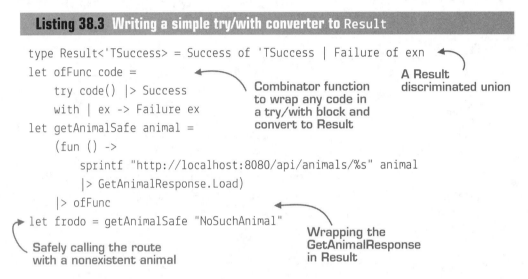

FSharp.Data is a lightweight, quick-and-easy way to start consuming JSON data enabled over HTTP. But it doesn't contain any mechanisms for discovering routes; you need to know them already, and you need to create a separate type for each type of data exposed.

Quick check 38.1

1 Why might you use FSharp.Data to consume a JSON resource over HTTP?
2 What limitations does FSharp.Data have with working with HTTP resources?

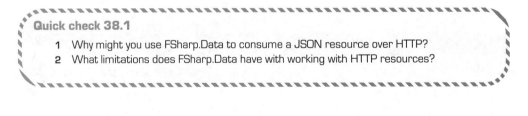

QC 38.1 answer

1 FSharp.Data is extremely quick and easy to use, and works with all JSON web services.
2 Works only with JSON services; no error handling is built in.

38.2 Working with HTTP.fs

HTTP.fs is a small, general-purpose NuGet package for working with data over HTTP, and enables close control over both creating requests and processing responses.

> **HTTP.fs versions**
> Newer versions of HTTP.fs have slightly increased the complexity of the library by intro-
> ducing a dependency on other third-party libraries. To keep things simple, you'll be using
> a slightly older version of the library (1.5.1), which has a smaller API surface area and is
> therefore, in my opinion, easier to work with.

38.2.1 Building requests as a pipeline

HTTP.fs follows a standard pattern you've already seen when working with immutable data and composable functions: you build a request by chaining together small functions that modify a request in some way, as shown in figure 38.3.

Figure 38.3   Creating an HTTP request by chaining small functions together

In the fictitious figure 38.3, you're creating a small pipeline to build an HTTP request. First, you create a basic GET request, before modifying the request in several ways before calling getResponse, which fires off the request and returns the data. Here's how that looks in code.

Listing 38.4 Mapping an HTTP composition pipeline in HTTP.fs

```
createRequest Get "http://host/api/animals"
|> withCookie { name = "Foo"; value = "Bar" }
|> withHeader (ContentType "test/json")
|> withKeepAlive true
|> getResponse
```

As you can see, the code maps closely to the diagram. You could use this mechanism to construct any sort of HTTP message, with security tokens as headers, or custom cookies.

Unlike FSharp.Data, HTTP.fs returns the optional response (as raw text) as part of an object that also contains any headers, cookies, the content length, and the response code.

Now you try

Now test HTTP.fs against your running Web API:

1   Add a reference to HTTP.fs 1.5.1 (if you're using the packages included in the code repository, it'll already be in the packages folder) and open the `HttpClient` namespace.

2   Create a request to the Animals endpoints.

Listing 38.5   Creating your first request with HTTP.fs

```
#r @"Http.fs\lib\net40\HttpClient.dll"
open HttpClient
let request = createRequest Get "http://localhost:8080/api/animals"
let response = request |> getResponse
```

The request object contains all the details needed for an HTTP request: the URI to hit, any cookies, headers, a body for POSTs, the type of request, and so forth. When you send this to the web server by using getResponse, you get back the following.

Listing 38.6   Getting a response from ASP .NET Web API with HTTP.fs

Status code of 200

Response body is a string option

```
{StatusCode = 200;
EntityBody =
Some "[{"Name":"Fido","Species":"Dog"},{"Name":"Felix","Species":"Cat"}]";
ContentLength = 66L;
Cookies = map [];
Headers =
Map
  [(ContentTypeResponse, "application/json; charset=utf-8");
   (DateResponse, "Mon, 16 Jan 2017 15:34:02 GMT");
   (Server, "Microsoft-IIS/10.0"); (NonStandard "X-Powered-By", "ASP.NET");
   (NonStandard "X-SourceFiles", <elided>)];}
```

Any headers from the server are provided.

Notice that the `EntityBody` property is an `Option<string>` to cater to when there's no valid payload returned. Now, continue by working on calling the "named animal" route. Remember from the previous lesson that this endpoint might return a valid animal if one was found, or none, or an HTTP 400 if the name contains numbers:

3 Now, add a reference to Newtonsoft.Json and create some helper functions:

```
open Newtonsoft.Json
let buildRoute = sprintf "http://localhost:8080/api/%s"
let httpGetResponse = buildRoute >> createRequest Get >> getResponse
```

Helper function to build
a route to your API

Creating a composed
function to go from a string
to an HTTP.fs response

Now that you have that helper function, you can easily write some API wrappers. Here's a simple one that gets the response, and if there's a payload, converts it to an F# record.

Listing 38.7 Creating a wrapper API function with HTTP.fs and Newtonsoft.Json

Getting the
response from Web
API via HTTP.fs

```
type Animal = { Name : string; Species : string }
let tryGetAnimal animal =
    let response = sprintf "animals/%s" animal |> httpGetResponse
    response.EntityBody
    |> Option.map(fun body -> JsonConvert.DeserializeObject<Animal>(body))
```

Checking the entity
body has a value

Converting it with
Newtonsoft.Json

It's easy to build a simple DSL around your own custom routes to allow you to create scripts (or even full APIs) around them. And because HTTP.fs is a simple library, and not a framework, you're free to use it however you want. For example, you could easily use the provided type that you generated in listing 38.1 to handle deserialization rather than an explicit F# record and Newtonsoft.Json. But the cost of this flexibility is that you have to usually create a wrapper façade around HTTP.fs; you wouldn't want to expose the outputs from a low-level library like this to callers. There are also no provided types here; you'll have to create your own types, share types across both server and client, or use something like the JSON type provider to give you types based on sample JSON.

38.3   Using the Swagger type provider

Swagger is rapidly becoming a standard for providing schematized metadata HTTP APIs (as well as an interactive browser application). It provides a web front end as well as a programmatic API for working with web APIs. It's a service to provide information about other services! Most languages and runtimes provide a Swagger generator, and .NET is no different, with the Swashbuckle package. Figure 38.4 shows what a Swagger endpoint looks like for your Animal web service.

38.3.1   Adding Swagger to ASP .NET Web API 2

To save you some time, I've made small modifications to the Web API project from lesson 37. You'll find the modified version in the lesson-38 folder. I've added the Swashbuckle NuGet package to the project, fixed the binding redirects that NuGet forgot to do, and then made several small changes to the code base. First, I've added Swagger support to the ASP .NET pipeline so that it runs on start-up.

Listing 38.8   Activating Swagger within ASP .NET Web API

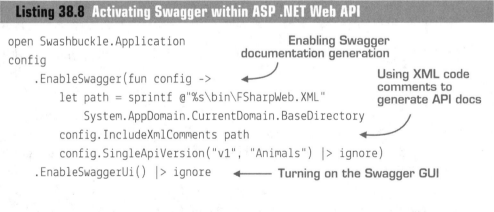

```
open Swashbuckle.Application
config
    .EnableSwagger(fun config ->
        let path = sprintf @"%s\bin\FSharpWeb.XML"
            System.AppDomain.CurrentDomain.BaseDirectory
        config.IncludeXmlComments path
        config.SingleApiVersion("v1", "Animals") |> ignore)
    .EnableSwaggerUi() |> ignore
```

Enabling Swagger documentation generation

Using XML code comments to generate API docs

Turning on the Swagger GUI

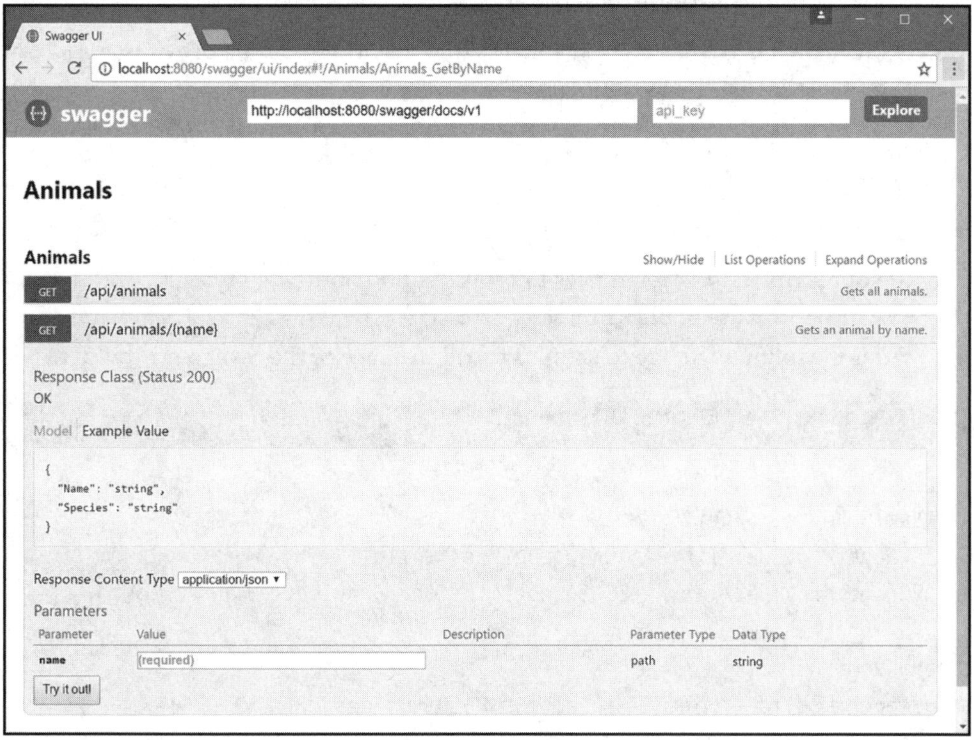

Figure 38.4 Viewing the Swagger-generated API documentation

Having turned on XML comments support, I applied comments and attributes to the HTTP routes so that they document what they do, as shown in figure 38.5.

```
[<Route("animals/{name}")>]
[<ResponseType(typeof<Animal>)>]
/// Gets an animal by name.
member this.GetByName(name) =
```

Figure 38.5 Decorating a route with the [<ResponseType>] attribute and XML triple-slash comments

Now that that's all working, you can launch the application and navigate to the Swagger docs endpoint. You'll now have a full web UI showing the different API methods you've surfaced, along with your XML comments on the right-hand side and an example response document. Neat!

38.3.2 Consuming Swagger APIs in F#

Swagger on its own is great, but even better is that the Swagger type provider for F# can generate a full API from the Swagger endpoint.

....

Now you try

Try it out yourself by consuming the API you just made:

1. In your script, add #r references to YamlDotNet and both SwaggerProvider and Swagger-Provider.Runtime assemblies in SwaggerProvider.

2. Enter the following code to create a typed instance of the Swagger provider.

Listing 38.9 Hooking up the Swagger type provider to a Swagger endpoint

```
#I @"..\..\..\packages"
#r "YamlDotNet/lib/net35/YamlDotNet.dll"
#r "SwaggerProvider/lib/net45/SwaggerProvider.dll"
#r "SwaggerProvider/lib/net45/SwaggerProvider.Runtime.dll"      Generating an
open SwaggerProvider                                            API from the
                                                                Swagger
type SwaggerAnimals =                                           endpoint
    SwaggerProvider<"http://localhost:8080/swagger/docs/v1">
let animalsApi = SwaggerAnimals()  ◀─────── Creating an instance of the API
```

Now, you can dot into animalsApi and get access to all the methods you've exposed. And not only that, but the full response types will also be generated for you, as shown in figure 38.6.

```
animalsApi.AnimalsGetByName("Felix")

        SwaggerAnimals.AnimalsGetByName(name: string) : SwaggerAnimals.Animal

        Gets an animal by name.
```

Figure 38.6 Consuming a Swagger endpoint by using the Swagger type provider

As you can see in figure 38.7, you also get generated comments based on the source XML comments—even at the field level.

This automatic API and type generation make it incredibly easy to start consuming web-enabled APIs in F#, since you get automatic route discovery and type generation. However, this means that the caller must expose an accurate schema via Swagger.

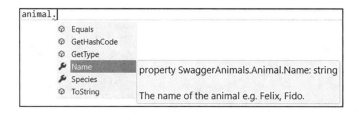

Figure 38.7 XML comments are generated by the Swagger type provider for fields as well as methods.

Quick check 38.3

1 What is Swagger?
2 What NuGet package is used in order to create Swagger documentation on .NET?

 **Summary**

That concludes the consuming side of the HTTP unit. Let's quickly review what we covered. In this lesson

- You saw how to use FSharp.Data to quickly and easily consume JSON-ready HTTP endpoints.
- You then worked with the HTTP.fs package, a low-level package that gives you full control over sending HTTP requests to web servers.
- You looked at the Swagger type provider, which provides you with full access to a generated HTTP client based on Swagger metadata.

Try this

Enhance the error handler in listing 38.3 so that failures have specific cases instead of just an exception (for example, `PageNotFound | InternalServerError of exn | BadRequest`). Then, enhance the `tryGetAnimal` function in listing 38.7 to check the `StatusCode` and emit logging if an HTTP 400 or 500 response is received. Finally, try to replace the explicit F# record in listing 38.7 with the provided type created in listing 38.1.

QC 38.3 answer

1 A standard for exposing schematized metadata on a web API.
2 Swashbuckle.

39

CAPSTONE 7

In this capstone exercise, you'll apply the lessons you've learned in this Web Programming unit to the Bank Accounts solution that you've been working on throughout the book. Start in src/code-listings/lesson-39.

39.1 Defining the problem

In this capstone, you'll first make your application web-enabled: you'll add a Web API layer on top, before consuming it via a script over HTTP. You'll also learn how to make your WPF application work over HTTP. Finally, you'll make your bank account use asynchronous data access.

39.1.1 Solution overview

At the end of the preceding capstone, you replaced the filesystem with a SQL database for storing transactions, along with a WPF application for the GUI. In this lesson, I've removed the GUI element completely (don't worry, you could plug it back in again without too much difficulty) as well as the database project (the schema hasn't changed at all). What I've introduced instead is an ASP .NET Web API project that you'll use to provide an API for the bank application. I've done all of the work to add the correct NuGet packages and set up the binding redirects already, so you can focus on the application coding.

39.2 Adding Web API support to your application

Start by making a controller for the bank account application. It should have endpoints reflecting the different functions exposed by the BankAPI interface—getting details on an account, getting the transaction history, withdrawing funds, and depositing funds.

39.2.1 Your first endpoint

Begin by creating a controller in the Controllers.fs file.

> **Listing 39.1 A basic Web API controller for the Bank API**

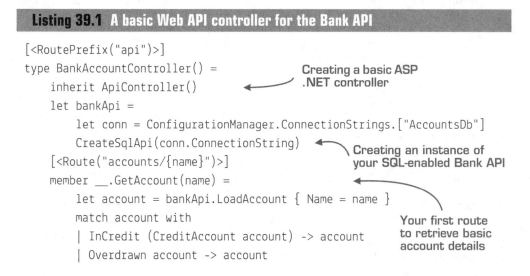

```
[<RoutePrefix("api")>]
type BankAccountController() =                    Creating a basic ASP
    inherit ApiController()          ◄──────────  .NET controller
    let bankApi =
        let conn = ConfigurationManager.ConnectionStrings.["AccountsDb"]
        CreateSqlApi(conn.ConnectionString)   ◄──  Creating an instance of
    [<Route("accounts/{name}")>]                   your SQL-enabled Bank API
    member __.GetAccount(name) =          ◄───────
        let account = bankApi.LoadAccount { Name = name }
        match account with                             Your first route
        | InCredit (CreditAccount account) -> account  to retrieve basic
        | Overdrawn account -> account                 account details
```

That's all that's needed! Notice how you're unwrapping the result of the load account so that you return the raw account object rather than the full discriminated union. This keeps things a little simpler in terms of the JSON that you expose. (By the way, I'm assuming that you still have the SQL database from the previous capstone. If not, go back and create it. Or you can replace the call to create the SQL layer with the FileApi, but doing this will stop you from doing some of the later exercises in this lesson.)

> ### Dependency injection with F#
> If you've been using ASP .NET for a while now, you've probably immediately spotted that you've tightly coupled the controller to the SQL API implementation. Shouldn't you be injecting this dependency into the controller based on the interface instead? Well, you can definitely do that; remember, F# can create interfaces just like C#. You'll need to create an implementation of an `IDependencyResolver` and assign it to the `DependencyResolver` property on the `HttpConfiguration` object.

You should now be able to run the web app, open a browser, and navigate to a URL similar to http://localhost:8080/api/accounts/isaac. You'll get back a response similar to this:

```
{"AccountId":"8e7a7909-5667-4cfb-8726-ac3c083ea621",
➥"Owner":{"Name":"isaac"},
➥"Balance":-3.0}
```

That was easy! You should now move along and create the transaction history route, `GetHistory` (I've used the route `transactions/{name}`). Again, test it out in a browser, and notice that transaction is serialized as follows:

```
{"Timestamp":"2016-12-30T17:02:53.757",
➥"Operation":{"Case":"Deposit"},"Amount":10.0}
```

Observe that the `Operation`, rather than being simply `"Deposit"`, is a full JSON object with a property called `Case`. In such situations, you can either replace the JSON serializer with another one, or create a JSON-friendly type—a simple F# record with no discriminated unions—and map from the complex F# type to the dumber JSON-friendly record. This has the added benefit that you decouple your internal domain with your public, user-facing contracts.

> ### Discriminated unions over JSON
> JSON.NET will happily serialize and deserialize F# discriminated unions for free. But the JSON that emits isn't the most idiomatic, as you've just seen. A couple of alternative serializers (such as FifteenBelow.Json) can plug into Newtonsoft to override the serialization for F# types, and they do a much better job of creating idiomatic JSON from F# types.

39.2.2 Posting data to the Web API

Next, create some handlers for Deposits and Withdrawals. You'll notice that we've prefixed both routes so far with the word `Get`. This convention tells ASP .NET that those methods should be bound to HTTP `GET` requests. Similarly, prefixing a method with `Post` tells ASP .NET to bind a method to HTTP `POST` requests. (You can explicitly state this with the [<HTTPPost>] attribute as well.) Because Deposit and Withdrawal are functions that save new data (rather than just reading data), mark them as Post methods. Here's an example to get you started.

Listing 39.2 Example routes for POSTing a Deposit request

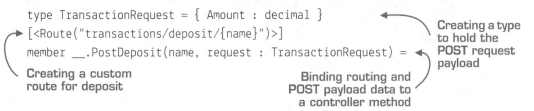

```
type TransactionRequest = { Amount : decimal }
[<Route("transactions/deposit/{name}")>]
member __.PostDeposit(name, request : TransactionRequest) =
```

Creating a type to hold the POST request payload

Creating a custom route for deposit

Binding routing and POST payload data to a controller method

Make sure that you also remember to unwrap RatedAccount to a raw Account, as you did with the initial controller method (you may want to create a reusable function that does this and call it from all three controller methods).

39.3 Consuming data with Swagger

It's not so easy to test these POST methods in a browser, so let's see how to expose this API over Swagger and then write a script to access the API programmatically. You need to do a couple of things to expose the data over Swagger: first, you need to turn on Swagger in the Web API pipeline, and then you'll have to add metadata to make Swagger a little easier to work with.

39.3.1 Activating Swagger

To turn on Swagger, you need to hook into the configuration phase of the Web API, just as you did earlier in this unit in the Configuration method of the Startup class.

Listing 39.3 Activating Swagger in ASP .NET Web API

```
config
    .EnableSwagger(fun config ->
        let path =
            sprintf @"%s\bin\Web.XML"
                System.AppDomain.CurrentDomain.BaseDirectory
        config.IncludeXmlComments path
        config.SingleApiVersion("v1", "Bank Accounts") |> ignore)
    .EnableSwaggerUi() |> ignore
```

Turning on Swagger with support for XML comments

Rerun the application. Navigating to http://localhost:8080/swagger/ui/index#/ should now present you with a documented API, as shown in figure 39.1.

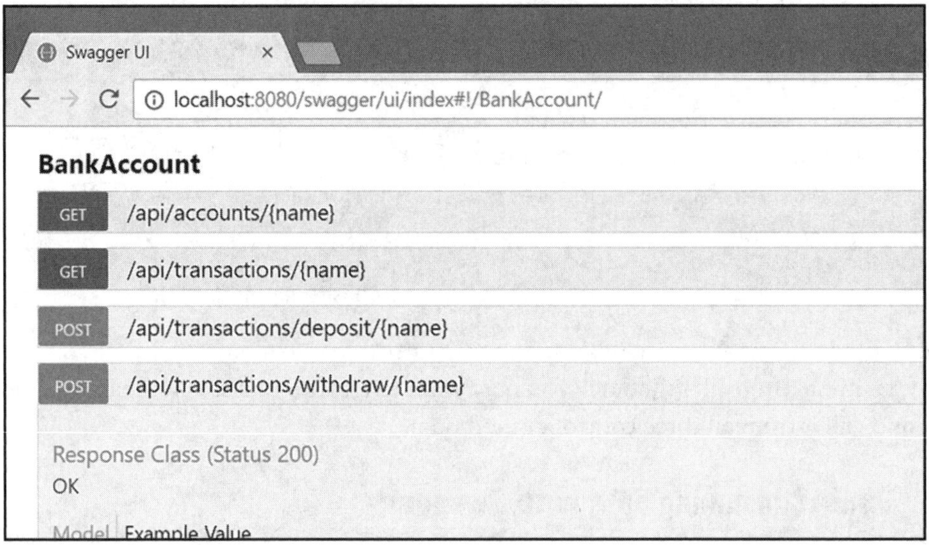

Figure 39.1   A Swagger API for your Bank Account API

39.3.2 Applying metadata

Now, you can improve the API a little by adding the following:

- *XML comments*—Apply triple-slash XML comments over any methods or data that are publicly exposed. This includes controller methods and any types (for example, Transaction Request, Account, and so forth). You can comment on both F# records and their fields.
- *Response types*—Place the [<ResponseType>] attribute on all controller methods, stating the type that they return—for example, [<ResponseType(typeof<Account>)>].
- *Mandatory metadata*—Swashbuckle generates Swagger metadata, with most fields marked as optional by default. The problem is that the Swagger type provider will process this metadata and generate optional types for you. This is a pity; Swashbuckle fields should be marked as mandatory by default. Nonetheless, you can override this by placing the [<System.ComponentModel.DataAnnotations.Required>] attribute on any fields that are mandatory (add a reference to the System.Component-Model.DataAnnotations assembly). For now, place it on the TransactionRequest's Amount

field, but you might want to also place it on decimal fields that are exposed by the core Bank domain (or alternatively, to avoid polluting the internal domain, create public types that live exclusively in your Web API domain and map across to them).

39.3.3 Consuming your API

Now you're ready to consume your API in F#. Open a new script and add references to Swagger as follows.

Listing 39.4 Consuming the Bank Accounts API via the Swagger type provider

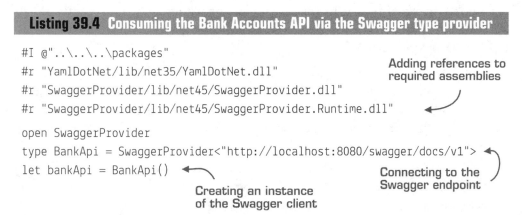

```
#I @"..\..\..\packages"
#r "YamlDotNet/lib/net35/YamlDotNet.dll"
#r "SwaggerProvider/lib/net45/SwaggerProvider.dll"
#r "SwaggerProvider/lib/net45/SwaggerProvider.Runtime.dll"

open SwaggerProvider
type BankApi = SwaggerProvider<"http://localhost:8080/swagger/docs/v1">
let bankApi = BankApi()
```

Adding references to required assemblies

Connecting to the Swagger endpoint

Creating an instance of the Swagger client

Now you're good to go! You can call methods on the provided client to call methods in your HTTP API, as shown in figure 39.2.

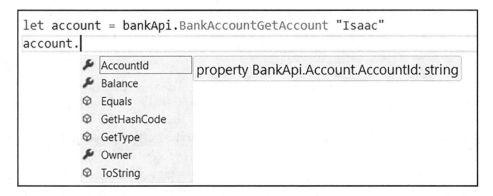

Figure 39.2 Strongly typed access to an ASP .NET API

Think about that for a moment. You're calling an HTTP API, with a full strongly typed domain, in six lines of code (and no code generation required). That API is itself performing some strongly typed business logic, which itself calls a pluggable data access layer (which in this case goes to a SQL database). In all, this needed perhaps a few hundred lines of code—not bad at all!

39.4 Enriching the API

Let's look at two final areas in this capstone: working with results, and async data.

39.4.1 Working with results

The eagle-eyed among you will have spotted that for the Withdraw method, you return a successful message even if the withdrawal fails (for example, if the user was already overdrawn). The problem is that the Bank API doesn't tell you whether a withdrawal was a success; it returns either the new account if the withdrawal succeeded, or the original account if it was rejected.

Listing 39.5 The existing Withdraw function

```
member this.Withdraw amount customer : RatedAccount =
    let account = this.LoadAccount customer
    match account with
    | InCredit (CreditAccount account as creditAccount) ->
        auditAs Withdraw saveTransaction withdraw amount creditAccount
        account.AccountId account.Owner
    | Overdrawn _ -> account }
```

An InCredit account is allowed to withdraw funds. New account state is returned.

An Overdrawn account can't withdraw funds. The existing account state is returned.

Notice that the return type is RatedAccount—here's our problem. You're going to change it so that the return type is Result<RatedAccount>. You'll return Success with the account when the account was in credit, and a failure with an error message if it was overdrawn. Create a Result type, and then change the logic so that you wrap the result of auditAs in either a Success or a Failure with the message "Account is overdrawn—withdrawal rejected!" Here's a Result type definition to get you going:

```
type Result<'T> = Success of 'T | Failure of string
```

In the controller, you should now expose either OK or BadRequest, for success or failure, respectively.

Listing 39.6 Surfacing errors from your domain as HTTP codes

```
open System.Web.Http
[<Route("transactions/withdraw/{name}")>]
member this.PostWithdrawal(name, request : TransactionRequest) =
    let customer = { Name = name }
    match bankApi.Withdraw request.Amount customer with
    | Success account -> this.Ok(account) :> IHttpActionResult
    | Failure message -> this.BadRequest(message) :> IHttpActionResult
```

Returning OK for   **Returns BadRequest for**
successful withdrawals   **failed withdrawals**

The only slight fly in the ointment is that you need to "safe upcast" from OK and BadRequest to IHttpActionResult so that both branches return the same type; F# won't implicitly upcast for you here. Quick tip: after you've done the explicit upcast for the first branch, you can simplify the second from :> IHttpActionResult to just :> _.

39.4.2 Making the API asynchronous

Let's spend a little time looking at what's involved in making the application asynchronous. The best place to start is at the bottom of the stack, and work upward—in this case, the SQL data layer. The only method you can truly make asynchronous is getAccountAndTransactions. The writeTransactions function uses DataTable.Update, which doesn't support async. You could wrap it in an async block anyway, but you'll just push the work onto another thread.

You'll first need to replace the Execute() calls to the database with AsyncExecute() calls instead. This will then cause everything to break, because these calls now return Async<T> instead of T. To fix it, you'll need to unwrap from Async<T> to T by using the let! keyword, and to do that, you need to wrap your code in an async { } block. Also, remember to explicitly return values—for example, return Some(accountId, transactions).

After you have that fixed, you'll see a cascading effect up the stack. All the calls will also need to be made Async-friendly, as in C# with async/await. The IBankApi will need to be updated so that all the methods return Async data, and the implementations of those methods will also need to be made Async aware so that you can let! them as needed.

Note that the filesystem-based API won't be compatible with BankApi anymore. You'll need to lift those functions so that they're also async. This is easily accomplished:

```
FileRepository.tryFindTransactionsOnDisk >> async.Return
```

async.Return takes a value and wraps it in Async. In other words, whatever the result of the function on the left is, push it into async.Return and give that result back out.

There's one, final area to fix: the controllers themselves. Be careful that you don't accidentally return Async<T> values; you'll need to convert them to Task<T> by using Async.Start-AsTask. You'll also find one last problem that's a bit of an F# oddity: you can't call protected class members (such as this.OK or this.BadRequest) directly within lambdas or async blocks. Some of your code will probably break with a lengthy error message, the key part of which is this:

```
Protected members may only be accessed from an extending type and cannot be
accessed from inner lambda expressions.
```

You might ask, where's the lambda expression? The answer is that async blocks (indeed, all computation expressions) are syntactic sugar to rewrite code as continuations, which are effectively lambda expressions. It turns out that there's a simple, rote solution to this, which is to make a member that explicitly calls the protected member manually, and then call that member instead, as the next listing shows

Listing 39.7 Working around F# restrictions with protected members

Manually calling a protected
base class member via a
top-level member method

```
member __.AsOk(account) = base.Ok(account)
member __.AsBadRequest(message:string) = base.BadRequest(message)

member this.PostWithdrawal(name, request : TransactionRequest) =
    async {
        let customer = { Name = name }
        let! result = bankApi.Withdraw request.Amount customer
        match result with
        | Success account ->
            return this.AsOk(account |> getAccount) :> IHttpActionResult
        | Failure message ->
            return this.AsBadRequest(message) :> _
    } |> Async.StartAsTask
```

Calling the delegating
member method

Don't worry if you're feeling confused now. I know that this workaround feels completely ridiculous. Hopefully, a future release of F# will automatically do this boilerplate for us, but for now this is one of the edge-cases where OO features of the CLR and F# language features don't mesh together that nicely.

 ## Summary

You're finished! You've now written an end-to-end application that's backed by SQL server with a WPF front end as well as a web-enabled, fully asynchronous API service. Not bad! Although the tools and techniques you've seen so far while building the application aren't the only ways to write F# applications, it's worth remembering some things that you might not have thought would be possible when you started creating the app:

- You've written an app that connects to SQL Server and can perform standard CRUD operations in a type-safe manner, quickly and easily.
- You've implemented some business rules and seen how to model a domain by using F# types.
- You hooked up a WPF application running in C# from an F# back end.
- You also exposed your data over an ASP .NET Web API app written entirely in F#, using asynchronous code and using Swagger to generate documentation, and then consumed it from a script within just a few lines of code.
- The application makes no use of mutable data, and you didn't need to resort to classes or inheritance. There are some impure functions—notably ones that write data to SQL—but the core app adheres to most of the core FP behaviors, such as separation of code and data and higher-order functions.

Try this

- Reincorporate the WPF front-end, but instead of connecting in process to the API, use the web API that you just created. Use either Swagger or another option for the HTTP client façade.
- Create a dedicated web domain model instead of directly exposing the types from the internal domain over HTTP.
- Write a full web front end that uses the Web API application as a data source.

Unit testing

We touched on the concept of testing early in the book but haven't looked at it since then. This unit discusses when and where you might want to unit test when working in F#, as well as exploring various unit-testing libraries. As with the other units, I'll show you how to get up and running with popular .NET libraries you might already know, and then you'll "go pro" and use libraries designed specifically with F# in mind that are seriously cool (or at least, as cool as you can get when it comes to unit testing!).

UNIT TESTING IN F#

Let's start this unit with a quick review of basic unit-testing tools and how they relate to F#. You'll see

- How to approach unit testing in F#
- How to write unit tests with F# and Visual Studio
- How to use F# DSLs for popular unit-testing libraries

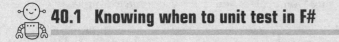 ## 40.1 Knowing when to unit test in F#

Earlier in this book, I touched briefly on unit testing and indicated that in F# you might not need as much unit testing as you have previously. This section provides an overview of what I consider different levels of unit testing, and how and where they're appropriate in F#. This section also covers various forms of unit-testing practices, including test-driven development (TDD).

40.1.1 Unit-testing complexity

Let's start by stating plainly and simply that, yes, there's still a place for unit testing in F#. Although its type system allows you to implement some kinds of business rules in code so that illegal states are unrepresentable (and this is a worthy goal), many rules aren't easily encoded within F#'s type system. Let's partition tests into three groups—

basic type system tests, simple rules, and complex rules—and see in which languages you might more commonly write these sorts of automated unit tests for them. Table 40.1 provides the details.

Table 40.1   Types of unit testing

Type of test	Example	Typical languages
Simple type	Is the value of the Age property an integer?	JavaScript
Complex type	Is the value of the Postcode field a postcode?	JavaScript, C#
Simple rule	Only an in-credit customer can withdraw funds.	JavaScript, C#
Complex rule	Complex rules engine with multiple compound rules.	JS, C#, F#

The point here is that the stronger the type system, the *fewer* tests you should need. Consider a language such as JavaScript: at compile time, there's no real type checking, and even at runtime you can assign a number to a property meant to store a string, while accidentally assigning a value to a misspelled property. (JavaScript will merrily carry on in such a situation, which is why languages such as TypeScript are becoming popular.) This explains why unit testing is so important in such a language; in effect, you're writing a custom compiler for each of your programs! Languages such as C# eliminate the need for such rudimentary tests, yet even in C#, anything more than the simplest rules can often lead to the need for unit tests in order to maintain confidence that your application is doing what it's meant to do. Finally, we have F#. In many cases, I'd suggest that unit testing doesn't make sense, but you might still want unit tests for complex rules or situations where the type system doesn't protect you. Here are some examples:

- *Complex business rules, particularly with conditionals*—For more-complex rules, or nested rules that combine to perform an overall feature, you'll still probably want some form of unit testing.
- *Complex parsing*—Parsing code can be tricky, and you might want some form of unit testing to ensure that regressions don't occur.
- *A list that must have a certain number of elements in it*—Some programming languages (such as Idris) do allow you to encode this within the type system. You can specify, for example, that a function takes in an argument that's a list of five elements, at compile time! These languages are known as *dependently typed* languages; F# isn't such a language.

Conversely, here are several cases in which you can often avoid the need for unit testing because the compiler gives you a greater degree of confidence that the code is doing the correct thing:

- *Expressions*—One of the fundamental principles of F# is that it encourages you to write code as expressions using immutable values. This alone helps prevent many types of bugs that you'd otherwise need to resort to unit testing for: functions that just take in a value and return another one are much simpler to reason about and test than those that require complex setup, with state based on previous method calls.
- *Exhaustive pattern matching*—The F# compiler will tell you that you've missed cases for conditional logic. This is particularly useful and powerful when pattern matching over tupled values, because you can perform truth-table-style logic and be confident that you've dealt with every case.
- *Single-case discriminated unions*—These provide you with confidence that you haven't accidentally mixed up fields of the same type (for example, Customer Name and Address Line 1) by providing a *type of type* such as Name of String or Address of String, which prevents this sort of error.
- *Option types*—Not having null in the type system for F# values means that you generally don't need to worry about nulls when working within an F# domain. Instead, you have to deal with the notion of absence-of-value only when it's a real possibility.

40.1.2 Test-driven development or regression testing?

We've discussed some high-level situations in which you might write unit tests, but I haven't said *when* to write them. Should you write them before writing production code (test-driven development) or after the fact? Based on my experience writing production systems in F#, and as someone who was a complete TDD zealot in C#, I can say that I don't perform TDD anymore. Not because I can't be bothered or because it's not possible in F#—I've tried it. It's that when using the language, combined with the REPL, I don't feel the need for TDD. My productivity feels much higher in F# without TDD—and this includes bug-fixing—than in C# with TDD.

Instead, I do write unit tests for low-level code that's either fiddly and complex, or at a reasonably high level (perhaps something that can be matched to a part of a specification). But, generally, I do this only after I've experimented with the code in the REPL, written the basic functionality, and made sure it works nicely within the rest of the code base.

The F# equivalent of TDD

As far as I'm aware, Mark Seeman coined the phrase *type*-driven development, which has become known as a kind of F# version of test-driven development. This refers to the idea that you use your types to encode business rules and make illegal states unrepresentable, thus driving development and rules through the type system, rather than through unit tests.

Your mileage may vary, and I don't want to sound dogmatic here. I recommend that you at least try by starting to write F# without unit tests, and see how you do. Alternatively, write the tests first; you'll most likely find that you don't need them (particularly with the REPL). Follow the sorts of rules and practices that you've learned in this book, and in many cases where you might have resorted to unit testing or even TDD in the past, you won't need to any longer. The first time you perform a compound pattern match and the compiler tells you about a case that you hadn't thought of yourself, is when it'll hit you that, yes, a compiler *can* replace many unit tests.

Quick check 40.1

1   What's the relationship between a type system and unit tests?
2   Name any two features of the F# language that reduce the need for unit testing.

40.2 Performing basic unit testing in F#

OK, that's enough theory. Let's get on with the practical stuff and see how to write some unit tests. I'm going to use the popular xUnit test framework here, but you can happily use NUnit or MSTest as well—they all work in essentially the same way.

QC 40.1 answer

1   Generally, the stronger the type system, the fewer tests that are needed.
2   Option types, expressions, exhaustive pattern matching, discriminated unions.

NUnit or xUnit?

Both NUnit and xUnit test frameworks are popular, and both work seamlessly with F#, so there's no need to move from one to another just for F#. But you might want to try a new F#-specific unit-testing library called Expecto. It's different; rather than a test framework with attributes, it's a flexible runner that can make tests out of any function. It's beyond the scope of this lesson to show it, but you should definitely check it out.

40.2.1 Writing your first unit tests

To start, you're now going to write a set of unit tests for arbitrary (simple) code in F#.

Now you try

Start by creating some basic unit tests using the popular XUnit test framework:

1 Create a new solution in Visual Studio and create a single F# class library. Normally, you'd probably create a separate test project, but it's not needed for this example.
2 Add the xUnit and XUnit.Runner.VisualStudio NuGet packages to the project.
3 Create a new file, BusinessLogic.fs, which will contain the logic that you'll test.

Listing 40.1 Business logic that can be tested

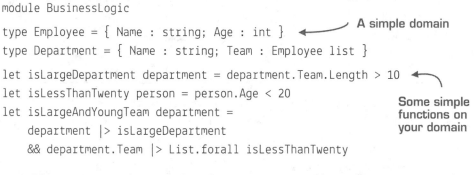

```
module BusinessLogic

type Employee = { Name : string; Age : int }        ◄──── A simple domain
type Department = { Name : string; Team : Employee list }

let isLargeDepartment department = department.Team.Length > 10  ◄──
let isLessThanTwenty person = person.Age < 20
let isLargeAndYoungTeam department =                            Some simple
    department |> isLargeDepartment                             functions on
    && department.Team |> List.forall isLessThanTwenty         your domain
```

4 Now write your first test. Start by creating a new file, BusinessLogicTests.fs (ensure that it lives underneath BusinessLogic.fs in Solution Explorer).
5 Enter the following code in the new file.

Listing 40.2 xUnit tests in F#

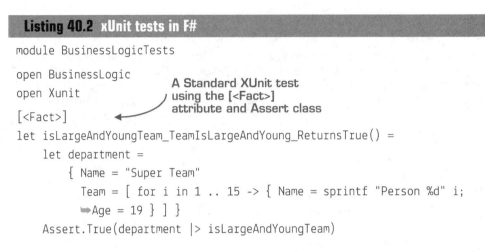

```
module BusinessLogicTests

open BusinessLogic                    A Standard XUnit test
open Xunit                            using the [<Fact>]
                                      attribute and Assert class
[<Fact>]
let isLargeAndYoungTeam_TeamIsLargeAndYoung_ReturnsTrue() =
    let department =
        { Name = "Super Team"
          Team = [ for i in 1 .. 15 -> { Name = sprintf "Person %d" i;
          ➥Age = 19 } ] }
    Assert.True(department |> isLargeAndYoungTeam)
```

6 Rebuild the project. You should see the test show up in Test Explorer in Visual
Studio as shown in figure 40.1; run it, and the test will go green.

Because a module in F# compiles down to a static class in .NET, and `let`-bound functions
in F# compile down to static methods, everything *just works*. You can use all the extra
features in xUnit and NUnit as well without a problem (for example, theories and
parameterized tests); they all work.

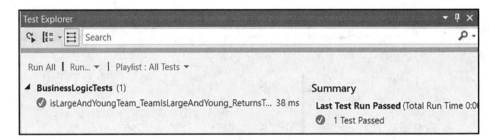

Figure 40.1   F# tests show up in the Visual Studio Test Explorer as you'd expect.

Removing class names from tests

In figure 40.1, you'll notice that the test name isn't prefixed with the class name. To
achieve this, you need to add an app setting key `xunit.methodDisplay` to the app.config file
of the test assembly and set its value to `method`.

40.2.2 Naming tests in F#

Entire blogs (and probably books) exist on how to name unit tests. This can be an emotive subject in many organizations, and can be difficult to keep consistent. I've seen many naming standards, from conventions such as Given-When-Then (which is a popular one for people following behavior-driven development) to ones such as Method Scenario Expected (recommended by Roy Osherove). There's nothing to stop you from following those standards (as I've done in the preceding listing), but thanks to F#'s backtick methods, you can eliminate this debate completely and name the method based on exactly what it's testing:

```
let ``Large, young teams are correctly identified``() =
```

Believe it or not, not only does this work, but it works beautifully. Try it: rename the test by starting and stopping the name with double-backticks, recompile, and then view Test Explorer again—much nicer! But don't stop there. You can go one step further by renaming the test module as well, so now Test Explorer looks like figure 40.2.

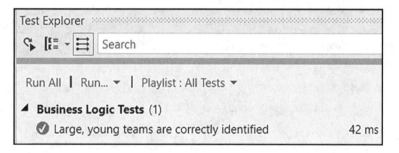

Figure 40.2 Using F# backtick methods can aid readability of unit tests.

Much nicer, isn't it? Aside from this, unit testing in F# acts pretty much exactly as you'd expect in C#.

> **What about BDD?**
> I touched on BDD before. You can certainly use frameworks such as SpecFlow to write BDD tests, and benefit from the extra readability that backtick members give you, with no problem. There's another option, though: TickSpec. This extremely lightweight F# library works with Cucumber format tests, but "automagically" binds tests to features based on naming convention—all cool and definitely worth looking at.

40.3 Testing DSLs in F#

You can easily create your own domain-specific language (DSL) on top of test libraries so that your tests take advantage of F#'s language features to make tests quicker and easier to read and write. For example, you can use the pipeline and even replace the Assert.True static method from xUnit with a helper function that can improve your test readability.

Listing 40.3 Creating a simple F# DSL wrapper over xUnit

```
let isTrue (b:bool) = Assert.True b          ◀────   Creating a simple
[<Fact>]                                              wrapper around
let ``Large, young teams are correctly identified``() =    Assert.True
    // existing code elided…

    department |> isLargeAndYoungTeam |> Assert.True
    department |> isLargeAndYoungTeam |> isTrue    ◀

    Using the pipeline with the          Using the wrapper function
    native xUnit assertion library       instead of Assert.True
```

You can immediately use the pipeline with xUnit's existing Assertion library, but by making a simple wrapper function, you can make your unit test even more succinct and readable.

To make your life easier, F# also has ready-made DSL wrapper libraries around the various test frameworks that take advantage of F#'s lightweight syntax. Let's look at a couple of them.

40.3.1 FsUnit

FsUnit is a NuGet package that takes the preceding approach for a DSL so that you can easily make fluent pipelines of conditions as tests. Wrappers exist for both NUnit and xUnit (via the FSUnit.XUnit package). Here's how you might write a couple of tests by using FsUnit (see listing 40.2 for the definition of the department value).

Listing 40.4 Using FsUnit to create human-readable tests

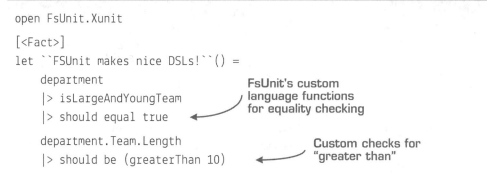

```
open FsUnit.Xunit

[<Fact>]
let ``FSUnit makes nice DSLs!``() =
    department
    |> isLargeAndYoungTeam          FsUnit's custom
                                    language functions
    |> should equal true            for equality checking

    department.Team.Length          Custom checks for
    |> should be (greaterThan 10)   "greater than"
```

FsUnit has a rich language, including functions for string comparisons (for example, "isaac" |> should startWith "isa") and collection tests (for example, [1 .. 5] |> should contain 3). If you like this style of unit testing, FsUnit is a great place to start.

Binding redirects with FsUnit

Note that FsUnit was compiled against F# 3.0, yet Visual Studio 2015 will by default set F# projects to build against F# 4.0. You'll need to add a binding redirect to the app.config file of the project (if NuGet doesn't create it). Place this in the <runtime> node:

```
<assemblyBinding xmlns="urn:schemas-microsoft-com:asm.v1">
  <dependentAssembly>
    <assemblyIdentity
        name="FSharp.Core"
        publicKeyToken="b03f5f7f11d50a3a"
        culture="neutral"/>
    <bindingRedirect
        oldVersion="0.0.0.0-65535.65535.65535.65535"
        newVersion="4.4.0.0"/>
  </dependentAssembly>
</assemblyBinding>
```

40.3.2 Unquote

Unquote is a test framework wrapper with a difference. It, too, works with both xUnit and NUnit, but unlike FsUnit, it provides a way to easily assert whether the result of a comparison is *true or false*—so, to check whether two values are equal to each other. At its most basic, Unquote gives a simple custom operator that can compare two values. Here's how it looks.

Listing 40.5 Using Unquote's custom comparison operator

```
open Swensen.Unquote
[<Fact>]
let ``Unquote has a simple custom operator for equality``() =
    department |> isLargeAndYoungTeam =! true
```

> The custom =! operator fails if the values on both sides aren't equal.

You can use this operator for more than comparing Booleans. For example, you can compare whether two lists are equal, or two records are the same (remember that F# types implement equality already!).

But Unquote goes one step further than this. Unquote, as its name suggests, takes advantage of F#'s *quotations* language feature, which allows Unquote to explain *why* two values don't equal one another.

> **F# quotations**
>
> F# quotations are beyond the scope of this book. Suffice it to say that they're roughly equivalent to C#'s expression trees. By enclosing a code block within an F# quotation, you can get back a typed (or untyped) abstract syntax tree to perform analysis on the code itself (treating code as data). Clear as mud? Don't worry; you don't need to understand F# quotations to take advantage of Unquote.

Here's an example of using Unquote's quotations support for a simple test.

Listing 40.6 Evaluating a quotation with Unquote

```
[<Fact>]
let ``Unquote can parse quotations for excellent diagnostics``() =
    let emptyTeam = { Name = "Super Team"; Team = [] }
    test <@ emptyTeam.Name.StartsWith "D" @>
```

> Wrapping a condition within a quotation block

A quotation is easy to create. You wrap around the condition to test with <@ @>, as shown in figure 40.3. (Visual F# Power Tools will also identify the quotation and display it in a different color for you.)

```
[<Fact>]
let ``Unquote can parse quotations for excellent diagnostics``() =
    let emptyTeam = { Name = "Super Team"; Team = [] }
    test <@ emptyTeam.Name.StartsWith "D" @>
```

Figure 40.3   VFPT highlights code quotation blocks for you

If the result of the expression inside the block returns true, the test passes. What's more interesting is when it fails (as in the preceding example). Let's look at a slightly simplified version of the error output from Visual Studio's Test Runner:

```
emptyTeam.Name.StartsWith("D")
{ Name = "Super Team";  Team = [] }.Name.StartsWith("D")
"Super Team".StartsWith("D")
false
```

The first three lines represent a *step-by-step* guide of how the test failed:

1 Line 1 represents the original test code.
2 Line 2 evaluates the test code by replacing emptyTeam with the actual contents of the record that this binding represents.
3 Line 3 simplifies this to just the value of the Name property that was being compared against.
4 You're finally left with a simple comparison, which returns false, so the test fails. But now you can see exactly how Unquote reached the value false.

This is a relatively simple example, but it's fantastically powerful. Imagine that your test code calls a function of production code, which itself calls two other functions that return data. It quickly becomes difficult to understand why a test failed. Unquote sheds light on this by allowing you to understand the code without needing to resort to a debugger.

Quick check 40.3

1   What is FsUnit?
2   What is a code quotation?

Summary

That's the end of basic unit testing in F#! In this lesson

- You learned when and where unit testing might and might not be appropriate in F#.
- You looked at basic unit-testing integration in F# with VS2015 and xUnit.
- You saw a couple of custom F# libraries that can make unit testing even better.

Try this

Try porting some unit tests in your own code to an F# library. Experiment with your own custom DSL functions, FsUnit, and Unquote; try performing a set of nested function calls that return a value, and test calling this through Unquote.

QC 40.3 answer

1   A DSL wrapper around xUnit and NUnit to allow fluent, human-readable tests to be written.
2   A block of code in which code is treated as data that can be programmed against.

PROPERTY-BASED TESTING IN F#

This lesson presents a different type of automated testing that you can do in F#, called *property-based testing* (PBT). You'll see

- What PBT is
- Why you might want to use it
- How to use the FsCheck library for .NET
- How to integrate FsCheck with popular test runners

At times, even if you've achieved "full test coverage"—where your tests are covering every branch of code in the system—you still might not be satisfied with your tests. Here are a few examples.

One common problem occurs when your code misses edge cases that you hadn't considered. This is common when working with strings or other "unbounded" inputs. How many times have you written code that expects a string to be a certain minimum length, but somehow an empty string creeps into your code? Or you wrote code that indexed into an array that turned out to be empty? Are these cases that you should've realistically expected?

Another example occurs when your unit tests appear to be fragile because they test only arbitrary cases. Imagine that you have a method, half(), being tested that takes in a number and returns half of it. To test this, you write a single test case that proves that when calling half() with 10, you get back 5. Why did you pick 10 as the test data? Is it easy to understand what the test is really proving? Have you tested all valid cases?

Finally, a system under test may be too complex for you to cover (or even identify) all the possible permutations with specific test cases. This is particularly common—but not unique—to integration tests. Normally, we unit test lower-level components well, but tend not to have great integration tests; they're too expensive to write to cover all combinations. But this omission often misses bugs that result from unintended interactions between two components when you finally bring them together. A good real-world example of this is the Mars Climate Orbiter that failed in 1999 because one team wrote a module using English units of measurement, while unknown to them, another team used the metric system! Both components worked well in isolation, but when plugged together, the system failed because of the unit differences. End result: a costly failed spacecraft. (Let's leave aside the fact that F# has a feature known as Units of Measure that would've prevented this.)

In all sorts of situations, conventional unit tests can feel fake or unsatisfactory; it's hard to put your finger on why, but sometimes something doesn't feel right! This is often a sign that another form of testing might be worthwhile.

41.1 Understanding property-based testing

Setting aside the whole area of mocking frameworks, regular unit tests generally work via a well-understood process:

1 You manually create test data.
2 You push that test data through production code.
3 You confirm that the outputs of that code are as expected.

Figure 41.1 shows a sample function, FlipCase, which takes in a string and flips the case of all the characters. You might normally test this with a single word as a unit test (for example, *Hello* becomes *hELLO*).

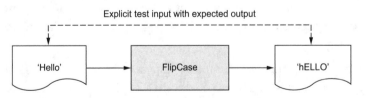

Figure 41.1   A function with an explicit test input and expected output

The idea behind property-based testing is that instead of testing code with arbitrary data that you create yourself, you allow the machine to *create test data* for you, based on guidelines that you provide. Then you test behaviors, or *properties* of the system that should hold true for *any* input values. Write enough properties, and you prove the functionality of the function as a whole. Figure 41.2 illustrates this principle.

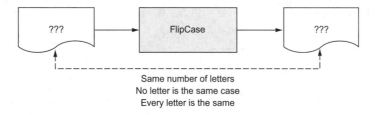

Same number of letters
No letter is the same case
Every letter is the same

Figure 41.2 A function with sample properties that should hold true for all possible input values

Property-based testing requires a different approach to thinking about tests; unlike conventional unit tests, the system generates test values for you. Therefore, you can't hardcode the expected result of a test. This is where the notion of *properties* comes in. A property is a kind of relationship that you can test on the output of your production code, without knowing the value of it. Figure 41.2 specifies three properties that should all hold true for your FlipCase function. You don't need to know the inputs or outputs; you just need to prove that those behaviors hold true against a large-enough sample dataset to prove that the code works.

Property-based testing can help with many kinds of tests, and can help identify corner cases (for which you might want to write specific unit tests).

41.1.1 How to identify properties

Identifying properties is one of the hardest parts of property-based testing, and it's not something that (in my experience) you can easily illustrate in a few pages. You could probably write a whole book on the subject! Nonetheless, here are some examples of how you *might* identify properties in your production code; think of this section as a taste of what property testing is about, rather than a detailed look at every possible aspect of it:

- *Identify specific properties about the behavior of the inputs and outputs*—How easy this is to do depends on the code being implemented and the functionality you're trying to implement. For example, figure 41.2 identifies three specific properties of the FlipCase function.

- *Identify a relationship between two functions*—You can pass the same input data into two different functions and see whether a relationship exists between the outputs of those two functions. For example, there's a relationship between the two functions "add two numbers together" and "subtract two numbers together" that you could define as a property. In figure 41.3, the relationship is that (c - d = b × 2). A property-based test would generate many pairs of numbers that you would pipe into that equation to prove whether it's true or not, through brute force.

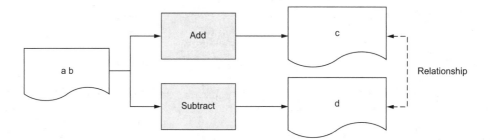

Figure 41.3   Using a secondary function is often a useful way to identify a property test.

- *Compare another implementation of the same function*—If you have an alternate function that does the same thing and is known to work correctly, you can compare the results to ensure that they're always the same. This is useful when refactoring a function (for example, to optimize performance); you can help ensure that the behaviors are the same for many arbitrary test cases. This is just a specialized form of the previous item; in this case, the relationship is that the values should always be equal!

The main point is that all of these sorts of tests can be achieved in a generalized way, without having to know a specific input or output value.

Property-based testing in the real world

Examples of using property-based testing to identify issues and prove the validity of a system include the Riak database system (which had several serious bugs that could result in loss of data, until the team ran it through a property-based test system) and Dropbox. Another example is the Paket NuGet package manager, which used FsCheck to create various types of package dependency graphs to ensure that the package resolution algorithm always picked an optimum set of versions for the packages specified.

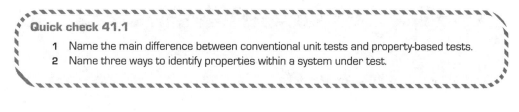

41.2 Introducing FsCheck

That's enough theory for now—let's move on to the practical side. FsCheck is a property-testing library that's effectively a port of Haskell's QuickCheck library. FsCheck allows you to provide it with a *parameterized* function that performs business logic, and then test the result of that logic. FsCheck calls the test function many times, each time with slightly different input values. In some ways, this isn't so different from NUnit or xUnit's TestCase or Theories features, except here you don't specify the data to test against; FsCheck does.

41.2.1 Running tests with FsCheck

Before jumping into the thick of things with full-blown property-based tests, let's start with a simple test that uses FsCheck so you can get a feel for the library itself.

Now you try

1 Create a new F# class library project and solution.
2 Download the FsCheck.Xunit NuGet package. (This will also download the core FsCheck package and xUnit).
3 Create a standard F# module and enter the following code. It creates a simple function that manually adds the numbers in a list, followed by a test that compares the values with a known good function, List.sum, that you use as a basis.

Listing 41.1 Your first FsCheck test

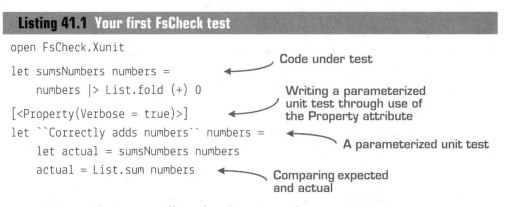

```
open FsCheck.Xunit                        ← Code under test

let sumsNumbers numbers =
    numbers |> List.fold (+) 0            ← Writing a parameterized
                                            unit test through use of
[<Property(Verbose = true)>]              ← the Property attribute
let ``Correctly adds numbers`` numbers =  ← A parameterized unit test
    let actual = sumsNumbers numbers
    actual = List.sum numbers             ← Comparing expected
                                            and actual
```

4   Now run the test; you'll see that this runs and turns green.

Let's review. This is a parameterized test. It takes in a list of numbers that you run against your code, and compares against the List.sum function. But what list of numbers?

5   To understand this, open the Test Explorer window and navigate to the appropriate test before clicking the Output link. You'll see something like figure 41.4.

```
Test Name:     Correctly adds numbers

Test Outcome:    ✓ Passed

┌─ Standard Output ──────────────────

  0:
  [2; 2]

  1:
  [2; 3]

  2:
  [3; -3]

  3:
  []
```

Figure 41.4 The output of an FsCheck test

If you scroll down the pane, you'll see a whole host of entries. FsCheck has seen the type of data needed by the test—a list of integers—and generated a set of samples for it. FsCheck creates and runs 100 test cases by default. The data isn't completely random, either. The data intentionally starts with simple cases and then expands to more-complex ones. In this example, you can see that FsCheck tries various scenarios, including a simple list with two items, empty lists, and different values. Even better, FsCheck can generate entire object graphs—full F# records (or lists of records), each with its properties populated.

6   Place a breakpoint on the first line of the unit test, as shown in figure 41.5.

7   Rerun the test but ensure that you choose Debug Selected Test in Test Explorer when you right-click the test.

8   Observe that the breakpoint is repeatedly hit, once for each test run, with different data.

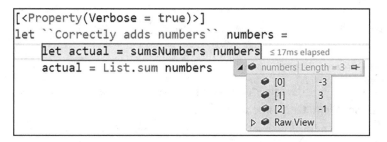

Figure 41.5   Setting a breakpoint within a unit test that's called by FsCheck

---

FsCheck and Microsoft Pex

Years ago, Microsoft Research came up with a testing framework named Pex. Pex would analyze your code and generate test cases based on that analysis. FsCheck doesn't do anything like that. It simply generates random test data across a known distribution that you can control, with the intent of proving or disproving your test cases.

41.2.2 Failing tests and shrinking

Let's look in detail at how FsCheck handles failing tests.

Now you try

First, make your production code fail and see what happens:

1   Change the implementation of sumsNumbers so that if the list of numbers contains 5, it always returns –1 (otherwise, it continues with normal logic).

2   Rerun the tests. You'll see that the test fails, as shown in figure 41.6.

```
FsCheck.Xunit.PropertyFailedException :
Falsifiable, after 5 tests (3 shrinks) (StdGen (382638564,296259880)):
Original:
[5; 5; -5; -4]
Shrunk:
[5]
```

Figure 41.6   A failing test with a shrunk test case from FsCheck

The key bits to notice here are twofold. In figure 41.6, you can see two items:

- *Original*—The initial data that failed the test, randomly generated by FsCheck. Notice that the list contains four values.
- *Shrunk*—A *simplified* dataset that fails the test based on the original data. Notice now that the dataset contains only a single element, 5! FsCheck has realized that the other values have no impact on the test, and so strips them out, leaving you with the simplest possible failure case.

Shrinking is the process by which FsCheck reduces, or simplifies, a failing test dataset to be the simplest possible failure case that it can be. This happens automatically and helps identify how and why a test failed.

> **Quick check 41.2**
>
> 1 What attribute do you place on a test to allow FsCheck to provide test data?
> 2 What is shrinking?

 ## 41.3 Controlling data generation

At times you might want to control up front the data generated by FsCheck. For instance, take your fictional FlipCase function and write one of the property tests for it.

QC 41.2 answer

1 The [<Property>] attribute.
2 The process of simplifying a failure case to its most basic form.

Listing 41.2 A function to flip case of all letters with a single property test

```
oen System
let flipCase (text:string) =
    text.ToCharArray()
    |> Array.map(fun c ->
        if Char.IsUpper c then Char.ToLower c
        else Char.ToUpper c)
    |> String

[<Property>]
let ``Always has same number of letters`` (input:string) =
    let output = input |> flipCase
    input.Length = output.Length
```

The problem with this is that this function is designed to work only with letters when no numbers or special characters are allowed, and no null values either. If you run this test now, there's a good chance that it will fail, because FsCheck will pick random strings, including those with nonletters. You could make the flipCase function throw out such values, but in this case, you want the test to tell FsCheck to supply only valid data to the test; you need a way to tell FsCheck to generate strings with only *letters*.

41.3.1 Guard clauses

Luckily, FsCheck offers a simple way to help, by using a *guard clause* in your test function.

Listing 41.3 Providing a guard clause for FsCheck

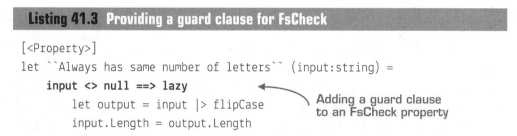

```
[<Property>]
let ``Always has same number of letters`` (input:string) =
    input <> null ==> lazy
        let output = input |> flipCase
        input.Length = output.Length
```

Adding a guard clause
to an FsCheck property

Here, you add a guard clause that says to prematurely exit any test where input is null. (FsCheck comes with the custom ==> operator, which says, "Run the code on the right only if the guard clause on the left passes.") Also, notice the lazy keyword; this is a language alias for System.Lazy and ensures that FsCheck runs the test code only when the guard check has passed.

41.3.2 Generators and arbitrary values

A limitation of guard clauses can be observed when you need a specific clause. For example, if you try to implement either of the other two properties we discussed, you'll need to enhance the guard clause so that it ignores not only null strings, but also empty strings or those with nonletters. In such a case, FsCheck will give up and complain with a message such as PropertyFailedException: Arguments exhausted after 3 tests. This means that FsCheck couldn't generate data 100 times to "pass" the guard clauses.

When guard clauses aren't sufficient for your needs, you'll need to create a custom generator. A *generator* allows you to specify a certain type of data, such as chars or strings, which then map into arbitrary values that FsCheck can run in its tests. FsCheck comes with many built-in arbitrary values in the FsCheck.Arb.Default module, such as the usual lists, sets, and numbers, and even things like nonempty strings and IP addresses. Let's see how to create your own generator that forces all generated characters to be only letters. In conjunction with the built-in NonEmptyString, you can achieve exactly what you need.

Listing 41.4 Creating a letters-only generator for FsCheck

```
open FsCheck                              Creating a class that contains
type LettersOnlyGen() =          ◄───── arbitrary generators
    static member Letters() =
        Arb.Default.Char() |> Arb.filter Char.IsLetter

[<Property(Arbitrary = [| typeof<LettersOnlyGen> |])>]
let ``Always has same number of letters`` (NonEmptyString input) =   ◄──
    let output = input |> flipCase
    input.Length = output.Length
```

Creating a generator that creates a stream of letters

Attaching the generator to the property test

The trickiest bit to understand here is the LettersOnlyGen type. This class has a single static method on it, Letters, that returns a type Arbitrary<Char>, the type that controls which set of data FsCheck can use to pick from randomly. You can create multiple generator methods with any name. No conventions exist, but you must have only one method per type that you want to generate (for example, strings, integers, or customers). In this case, you're creating the set of all characters, filtered by whether the character is a letter. This is essentially the same as using Seq.filter or something similar, except instead of operating on a real list of items, you supply the *logic* to FsCheck to tell it how to generate data.

Next, you apply that generator to the test by setting the Arbitrary value of the Property attribute. This ensures that all characters generated for this test are letters. And you can replace the null-check guard by using the NonEmptyString discriminated union that was previously mentioned, which FsCheck guarantees will never be null. Now if you rerun the test (and turn on Verbose mode by passing Verbose = true to the Property attribute), you can observe that the test cases will all be valid test data:

```
NonEmptyString "cAv"
NonEmptyString "S"
NonEmptyString "Yo"
NonEmptyString "UkUr"
NonEmptyString "NBwhlF"
NonEmptyString "el"
NonEmptyString "UI"
NonEmptyString "CxyP"
NonEmptyString "xeuZepyl"
NonEmptyString "bUIxl"
NonEmptyString "Pf"
```

Creating your own generators isn't always trivial, but the time and effort required is definitely worthwhile. I've used only simple types in this sample, but imagine creating a generator that provides customers of a certain type for you to test, or user requests meeting a certain specification. This can be absolutely invaluable in rapidly creating test data for multiple tests, quickly and easily.

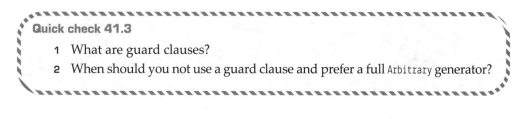

Quick check 41.3

1 What are guard clauses?

2 When should you not use a guard clause and prefer a full Arbitrary generator?

QC 41.3 answer

1 Simple predicates that tell FsCheck that data is invalid for a given PBT.

2 Guard clauses are useful only for simple filters. If the filters are too constraining, FsCheck won't be able to generate sufficient test data that meets the requirements. In these situations, Arbitrary generators should be used.

Summary

Property-based testing is a different way to approach automated testing. But it's also a useful tool to have in your arsenal, particularly for certain types of problems that are difficult to white-box test (testing the internals) and that are easier to black-box test (testing the external behaviors). This lesson has only scratched the surface of PBTs, and you should seriously consider checking out this type of testing in more detail.

Try this

Try implementing tests with the other two properties for the FlipCase function. Then write example functions and associated PBTs for the data model in the previous lesson, before writing a set of property-based tests against a method in a class in the BCL (for example, System.Collections.Generic.Queue.Enqueue).

42

WEB TESTING

This short lesson will round off our trip around testing in F#. You'll learn about

- Web testing, and where it fits into the testing landscape
- Selenium
- Canopy
- Using Canopy for web automation

Often unit testing—even property-based tests—aren't enough to test an entire system from end to end. Perhaps you've written code that has excellent test coverage against individual components, such as a class that calculates the interest on a loan payment, or perhaps across two or three layers—but then tested the real application and found that the interest that was calculated and saved to the database was incorrect. You need something that can ideally cover the entire spectrum of tiers within your application, yet you want this to run in a repeatable way.

In my experience, there are two popular ways of doing this. One is through an acceptance testing framework such as *Fitnesse*, a system that allows business users to specify tests through *tables* in a wiki website, which then calls production code behind the scenes. It's powerful but also requires a reasonable learning curve. That's fair enough—after all, F# also has a learning curve associated with it—but it's more than just the investment in learning it. It's a full application, so you need to manage it within your application tier somehow, as well as consider how it works within the context of a continuous integration environment. And finally, the .NET SDK for it is somewhat unusual; certainly, it's not what I'd call idiomatic.

An alternative to this when working with a website is to write web-based tests. These are often step-by-step tests that people can follow and then record the results in a bug-tracking system. This process is so popular that some versions of Visual Studio (and its sibling, Team Foundation Services) even have a test recorder that allows you to record a video of your test along with the results of the test, plus capture information such as a call stack to more easily enable error reproductions. That's nice, but it's ultimately a manual system; the more tests you have, the longer (and more expensive) it becomes to run through the test suite.

42.1 Web automation with Canopy

In this section, you'll look at how to run web-based tests in an automated fashion, by writing simple, declarative programs in F# that can state how a web application should behave. You'll fill in fields on a web page, click buttons, and so forth—interacting with a web site to simulate a real person—and then test the results, to see, for example, the value of a field or the URL you're now on. But before looking at the testing side of things, let's start with the basics—controlling a browser through code.

> **Selenium**
>
> Selenium is a freely distributable WebDriver plugin to your web browser, plus an SDK and IDE, that allows you to perform web automation. In other words, you can program-matically automate the control of your web browser. Selenium can be run as a stand-alone tool and can generate scripts via an IDE, but as you'll see, there's a much nicer way of doing this in F#.

42.1.1 What Is Canopy?

Canopy is an open source, free-to-use library that wraps around the Selenium plugin. It provides an extremely simple, easy-to-use DSL for writing basic scripts that can control your web browser. Because it's just a wrapper on top of Selenium, any browser that Selenium supports is also supported by Canopy (this includes IE, Chrome, and Firefox). You can use Canopy to perform all manner of tasks, such as filling in fields, clicking buttons, and dragging elements from one location to another. This can be exceptionally useful for automating processes that must be done through a web-based UI. I've seen individuals use this for anything from uploading information from a spreadsheet into a web portal, to filling in timesheets at the end of every week!

42.1.2 Creating your first Canopy script

Let's take Canopy for a quick spin to see how it works firsthand.

Now you try

This exercise uses the Google Chrome browser. The majority of the exercise will be identical for other browsers, but in the interest of keeping things simple, I focus on Chrome (the Canopy site documents any differences). In this exercise, you'll open Chrome, navigate to the Manning website, and fill out a form to buy another copy of *Get Programming with F#*; two copies are better than one, right? (Don't worry; you won't complete the checkout!)

> *The Manning website may have changed since this book was written, in which case some of the IDs or element names may no longer be correct.*

1 Download the latest version of the Chrome web driver from https://sites.google .com/a/chromium.org/chromedriver/. This driver allows you to communicate with Chrome programmatically, so copy it to the drivers/ folder in the source code repository.

2 Create a new F# script. As usual, I recommend putting it either in the src/code-listings folder or at least one that's parallel to it, so that the package references in this lesson's code listings work straightaway.

3 Enter the following code into your script. This references the core Selenium and Canopy assemblies and then sets the path to where the Chromium web driver is located. (`chromeDir` is a global mutable variable exposed by Canopy!):

```
#r @"..\..\packages\Selenium.WebDriver\lib\net40\WebDriver.dll"
#r @"..\..\packages\canopy\lib\canopy.dll"
open canopy
chromeDir <- "drivers"
```

4 Start a new instance of Chrome under Canopy's control:

```
start chrome
```

You should see output similar to the following in the FSI window. (If Canopy can't find the driver in `chromeDir`, try copying it to the root of the C:\ folder.)

```
Starting ChromeDriver 2.27.440174 (…) on port 3732
Only local connections are allowed.
```

You'll notice that Chrome opens by default, tiled to the right of the desktop. If you tile VS to the left, you can send commands to Chrome and watch them take effect.

5 Navigate to the Manning site: url "https://www.manning.com/books/get-programming-with-f-sharp". Observe that the DSL makes commands extremely easy to read (for example, start chrome, url <url>). You don't use brackets or curly braces, and you can execute arbitrary commands from the script.

6 You can choose from two versions of the book, as shown in figure 42.1; buy the combo version.

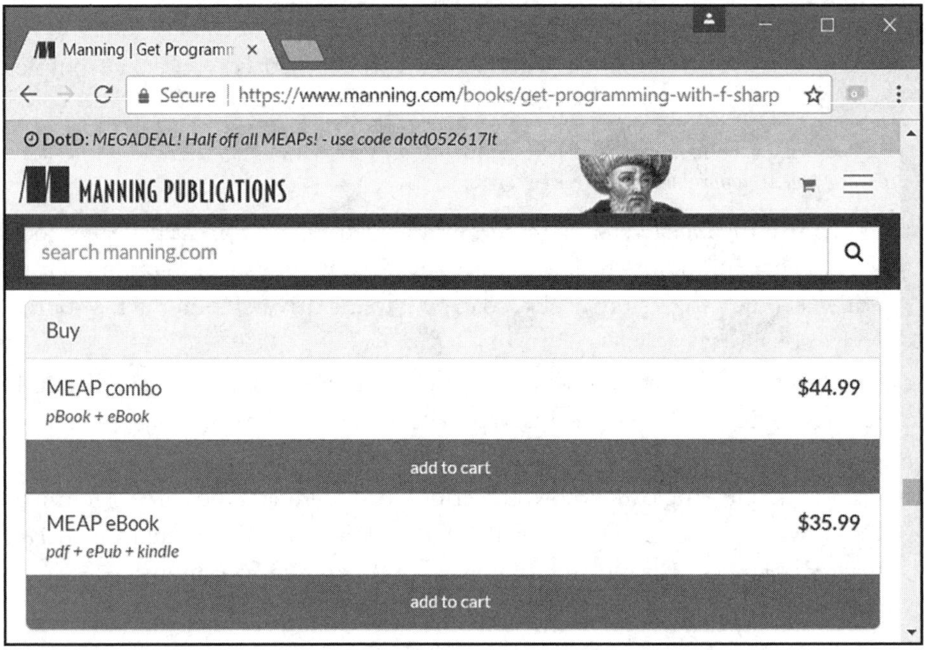

Figure 42.1   Buying Get Programming with F# on the Manning website

Both of the Add to Cart buttons are submit buttons. You'll use Canopy to get the first element that has an ID of submit and then click it:

```
first "#Submit" |> click
```

The identifier for the element can be any valid CSS selector. After you click the button, you receive a notification that the item has been added to the cart. You can also confirm this at the top of the page by looking at the cart icon, shown in figure 42.2.

Figure 42.2 Adding an item to the shopping cart on the Manning website

Getting element names for Canopy

You'll see in step 9 that I've used a set of IDs and classes to identify elements that you can access. I manually went through the page in Chrome's developer panel to pull out the IDs, but another option is to search for elements with specific text by using Canopy's elementWithText function.

7 Now proceed to checkout. You do this by first going to the cart and then clicking the checkout button on that page:

```
click ".cart-button"
click ".btn-primary"
```

8 You're asked to either sign in or check out as a guest—use the second option. Set the Email address textbox to a random name before clicking the Check Out as a Guest button on the form:

```
"#email" << "Fred.Smith@fakemail.com"

elements ".btn-primary"
|> Seq.find(fun e -> e.Text = "checkout as a guest")
|> click
```

Note the << operator, another feature in the Canopy DSL. This allows you to set the content of any element on the left side with the content on the right side!

9 You're now on the final page, which captures details of the guest. Fill in all the form fields as follows:

```
"#firstName" << "Fred"
"#country" << "United States"
"#firstName" << "Fred"
"#lastName" << "Smith"
"#company" << "Super F# Developers Ltd."
"#address1" << "23 The Street"
"#address2" << "The Town"
"#city" << "The City"
"#USStateSelector" << "CA"
"#zip" << "90210"
"#addressPhone" << "0800 123 456"
```

At this point you can stop there (you can close the browser by using quit()). The main point is that you can create a repeatable script to easily control a web browser to perform various actions. Canopy has a rich set of helper functions that allow you to easily interact with a browser, including reading the contents of an element, double-clicking, and switching tabs—a whole host of functions. (You can find out more at http://lefthandedgoat.github .io/canopy/actions.html.)

Quick check 42.1

1   What must you manually download before using Canopy?
2   Does Canopy work only with Google Chrome?
3   What custom operator do you use in Canopy to assign text to an element?

42.2 Web tests with Canopy

Now that you've seen the basics of how Canopy works, let's briefly look at the second half of Canopy, which is a full test runner designed to create and run automated tests.

QC 42.1 answer

1   You must download the appropriate web driver for your browser.
2   No—Canopy works with multiple browsers.
3   The << operator is used to assign text to an element.

42.2.1 Hooking into Canopy events

Canopy has a simple test runner that can launch directly from a script or a console application. There's no need to shoehorn it into a class library that supports the VS test runner if you don't want to. You declare events and tests through a set of functions, before starting a test run. Let's first see how to hook into events when tests start and finish.

Listing 42.1 Setting up a basic test run suite in Canopy

```
                                        Run once before
                                        starting the test run.
once (fun _ -> start chrome)       ◄──
before (fun _ -> url "https://www.manning.com/books/get-programming-with-
   f-sharp")                       ◄──   Run before each test
lastly (fun _ -> quit())           ◄──
                                        Run once after all tests.
```

Before you start your test run, Chrome will load. At the start of each test, Canopy navigates to the Manning website, and after all the tests are complete, the browser will close. These functions relate roughly to the [<SetUp>] and [<TearDown>] attributes in NUnit or xUnit. You can find out more about Canopy functions and features at https://lefthandedgoat.github .io/canopy/testing.html.

42.2.2 Creating and running tests

Creating tests with Canopy is just as simple; you call one of two functions to create (but not run!) a test case. Both are higher-order functions. The simplest form creates a case with an autogenerated name of Test #n (for example, Test #1, Test #2, and so forth):

```
test <test function>
```

The test function is simply a function that takes no arguments and returns no arguments. Inside, it performs test code by using Canopy's assertion test functions (see the following code). The alternative form allows you to specify a custom test name:

```
<test name> &&& <test function>
```

Each test case that gets executed adds the test case to a list that Canopy maintains of all test cases. When you're finished, calling run() will execute all the test cases.

42.2.3 Working with assertions in Canopy

Canopy has a large set of common test functions that can do the usual comparisons of elements as well as several others. Here I've created three tests within a test context called Sample Tests.

Listing 42.2 Listing 42.2 Creating a simple test suite in Canopy

Testing the value
of an element

Testing the count
of elements

```
context "Sample Tests"

test (fun _ -> "#chapter_id_1" == "LESSON 1 THE VISUAL STUDIO EXPERIENCE")
"49 lessons in total" &&& fun _ -> count ".sect1" 49
"There's a web programming unit" &&& fun _ ->  ".sect0" *= "UNIT 8:
➥WEB PROGRAMMING"

run()
```
⟵ Running the tests

Testing that a value
exists in a collection

Let's take these tests one by one:

- The first test checks that the value of a specific element (identified by the ID chapter_id_1) is equal to LESSON 1 THE VISUAL STUDIO EXPERIENCE. Note the custom == operator that Canopy uses to perform the equality check.
- The second test is titled 49 lessons in total and confirms that 49 elements have the sect1 CSS style.
- Finally, the final test gets all the sect0 elements and checks that at least one of them has the value UNIT 8: WEB PROGRAMMING.
- You can read up on more helper functions and operators at the Canopy website at https://lefthandedgoat.github.io/canopy/assertions.html.
- After you've compiled your tests, you can run them by using the run() function. The output should be something like this:

```
Starting ChromeDriver 2.27.440174 on port 3446

Test: Test #1
Passed
Test: 49 lessons in total
Passed
Test: There's a web programming unit
Passed

0 minutes 10 seconds to execute
3 passed
0 skipped
0 failed
```

> ### Integration with other libraries
>
> Canopy is an extensible library, so you can choose how you output data. There's a Team-City plugin that outputs test results in a manner that TeamCity can read, or you can create your own. And remember, there's nothing to stop you from using Canopy's assertion libraries and using, for example, NUnit's test runner. Similarly, there's nothing to stop you from using FsCheck to generate test data for you that you can then plug into Canopy!

There's even a web page version of the test reporter, shown in figure 42.3, so that you get an interactive web page showing test results rather than just the console.

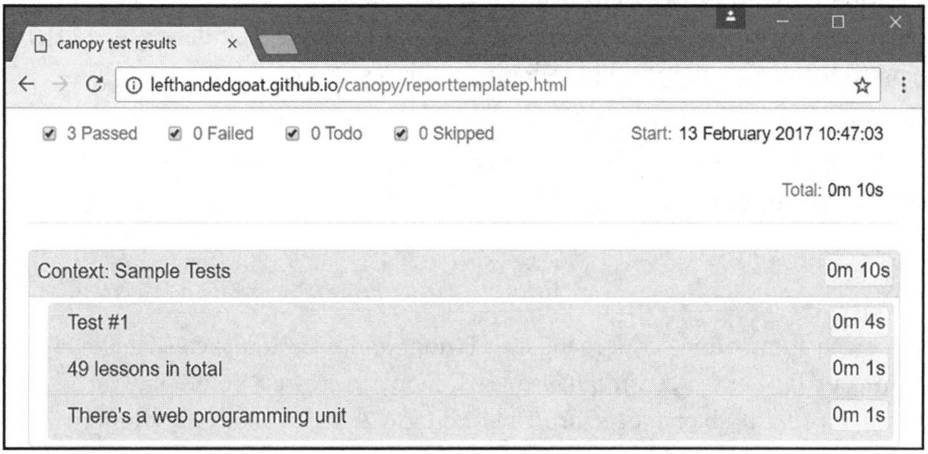

Figure 42.3   The Canopy UI test runner

You can activate this by adding the following code before you start your test run:

```
open reporters
reporter <- LiveHtmlReporter(BrowserStartMode.Chrome, "drivers") :>
IReporter
```

I strongly advise you to try this section for yourself and see it working firsthand. After you realize how easy Canopy is to use, you'll see that there are endless possibilities for easily creating repeatable tests!

Quick check 42.2

1 Can you use Canopy with other test runners?
2 What's the difference between test and &&&?
3 What does the == operator represent in Canopy?

Summary

That's the last testing lesson. You've touched the edges of Canopy and seen how to write automated tests within F#, using a powerful yet simple-to-use DSL. Although it's not necessarily a pure functional library (a global state exists behind the scenes with mutable properties), Canopy is an extremely practical library that does a terrific job of making web automation incredibly simple. In this lesson

- You learned how to install Canopy and Selenium.
- You learned how to perform basic web automation with Canopy.
- You wrote automated tests in Canopy.

Try this

Create a web automation script to log into Twitter and print to the console the top five posts in your Twitter feed. You can also use Canopy to create a bot to play the game 2048; see https://github.com/c4fsharp/Dojo-Canopy-2048 for a starting solution. Finally, write automation code that searches GitHub for all F# repositories, sorting by Most Stars, and prints out the first ten repositories.

QC 42.2 answer

1 Yes, you can use Canopy from within, for example, xUnit or NUnit.
2 test generates a name for a test case, whereas &&& allows you to specify a name.
3 The == operator performs an equality test equivalent to, for example, Assert.Equals.

43

LESSON

CAPSTONE 8

Phew—this is the last capstone exercise in this book! You'll be performing unit testing here, and applying some of the techniques and tools presented in this unit to the Bank Accounts system you've been working on throughout the book.

 ## 43.1 Defining the problem

In this capstone, you'll add a set of tests to the business logic domain of your application, using various test libraries that you've seen in this unit, from simple unit testing with xUnit, to DSL-based testing with Unquote, before finally writing a couple of property-based tests. You'll test a couple of tiers as well. In this example, you won't be writing any Canopy-based tests, but you'll test a couple of internal layers within the application: the Web API tier and the internal Bank API, as illustrated in figure 43.1.

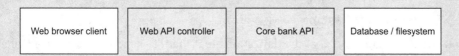

Figure 43.1 The API layers selected for unit tests

43.1.1 Solution overview

The solution you'll be working with is what you finished up with at the end of the pre-ceding capstone—a web-enabled version of your Bank API; you'll find it in the lesson-43 folder. The main difference is that I've added a new test project to the solution. Once again, to save you from working with the hassles of NuGet binding redirects, I've done all the hard work for you. But so you know what's been done

- The project has the following NuGet packages (plus their dependencies):
  - xUnit (and the Visual Studio runner)
  - Unquote
  - FsCheck (and xUnit integration)
  - ASP .NET Web API Core
- The versions of the dependencies have been set to match those in the other projects. For example, Newtonsoft.Json is set to 9.0.1.
- A set of binding redirects ensures that everything works nicely.

(If you used Paket, none of this would be a problem, because packages are automatically kept consistent *across* projects.)

> **100% test coverage?**
> Don't expect to go through a full set of exhaustive tests in this capstone exercise. As I've mentioned, I'm not a fan of trying to achieve 100% test coverage across your applica-tion, particularly with F#. Instead, you'll apply some of the techniques and tools from this unit in a code base that by now you're (hopefully) familiar with.

43.2 Writing API tests

Start by writing a few simple API tests for your core bank API—in-memory tests that can prove various cases of the API.

43.2.1 In-memory testing

You'll notice in figure 43.1 that the data store area is faded compared to the controller and API boxes. This is because you aren't going to be doing full end-to-end tests that "hit the database." Instead you'll need to create an in-memory version of the data tier so that you can easily set up different test cases. Let's refresh your memory as to what the data tier looked like in your application. First, let's look at save:

```
accountId:Guid * customerName:string * Transaction -> unit
```

This says that given an account ID, a customer name, and a transaction, you can perform a function that performs a side effect for that transaction (in this case, save to the database). Now let's see the signature to load all transactions:

```
customerName:string -> (accountId:Guid * Transaction seq) option async
```

This time, you give a customer name and get back Some accountId plus the associated transactions. If no customer exists, you get back None instead. And to further complicate matters, this function returns asynchronously.

Now you try

Start by creating a function that will create an IBankApi but use ResizeArray as an inmemory backing store rather than the filesystem—perfect for quick unit tests:

1. Implement the function Helpers.createInMemApi(), which will create a fake IBankApi whenever called.
2. The existing buildApi function in the Api module will do the bulk of the work for you; it requires both a load and a save function (with the signatures previously identified) and returns IBankApi.
3. The buildApi function is currently private, so won't be accessible to the test project. You can do one of the following:
   a. Make it public so that it's visible to the test project (my preference).
   b. Make it internal and add an InternalsVisibleTo attribute to the project.
   c. Implement the createMemApi function in that module.

To get you on your way, here's a stub function for you.

Listing 43.1 A stub function to create an in-memory IBankAPI

```
open System
open Capstone8.Api

let createInMemApi() =
    let dataStore = ResizeArray()
    let save accountId owner transaction = ()
    let load (owner:string) = None |> async.Return
    buildApi load save
```

In-memory backing store for transactions

Save and Load function stub implementations

Building the Bank API using these in-memory functions

4   The save function should be easy to implement—simply add the supplied data as
    a tuple to the dataStore.

5   The load function involves a slightly longer query. You need to filter out rows that
    aren't for the requested owner, and then extract the account ID from the list as
    well as the transaction elements. (One way is to use a groupBy over the account ID
    in order to easily extract it, and take the first group that's returned; there should
    be only one group per customer.)

6   Don't forget to wrap the result in an async. You can use the shortcut method
    async.Return to do this.

43.2.2 Example API tests in xUnit

I advise writing a few API tests to get your muscle memory up and running, such as the
following:

- *Create an account if none exists*—Prove that you get a new account with an empty
  balance if you call LoadAccount for a nonexistent customer.
- *Multiple deposits are stored correctly*—Make several deposits to a new account;
  determine that the final balance on calling LoadAccount is correct.
- *Cannot withdraw if overdrawn*—If you go into an overdrawn state, trying to withdraw again returns a Failure result.

Here's the first test to get you going.

Listing 43.2 Your first API unit test

```
[<Fact>]
let ``Creates an account if none exists``() =          Creating a sample
    let customer = { Name = "Joe" }                     input customer
    let api = createInMemApi()                          Creating a clean
    async {                                             in-memory API
        let! account = api.LoadAccount customer
        test <@ account.Balance = 0M @> }              Forcing synchronous
    |> Async.RunSynchronously                           evaluation of your test
```

There are important things to note about this test. First, you create an in-memory API as
part of the test. It's stateful, and you don't want the effects of this test shared with
another test! Second, notice that you *explicitly* execute this test synchronously. xUnit has
support for asynchronous tests, so you could also call Async.StartAsTask if you wanted.
(xUnit 2.2 will have native support for F#'s async { } blocks but at the time of writing is
still in beta.)

43.3 Testing the Web API tier

Now that you've written some basic API tests, let's move up a level and see how to test your Web API controllers. In my view, your Web API controllers should be extremely thin—a mapping exercise before your internal and public domains in both directions, and at most some extremely simple orchestration; anything more should probably be moved into your internal domain.

Testing Web API controllers isn't especially difficult. You create your controller object as you would any other object, passing in any dependencies as needed (in our case, a Bank API that talks to an in-memory list). But you do have to ensure that the request and configuration properties are correctly set on the controller object. Here's a function that will create a test controller with everything needed.

Listing 43.3 Creating a Web API controller under test

```
open Capstone8.Controllers
open System.Web.Http
open System.Net.Http

let createController() =
    let api = Helpers.createInMemApi()          ⎫ Creating dependencies
    let request = new HttpRequestMessage()      ⎬ for the Bank Account
    let config = new HttpConfiguration()        ⎭ Controller class
    new BankAccountController(api, Request = request, Configuration = config)
```

Now you try

Create a set of tests for the HTTP layer. Again, I advise you to stick to focusing on the mapping between data from the web layer to the internal Bank domain model and back again. With that in mind, here are some examples you can try:

- *Successful withdrawal returns OK*—Check that the Withdrawal controller returns `HttpStatusCode.OK` if the withdrawal worked.
- *Unsuccessful withdrawal returns Bad Request*—Check that the Withdrawal controller returns `HttpStatusCode.BadRequest` if the withdrawal was rejected.
- *Returns correct balance*—The balance of an account is correctly entered onto the response message.

One thing that's interesting is that Web API methods that return an `IHTTPActionResult` rather than arbitrary objects (for example, `PostDeposit` compared to `GetHistory`) need to be unwrapped to get the `HttpResponseMessage`. To save you some time digging around, here's a helper method that will do it for you.

Listing 43.4 Unwrapping a `Task<IHttpActionResult>`

```
open System.Threading
open System.Web.Http
open System.Threading.Tasks

let executeRequest (request:IHttpActionResult Task) =
    async {
        let! request = request |> Async.AwaitTask
        return! request.ExecuteAsync CancellationToken.None |>
        ➥Async.AwaitTask }
    |> Async.RunSynchronously
```

Mocking libraries

It seems strange that we've gotten all the way here and not touched on mocking frameworks! This is a question that I see coming up now and again, so it's worth briefly addressing. First, you can absolutely use standard mocking libraries with F#, such as Moq (there's even a library designed specifically with F# in mind, called Foq!). But as you've seen throughout this book, often you're simply varying code by injecting individual functions, rather than entire objects and interfaces—in which case, it's trivial to mock them by creating arbitrary test functions by hand and passing them in.

There's also a tendency in F# to lean toward passing simple data structures around to pure functions rather than objects with behavior on them—and again, these are generally extremely easy to test.

Try not to get hung up about mocking frameworks—you'll very rarely need them.

43.4 Using property-based tests

OK! Almost done—you have just one more type of test to try! You'll put in a couple of property-based tests for the Bank API, just to prove that you can.

43.4.1 Thinking about property-based tests

As you may recall from lesson 41, we identified a few ways to discover tests. I'm going to opt for a couple of simple tests to get you started, which will hopefully give you some good ideas of how to find further properties to test:

- *Going under 0 makes the account overdrawn*—If you make a withdrawal that pushes the account below 0, the account should become overdrawn.
- *Withdrawal fails if the account is overdrawn*—If the account is in an overdrawn state, trying to withdraw funds should fail.

These are similar to the tests you wrote at the start! The difference here is that rather than use hardcoded inputs and outputs, you'll have to write general tests that prove the rule. In these cases, the logic to test should be fairly obvious.

43.4.2 Your first property-based test

I'll get you started on the first test by at least providing the signature for you. It declares a test method that takes in a value that you'll use as the starting balance of the account. From there, it's up to you to write code to force the account to go overdrawn and then prove that the account is correctly identified as such.

Listing 43.5 A stub property-based test

```
[<Property(Verbose = true)>]
let ``Going under 0 makes the account overdrawn``(PositiveInt startingBalance) =
    let startingBalance = decimal startingBalance
    // ... complete the test!
```

> Converting the integer to a decimal

> Using FsCheck to generate only positive integers

The test implementation shouldn't prove too challenging:

1 Create an instance of the test Bank API.
2 Make a deposit for the starting balance supplied.
3 Make a withdrawal of the starting balance + 1.
4 If the returned result is Success (Overdrawn _), return true.
5 Otherwise, return false (the test fails).

The important bit here is that you make a withdrawal amount based on the value used as the starting balance. By always withdrawing one unit more than was deposited, you can ensure that you always go overdrawn (indeed, you could start with an empty balance to try to prove this, but starting from different amounts at least makes the test a little more interesting).

Summary

That's the end of the final capstone! You've written a set of unit tests by using tools and techniques covered in this unit, and applied them to a domain that you've worked on throughout the book.

Try this

Here are some ideas for further types of tests you could write:

- Write a set of tests using FsUnit.
- Create a mock Bank API for the controller tests, instead of using the real Bank API logic. Use F# object initializers to avoid creating a real mock type!
- Read up on FsCheck's model-based testing feature (also known as stateful tests). Create a set of model-based tests proving that the Bank API correctly works with a random sequence of withdrawals and deposits.

10

Where next?

Congratulations—you've made it! That's the end of the learning phase of this book. Remember that this book is split into two distinct halves; the first half covered a core subset of the F# language, and the second half covered applying F# in real-world scenarios using various technology stacks.

Having worked diligently through this book, are you now an expert in F#? Probably not. But I'm hoping that you have the confidence to attack nearly any problem that previously you would've solved by reaching for C# without a second thought. Instead, you now know that you can use F# for just about any use case that you'd have looked to C# for, as well as other use cases that you previously might not have even considered .NET a viable option for at all.

Are you a functional programming expert? Again, probably not. Remember, this book focused on some of the *fundamentals* of FP, including expressions over statements, functions as values over classes and methods, and composition over inheritance. There's a whole world of information for you to find out more about FP and its use within F#— compare this to learning more design patterns in the OO world to enrich your ability to effectively solve problems.

The final unit of this book doesn't contain many code samples or any practical exercises. Instead, it consists of several small appendixes that aim to address questions or issues you may have, such as the following:

- How can I convince my boss to give me permission to use F#?
- What's the best way to start using F# in an existing system and team?
- How can I learn more about F#?
- What features of F# didn't you cover?

Without further ado, let's dive in!

THE F# COMMUNITY

Since 2015, Microsoft has openly been a fan of moving to an open source model. Lots of .NET has been open sourced, and the impending delivery of .NET core—which includes a lighter, cross-platform version of the CLR—suggests that Microsoft sees the long-term future of .NET as running on equal footing on Windows, Mac, and Linux. Microsoft has a long way to go, though, in my opinion, until it *truly* adopts open source—there's a world of difference between putting a repository on GitHub and embracing a community-led approach to development. Nonetheless, it's something to be applauded.

If you're not familiar with working with open source, community-led projects, doing so can be a great learning experience. Not only are you exposed to different coding styles and techniques, but you also learn about a different way of developing software, through features such as pull requests and (almost certainly) through Git and GitHub.

A.1 The F# community

F# is way ahead of the curve here in terms of the .NET community. The language and compiler itself was open sourced several years ago, and it has a vibrant, active, passionate (some might say *too* passionate!), and growing community behind it. F# has channels of communication through Twitter, hangouts, real-world meetups, mailing lists, and websites (see appendix D). But what does this mean for you as a software developer in terms of day-to-day development, sourcing reusable libraries, and working with others?

A.1.1   Microsoft and F# libraries

First, you have to get used to the idea of not relying on Microsoft to provide every library, framework, or tool. Instead, many of the libraries and tools you'll use are open source, run by the community, for the community. On the one hand, many people work on these tools in their spare time rather than as a full-time job. But I should point out that many people are able to contribute to open source projects as part of their day-to-day jobs, because their organizations use (or maintain) those tools. At the same time, you'll have open, direct access to the code base (and authors), and can make fixes or enhancements yourself, as well as encourage others to chip in. That's not to say that code bases in, for example, Microsoft's repositories don't allow changes, but you might find a slightly higher barrier to entry to contribute to the C# compiler (and perhaps with good reason!).

Think of all the F# libraries you've seen in this book: FSharp.Data, Paket, Suave, XPlot, and FsCheck. All are open source projects that are managed by individuals within the F# community—not Microsoft. The community, not Microsoft, dictates where the tools go, and, ultimately, the ecosystem of tools that are available. This mentality is a sort of survival of the fittest: tooling can rapidly evolve, benefitting everyone. This is very different from the typical C# library stack of Nuget, Entity Framework, ASP .NET, and so forth, all of which are ultimately owned by Microsoft. If Microsoft decides to make a change to these tools, you may be able to comment on the direction they take, but, ultimately, you'll have little choice but to accept the decisions that are made in Redmond.

Note that the F# community *includes* the Microsoft F# team, which contributes to these tools as well, but doesn't own them. In this way, the F# community stands out a little from the C# and VB .NET communities, in that a much higher proportion of F# users are actively involved in community activities. Part of this is drawn out of necessity; because Microsoft doesn't invest quite as much in F# as, say, C#, the F# community has matured extremely rapidly and is remarkably self-sufficient. Frankly, this attitude is something that the C# and VB .NET communities need to imitate in the future in order to ensure that those languages (and associated libraries) evolve in the right way and stay relevant, particularly with the move to .NET Core. A few years ago, a similar movement known as the "alt .net" movement arose within the C# community. It encouraged developers to not only look to Microsoft for tooling and libraries but to the community itself. It kind of died off a few years ago, although it looks like it might resurrect itself with the coming of .NET Core.

A.1.2 Impressions of the F# community

The F# community has become known in some circles within the .NET community—somewhat unfairly, in my view—as the awkward sibling that operates differently than the rest of the .NET ecosystem. Why? One reason is that although today Microsoft is publicly committed to the future of F#, that wasn't always the case. The F# community is used to having to fix things that aren't up to scratch in order to improve tooling or processes, because for several years there was no alternative than to do it themselves. This led to the misconception that the community was often going against the grain of established tools and processes just for the sake of being different. As a result, the F# community often uses alternatives to many of the common tools and libraries that you might be familiar with; we'll cover more of this in appendix C, which details specific libraries and tools that make up a key part of the most common F# toolchains.

> ### F# elitists
>
> There's also a tendency to think of the F# community as somewhat elitist, looking down on the "inferior" C# and VB .NET developers who haven't "seen the light." There's unfortunately an element of truth here, as occasionally people in the community have allowed their enthusiasm for F# to bleed over into maligning those languages.
>
> But by and large, even though many people in the F# community firmly believe that F# offers a way to solve many types of problems that's superior to C# or VB .NET, most don't feel the need to disparage the use of other languages or people who haven't tried F# yet.

In the past, this do-it-yourself approach led to the relationship between the community and Microsoft being somewhat uncomfortable; at times Microsoft ignored many of the excellent .NET technologies that were created by the F# community just because of a lack of awareness or a misconception that F# libraries couldn't be used by .NET in general. Other times, Microsoft teams actively attempted to thwart tools being created within the F# community, which ultimately led to public squabbles on social media. Hopefully, those days are now past us!

Within Microsoft, there's a growing acceptance and acknowledgment that F# *does have* a valid place within .NET in many spaces, and has a valuable role to play in moving .NET out from the closed world it inhabited for many years and into the open.

> **The F# foundation**
>
> The F# Software Foundation (http://foundation.fsharp.org/) is a not-for-profit organization whose goal is to "promote, protect, and advance the F# programming language and facilitate the growth of a diverse and international community of F# programmers." The foundation has a board, elected annually by the members of the foundation, whose responsibility is to help shape and promote the evolution of F# as a whole. The foundation runs several working groups and programs, such as a 1:1 mentoring program, core engineering, and communications, and also helps connect people looking for speakers and those giving presentations.

A.2   Coding in the open source world

As an example of what I mean about community involvement, let's take a simple scenario: you're using an open source library and find a bug, or maybe you have a feature request to improve it. How do you report this? It's pretty easy. You go to the GitHub repository for the library and raise an issue; usually, someone who maintains the project will respond within a few hours, sometimes less. Sometimes the feature will already be there. Other times it won't be appropriate, and still other times it'll be accepted and placed on the to-do list. At this point, rather than waiting until one of the maintainers makes the appropriate changes—particularly if the change is relatively small—you might be asked to submit a pull request with the changes yourself! The maintainers will usually help you by providing the area of code that needs to change, and then suggesting what you might do for the change. Although it would undoubtedly be quicker for the maintainers to make the change, there's a reason they're keen to get a new contributor involved with the project: this grows the team of people who can help with the project. The next time you have a feature request or bug fix, you'll already have the source code on your machine, and it'll be much quicker for you to make a change.

A.3   A real-world example of open source contributions

Here's a real-world illustration of three people on Twitter discussing a feature request for the FsReveal project:

29th January 2016

08:39 [PI]: Hello #fsharp nation! Is there any way to do links between slides in #fsreveal?

10:03 [IA]: Can't they just point to the URI (every slide has a #page bit in the URI)?

10:04 [PI]: Yes, but I'd like the URI to be dynamically generated. Define an anchor in a slide and reference it from another one ☺

10:05 [PI]: But I know the correct answer is to open an issue on GitHub and write a pull-request!

10:13 [SF]: Maybe there is already a trick in reveal.js?

14:18 [PI]: Indeed there is!

30th January 2016

10:25 [PI]: And here comes the pull request ☺

11:27 [SF]: Awesome!

Notice the use of the #fsharp hashtag, designed to get the attention of the active F# community on Twitter. From there, it takes about 24 hours from the idea for a feature first being formed to the solution being submitted as a pull request into the proper code base.

Let's look at the pull request in more detail (see figure A.1). In this case, having already spoken about a new feature for this project on Twitter with a couple of maintainers of the project, pirmann submits a pull request (PR) with the code changes required for a specific feature. forki (one of the project maintainers) then replies and asks for documentation to be added; shortly after, it arrives. Only then does forki accept the pull request, and thanks pirmann for his contribution to the project. He might have also done a quick code review of the changes to see what's been added. Total turnaround time from idea to release in this case was around 24 hours—not bad!

Pull requests are a low-ceremony, quick-and-easy way to help shape a system that you use and benefit from. The feature may not have been particularly large, but by accepting lots of small PRs, a system can rapidly grow in features and complexity.

Again, this collaborative approach is something that might be completely foreign to you; you might even find it rude the first time someone on a project asks you to do a fix yourself, but this attitude is perfectly normal. Working together in this manner empowers us all to shape libraries and frameworks as we see fit, and with a much quicker turnaround than you might be used to. Of course, this quick turnaround means that rapid change often occurs within a library, which can be unsettling. There's also the increased risk of bugs. Some projects are more "bleeding edge" than others and are willing to push out new versions of tools much more quickly (the flip side is that bugs are often fixed much more quickly, too!).

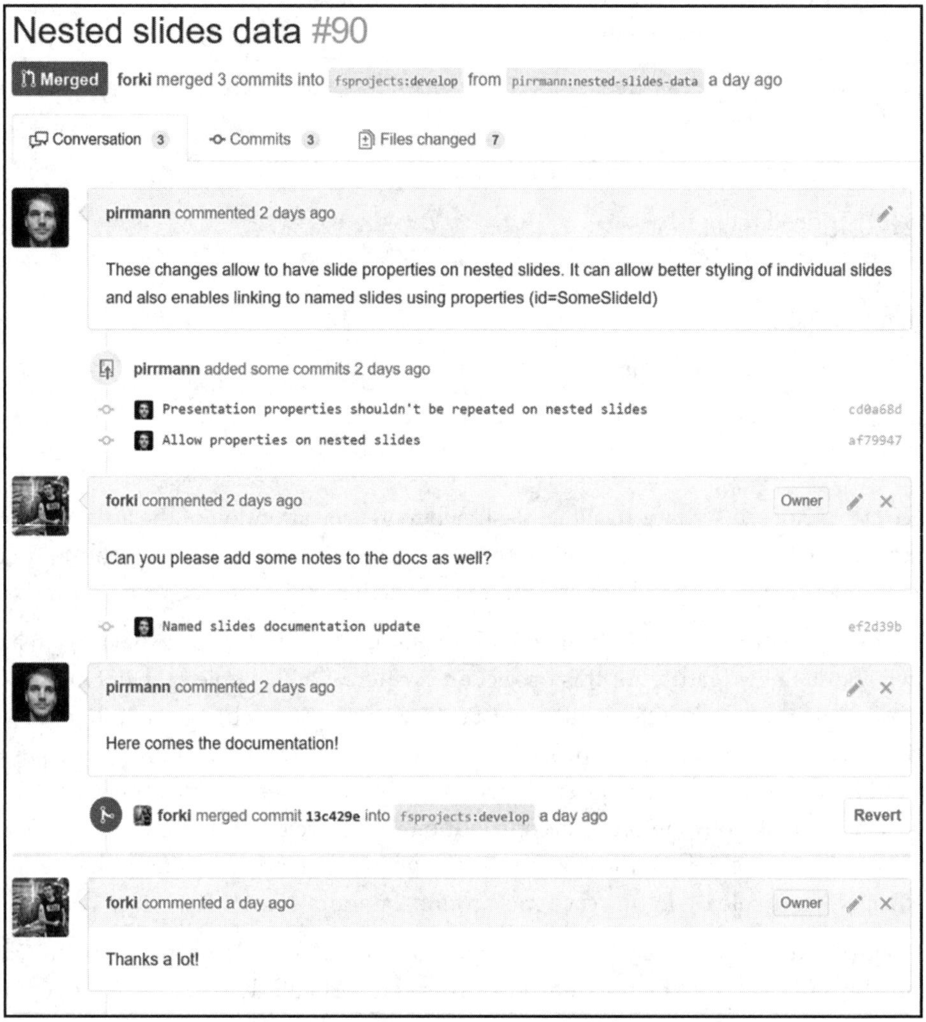

Figure A.1 A real-world example pull request from the FsReveal project

Summary

The F# community is friendly, welcoming, and enthusiastic. But it also operates on a different mind-set than you might be used to if you're comfortable with the approach that we should adopt—and rely upon—everything Microsoft serves us. If you can accept that there's another way to get things done, and are interested in becoming an active member of the F# community, you'll find it's a fun, vibrant, and extremely productive way to collaborate and get things done! You'll see how to get involved in appendix C.

F# IN MY ORGANIZATION

One of the most common difficulties that developers have after they've tasted F# is adopting it into their real-world, day-to-day jobs. I see this difficulty play out in three ways:

- Making the leap from writing scripts and console applications into integrating with the full .NET stack—things such as interoperability between C# and F#, working with NuGet, and using frameworks such as the ASP .NET Web API.
- Convincing others of the value of using F#, and ultimately getting permission from colleagues or management to give F# a go.
- Understanding how to start using F# in a practical way in an existing tech stack. What areas are safe bets to start using F# that will show its strengths? How should you start applying F# within an existing solution?

I hope that over the course of this book, you've gained confidence in carrying out tasks that fulfill the first of these three points, and can see enough to assure you that F# works fine in basically the same contexts as C# or VB .NET. This appendix covers the latter two points: dealing with common misconceptions regarding F#, and learning how to incorporate it into your existing tech stack.

B.1   Introducing F# to others

Let's first discuss the human element. This section provides pointers on how to show F# to the rest of your team, or your boss, in such a way that they're happy for you to start adopting it within your organization, and how to answer many of the common fears about adopting F#. But before reading this, have a quick look at this tongue-in-cheek YouTube video that demonstrates a common outcome to such a conversation: www.youtube.com/watch?v=Hd9Z9s4_DII. Then read on to see ways to avoid this happening to you!

B.1.1   Show the advantages of F#

First and foremost, I encourage you to start by stating the overall benefits of F# in simple terms that all developers can understand. You can talk about improved productivity, reduced bug rates, and the ability to write code that's easy to reason about. Give tangible examples, such as showing how easy it is to work with data in F# by using type providers; give examples that relate to concerns or difficulties you might be facing in your current project or have had in the past, such as areas where bugs crop up often and F# could help, or where you're doing something such as CSV-parsing. Features such as exhaustive pattern matching and discriminated unions, or even structural equality with records—all of these are relatively simple ways of illustrating some of the quick wins of F#. You can use many useful online resources, such as demos or presentations that people have done in this vein.

B.1.2   Avoid dismissing C#

By far, the biggest mistake people make when showing F# to their colleagues is to suggest that C# is somehow obsolete or bad. There are two reasons for not doing this:

- No one likes being told that something they've invested years learning and growing fond of is somehow wrong; it becomes an emotional discussion that's not worth spending time on.
- C# is not suddenly a bad language. As far as modern OO languages go, it's probably one of the best ones out there. The question is more about whether using it in specific areas is going to be the best fit for you and your team compared to working with perhaps a hybrid stack that also uses F#.

There's nothing wrong with being enthusiastic about F#. The trick is to show the benefits of F# without presenting them as a direct comparison to the "shortcomings" of C#.

Instead, focus on the strengths of F# as a language on its own, and then as an afterthought relate this to how you'd perform the equivalent task in C# (avoiding straw-man examples wherever possible). Ideally, show real examples of your existing code base and how you might have approached the problem differently using F#, and where the pain points are. Explain that if you like working with mutable data, statements, and side effects with inheritance, then F# probably isn't a great fit; but if you like working with expressions that can be reasoned about, simple functions that compose together, and lightweight modeling without the need for a myriad of design patterns, then F# might well be a better fit.

B.1.3 Dismiss the zero-sum game

A common misconception about a new way of doing things—particularly something like F# or FP in general, of which there's sadly a lot of fear, uncertainty, and doubt (FUD) out there—is that to gain the benefits of F#, there must also be a cost associated with it. For example, it can't be ready for production usage, or it can't possibly be used for general-purpose programming.

Explain to colleagues that this isn't true and that, yes, it's entirely possible to reduce bug rates *and* increase developer productivity *and* improve developer satisfaction at the same time! Plenty of case studies are available online that you can use to prove this as well (see appendix D). Is your company or development team so unique that these studies don't apply to your organization?

B.1.4 Reduce the fear of learning

It's often taken as truth that F# carries a high cost. Again, this idea perpetuates the zero-sum-game theme: that it must be hard to learn F# if the benefits are so great! Yes, learning F# has an up-front cost, but by the same token, there was an up-front cost to learning LINQ in C# 3, or async/await in C# 5. Because F# sits on top of the .NET Framework, you can reuse virtually all of the frameworks and libraries that you already know; you're just going to be orchestrating the use of them against data in a different way. Explain that there are ways to start small (see section B.2) and gently introduce the use of F# without the need to throw away all your existing code. And best of all, you're holding a book that provides a great way to start learning F# (although perhaps you'll need to buy a few more copies to share with your colleagues)!

B.1.5   We're already productive enough!

More often than any other argument against adopting F#, I hear that a team is "already productive enough in C#." This is also one of the most ridiculous arguments of all. Against what yardstick is your team measuring itself? Have you arbitrarily decided that it's going to be *impossible* to make any more productivity gains in the future? Is your team not even interested in exploring the possibility of reducing the cost of development for your organization?

Ask your team about the areas of development that they would consider for using F#. If the reply is "math or science," their information about F# is almost certainly hearsay (F# was initially marketed as such when it first came out many years ago). If the reply is "only when we're doing something especially difficult," you can dispel this easily enough; although F# does allow you to solve *difficult* problems with *simple* code, F# also allows you to solve *simple* problems with *extremely simple* code!

B.1.6   It's not fully supported by Microsoft

Until not so long ago, I might have said that there was some weight to the argument that F# isn't fully supported by Microsoft. Yes, the F# team is smaller than the C# team, but that doesn't mean that F# isn't an important part of the Microsoft development stack. Indeed, Microsoft has recently indicated several times that F# is here for the long haul, that Microsoft knows there's real value in having it as a core part of the .NET stack, and that it's committed to bringing F# more in line with support for tools such as VS2017.

B.1.7   Specific use cases

Your product or project might have some areas that are especially applicable to F#, such as data manipulation, complex modeling, or working with scripts, where C# doesn't necessarily fit especially well. You can explain, with real examples, how F# would eliminate a bottleneck in your process or current development project. The problem with going down this route is that you run the risk of F# being thought of as only applicable to solving problems in that specific area. You then might find it difficult to "break it out" later. On the other hand, if using F# is a roaring success, you can always use it as a springboard from which to justify adopting it in other areas.

B.1.8   Cost/benefit analysis

Particularly when you're dealing with decision makers rather than pure technologists, those people who hold the purse strings will need to see why F# is of interest to them. There's always an inherent risk when doing anything new or different, so you'll need to explain in nontechnical terms why this is important for your organization.

Look at F# as providing your company with a competitive edge over others. Explain how F# can reduce development costs, both in terms of time-to-market as well as maintenance costs. Show how F# is consistently one of the most loved languages in developer surveys, which could lead to improved staff retention. For example, in the 2016 Stack Overflow survey, F# placed third as the most loved language, with an approval rating almost 10% higher than C#. There's also some evidence that developers are willing to take a pay cut in order to work on F#, as they understand the benefit it'll give them in their careers.

Jet.com is a great case study of a large organization that bet the farm on F#, building its entire back-end stack in F# on top of Microsoft Azure. Just 18 months after launch, Jet was bought by Walmart for a whopping $3.3 billion, due in no small part to the technical assets Jet had developed. Many other excellent case studies exist on fsharp.org in a variety of verticals, from finance to e-commerce to gaming.

B.1.9 Hire new staff

Another common concern exists, and a fair one. If you look at the number of available jobs for F# positions, it'll always be lower than C# jobs—no surprises there, because C# is used around 100 times more than F#, according to high-level figures from Microsoft.

But that's no reason to avoid using it—developers can always cross-train to F#. In my experience, when using F# day in and day out, it takes a few weeks for a competent developer to become reasonably productive in the language, and a few months to be completely comfortable in the language. (This time can be reduced further if the developer is already familiar with either .NET or functional programming.) It's certainly nothing that should be a major blocker, although I've seen this concern block adoption of F# before.

B.1.10 Simply start using it

This approach is riskier, and depends on the level of control you have within your organization. I know of developers who have started using F# without even asking the customer or management for approval. Potentially, this is a high-risk strategy, because if things don't work out—for example, you struggle with a specific part of the project, or for some other reason the project isn't a success and someone else blames it on "that weird language" (this has been known to happen!)—you could end up facing difficult questions. Also, bear in mind that doing this could mean going against the wishes of other team members who might have a vested (and even emotional) interest in staying with a language that they feel comfortable with.

The flip side to this is that if things go well, you could end up being the superstar, someone who was able to get things done by using the right tool for the job. Getting noticed like this will probably also win you points with management, as someone who was able to take personal responsibility and showed initiative to make a positive difference in the company.

B.2   Introducing F# to your code base

OK! You have buy-in from the powers that be to start using F#, and your fellow developers are all eager to start trying F#—ideally, on your current project. The question now is, how do you start? This section outlines a few approaches that you can take in order to adopt F# in an existing team and project.

B.2.1   Exploratory scripts

Probably the easiest way to start using F# is with scripts. A script allows you to start to learn the language in a relatively low-risk manner, while quickly building confidence in the language and getting immediate benefit. In my experience, scripts are always needed in a project (even a project whose code base is 100% C#), whether it's to quickly test a subset of the application (instead of the dreaded console application) or to quickly try a new NuGet package. Alternatively, you might also use a script to aid with bugfixing or fault reproduction, to quickly identify a record in a database, hit an HTTP API, and then call some code with a mashup of both. You'll be surprised just how quickly you'll naturally start to use a variety of F# features even within a script!

Note that as of VS2015, C# has some support for scripts (as well as third-party tools and systems), and this will no doubt improve in time. But for the moment, F# scripts reign supreme in terms of experience. If you acknowledge that you'd like to use scripts to not only provide business benefit but also to help learn F#, they are probably the lowest hanging fruit.

B.2.2   Ad hoc processes

Some ad hoc processes are nearly always needed within a system. These processes may take the form of scripts, but rather than as a means to explore code, they might be something to aid the day-to-day running of your system. For example, you may use a maintenance process that clears certain records in a database based on the result of another query, or the results of a text file that needs to be parsed that's delivered on a daily basis from a third party. Or you might use the process to generate a report once a day, every day, by pulling in data from your source systems and emitting a PDF or HTML report (see appendix C for details on the FsLab project).

B.2.3   Helper modules

If you're ready to start bringing F# into your main code base, you have several options. The easiest one to start with is to write standalone helper functions or modules of functions. These show up as static classes in C# and so are easy to work with from a consumption point of view, and can help you build confidence in writing hybrid applications within your team.

But beware of underselling F# here. It's easy to think that F# is great for small functions that take a number and give back another number, but can't be used for anything more than that. You'll also be somewhat hamstrung in that you won't be able to use F#'s type system for modeling if you rely on your C# domain model. Again, this is missing out on much of the power of the language.

B.2.4   Horizontal tiers

One way to allow F# to flex its muscles a little more is to say that from an architectural perspective, a single horizontal tier of the application will be written in F#. For example, you might use F# for the validation tier, or data access layer, or even a large module within a system (such as a calculation engine). You can provide a contract that you expose to consumers (and even wrap in a lightweight OO interface to make it natural to consume from C#), but internally you're free to use the full power of F#, with a rich internal domain model built on discriminated unions, with exhaustive pattern matching and type providers.

In figure B.1, you can see a fictional web stack that uses F# for the validation and business logic, while leaving C# for implementing the MVC controllers and data access. Note that I'm not suggesting that this is a recommended partition of concerns to language!

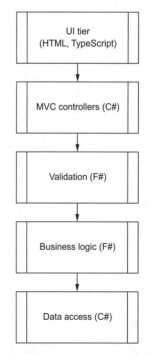

Figure B.1   A sample hybrid language application stack with different languages used for different tiers

Adopting a horizontal-tiers approach means that you can pick and choose which areas you'd like to tackle, one at a time, and gain the benefit of the F# code across all the modules within the application. But if this is an existing application, you'll need to gently phase in the F# code to replace the C# code. This might prove challenging if your team is actively developing at the same time across the application.

B.2.5   Vertical tiers

An alternative to partitioning by horizontal tiers is to pivot this, and partition by vertical tiers. In this case, you provide a full end-to-end stack implementation in a single .NET language, but only for specific business areas of the system (for example, the customer module or the order management module). You could therefore reorganize your architecture as shown in figure B.2.

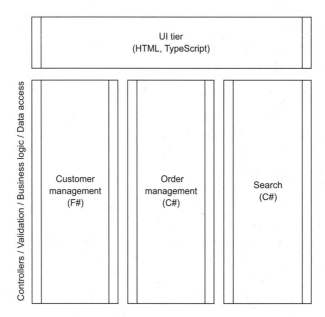

Figure B.2   Partitioning an application into vertical tiers

This approach has several benefits:

- You can see how a full F# stack works compared to an equivalent C# stack. Is it any easier to work with? What are the pain points?
- The next time you create a new area of the system, you can adopt this without treading on anyone else's toes or affecting the existing product.

The cost of this approach is that for cross-cutting code (for example, logging or caching), you might end up having two versions of code that do the same thing, one in C# and one in F#. It's also somewhat bolder than the horizontal version, as you'll rely on a new language for an entire business area of the system.

You could try a hybrid approach, perhaps creating some cross-cutting concerns in F# (such as a cache layer) and a subsection of the Customer module in F#. But you'll need to be careful that your code base doesn't turn into a patchwork of seemingly random language choices across your application stack!

One thing I can tell you from experience is that working in hybrid stacks often leads to a bleed of F# code into what is historically the C# stack, because the ability to rapidly and accurately model domains in F# quickly becomes addictive. As you move between the two languages, you'll probably find yourself wanting the F# side of things to expand across the stack as you miss the extra type safety and security that the language affords you.

B.2.6   Unit tests

I'm not a huge fan of using F# for unit tests in C# projects, but some people swear by this. You can certainly use F#'s backtick methods to improve readability, and can use its succinct syntax to more rapidly write tests. But you'll probably still be working with an object-oriented API, so you won't easily be able to use more powerful F# features such as currying.

The only exception to this is with something like Canopy, which has a specific DSL that makes writing tests easy. But the flip side is that because Canopy has such a specific DSL (with several custom operators and global mutable variables), it can be difficult to know where "F# the language" stops and "Canopy the DSL" begins.

B.2.7   Build scripts

FAKE is a popular project in many .NET (not just F#) solutions to provide a succinct, simple-to-use build system that can replace TeamCity for build orchestration (see appendix C). Because the build is completely separate from your application code, you're isolated from the main code base, so in one sense it's fairly low risk. But once again, because FAKE provides a DSL on top of F#, it can be tricky for beginners to distinguish between FAKE and F#.

Summary

Adopting F# in your team is a two-step process. First, you need to get buy-in from those you work with (and under!). Second, you need a plan for easing F# into your existing development process and stack. There's no right or wrong here. A lot depends on your team's appetite for learning something new (and the apparent risk of adopting something different), as well as the ease with which you can integrate F# into your product stack. Spending a few days in advance trying out a proof of concept (or speaking with someone who has done this before) is always a good idea.

MUST-VISIT F# RESOURCES

One of the goals of this book is not just to give you confidence in using F#, but also to give you the ability to join the F# community and to learn about new areas of F#. The objective of this appendix is to point out some of the many excellent online resources that you can take advantage of that will enrich your use of F#. I should also point out that there are many excellent offline resources—books—by which you can further your knowledge of F#. You can probably find the ones that are right for you by speaking to people within the community.

C.1 Websites

Many websites are dedicated to F#; this section lists a few of the most popular ones that you'll definitely want to check out.

C.1.1 FSharp.org

http://fsharp.org/

The official home of F#, this contains all sorts of goodies, from customer testimonials to Getting Started guides on a variety of platforms, to helpful guides in several areas. The site also has details about the F# Foundation, including how to become a member, how to contribute, and how to take part in some of the programs that the foundation runs.

C.1.2   Community for F#

http://c4fsharp.net/

The C4FSharp site provides a list of information regarding events and user groups happening in the F# world. It also contains a list of webinars and recorded user group talks demonstrating various aspects of F#. If you're looking to go to a meetup or user group near you, there's a good chance it'll be registered here!

The site also contains great coding *dojos*. These are challenges that usually last a few hours, with a set task and model solution, usually best done in groups or pairs, often in a user group session.

C.1.3   F# for Fun and Profit

http://fsharpforfunandprofit.com/

There's no way you could use F# and not know about this site. F# for Fun and Profit has been running for several years and contains many educational posts on various aspects of F#, from error handling to domain modeling, to more complex areas of F# such as monads. The series of posts has evolved organically over time, so they don't necessarily follow a clear "path," and the content is *very* detailed—many of the posts have a large number of examples that explain (very clearly!) the concepts. Although it's not a site that you might quickly look at for a five-minute answer to a specific question, the concepts it deals with are definitely worth your time to read. The series on error handling and railway-oriented programming alone is worth it, but dozens of series are available to read up on. Scott Wlaschin (the author of the site) is also a regular (and excellent) speaker on F#, so if he's in a user group in your area, it'd be well worth your time to go listen to him.

C.1.4   F# Weekly

https://sergeytihon.wordpress.com/category/f-weekly/

F# Weekly performs an excellent news aggregation function for F#, based on new libraries that have been released, news on the F# language, blog posts and videos, as well as generally anything that's happening in the community. Subscribing to it is definitely worthwhile, and probably the easiest way to quickly catch up on what's been going on in F# over the past seven days.

C.2 Social networks

If you want to quickly interact with the rest of the F# community, whether it's to ask someone's opinion on something or for advice on a problem you're facing, F# has you covered with a great presence on various social media.

C.2.1 Twitter

https://twitter.com/hashtag/fsharp

The #fsharp hashtag is your friend on Twitter. Whether it's someone's ideas or news on F#, a new library that's just been released, or the latest debate as to whether F# should adopt type classes or not, it'll almost certainly have a discussion here.

C.2.2 Slack

Slack, shown in figure C.1, is an excellent browser-based medium for discussions that need more than 140 characters in a tweet, allowing users to chat in groups on a variety of topics.

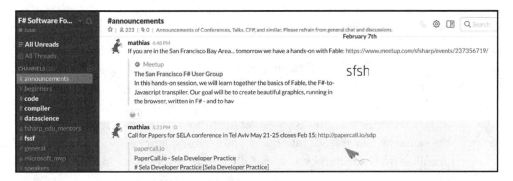

Figure C.1 The F# Software Foundation Slack channel

There are two Slack forums for F#:

- https://fsharp.slack.com/—The F# Software Foundation slack channel, with chat rooms for beginners, general discussions, and data science to the compiler
- https://functionalprogramming.slack.com—An unofficial F# channel, but also equally popular

Many of the F# community will crop up on here as well, so it's often worth having both Slack channels open in separate tabs in your web browser just in case!

C.2.3   Reddit

https://www.reddit.com/r/fsharp/

The F# subreddit contains many news items and discussion topics that are worth looking into, on a wide variety of topics. If you use the Reddit website already, this is a good subreddit to belong to.

C.2.4   The F# mailing list

https://groups.google.com/forum/#!forum/fsharp-opensource

You can also subscribe to the F# Google group and mailing list. Since the increase in popularity of Slack, the content on the group has dropped a little, but there are still interesting discussions to be had on it. In addition, the F# Weekly is always sent here, so this is an easy way of getting weekly news on F# delivered to your inbox!

C.3   Projects and language

This section presents source code repositories that are important for F#.

C.3.1   The F# compiler

There are two repositories for F#: the Microsoft Visual F# repository, which contains the core compiler and the open sourced tooling elements (https://github.com/Microsoft/visualfsharp), and the "open" edition of the core language and tools (https://github.com/fsharp/fsharp). The former feeds directly into Visual Studio and the official F# NuGet packages, whereas the latter is based off the former (theoretically, they should always be the same) and then feeds into many of the cross-platform initiatives such as Mono. In time, the two repositories will hopefully be merged into one, but I suggest that for any issues (or if you want to keep up-to-date with the changes being made to the F# language and compiler), you look at the Microsoft repository. Pull requests to the repository are definitely accepted and encouraged, although the toolchain for the compiler is complex, so you'll need to have your wits about you before you dive in and start to add higher-kinded types to F#.

C.3.2   Language suggestions

The GitHub repository at https://github.com/fsharp/fslang-suggestions is used for managing suggestions to F#, and is curated by both the Microsoft Visual F# team and Don Syme (the creator of F#). You'll see many language suggestions here, all of which will be read by the F# team (see figure C.2). You can also participate in existing issues by upvoting those that you agree with; this helps the team understand demand from developers for new features in the next version of F#.

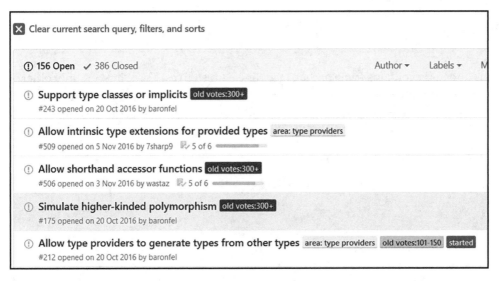

Figure C.2   Some of the issues on the F# language suggestions repository

C.3.3   FS projects

The FS Projects website (http://fsprojects.github.io/) is a kind of semiofficial list of popular F# projects that are on NuGet and GitHub; see figure C.3.

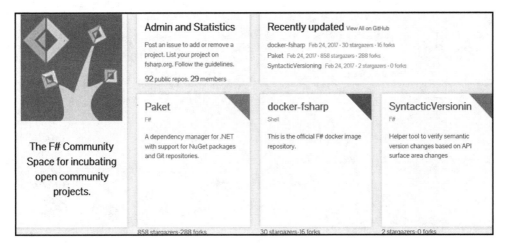

Figure C.3   The FS Projects website

FS Projects is definitely worth a look if you're seeking a specific library, but it's by no means a complete list. Appendix D contains some libraries from here, as well as others that are not included here.

Summary

This appendix contains some of the key online F# resources. There are certainly other resources available, but the ones presented here are a great base for you to start engaging with the F# community, learning from others, and sharing your knowledge and experiences with the community at large.

MUST-HAVE F# LIBRARIES

As an aside to all the NuGet packages you use today (almost all of which can be used seamlessly with F#), this appendix contains a list of popular libraries and tools unique to the F# ecosystem. It's by no means an exhaustive list of all libraries out there (new libraries are always cropping up), but there should be enough here to give you a few ideas of how to start using F# in new and interesting ways.

D.1   Libraries

First, we'll cover a whole set of F# libraries that we haven't touched on yet in this book. But don't forget the ones we've already covered, such as Paket, FSharp.Data, and Canopy! Note that many of these libraries are just that: libraries, not frameworks. They can be used interchangeably in a flexible manner, without forcing you down a specific path. They're nearly all open source and free to use (available on GitHub and NuGet), and most work cross-platform without relying on Visual Studio tooling.

D.1.1   Build and DevOps

F#'s unique syntax, scripting, and language features make it a great choice for part of (or to replace!) your build pipeline. The ability to create custom operators enables you to perform some impressive tricks that can replace MSBuild and PowerShell for orchestrating build pipelines.

Fake

http://fsharp.github.io/FAKE/

FAKE (F# Make) is a build automation system with capabilities that are similar to make and rake.
FAKE comes with a large set of helper libraries to perform common tasks, such as copying files, building projects, versioning assemblies, rewriting configuration files, running unit tests—all sorts of goodies. It can, in effect, replace your reliance on a central build platform such as TeamCity and allow you to run builds locally as well as remotely. Builds are made up of tasks, which are arbitrary functions that have a name; these are then composed together using the FAKE DSL into a pipeline, as shown in figure D.1.

```
"Clean"
    ==> "BuildDatabase"
    ==> "DeployCIDatabase"
    ==> "ConfigureDbConnection"
    ==> "BuildWebsite"
    ==> "CopyArtifacts"
```

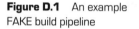

Figure D.1   An example FAKE build pipeline

One of FAKE's great strengths is that it runs as simple F# scripts, so you have *total* control; if you need to make your own custom build task, you can easily do so—just write some F#! In addition, you avoid tying yourself into a particular CI server (for example, TeamCity, AppVeyor, or VSTS). Instead, FAKE handles your build process, and because you can run it locally, it's much easier to reproduce problems in your CI build chain; your CI server simply has a single task in it, which is to run the FAKE script.

ProjectScaffold

http://fsprojects.github.io/ProjectScaffold/

ProjectScaffold helps you get started with a new .NET/Mono project solution with everything needed for successful organizing of code, tools, and publishing.
The F# ProjectScaffold was designed to create a framework to support many common features you'll want in an open source project, such as automated build, dependency management, automatic NuGet package creation, HTML documentation generated from F# scripts, and a full, one-click release process with automatic labeling and versioning to Git.

ProjectScaffold is commonly used for many open source F# projects (including many that you'll see in this appendix), and the tools it uses are popular and well understood in the community, such as Fake, Paket, and FSharp Formatting. But the build scripts can be complex, so there's a lot to get your head around.

D.1.2 Data

You've already seen how well suited F# is to working with data, but we haven't covered all the libraries out there. This section covers a few more libraries that can make your life much easier when trying to perform more than the typical day-to-day sort of data operations you've seen so far.

ExcelProvider

http://fsprojects.github.io/ExcelProvider/

As much as you might not like to admit it, Excel is everywhere and isn't going away any time soon. Sooner or later, you'll need to work with data that a customer sends you in Excel.

The ExcelProvider is a type provider that sits on top of Excel files. You can then work with Excel files directly in F#, just as you can use the FSharp.Data type provider to work seamlessly with CSV, JSON, or XML files. ExcelProvider has a great deal of flexibility, and you can use cell ranges to work with only subsets of data within an entire sheet; this is great if you have multiple datasets within a single worksheet.

Deedle

http://bluemountaincapital.github.io/Deedle/

> *Deedle is an easy-to-use library for data and time-series manipulation and for scientific programming.*

Deedle is F#'s equivalent of R's DataFrames, or Python's Pandas. It allows you to work with datasets in a two-dimensional *frame* (think of old-school .NET DataTables) and perform operations on the frame, such as inferring missing cells based on surrounding rows, time-series analysis, groupings, and aggregations. It's also used within the finance domain for things such as stock tickers and price analysis. The API definitely takes a bit of getting used to, but it's extremely powerful.

FsLab

https://fslab.org/

> *FsLab is a collection of libraries for data science. It provides a rapid development environment that lets you write advanced analysis with a few lines of production-quality code.*

If you're interested in machine learning but thought you'd need to leave the comfortable world of .NET to get involved, this package is for you. FsLab is a one-stop shop for machine learning on .NET. In and of itself, it doesn't do much; it's a NuGet package that references a set of other NuGet packages, including the usual data ones (such as FSharp.Data and Deedle), charting libraries, machine learning libraries, and the R Type Provider, which allows you to seamlessly call out to R packages and libraries from F#. It also contains project templates that can make your life a little easier with regard to getting up and running (although it's not strictly necessary to use them).

FSharp.Charting

https://fslab.org/FSharp.Charting/

Unlike XPlot (which uses Google Charts and Plotly to render visuals), FSharp.Charting uses the charting components built into .NET to create charts, as shown in figure D.2. Although the results aren't quite as flexible as XPlot (nor are they quite as pretty), the API is easy to use, and it has support for streaming and animated charts, something XPlot doesn't support.

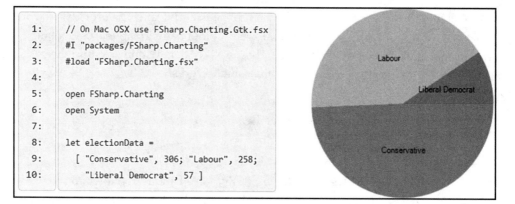

```
1:    // On Mac OSX use FSharp.Charting.Gtk.fsx
2:    #I "packages/FSharp.Charting"
3:    #load "FSharp.Charting.fsx"
4:
5:    open FSharp.Charting
6:    open System
7:
8:    let electionData =
9:      [ "Conservative", 306; "Labour", 258;
10:        "Liberal Democrat", 57 ]
```

Figure D.2   Using FSharp.Charting to quickly and easily generate visual charts

D.1.3   Web

F# is close to achieving an exceptionally good web story. You've already seen how F# and functional patterns are a great fit for the web on the server, but what about on the client? F# has two choices here, Fable and WebSharper, that allow you to do just that.

Fable

http://fable.io/

Something that this book has steered away from is F# on the client, or running F# code *in the browser*. You can't directly do this, but what you can do with the Fable project is *transpile* F# into JavaScript, in the same way that you can create JavaScript from Type-Script or Dart or CoffeeScript (see figure D.3). The Fable project (and the FunScript project it replaced) do an excellent job of this. The generated JavaScript is not only easy to read, but also maps across many calls from the BCL to JavaScript libraries automatically.

A lot of superb work is being done in this area, including libraries that allow you to design web pages in F# by using custom DSLs; developers are already reporting fantastic productivity gains by having F# on both sides of the fence. There's no reliance on specific Visual Studio tooling, and it works cross-platform. If you're doing any web programming, you should check it out. Check out http://fable.io/repl for a page that converts F# to JavaScript in the browser—seriously cool!

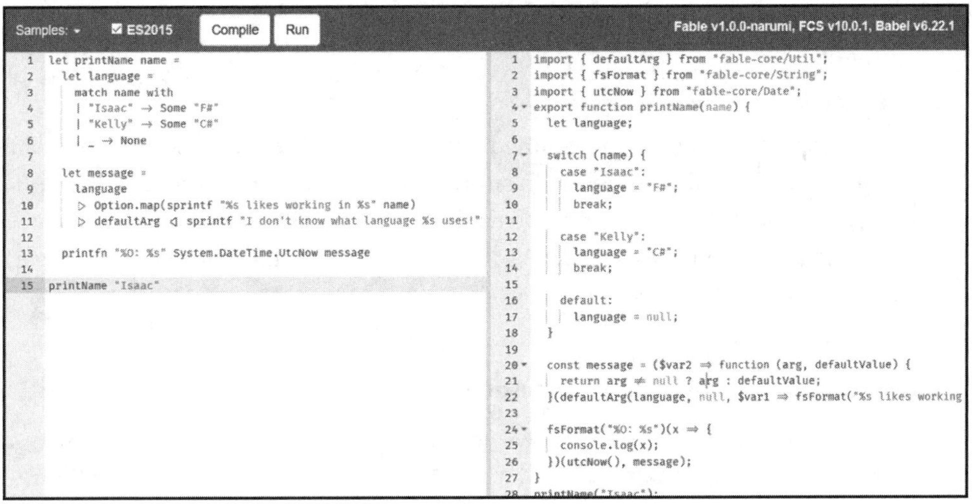

Figure D.3 Using Fable's browser REPL to try out F#-to-JavaScript compilation

WebSharper

http://websharper.com/

A fundamentally different web framework for developing functional and reactive .NET applications.

WebSharper is a more mature project than Fable that has the same aim—F# on the client—but tries to achieve this via a more prescriptive framework plus some Visual Studio templates. It's extremely smart, using its own custom compiler to generate JavaScript from F#, and allows you to write reactive (event-driven) applications entirely in F#.

WebSharper began as a commercial platform, and although it has become free to use now, it's not quite the same in terms of open source as Fable. The flip side is that it has a team of developers who maintain the project, as well as consultants who offer training, so it's not necessarily the case that you'll be on your own if you use it. It's not the easiest framework to pick up, and being a framework, it's not only prescriptive but also locks you into a specific way of working.

FREYA

https://freya.io/

Elegant. Modern. Powerful. Functional web programming for F#.

Freya is another F#-first web programming framework, just like Suave, although Freya has a different programming model. Both support the idea of composing small bits of functionality together to build larger systems. Freya is actively updated and uses several other libraries to provide excellent performance (in fact, it sits on top of Kestrel, part of the new ASP .NET core framework).

F# Formatting

http://fsprojects.github.io/FSharp.Formatting/

F# Formatting is a fantastic tool that allows you to generate HTML documentation based on F# scripts or a combination of Markdown files with embedded F# (see figure D.4). Indeed, the documentation states that most F# open source projects are created using this library. It also has support for embedding images, charts, tables, and even source code (with tooltips!) inline.

You can use F# Formatting for more than just documentation of a site. You can also use it for generating reports. For example, imagine you want to create a daily report that contains the latest sales figures—no problem. Create an F# script with the F# Formatting library and generate your report as an HTML document. When you're done generating it, email it off to key stakeholders, perhaps using a FAKE script to orchestrate the tasks!

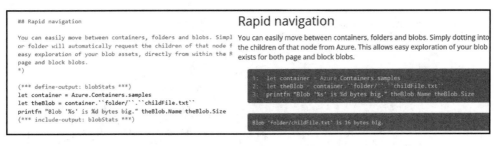

Figure D.4 Using F# Formatting to generate HTML content from combined Markdown and F#

D.1.4 Cloud

I spend a lot of time working with cloud applications, and F# is well placed to take advantage of the cloud (something Microsoft is well aware of). If writing multithreaded applications is difficult to reason about, think about the difficulty of writing applications that run across multiple machines across an unreliable network. F#'s approach to immutable data and expressions helps reason about things here!

FSharp Azure Storage

https://github.com/fsprojects/FSharp.Azure.Storage

The Microsoft Azure storage service provides access to multiple services, one of which is Tables, a cheap, simple, two-dimensional storage system. FSharp.Azure.Storage provides a pleasant F# DSL on top of the table service, with support for easy insertion, updates, and queries of data directly from F# records.

Azure Storage Type Provider

http://fsprojects.github.io/AzureStorageTypeProvider/

The Azure Storage Type Provider gives you a full type provider over the three main Azure Storage services: Blobs, Tables, and Queues. You can point the type provider to a live Azure Storage account and receive IntelliSense over the assets in the account (see figure D.5). It supports safe querying over tables (in that it guarantees not to generate queries that the service will reject at runtime), and intelligently generates table types based on the contents of a remote table; there's no need to create F# records in advance.

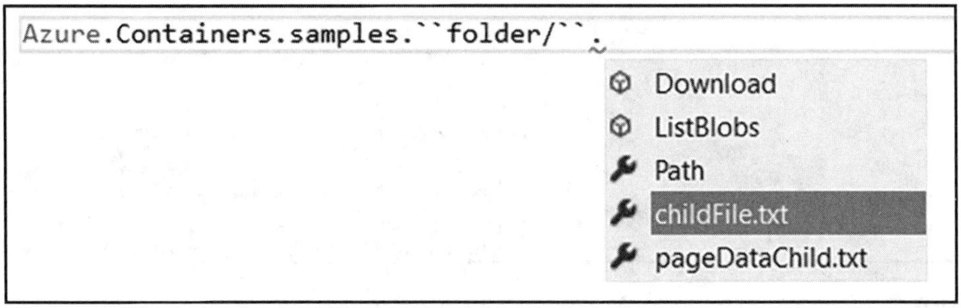

Figure D.5   Navigating through a live Azure blob storage account in real-time with IntelliSense

FSharp AWS DynamoDB

https://github.com/fsprojects/FSharp.AWS.DynamoDB

If you're an Amazon Web Services developer, rather than Microsoft Azure, you can use the FSharp AWS DynamoDB library. It's similar to the FSharp Azure Storage library in that it's not a type provider, but rather aims to provide a simple API that takes advantage of F#'s language features to make it easier to work with the DynamoDB storage system.

MBrace

http://mbrace.io/

> *Integrated data scripting for the cloud—get started with MBrace today.*

MBrace is possibly the most exciting project of all here. It's a general-purpose, flexible framework for distributed computing on .NET. It allows you to wrap arbitrary code blocks—whether they're accessing F# functions, values, or even VB or C# code—and distribute work across a cluster of machines, before returning with the result. It's extremely smart, handling distribution of captured values, exception propagation, parallel workloads; there's even a big-data library that supports LINQ-style queries against massive datasets. The programming model is extremely easy to grok if you understand how `async { }` blocks work, as it's effectively the same; you simply replace `async { }` with `cloud { }`! There's support for both Azure and Amazon cloud systems as well as an on-premises model.

D.1.5   Desktop

When we touched on WPF in this book, it was explicitly left as the domain of C# for the presentation layer, with F# providing the business logic. But that's not entirely necessary, as F# also has several excellent libraries for working with WPF.

FsXaml

http://fsprojects.github.io/FsXaml/

FsXaml is a type provider that can create a strongly typed view based on an XAML file. In effect, it replaces the need for the code-generation phase used in Visual Studio when working with XAML in C#. Using FsXaml, you can start to create complete WPF applications in F# projects, with full IntelliSense over controls that live in those views. If you already know WPF, this type provider will allow you to continue to work with WPF but in a 100% F# environment.

Although the official documentation is very sparse, the source code repository has some useful samples, as well as a collection of F# WPF templates that you can add to Visual Studio that show larger examples of working with it.

FSharp.ViewModule

https://github.com/fsprojects/FSharp.ViewModule

The companion project to FsXaml, FSharp.ViewModule, provides a framework for creating GUI applications that adhere to the Model-View-ViewModel (MVVM) pattern that's popular in the WPF world. The MVVM pattern is typically object-oriented, with changes to your state combined with the `INotifyPropertyChanged` interface to push changes to the view.

FSharp.ViewModule encapsulates much of this and allows you to focus on working with simple mutable objects with automatic change tracking. There's also an excellent set of helpers for binding XAML commands to standard F# functions; this abstraction means that you can write code that doesn't stray too far for F# patterns and practices while still being able to work with WPF views.

D.1.6   Miscellaneous

Alongside the preceding libraries, a few other miscellaneous libraries, although not necessarily fitting into any specific category, are nonetheless useful and worth pointing out.

Argu

http://fsprojects.github.io/Argu/

How many times have you written a console application and needed to parse configuration arguments supplied to it? Argu solves this problem for you. You define a declarative model that represents the possible arguments that can be supplied, and the tool maps the model to the input arguments. There's support for mandatory and optional arguments, automatic help, and friendly error messages, as well as automatic parsing of types.

FSharp.Management

http://fsprojects.github.io/FSharp.Management/

The FSharp.Management package contains a set of utility-type providers that you'll always want to have around when working on Windows with local resources:

- *File System*—Strongly typed access to files on the local filesystem
- *Registry*—Strongly typed access to the Windows registry
- *WMI*—Strongly typed access to the Windows Management Instrumentation service (see figure D.6)
- *PowerShell*—Provides the ability to call PowerShell functions and modules directly from F#
- *SystemTimeZonesProvider*—Strongly typed access to all time zones in .NET

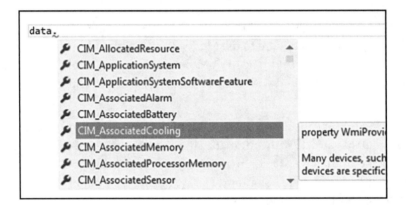

Figure D.6   Accessing WMI components through IntelliSense via the WMI type provider

FsReveal

http://fsprojects.github.io/FsReveal/

If you're fed up with creating presentations using PowerPoint, FsReveal is an easy-to-use tool that can generate web-ready slide decks based on simple Markdown files. You don't need a full application such as PowerPoint; you simply open a text editor (ideally, one that can preview Markdown), and off you go. Instead of heavyweight tooling, a simple FAKE script converts the Markdown files into a fully interactive website.

Because FsReveal sits on top of the JSReveal library to do most of the heavy lifting, it has all the nice features that JSReveal has, such as speaker notes, support for clickers, animated images, tables, and more. And because it also uses F# Formatting, you can embed code in your slide decks and have it automatically generated in a pleasant HTML web-based slide deck, complete with tooltips!

FSharp.Configuration

http://fsprojects.github.io/FSharp.Configuration/

FSharp.Configuration is a set of easy-to-use type providers that support the reading of various configuration file formats:

- *AppSettings*—Application settings (and connection strings) for a .NET config file (see figure D.7)
- *ResX*—.NET resource files
- *Yaml*—YAML configuration files
- *INI*—Old-school .ini files

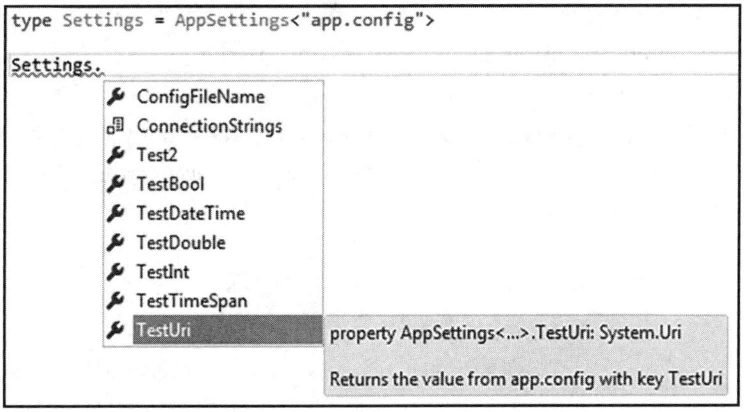

Figure D.7   Accessing application settings from an app.config file by using the Configuration type provider

Most projects have some form of configuration settings, so you'll probably be using this package more often than not!

Chessie

http://fsprojects.github.io/Chessie/

The last project we'll address in this appendix is Chessie, a ready-made library for working with Result code (code that might be a Success or Failure), also known as railway-oriented programming. F# 4.1 will have a built-in Result type, so I imagine that Chessie will change at some point to build on top of that. For now, it contains a complete Result type along with many useful helper methods, such as mapping, binding, and so on—in effect, the same sort of behavior that you can achieve with the Option module.

If you find that Option isn't quite enough for you, and you want to encode error details along the way rather than simply throwing away the None path, Chessie is a ready-made library for you (and one that has some good documentation).

D.2   The F# toolchain

Now that you've looked at all of these libraries, many of the points I made at the start of this appendix (and indeed at the start of the book) should now become clear about the F# toolchain:

- No reliance on custom tooling in Visual Studio
- Emphasizing a code-first approach to development
- Type providers instead of code generation
- Simple, independent libraries that can be composed together
- Open source, community-led projects
- With that in mind, let's compare a typical tooling stack that you might be used to today, and an alternative stack that an F# developer might choose to adopt. Table D.1 details the comparison.

Table D.1   Comparing alternative technology stacks on .NET and F#

Function	Microsoft stack	Pure F# stack
Complex build process	MS Build custom tasks	FAKE script with MSBuild
Continuous integration	TeamCity, TFS pipeline, etc.	FAKE script on TeamCity, TFS, etc.
Dependency management	NuGet	Paket with NuGet + GitHub dependencies
Project system	Solution and projects	Standalone scripts and/or project + solution
Ad hoc processing	Console applications	Standalone scripts
Test libraries	xUnit, NUnit	Expecto, QuickCheck, Unquote, FsTest
SQL ORM	Entity Framework	SQLProvider
SQL micro-ORM	Dapper	FSharp.Data SQLClient
Server-side web	Full-blown Web API project	Bare-bones NET Web API OWIN, or Suave

Table D.1 Comparing alternative technology stacks on .NET and F# (continued)

Function	Microsoft stack	Pure F# stack
Front-end web	ASP .NET MVC, TypeScript	F# with Fable
IDE	Visual Studio	VSCode, Emacs, Visual Studio, and so on

The main point is that although you can definitely continue to work with virtually all of the technologies and tools in the Microsoft stack in the F# world, you'll also find an alternative stack on the right-hand side, which more fully embraces the points previously made, with the overall aim of trying to improve productivity (and developer satisfaction!).

Nothing says you must pick everything on one of the two sides; the key takeaway is to understand that there's more than one way to solve many of the problems that previously you might have assumed had only a single option.

Summary

This appendix has hopefully given you a whirlwind tour of some of the tools and libraries that weren't introduced in the book, and shown you that there's a wide-ranging ecosystem in the F# world that takes full advantage of its features, in addition to the standard set of .NET libraries you're already familiar with. Undoubtedly, other libraries could just as easily have made this list, and you should investigate finding new libraries through the community on a regular basis.

OTHER F# LANGUAGE FEATURES

Get Programming with F# focuses on a core subset of the F# language. Some features were only partially demonstrated, referenced but not shown, or completely ignored. This appendix contains a list of many of those features (based on the current production version of F#, F# 4.0) for you to read up on in your own time. The best place to start is probably the F# language reference on MSDN (https://docs.microsoft.com/en-gb/dotnet/articles/fsharp/language-reference/).

E.1   Object-oriented support

This book deliberately steers clear of the rich OO support in F#, as the aim of the book isn't to show you how to write code like what you write today but in another syntax, but to get you thinking about solving problems in a different way. Nonetheless, here's a quick sample of typical OO features in F#. This should map relatively closely to C# and VB .NET OO features that you know, although a few differences may surprise you!

E.1.1   Basic classes

Listing E.1 Basic classes in F#

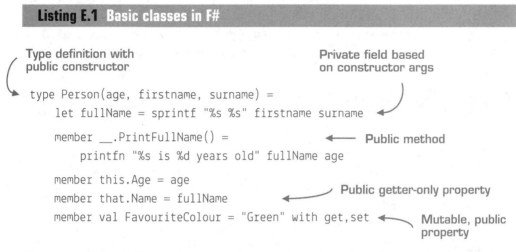

Type definition with public constructor

Private field based on constructor args

```
type Person(age, firstname, surname) =
    let fullName = sprintf "%s %s" firstname surname

    member __.PrintFullName() =                          ← Public method
        printfn "%s is %d years old" fullName age

    member this.Age = age
    member that.Name = fullName                  ← Public getter-only property
    member val FavouriteColour = "Green" with get,set  ← Mutable, public property
```

Of interest in this listing is that you still can reap the benefits of type inference, while also taking advantage of the fact that member methods and properties can access constructor arguments without the need to set them as private backing fields first. Also of interest is that if a member doesn't need to access other members, you can omit the `this.` and replace it with `_` (as per the `PrintFullName` method). Although it's not common practice, you can also place members on records and discriminated unions. This is occasionally useful, but I recommend that you prefer modules with functions that act on the record/DU rather than members on those types.

E.1.2   Interfaces and inheritance

Listing E.2 Interfaces in F#

```
type IQuack =
    abstract member Quack : unit -> unit          ← Defining an interface in F#

type Duck (name:string) =
    interface IQuack with                         Creating a type
        member this.Quack() = printfn "QUACK!"     ← that implements an interface

let quacker =
    { new IQuack with
        member this.Quack() = printfn "What type of animal am I?" }
```

Creating an instance of an interface through an object expression

This should be familiar to you, except for the last section, which shows how F# can create an instance of an interface without first formally defining a type. This is extremely useful if you're creating an abstract factory, as you don't need to formally define the types behind the interface first. Finally, interfaces don't need to be explicitly marked as such; in F#, any type that contains only abstract members is automatically declared as an interface.

Listing E.3   Inheritance in F#

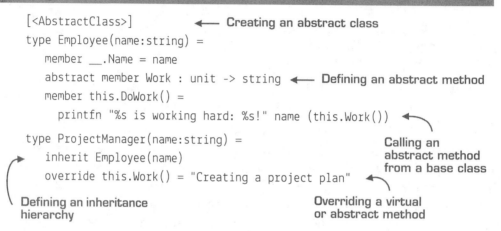

```
[<AbstractClass>]               ◄— Creating an abstract class
type Employee(name:string) =
  member __.Name = name
  abstract member Work : unit -> string  ◄— Defining an abstract method
  member this.DoWork() =
    printfn "%s is working hard: %s!" name (this.Work())  ◄
type ProjectManager(name:string) =
  inherit Employee(name)
  override this.Work() = "Creating a project plan"  ◄
```

Calling an abstract method from a base class

Defining an inheritance hierarchy

Overriding a virtual or abstract method

I'm not going to explain all the ins and outs of inheritance to you here. The preceding sample maps almost directly 1:1 with equivalent C# code in terms of concepts. The only real thing to note is that in F# you need to mark the type with the [<AbstractClass>] attribute.

E.2   Exception handling

You've seen exception handling occasionally in this book. Again, there's not much to say except that in F#, we tend to avoid exceptions as a way of message-passing, and use them for only truly exceptional cases. F# allows you to use pattern matching on the type of exception in order to create separate handlers; VB .NET has had this for some time, and C# recently added a similar feature.

Listing E.4   Exception handling in F#

```
open System
let riskyCode() =
    raise(ApplicationException())
    ()
```

Throwing a specific exception by using the raise() function

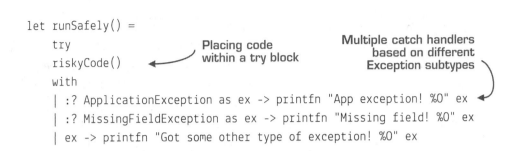

```
let runSafely() =
    try
    riskyCode()
    with
    | :? ApplicationException as ex -> printfn "App exception! %O" ex
    | :? MissingFieldException as ex -> printfn "Missing field! %O" ex
    | ex -> printfn "Got some other type of exception! %O" ex
```

Placing code within a try block

Multiple catch handlers based on different Exception subtypes

E.3   Resource management

The dispose pattern still exists within F# and has language support, as in C#. Unlike C#, F# has two ways to work with automatic disposal of objects. The first is the use keyword, and the second is the using block. Here's how they look.

Listing E.5   Exception handling in F#

```
let createDisposable() =
    printfn "Created!"
    { new IDisposable with member __.Dispose() = printfn "Disposed!" }
let foo() =
    use x = createDisposable()
    printfn "inside!"
let bar() =
    using (createDisposable()) (fun disposableObject ->
        printfn "inside!")
```

A function that creates a disposable object

The use keyword with implicit disposal of resources

The using keyword with explicit disposal of resources

As you can see, the main difference between the two alternatives is that the former one lets the compiler determine when a disposable object goes out of scope, whereas the latter allows you to explicitly determine when scope ends, by virtue of a lambda function.

E.4   Casting

F# has support for two types of casts: *upcast* and *downcast*, shown in listing E.6 and illustrated in figure E.1. These are similar, but not quite the same as the as keyword and the cast functionality offered by C# or VB .NET:

- Upcast (:>)will *safely* upcast to a parent type in the type hierarchy. It will allow you to do this only for a type *known* to be "above" in the hierarchy.
- Downcast (:?>) will allow you to unsafely downcast from one type to another, but only if the compiler knows that this is possible. For example, you can't downcast from string to Exception because the compiler knows that this will never pass. This isn't the same as the cast functionality in C#, which will blindly allow casts that can be proved to be invalid even at compile time.

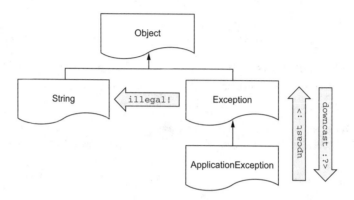

Figure E.1   Upcasts and downcasts in F# are stricter than in C#.

Listing E.6   Casting in F#

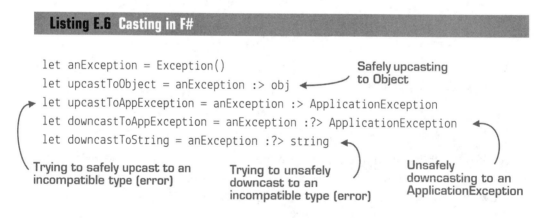

The first and third casts will compile—the first is guaranteed to work at compile time and at runtime, and the third compiles but *could* cause a runtime exception. The second and the fourth won't compile at all—the second fails because ApplicationException isn't above Exception in the type hierarchy. The last one fails because the compiler knows that Exception can never be treated as a string.

Don't forget that F# can safely pattern match on types (as seen with exception handling), so you can safely try to cast across, and handle incompatibilities without the risk of run-time exceptions.

E.5   Active patterns

This book briefly touched on active patterns. They're a form of lightweight discriminated unions, and a way to categorize the *same* value in *different* ways. For example, you could create an active pattern that categorizes strings into long/medium/short and then pattern match directly on any string. Two more sophisticated forms of active patterns are *partial* active patterns and *parameterized* active patterns. Both allow you even more flexibility when pattern matching, but are beyond the scope of the book. I definitely recommend that you look into these after you've mastered the basics of pattern matching and discriminated unions, because they allow for powerful abstractions.

Listing E.7   Active patterns

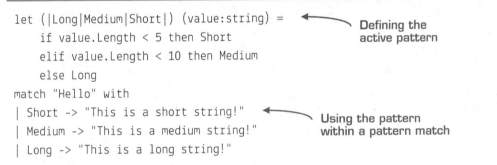

```
let (|Long|Medium|Short|) (value:string) =       ◄───    Defining the
    if value.Length < 5 then Short                        active pattern
    elif value.Length < 10 then Medium
    else Long
match "Hello" with
| Short -> "This is a short string!"    ◄───    Using the pattern
| Medium -> "This is a medium string!"          within a pattern match
| Long -> "This is a long string!"
```

E.6   Computation expressions

This book has mentioned computation expressions several times. Computation expressions allow you to create language support for a specific abstraction, directly in code—whether that's asynchronous work, optional objects, sequences, or cloud computations. F# also allows you to create your *own* computation expressions to capture a type of behavior that you want to abstract away, with your own "versions" of let!. Here's a quick example of a computation expression for working with options.

Listing E.8   A custom computation expression

```
type Maybe() =
    member this.Bind(opt, func) = opt |> Option.bind func    Creating your
    member this.Return v = Some v                            own computation
let maybe = Maybe()                                          expression
let rateCustomer name =
    match name with | "isaac" -> Some 3 | "mike" -> Some 2 | _ -> None
let answer =
    maybe {                             ◄─── Creating a maybe { } block
        let! first = rateCustomer "isaac"    ◄─
        let! second = rateCustomer "mike"        Safely "unwrapping"
        return first + second }                  an option type
```

Try this in a script yourself. I don't expect you to understand all of this code, but the methods in the Maybe type map to calls in the maybe{} block. (F# automatically maps let! to Bind(), and return to Return()). Next, you have a fictional function that rates customers based on their name. Finally, you call that function from within the maybe block. Notice that rateCustomer returns Option<int>, yet inside the block you don't need to check for Some or None; the value is safely unwrapped by let!; if you try to get a customer that doesn't exist, the entire block will prematurely return with None.

You can even create your own custom keywords in the language when inside the computation expression. They're powerful and commonly found within custom DSLs—definitely a more advanced feature, but one that's worth looking into.

E.7   Code quotations

Essentially the equivalent of C#'s expression trees, code quotations allow you to wrap a block of code inside a <@ quotation block @> and then programmatically interrogate the abstract syntax tree (AST) within it. F# has two forms of quotations: *typed* and *untyped*. You won't find yourself using these in everyday code, but if you ever need to do low-level meta programming or write your own type provider, you'll come into contact with these.

E.8   Units of measure

Units of measure (UoM) are an *incredibly* useful feature of F#. The only reason they weren't included in the book is that they're not needed often. UoMs allow you to create a kind of "generic" numerics, so you can have 5<Kilogram> as opposed to 5<Meter>. You can also combine types, so you can model things such as 15<Meter/Second> and so on. It's extremely useful because the compiler will prevent you from accidentally mixing and matching incompatible types. UoMs are erased away at compile time, so there's no run-time overhead.

E.9 Lazy computations

Lazy computations in F# allow you to create System.Lazy values by wrapping any expression in a lazy scope:

```
let lazyText =
    lazy                          ◄——— Creating a lazy scope
        let x = 5 + 5
        printfn "%O: Hello! Answer is %d" System.DateTime.UtcNow x
        x
let text = lazyText.Value
let text2 = lazyText.Value
```

Explicitly evaluating the result of a lazy computation

Returning the result without re-executing the computation

In the preceding example, the code to print the answer to the console will occur only the first time the Value property is accessed.

E.10 Recursion

Finally, as a functional-first language, F# has excellent support for recursion, with special CLR support for *tail recursion* (the ability to call a recursive function without risking stack overflow). To create a recursive function, prefix it with the rec keyword:

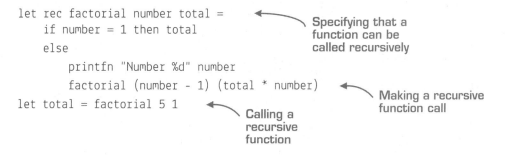

```
let rec factorial number total =
    if number = 1 then total
    else
        printfn "Number %d" number
        factorial (number - 1) (total * number)
let total = factorial 5 1
```

Specifying that a function can be called recursively

Making a recursive function call

Calling a recursive function

INDEX